Braxton Bragg

Civil War America

Peter S. Carmichael, Caroline E. Janney,
and Aaron Sheehan-Dean, editors

This landmark series interprets broadly the history and culture of the Civil War era through the long nineteenth century and beyond. Drawing on diverse approaches and methods, the series publishes historical works that explore all aspects of the war, biographies of leading commanders, and tactical and campaign studies, along with select editions of primary sources. Together, these books shed new light on an era that remains central to our understanding of American and world history.

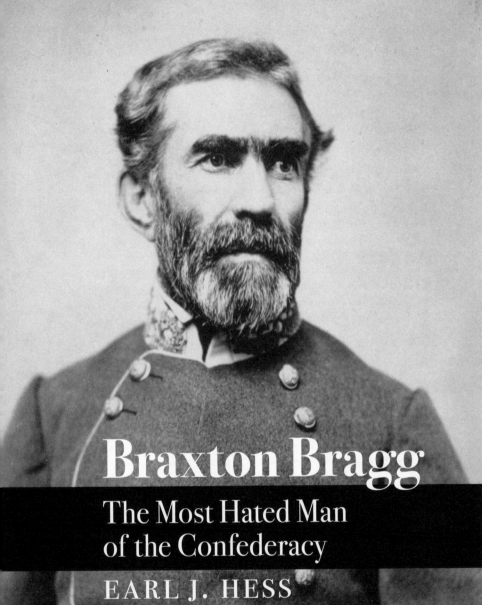

Braxton Bragg

The Most Hated Man of the Confederacy

EARL J. HESS

The University of North Carolina Press *Chapel Hill*

*This book was published with the assistance of the
Fred W. Morrison Fund of the University of North Carolina Press.*

Manufactured in the United States of America. Designed and set in Merlo by
Rebecca Evans. The paper in this book meets the guidelines for permanence
and durability of the Committee on Production Guidelines for Book Longevity
of the Council on Library Resources. The University of North Carolina Press
has been a member of the Green Press Initiative since 2003.

Cover illustration: Braxton Bragg (Library of Congress, LC-USZC4-7984)

Library of Congress Cataloging-in-Publication Data
Names: Hess, Earl J., author.
Title: Braxton Bragg : the most hated man of the Confederacy / Earl J. Hess.
Other titles: Civil War America (Series)
Description: Chapel Hill : The University of North Carolina Press, [2016] |
Series: Civil War America | Includes bibliographical references and index.
Identifiers: LCCN 2015049262| ISBN 9781469628752 (cloth : alk. paper) |
ISBN 9781469628769 (ebook)
Subjects: LCSH: Bragg, Braxton, 1817-1876. | Generals—Confederate States of
America—Biography. | Confederate States of America. Army—Biography. |
United States—History—Civil War, 1861-1865.
Classification: LCC E467.1.B75 H47 2016 | DDC 355.0092—dc23 LC record
available at http://lccn.loc.gov/2015049262

An earlier version of chapter 7 was published as "Braxton Bragg
and the Stones River Campaign," in Kent T. Dollar, Larry H. Whiteaker, and
W. Calvin Dickinson, eds., *Border Wars: The Civil War in Tennessee and Kentucky*
(Kent, Ohio: Kent State University Press, 2015). © 2015 by the Kent State
University Press. Reprinted by permission.

For Pratibha, with love

Contents

Figures and Maps

Figures

Maps

Preface

Braxton Bragg has always been a controversial figure of the Civil War. His contemporaries began the process of making him into a hero, a fool, a bloodthirsty disciplinarian, and an old-fashioned scapegoat, all wrapped up in one package. Historians have tended to do similar things, followed by a legion of Civil War enthusiasts who seem to delight in making of Bragg the Confederacy's chief whipping boy.

It is not easy to gain a proper perspective on Bragg because of these kaleidoscopic views of his personality and generalship. His image has been warped and tainted by them. One need only mention his name at a Civil War round table meeting to bring a guffaw from someone who will make a snide comment about the general. Nearly everyone has a negative view of Bragg, and yet he remains one of the most popular figures of the Civil War. Even those who think poorly of his war career are fascinated by it, and almost any group of Civil War students or historians will engage in a heated discussion about his impact on the course of the conflict.

This book is an effort to understand many things about Bragg the man and the Civil War general. To understand the man, it delves into his personality, his family life, and his views of Southern culture when slavery was at its height and most of the South fought a desperate war for independence. Bragg fully embraced that war because he had come to embrace the plantation culture that he thought was at the heart of the Southern independence movement. Bragg's career as a Confederate general is probed deeply, including the many controversies surrounding his handling of Confederate troops in the field. The connections between Bragg's personal life and his military career are explored as well. The deep and intense controversies about his generalship unfortunately have had the effect of dehumanizing Bragg. He has become almost a cardboard figure among Civil War enthusiasts and even among some professional historians.

This book is a study of Braxton Bragg's Civil War career, not a full-fledged biography of the man. It also is not simply a generic narrative of the campaigns and battles he conducted, a fault of too many histories of prominent figures in the conflict. How Bragg handled his army in the field is important, but the reaction of a myriad of people to his success or failure as a general is even more important in this study. His immediate colleagues, his chief subordinates, and the middle-ranking officers and privates in his command all had differing opinions of their general. Men and women in the civilian society of the South had their views, and prominent politicians in Richmond also formed their assessments of Bragg. Even his Federal opponents weighed in with evaluations of their gray-clad adversary.

Digging deeply into all these opinions and weighing their significance on Bragg's ability to command are important objectives of this work. But it is also important to understand how these opinions affected Bragg the man as well as the general. Historians have tended to see Bragg as the actor in creating a circle of negativity around him, but we also must understand that he was in turn deeply affected by the actions and opinions of others.

Setting Bragg within his proper context is another important objective of this book. Comparing his Civil War career with that of other generals, especially Robert E. Lee, helps us to understand whether he really deserves to be blamed for causing Confederate defeat. In other words, did the problems inhibiting Bragg's ability to win campaigns and battles stem mostly from his own failings or from a set of strategic problems encountered by all other Rebel generals? Could Lee have done better if plucked from the Army of Northern Virginia and planted in the Army of Tennessee? How did Bragg's generalship at Stones River compare to that of Lee at Chancellorsville? Comparison and context always enlighten historical questions in one way or another.

We must also consider Bragg the family man—the husband and domestic provider. His wife Elise was the primary emotional support of his life. Bragg certainly possessed the ability to make and keep male friends, but no one came close to sustaining him in an emotional way as did Elise. Understanding these personal relationships helps us to humanize Bragg, turning him from a cardboard figure into a real person with admirable personal qualities as well as distressing personal faults.

This book gives shape and contour to Bragg's career as the most hated general of the Confederacy, trying fairly to assess where he deserves credit as well as where he deserves blame. We need to stop automatically assuming Bragg was a bad general, an ogre who casually shot his men for minor infractions of discipline, or a cold, callous person who deserved the op-probrium heaped upon his head by generals, enlisted men, and civilians alike. Instead, it is important to include his own view of the war and to pay special attention to his supporters both in and out of the army in order to counter the tendency among historians to assume he was hated by everyone.

Just as most people automatically assume Lee was a great general who made no mistakes, they have placed Bragg at the opposite end of the spectrum and assume he was a bad general who never did anything right. We have to approach Bragg from a clean perspective and take him for what he was, while rejecting the old image that has become a comforting but unfair view of the man and his military career.

Bragg's appearance and personality certainly did not invite approach and easy conversation, and that fact severely hampered his popular image. Edmund Kirby Smith described him as "a grim old fellow, but a true soldier." Walter Bullock happened to see him at the railroad depot in Salisbury, North Carolina, one day in early 1864 and found him "a very stern looking old man with gray hair" who also had "a gray eye and seems to be very restless." Thomas H. Malone, who served on a brigade-level staff in the Army of Tennessee, never forgot the only time he personally interacted with the general. He had the unpleasant task of telling him that a Unionist citizen under arrest had escaped custody. Bragg was displeased, acting "in great anger and with an exceedingly harsh manner." Although standing only a few feet away, he did not talk directly to Malone but communicated with him through one of his own staff members. Of all the officers Malone served under during the war, Bragg was the only one he personally disliked. "General Bragg was a stranger to his men to the last," commented Philip D. Stephenson.[1]

Negative views such as these by some of Bragg's contemporaries have often influenced the attitude of students to come. "Generations of Civil War historians have succeeded in making Braxton Bragg's name synonymous with pettiness, bitterness, incompetence, and in some cases even paranoia and insanity," as Kenneth W. Noe has aptly put it in his history of the battle of Perryville. Those historians have included eminent figures such as Bruce Catton, T. Harry Williams, Douglas Southall Freeman, and David Donald, according to Bragg's biographer Grady McWhiney.[2]

The first major biographer of Bragg was Don C. Seitz, whose *Braxton Bragg: General of the Confederacy* appeared in 1924. "It is not a grateful task to write the biography of a much hated man whose military efforts led to defeat," Seitz wrote in the foreword of his book. Despite that caveat, Seitz was prudent in his judgments about the general. He declared his aim as "neither to defend nor vindicate" but to "put into concrete form the circle of events around the life of an important figure in the great contest between the States." But Seitz was not a trained historian. As general manager of the *New York World*, he was an effective writer and managed to gather and consult a pretty good base of primary material for his work. The book is sympathetic to Bragg but amateurish. Thomas Robson Hay, also an amateur historian but one who had a deep interest in plumbing the primary sources, criticized Seitz in a long review of the biography for not doing enough research. It is true that Seitz made little effort to analyze anything or craft an effective argument, preferring to provide long quotations from documents and then let readers make up their own minds about Bragg. Those long quotes are about the only way to know how far Seitz's research went, for he did not provide footnotes or a bibliography.[3]

Seitz's conclusions are fair as far as he was able to make them in 1924. He thought Bragg's "stern sense of duty and discipline" and the view that he was a pet of Jefferson Davis were the roots of ill will sent his way by critics. Seitz noted that the Federals generally respected Bragg's ability on and off the battlefield far more than the Confederates. He also felt that Bragg's place in Confederate history remained vitally important no matter what one thought of the man or his generalship.[4]

By far the worst treatment accorded Bragg by a historian came from the pen of Stanley Horn, a Tennessee newspaper editor who turned his hand to Civil War history. Horn detested Bragg with a passion. He was critical of every decision made by the general and blamed him for the loss of the western Confederacy. Horn often made conclusions about Bragg that are clearly disproved by the evidence, in part because he hardly read any primary sources. In fact, his history of the Army of Tennessee (1941) is based on scant research of any kind. Horn did not even bother to call the army by its correct name from the time it was created in March 1862 until the Army of the Mississippi became the Army of Tennessee eight months later.[5]

Horn was able to conclude, however, that Bragg was personally devoted to the Confederate cause. But he criticized the general for his "innate vagueness of purpose" and noted his "unpopularity with practically everyone he encountered." While Horn excused this, in part, by noting that Bragg suffered chronic health problems, it hardly palliates the hatred Horn felt for the general, which suffuses every chapter that deals with the Bragg era in the army's history.[6]

Thomas L. Connelly's two-volume history of the Army of Tennessee easily supplanted Horn's book on that army and inspired other academic historians to study Bragg as a commander. On the basis of extensive research and delving deeply into the army's command history, Connelly offered the reader a largely negative view of Bragg. However, many of Connelly's conclusions do not ring true. "His worst fault as a leader was probably his constant fear of making a mistake," Connelly wrote in 1967, "and his consequent hesitation in committing his troops. He could drill, but he could not engage; he could plan, but he could easily change his mind." These conclusions are difficult to understand considering that it was Bragg who made the decision to attack at Perryville, Stones River, and Chickamauga, often against the advice of his chief subordinates.[7]

Connelly continued to denigrate Bragg's combat effectiveness by arguing that he "had lost his nerve, and the ability to see a battle to the end." Bragg was "not a fighter," in Connelly's view. Ironically, he was speaking in these last two quotes of the time period around July 1862, even before Bragg had an opportunity to demonstrate whether he could command an army on the battlefield.[8]

When it came to Bragg's personal life, Connelly made more outlandish claims. "Even his letters home to his wife resembled battle reports and lacked any semblance of affection," he wrote. On the contrary, Bragg's personal letters reveal that he was ardently in love with his wife and was not shy about expressing it. Connelly also unfairly accused Bragg of having no compassion for others. As Surgeon Samuel Stout amply testified, Bragg felt deeply for the welfare of his men, especially when they were wounded or taken ill. Connelly further exaggerated Bragg's sense of combativeness in tussles with his subordinates. "He never left his enemies any escape mechanism, but instead relished complete victory in any dispute. Within the army, he drove his enemies to the wall, humiliated them, and forced them into the anti-Bragg element. Then he never let the matter subside." There is little evidence to support such a charge. In fact, Bragg acted leniently toward many subordinates who deserved more punishment than he gave them, as seen later in this book. Such figures as Leonidas Polk and Benjamin F. Cheatham got away with a great deal of backbiting against him because Bragg hesitated to act in their cases. Despite his many unsubstantiated conclusions, Connelly was able at times to give Bragg the benefit of the doubt by admitting that his tactical and strategic decisions were about the best choices any other general could have made under the circumstances.[9]

Grady McWhiney authored a prominent biography of Bragg that was published in 1969. It only takes the general up through the midpoint of the Civil War. The study is one of the more even-handed treatments of Bragg, even though the title of the book links his name with Southern failure. "I have emphasized how and why Bragg, as commander of the Army of Tennessee, contributed to Confederate defeat," McWhiney admitted. "My purpose is neither to defend nor to denigrate the man himself but to untangle many of the exaggerated opinions about him, to present him as his contemporaries saw him and as he saw himself, and to analyze his successes and failures." McWhiney succeeded to a large degree in this purpose, but his contribution to our understanding of Bragg's life and army career *before* the Civil War is more important, in my view, than his contribution to our understanding of Bragg's Civil War experiences. McWhiney did admirable research into and clearly explained Bragg's triumph in the Mexican War and his contentious relations with many people high and low in the U.S. Army before the Civil War.[10]

"Tolerance of those he disliked was impossible," McWhiney has stated of Bragg's widespread criticism of many things in the old army. "He passed moral judgments quickly and constantly sought to justify his own and his heroes' prejudices. He rarely saw more than one side to any question. Things were either right or wrong; people were either good or bad, friends or enemies. Bragg invariably denounced his enemies openly and in the most sarcastic manner." This is a fair assessment of Bragg the young army officer, but I think his tendency to see others in this way toned down under the pressure of dealing with large armies and his declining health during the Civil War.[11]

McWhiney reportedly became tired of his work with Bragg and decided not to pursue the second and concluding volume in his projected biography. One of his graduate students, Judith Lee Hallock, continued the work with the publication of volume two in 1991. The study is relatively superficial in research and treatment, but distinguished by Hallock's effort to medically and psychologically analyze Bragg as a way to understand his career. Not only is that a comparatively unusual approach, but the conclusions are speculative at best. For example, she writes, "Bragg's harshness may have been prompted by fears of his own inadequacy. His unreasonable efforts to discipline and organize his soldiers may have provided him some measure of comfort as a way of making up for his inadequacies on the battlefield."[12]

Such overarching statements beg several questions. Was Bragg's discipline really too harsh? Was the general who authored brilliant tactical victories at Perryville, Stones River, and Chickamauga really inadequate on the battlefield? And, do we really need to psychoanalyze Braxton Bragg to understand the man and his career? I argue that the answer to all such questions is no and will explain why in the rest of the book.

Work by Steven E. Woodworth, Alexander Mendoza, and Peter Cozzens has painted Bragg in more positive tones than many previous historians have done. All of them have examined specific aspects of Bragg's career rather than its totality. Woodworth argues that Bragg owed his longevity as commander of the Army of Tennessee to his genuine ability rather than to any supposed friendship with Jefferson Davis. Woodworth has crafted two defenses of Bragg's actions during the Tullahoma campaign and at McLemore's Cove during the Chickamauga campaign in which he argues that the general's plans were sound and promising but destroyed by subordinates who had no faith in him. His arguments are convincing. Mendoza has written in similar vein that D. H. Hill failed Bragg during the Chickamauga campaign. Cozzens has not been such a forthright defender of Bragg's image, but he has pointed out the general's strengths as well as his weaknesses. "Bragg had an excellent strategic mind," Cozzens wrote in his history of the battle of Chickamauga. "His campaigns were well conceived. It was in the execution that he faltered."[13]

Woodworth also has treated Bragg's personality with care. "He was himself highly self-disciplined and valued self-discipline in others. When a person fell short in that trait, as was often the case, Bragg could be a very strict disciplinarian. This had made the troops he commanded some of the best drilled and trained in the Confederate army. Even so, he exercised a paternal care for his men, seeing to their welfare and even visiting hospitals and making attempts (however clumsy) at joking with them."[14]

Yet Bragg's personal limitations inhibited his ability to succeed in command, as Woodworth has recognized. The general lacked "the ability to inspire and motivate those around him. One might call it charisma, or simply a winning personality." Woodworth in fact faults Bragg for not trying harder to develop good relations with recalcitrant officers under his command. Bragg also failed to develop the kind of relationship with Jefferson Davis that Lee cultivated, a relationship wherein Lee could obtain favors from the Confederate president that allowed him to get rid of poor subordinates and maximize the amount of resources allocated to his army.[15]

Samuel J. Martin's recent biography of Bragg, published in 2011, takes a thoroughly positive view of Bragg, but Martin fails to make a convincing case for his view. An amateur historian, Martin's research is good but somewhat spotty as well. He is to be applauded for seeing Bragg in a way that is different from the general trend among historians, but he too often tends to simply state that Bragg was right in every controversy without crafting an argument to prove his position. Nevertheless, Martin has correctly pointed out that many ideas about Bragg are mere myths that have been taken at face value by generations of historians. He also asserts that Bragg cared for his men, and he blames subordinates such as Leonidas Polk for most of Bragg's battlefield failures.[16]

"There has never been a comprehensive, balanced presentation of Bragg's life, until now," Martin stated early in his book. While I do not think he has written such a study, I agree that no one else has accomplished that feat.[17]

A story about Braxton Bragg circulated so widely that it has become commonly accepted as fact. It relates to Bragg's contentious personality and was started by Ulysses S. Grant, who had no evidence that it was true. "I have heard in the old army an anecdote very characteristic of Bragg," Grant wrote in his memoirs, which were published in 1885. Bragg served as both the quartermaster and commissary at an army post before the Civil War. For a time he also commanded one of the companies at the place. "As commander of the company he made a requisition upon the quartermaster—himself—for something he wanted. As quartermaster he declined to fill the requisition, and endorsed on the back of it his reasons for so doing. As company commander he responded to this, urging that his requisition called for nothing but what he was entitled to, and that it was the duty of the quartermaster to fill it. As quartermaster he still persisted that he was right." By now, Bragg referred everything to the post commander for his review. That officer was astonished. "My God, Mr. Bragg, you have quarreled with every officer in the army, and now you are quarrelling with yourself!"[18]

Most people who have read this story accept it without question, in part because it is too good to pass up. But there is no reason to believe it is anything more than an amusing story without foundation. Grant himself admitted that he knew nothing of its veracity, and no one else claimed to know that it was true. Grady McWhiney does not say if it is false but does admit that Grant is the only source for the story.[19]

From my own work with Bragg, I cannot believe this story has any foundation in truth. Bragg was a very intelligent and practical man, and the notion that he would waste his time in senseless activity such as this defies belief. Yet the story is emblematic of the problem with Braxton Bragg;

most people's view of the man is such that they readily accept such a farce as real. Such a story actually becomes a substitute for truly understanding a complex and important individual who deserves much more from students and historians than to be made the butt of unfounded ridicule.

Two comments on Bragg by contemporaries seem to sum up much of the maligned general's problems. "I believe Bragg lost us our independence," wrote William Dudley Gale, staff officer to Leonidas Polk, after the war. Gale offered a damning appraisal of Bragg when describing him as "Cruel yet without courage, Obstinate, yet without firmness, Restless, yet without enterprise, Crafty, yet without strategy, suspicious, envious, jealous, vain, a bantam in success & a dunghill in disaster, and yet in command of a better army than Hannibal & Scipio had to conquer Rome or Carthage."[20]

John C. Spence, who survived the battle of Stones River at his hometown of Murfreesboro, Tennessee, saw a better side of the man. Bragg was "generally underrated," Spence mused after the war and "does not at all times get the credit he is entitled to. Is sometimes charged by some for the want of tact in the management of his affairs. This may be by those who know the least of what his designs are. He has one trait—he can make a hard fight, and if pushed close can get out of the way and not be caught. His men respect him but are not disposed to worship."[21]

The passionate denunciation of Gale well represents a general view of Bragg among his detractors, although few expressed it quite as vehemently as the staff officer who married Leonidas Polk's daughter. But Spence's more sober assessment comes far closer to my own. Bragg was an officer of undoubted qualities. He was hardworking, meticulous, detail-oriented, and extremely self-disciplined. The intense way he did everything led him to burn out in his job of guiding the main Confederate field army in the West. Bragg also held the world up to his own standard and had little regard for those who did not meet that very high mark. He had a strong tendency to act with energy and aggression when dealing with tactical problems—his actions at Perryville, Stones River, Tullahoma, and Chickamauga indicate that he was by no means afraid to attack the enemy. In the beginning of his tenure as commander of the main Confederate army in the west, at least, he also planned bold strategic offensives.

Bragg's chief failure in the Civil War lay on the personal level rather than in the military sphere. He saw life in black-and-white terms, had scant ability to accept the complexities to be found in others, and possessed a stubborn streak that served him ill in his relations with subordinates. He had no tact in dealing with newspaper correspondents and only clumsily tried to manipulate his public image or ingratiate himself with politicians. If not for Jefferson Davis's keen appreciation for his talents, Bragg would have had no important supporter in Richmond. When Bragg unwisely began to challenge his generals to demonstrate whether they supported him, his effectiveness rapidly declined. Their frank admission that he ought to be replaced merely sparked the stubbornness in him. Bragg desperately held on to a command that he sometimes wanted to give up, out of sheer determination to impose the sort of discipline on others he demanded of himself. This course of action benefited no one in the end. Despite this, Bragg retained the support of far more men in his army than historians tend to admit. His record of success while shaping the Army of Tennessee and leading it longer than any other individual was severely tarnished and corrupted by the controversies that erupted from his ill-advised dealings with recalcitrant officers.

Bragg was not responsible for Confederate defeat, nor was he a monster or an imbecile. It is true he had some glaring weaknesses, but he also had admirable strengths. His impact on history was mixed but important, and it is time to attempt a balanced view of it. This book to a degree defends Bragg; it is inspired by a sense of historical justice. In balancing historical accounts, Bragg will inevitably come out the winner because he has suffered such a deficit of goodwill in the eyes of history that his reputation can only go up if one looks at his Civil War career with care. Bragg was keen on finding someone to write *his* version of history after the Civil War. He thought he found that person in W. T. Walthall and then in E. T. Sykes, but both men did not want to fill that role. I do not either. The raw material for Bragg's story is richly laid out in the published and unpublished primary material, and what is needed is a professional study of that material, not a partisan historical account either for or against Bragg. This is what I have tried to do. While I defend or sympathetically explain him in many cases, he often did not think, say, or do the right thing, and I fully include those instances as well.

I WISH TO THANK all the staff members at the archival institutions listed in the bibliography for their assistance in gaining access to the many unpublished collections containing relevant material on Bragg's Civil War career. Also, my gratitude to several graduate student researchers who aided me in exploring holdings I was unable to visit personally.

Most of all, my gratitude and love for my wife, Pratibha, for her insightful comments on the first draft of this book and for all she is.

Braxton Bragg

The Making of a Southern Patriot

Braxton Bragg came from a successful middle-class family in the Upper South. His father Thomas Bragg owned slaves and made a living by contracting the construction of various buildings in the state. Born in Warrenton, North Carolina, on March 21, 1817, Braxton had eleven brothers and sisters. The eldest, John, graduated from the University of North Carolina and served in the U.S. Congress and as a judge in his adopted state of Alabama. Thomas Bragg Jr. graduated from Captain Partridge's Military Academy in Middleton, Connecticut, and later served as governor of North Carolina and attorney general of the Confederate government. Brother Alexander was an architect, Dunbar was a merchant in Texas, and William, the youngest son, was killed in the Civil War. Thomas Bragg Sr. fathered six daughters as well.[1]

A tragic incident accompanied the family history. Braxton's mother, Margaret Bragg, shot and killed a free black man who apparently spoke impertinently to her one day. She was arrested and held in jail for a while before being acquitted in a jury trial. The exact date of this incident remains unclear, leading some historians to speculate that she may have been pregnant with Braxton at the time. Moreover, historians have also speculated that the incident made an impression on the young Braxton when he became old enough to understand it. Grady McWhiney states that "this unquestionably affected Braxton." "Consciously or subconsciously he may have been ashamed of his mother's jail record," McWhiney continued, even though there is no evidence to support such a conclusion. This incident seems the only explanation for Bragg's sensitivity and fierce resolve to prove his standing in society, in McWhiney's view.[2]

One ought to be able to support such a conclusion with documentary evidence, but there simply is none to use in this argument. Bragg's many battles with other men throughout his life do not need such a hypothetical

THOMAS BRAGG SR. A builder and contractor in North Carolina, Bragg fathered five sons and six daughters. One son, John Bragg, served in the U.S. Congress; another, Thomas Bragg Jr., was governor of North Carolina and attorney general in the Confederate government; and Braxton Bragg was a full general in the Confederate army. (Bragg Family Photographs, ADAH)

explanation, for there are many other ways of interpreting that part of his contentious personality.

Bragg's lot in life was a military career; it suited him professionally and temperamentally, and he became a superb soldier. After graduating fifth in a class of fifty cadets from the U.S. Military Academy in 1837, the very year that the Second Seminole War broke out, his first assignment was in Florida to fight Native Americans as a second lieutenant in the 3rd U.S. Artillery. The next year he became seriously ill and never fully recovered from the effects of malaria. In fact, the young lieutenant was given a sick leave in 1838 to recuperate before returning to duty.[3]

Although Bragg saw no combat in Florida or during his participation in Indian Removal, his professional advancement was impressive. He served as adjutant of his artillery regiment and was promoted to first lieutenant on July 7, 1838, captain eight years later, major in 1846, and lieutenant colonel dating from the battle of Buena Vista in 1847.[4]

But Bragg's rise was not without trouble. His contentious personality came to the fore within the context of soldiering. Because he had a strong tendency to analyze the army's system and find it wanting, he often wrote testy letters to officers as well as politicians who might be interested in reforming the military establishment. While serving at various posts, Bragg became acquainted with many other officers and developed friendships with some, including William T. Sherman. But he also rubbed many other colleagues the wrong way. Erasmus D. Keyes remembered Bragg from their mutual service in South Carolina as ambitious, "but being of a saturnine disposition and morbid temperament, his ambition was of the vitriolic kind." Keyes recognized that Bragg was intelligent "and the exact performance of all his military duties added force to his pernicious influence."[5]

Keyes also recalled that Bragg had already developed into a fierce defender of his native region by the mid-1840s. "He could see nothing bad in the South and little good in the North, although he was disposed to smile on his satelites and sycophants wheresoever they came." Keyes failed to get along with Bragg because the Northerner was "not disposed to concede to his intolerant sectionalism." Forty years later, Sherman recalled an incident wherein he mediated to prevent a duel between Bragg and a correspondent of the *Charleston Mercury*. The newspaperman disparaged North Carolina while making a toast at an Independence Day banquet in 1845, calling it a "strip of land lying between two States." Bragg challenged him to a duel. Friends asked Sherman and John F. Reynolds to stop it, and Sherman was able to convince the correspondent to "admit that North Carolina was a State in the Union, claiming to be a Carolina, though not comparable with *South* Carolina." Sherman recalled this incident with a good deal of sardonic humor, but it is obvious that Bragg's hotheaded defense of his home state nearly resulted in bloodshed.[6]

Bragg was ready, in short, to take on all comers. He certainly had no hesitation in taking on the U.S. Army. The young officer wrote a series of nine articles that were published in the *Southern Literary Messenger* in 1844–45, all of them highly critical of army administration and organization. He did not spare certain high-level individuals as well. Although Bragg signed these articles "A Subaltern," it soon became common knowledge that he was the author. The person targeted for the most criticism was Winfield Scott, general-in-chief of the army. Many of Bragg's suggested reforms were needed, but the tone of his articles was very unkind and unprofessional. That tone brought nothing but trouble. Bragg applied for a leave of absence, being deliberately vague about its purpose, and used it to travel to Washington, D.C., in March 1844. There he lobbied various congressmen regarding his proposed army reforms. When the adjutant general learned of this, he ordered Bragg to leave, but the ambitious young man refused and continued his lobbying efforts, testifying before a congressional committee. Bragg was arrested, tried, and found guilty of disrespect. Unfortunately, he was given a light punishment, and it failed to instill any sense of regret or repentance.[7]

Grady McWhiney has aptly written of "Bragg's distinction as the most cantankerous man in the Army. He had been court-martialed and convicted; he had been censured by the Secretary of War, the Adjutant General, and the Commander of the Eastern Division. No other junior officer could boast of so many high ranking enemies."[8]

The Mexican War offered Bragg a distraction from his obsession with military reform. He commanded one of only two light batteries in the army, joining Zachary Taylor's field force in southern Texas in 1846. His unit participated in Taylor's capture of Monterey in September of that year, but the battle of Buena Vista on February 23, 1847, created national fame for the young officer. Outnumbered three to one, Taylor's army of mostly untried volunteer troops was sorely pressed. If not for the steadiness of the few regular units, the American position might well have collapsed. The widely circulated story that Taylor encouraged Bragg by telling him to fire "a little more grape" is certainly apocryphal. Bragg himself later told acquaintances that Taylor really said, "Give them hell!"[9]

Buena Vista marked the beginning of Bragg's relationship with Jefferson Davis, whose Mississippi regiment did well in the battle. In his official report, Davis praised Bragg's handling of the guns: "We saw the enemy's infantry advancing in three lines upon Capt. Bragg's battery; which, though entirely unsupported, resolutely held it's position, and met the attack, with a fire worthy of the former achievements of that battery, and of the reputation of it's present meritorious commander." In fact, Davis moved his Mississippians to support Bragg and helped the artillery drive away yet another Mexican attack.[10]

Bragg praised Davis's regiment as one of the few reliable volunteer units with Taylor's army. In general, his criticism of volunteers was deep and intense. Humphrey Marshall had graduated from West Point but commanded volunteers in Mexico. "He was at Buena Vista," Bragg told his brother John, "where his regiment did some fine running & no fighting, as all mounted volunteers ever will do. He is a great humbug and a superficial tho fluent fool."[11]

The fame accorded Bragg at Buena Vista did not turn the officer's head. He continued to serve dutifully even though suffering "two severe attacks" of malaria in the summer of 1847. During this time period one of Bragg's artillerymen tried to kill him, but the motive remains obscure. Samuel B. Church placed a loaded and fused twelve-pounder shell outside Bragg's

ELISE BRAGG. Commonly known as Elise, Eliza Brooks Ellis was born in Mississippi and lived on the family's Evergreen plantation near Thibodeaux, Louisiana. She and Braxton Bragg married in 1849. (*Confederate Veteran* 4 [1896]: 103)

tent on August 26, 1847. Although exploding only two feet from the sleeping officer, the shell failed to injure him. At the time no one knew who planted the bomb, and Church was free to try another in October 1847 but failed again. He later deserted the battery and was hanged as a horse thief.[12]

Buena Vista fame translated into social advancement for Bragg. He was greeted as a hero in many Southern cities after the war, and it was during one such reception that he met his future wife. Eliza Brooks Ellis, more familiarly known as Elise, was the oldest daughter of Richard Gaillard Ellis and Mary June Towson Ellis. She had been born in Mississippi and was for a time a schoolmate of the future Mrs. Jefferson Davis. The family estate, a sugar and cotton plantation called Evergreen, was located in Terre Bonne Parish, Louisiana. Elise met Bragg at a ball given in his honor at Thibodaux, forty miles west of New Orleans. The couple was married on June 7, 1849.[13]

Soon after her marriage, Elise confided to a correspondent that she initially believed Bragg was a bit too reserved and cold, but she had been attracted by his strong character and commitment to the truth. Now that she had come to know him better, Elise was surprised by the "depth of affection" that lay behind "such an exterior—he is an ardent & devoted husband." Bragg fully reciprocated her feelings. He wrote of his longing for her upon leaving to attend court-martial proceedings six months after their wedding. "My first thought is for you . . . what in this world can make a man so happy, especially when he possesses such a wife."[14]

Bragg's army career after Mexico became more complex, and he was shifted around to a number of army posts largely along the frontier, causing numerous separations from Elise. He continued to criticize high-level administrators in the army and in the executive branch of the national government and pushed for army reform, hoping for a time that his brother John could capitalize on his tenure in the U.S. Congress to aid the cause. As with the Subaltern articles, his ideas made sense. Now, however, he pursued them with more tact and less bristle. Bragg also proved loyal to trusted subordinates and colleagues. He wrote glowing letters of recommendation for George H. Thomas and Daniel Harvey Hill, both of whom had served in his battery. Given the bitter controversy that erupted between Bragg and Hill growing out of the Chickamauga campaign, it is interesting to see that Bragg referred to him as "my young friend" in 1848. He praised Hill as "without a superior for gentlemanly deportment and high moral character." Bragg also thought very highly of Henry J. Hunt, another friend of the post-Mexico era, who, like Thomas, would fight in the Union army.[15]

Numerous partings with Elise were hard to bear. "I am lost without you, dear wife," he wrote from Fort Leavenworth in June 1853. Bragg often complained that he rarely heard from his numerous siblings. What Bragg called "my old Florida complaint of the *liver*" continued to trouble him. "Every summer I have these attacks, and I can . . . only keep about by almost living on Mercury (Blue Mass & Calomel). No constitution can stand it," he told his friend Sherman. An undated prescription "for Chronic Chill & fever," written in Bragg's hand but coming from a doctor in North Carolina, probably relates to this time period in the officer's life.[16]

By the mid-1850s Bragg's army career reached a crisis point. Jefferson Davis, as secretary of war in the Franklin Pierce administration, instituted significant army reforms. One of them involved introducing rifled artillery and phasing out light batteries. Bragg was devastated by the decline of efficiency in his battery, and he was ordered to join a cavalry regiment on the frontier. The distant but respectful relationship between Bragg and Davis now became bitter, with the officer sarcastically referring to the secretary as "our friend" in his correspondence. Bragg resigned his commission in the U.S. Army on January 3, 1856, "disgusted & worn down" as he told a correspondent. Davis was "absolutely bent on substituting long range rifles for Light Artillery, though *nominally* keeping it up at a heavy expense." As a result, "my command was destroyed, my usefulness gone. . . . The finest battery I ever saw was destroyed in two years at a cost of $100,000."[17]

As Grady McWhiney has indicated, Bragg was possibly motivated to resign because he was nearly forty years old and looking for other avenues

Sugar Plantation along Bayou La Fourche. This Civil War–era photograph
of an unnamed sugar plantation in the Bayou La Fourche region is a good
indication of what Bragg's Bivouac might have looked like. (Marshall
Dunham Photograph Album, Special Collections, LSU)

to keep Elise in the comfort she had grown accustomed to in her father's
house. He became interested in using Elise's inheritance to purchase a sugar
plantation in Louisiana. In fact, Bragg had been looking for a good bargain
as early as the summer of 1855. He found one called Greenwood, only three
miles north of Thibodaux, and purchased it on February 8, 1856, only one
month after leaving the army. Title to Greenwood, which contained 1,600
acres of land and 105 slaves, catapulted Bragg into the elite ranks of the
slave-owning aristocracy with the stroke of a pen. Of the 330 estates along
the left bank of Bayou Lafourche, only 10 others were more valuable than
Greenwood. Bragg renamed the plantation Bivouac, reminiscent of his
recent army career.[18]

Two days after finalizing the purchase, Bragg informed Elise what he
had done. The estate had been purchased two years before by J. Sherman
Shriver from a Creole owner named Pierre Loria. In fact, in assessing the
place, Bragg called all the buildings on it "Creole (*inferior*) but habitable.
Sugar House tolerable. . . . Stock tolerable. Cows enough for the present,
40 or 50 sheep. Fair lot of fruit trees, some sweet oranges at the overseers.

Much of the furniture is good—for creole." As far as his slaves were concerned, Bragg found them "a fair lot, the children very fine and of a pretty age just getting to the field."[19]

Bragg threw himself into managing Bivouac with enthusiasm and detail, learning the sugar industry from the ground up. "My army experience is of infinite benefit to me," he told Sherman. "The planting & cultivation is nothing, management is everything in a business wielding such capital." It took several years of improvement to make Bivouac profitable but Bragg applied himself to the task. By the fall of 1859, he proudly reported that his net profit for that year was $30,000 from an outlay of $45,000 for the season. Bragg admitted that he worried over every detail of his plantation affairs, but that was his nature, "not having been accustomed to manage my business by a proxy." Yet he hoped to arrange for a two-month vacation to the mountains in the summer of 1860. Meanwhile, Elise filed a will in 1858, leaving everything to "my most kind & beloved husband," who also was named executor.[20]

Somewhat reluctantly, Bragg allowed himself to be drawn into a variety of civic duties, imitating the role of large planters all across the South. He served as levee inspector and school director in his locality and permitted his name to be placed in nomination by the Democrats for commissioner of the board of public works in the fall of 1859. It was a new position, designed to combine the posts of land commissioner and engineer for the state of Louisiana. Bragg had no great enthusiasm for the job but was urged by many, especially state senator Richard Taylor, to embrace it. Bragg was impressed by Taylor, the son of his much-respected commander in the Mexican War. "He is a very plain, strait forward man," Bragg wrote of the future Confederate general, "of great independence; candid, honest, and clear headed." There was no one running against him for the position, so it was a certainty he would have to shoulder its responsibilities in 1860. Those responsibilities involved handling improvements such as levees and drainage canals valued at more than $1 million and dealing with corruption. The position contrasted sharply with his two parish jobs of levee inspector and school director, positions that Bragg called "trifles its true." He vowed to do his best as state commissioner but expected much criticism to attend his work.[21]

The project that drew most of Bragg's interest was the creation of a state institution of higher learning. He was involved in the conception of what today is Louisiana State University at Baton Rouge, but in 1859 it was called the Louisiana Seminary of Learning and Military Academy and was located at Alexandria. Tension among the founders as to whether it should be a traditional college with a classical curriculum or a true military academy led to its convoluted name. In fact, if it had been created as a true military academy, Bragg would have been very interested in becoming its superintendent.[22]

Bragg supported the appointment of Claudius W. Sears, who currently was a professor of mathematics at what would later be called Tulane University, as superintendent of the new state college. But William T. Sherman was hired instead. Bragg was very pleased at the choice, although he had not known that Sherman was an applicant. As Sherman was careful to point out in his memoirs, his selection for the post was not due to his friendship with Bragg.[23]

Louisiana needed an institution of higher learning that emphasized a military style of discipline coupled with intense scientific and technical instruction, according to Bragg. He thought the state had enough "High Literary Institutions" and was convinced that "no class of people on the face of the earth are more dependent on Science and discipline for success than the Southern planters." After the seminary opened on January 1, 1860, Bragg strongly supported Sherman in his attempts to discipline unruly students. It was important, in his view, that Southern young men learn they had to become something other than an "aggregation of loafers charged with the duty of squandering their fathers legacies and disgracing their names."[24]

Seminary matters allowed Bragg to indulge in one of his favorite trains of thought, the importance of discipline in a successful life. "Discipline to amount to anything must be firm, decisions prompt, and their execution immediate and irrevocable, except in very extraordinary cases," he told G. Mason Graham, a Mexican War colleague who also was deeply involved in seminary affairs. "Hard cases arise under all laws, and it is better to do some injustice than to break down from laxity. This duty is the more difficult and trying from the very loose system which prevails in our southern society, and which has reduced parents to a subordination to children." Bragg pushed to have the administration of the college veer strongly toward military discipline rather than "*University theories*," as he called them.[25]

Deeply immersed in his plantation, Bragg was willing to encourage and support but hesitated to take a more active role in the affairs of Sherman's institution. He was not interested in serving on the board of visitors. "I have done my share of public duties in this life," he informed Graham, "and seek no more of them for honor or profit. Yet I am always ready to do my share in the advancement of a good cause and to fill my station as a good citizen." Sherman was pleased when he learned that Bragg had been invited to give a speech at the seminary. "He writes, as you know, well and can speak his thoughts clearly and with emphasis," Sherman told Graham; "still I don't think he has an ambition to be styled an orator." Bragg also tried to get the guns of his old Buena Vista battery donated to the seminary, but that did not happen. The weapons were stored in Washington, D.C., and were considered national trophies that could not be issued to the state government of Louisiana.[26]

The relationship between Bragg and Sherman was never so close as during the few months that the latter ran the seminary, and Bragg often wrote long letters to his friend expressing his views on Southern life. "We have a large class of our population in subordination—just & necessary," he wrote of slavery. "Give me well disciplined masters, managers and assistants, and we shall never hear of insurrections." Like most Southerners, Bragg considered the peculiar institution of slavery to be not so peculiar after all. "Human nature is the same throughout the world," he concluded.[27]

The large Southern plantation was a fit venue for applying Bragg's theories of discipline and success. He viewed every estate as "*a small military establishment—or it ought to be*. By military, I don't mean the old fogy notion of white belts, stiff leather stocks, and 'palms of the hands to the front'— but *discipline*—by which we secure system [and] regularity: methods securing of time, labor, and material, this all tends to secure better health, more labor at less exertion, and with infinitely less punishment. More comfort and happiness to the laborer, with more profit & pleasure to the master."[28]

Bragg found his fit venue in the Louisiana sugar plantation culture. It was a more demanding task to run one of these complex operations than a cotton plantation because processing the raw cane into usable sugar required specialized equipment and a rigid work regimen from October to January of each year. The slave laborers often engaged in eighteen-hour days, working in shifts, during those months. They used iron rollers to squeeze the juice out of the cane, boiled the juice until it crystallized, cooled it, and stored the result in large hogsheads. The liquid that continued to drain out was later made into molasses. Larger, better-organized, and more efficiently managed sugar plantations had a higher chance of producing a profit.[29]

Successful sugar planters tended to be effective businessmen as well as managers of their labor force. They also became "aggressive promoters of the most industrialized sector of southern agriculture," in the words

Braxton Bragg in civilian clothes.
The first known photograph of Bragg,
taken sometime just before the outbreak
of the Civil War by Theodore Lilienthal
at his studio, 102 Poydras Street,
New Orleans. (Goelet and Buncombe
Family Papers, Southern Historical
Collection, UNC)

of historian Richard Follett, seeing themselves both as "slaveholders and as thoroughly modern businessmen." While the sugar masters sometimes extolled the paternalistic nature of their role as slave masters, they more often spoke of economic efficiency and managerial skill in a world view that embraced both business enterprise and human slavery. Many of them led the secession wave in 1861 to protect the profitable world they had created for themselves.[30]

Bragg bought into this world of the Louisiana sugar planter, both figuratively and literally. Given his huge personal investment in slavery, he reacted harshly to any sign that the North threatened the plantation system of the South or encouraged the freeing of its slaves. He applauded the caning of Massachusetts senator Charles Sumner on the floor of the U.S. Senate in May 1856 by Preston Brooks, a South Carolina member of the House of Representatives, for making remarks derogatory of the South and of Brooks's cousin in the wake of turmoil over slavery in Kansas territory. Brooks nearly killed Sumner, and the senator took several years to recover before resuming his political career. Bragg callously remarked that "old Sumner [was] severely chastised for his impertinence. You can reach the sensibilities of such dogs only through their heads & a big stick. The place was probably injudiciously chosen, but the balance was well, and were I in the House I should certainly propose a vote of thanks to Mr. Brooks." According to a family friend, Bragg's only hope for the future lay in the influence of Northern Democrats, for he thoroughly distrusted the Republicans to take Southern interests into consideration.[31]

The election of Abraham Lincoln in November 1860 propelled South Carolina out of the Union and aroused the spirit of secession across the Deep South. In Louisiana, Bragg offered his advice regarding the creation of a state military force for self-defense. He thought the existing militia system was inadequate and distrusted the rush of volunteer spirit that initially appeared, arguing that all volunteers wanted to be mounted. From his Mexican War experience, Bragg was convinced that putting a volunteer on a horse was giving him an excuse for running away from battle. In his own parish around Thibodaux, "nothing is doing, our leaders are incompetent, and a large portion of our population are unreliable." Bragg was deep in plantation problems, his crop "almost a failure," yet he was willing to do something to prepare the state for possible conflict.[32]

With the start of national disintegration, Bragg came to accept secession as the only viable course for the South. "The Union is already gone," he told Sherman in late December, 1860. "The only question now is, can we reconstruct any government without *bloodshed*. I do not think we can." Bragg sympathized with Sherman, a Northerner in charge of a semimilitary academy in the Deep South, and understood that he would probably resign and head back home. "A similar duty on my part may throw us into an apparent hostile attitude," Bragg confided to his friend, "but it is too terrible to contemplate, and I will not discuss it."[33]

Even before Louisiana seceded, events propelled Bragg into action. Governor Thomas Moore was anxious to secure Federal property in the state and called on Bragg for help. The Mexican War hero was in New Orleans on January 8 when he received the governor's telegram and left that evening for Baton Rouge. Moore decided to act the next day. Leading a handful of state troops, Bragg talked the commander of the U.S. arsenal in Baton Rouge, a personal acquaintance, into giving up the place without resistance on January 11. Then Bragg worked hard to create a strong state army. His brothers in Alabama and North Carolina read of his leading role in these stirring events and concluded that Braxton was "acting, virtually, as Sec'y of War of Louisiana, and is rapidly organizing her military force." Louisiana seceded on January 26, and Bragg was named major general of the state forces. "We hope this course will lead to a peaceable solution of the matters," Bragg told Sherman. "A separation is inevitable—nothing can prevent it now. Why should there be any strife over it?"[34]

Moore's seizure of the arsenal and of Federal forts in Louisiana, with

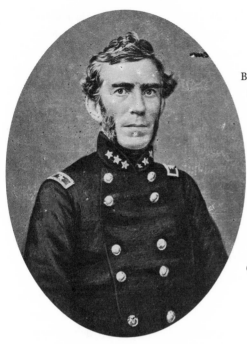

Braxton Bragg in Louisiana State uniform. Bragg held a commission as major general and commander of the forces of his adopted state for a couple of months early in 1861, during which he engineered the takeover of the U.S. Arsenal at Baton Rouge and the raising of three regiments for state service. The face in this image is exactly the same as in the photograph depicting Bragg in civilian clothing. (Library of Congress, LC-DIG-cwpb-07427)

Bragg's help, was the turning point in Sherman's view; he decided to resign as superintendent of the academy and leave the South. Sherman counted Bragg among his "most intimate friends" and often dined with him and Elise while spending time in New Orleans to wrap up business attending the seminary. One day at tea, Elise brought up her husband's relations with Jefferson Davis, who by then had been selected provisional president of the Confederate government. Sherman knew that "Bragg hated Davis bitterly" and had resigned from the army because of his policies.[35]

Sherman recalled in his memoirs that, during the 1840s, Bragg had often ridiculed the idea that South Carolina might secede from the Union. But that had all changed now. During his dinners with the Braggs in New Orleans during those few days in February 1861, Bragg was an enthusiastic defender of the South's right to secede. In fact, according to Sherman, Bragg thought it was best for everyone that the South leave and form a new nation "because the possibility of a successful effort was yearly lessened by the rapid and increasing inequality between the two sections, from the fact that all the European immigrants were coming to the Northern States and Territories, and none to the Southern."[36]

Bragg now filled a prominent role in Louisiana's history, and friends and family members were keenly aware of it. As he set about to organize three regiments for the state army, Sherman was convinced he would succeed brilliantly and train those troops to a high state of efficiency. Bragg was troubled by an outbreak of boils on his hand at this time but used home remedies to treat them and simply put up with the inconvenience. His position as major general and commander of the state forces of Louisiana compelled him to be in touch with the new Confederate government at Montgomery, Alabama. Federal troops who gave up their forts in Texas were passing through the state in late February and Bragg telegraphed Confederate secretary of war Leroy P. Walker for instructions on how to handle them. Walker passed the question on to Davis, who told Walker to inform Bragg that he had "entire confidence in your discretion and prudence" to handle the situation so as to protect the interests of the new Southern government and avoid an outbreak of violence at the same time.[37]

In fact, far from holding any grudge against Bragg, Davis was interested in bringing him into Confederate service. There was even talk of Bragg filling a post in Davis's cabinet, but a military appointment seemed more appropriate. On March 7, 1861, Walker telegraphed Bragg proposing the rank of brigadier general in the provisional Confederate army. Bragg accepted without hesitation.[38]

A Southerner by birth, Braxton Bragg had become more than that by the late 1850s. His service in the U.S. Army represented a career spent in national, not just regional, service. But his disenchantment with the army changed his life. Bragg moved into the planter class where he became a thorough Southern patriot, protective of the institution of slavery and determined through the seminary to instill a higher degree of efficiency in the younger generation of Louisiana. He embraced and promoted the secession of his state, acted to seize Federal property even before the secession ordinance was passed, and then organized and commanded the state's military forces. Bragg was not enthusiastic about his visible role in secession and the drift toward war, but he certainly did not regret it or shun the responsibility offered him to be an important part of state and Confederate national affairs. He was convinced it was the right thing for his section and for himself to do.

2

Pensacola

When Bragg received the offer of a commission in the Confederate army, he rushed to respond. Making arrangements to leave New Orleans immediately for his assignment at Pensacola, he could not return to Bivouac and say goodbye to Elise in person. The new brigadier wrote a letter to her explaining the need for haste and then rushed to finish his business in the city before leaving on March 8.[1]

"What is to become of all this I do not see except war," Bragg told Elise. "Mr. Lincoln says he will not recognize our government, and if he does not we must take the Forts in our limits: To do that is war, and when it commences it will rage from one end of the country to the other." Bragg went from believing that secession would be a peaceful process to expecting a bloody conflict to erupt from it, but he was confident. "Our course is just, and we must triumph. I deplore the necessity, but neither you nor I could wish me out of it. Come what will I must be in it."[2]

Davis assigned Bragg to one of the Confederacy's hot spots: control of volunteer troops assembling at Pensacola where the U.S. government held a coastal defense called Fort Pickens. Bragg would be the first Confederate officer to take charge of affairs at Pensacola. Florida had seceded on January 10, 1861, and the Federals had evacuated their mainland posts at Pensacola the next day. The state government decided not to attack Fort Pickens, which was located near the west end of Santa Rosa Island with Pensacola Bay separating that island from the mainland. The Federal garrison had agreed not to accept reinforcements if the Florida troops allowed mail to be delivered to the fort and refrained from attacking Santa Rosa Island. As Confederate troops moved in during February, they replaced state forces at Fort McRee and Fort Barrancas on the mainland as well as at the U.S. Navy Yard and the small village of Warrington. The situation was similar to that at Charleston, South Carolina, where a small Federal garrison continued to occupy Fort Sumter on a sandbar at the entrance to the harbor although

Braxton Bragg in *Frank Leslie's Illustrated Newspaper*. Bragg became one of the very few Confederate generals to have his portrait printed in a Northern illustrated newspaper. The editors chose to reproduce the Lilienthal photograph of the future general in civilian clothes. (*Frank Leslie's Illustrated Newspaper*, June 22, 1861, p. 91)

confronted on three sides by Confederate mainland fortifications. Davis assigned trusted generals to these two flashpoints, relying on Pierre G. T. Beauregard to handle the military resources at Charleston.[3]

When Bragg reached the area on March 10, 1861, he found 6,804 men organized into four brigades. This became the nucleus of the Army of Pensacola. The men who commanded these brigades, James R. Chalmers, S. A. M. Wood, H. B. Tyler, and John K. Jackson, became some of his warmest supporters. He later consolidated these four brigades into two under Daniel Ruggles and Richard H. Anderson.[4]

If Bragg worried that his old feud with Davis would create difficulties, he was wrong. The president of the Confederacy treated him with respect and confidence. Given the significance of Pensacola, Davis communicated freely with his new general about Fort Pickens. "I wish you to regard this not as a letter of the President," he told Bragg on April 3, "but of your old comrade in arms, who hopes much, and expects much for you, and from you." Bragg wanted to know from Secretary of War Leroy P. Walker whether he had authority to attack the Union fort. He fully understood that this was a political as well as a military matter, for it could propel the South into war. From a military standpoint, he believed his men could do it by distracting the small Federal garrison and then scaling the walls at a different point. Bragg believed that "the ardor and ignorance of my troops

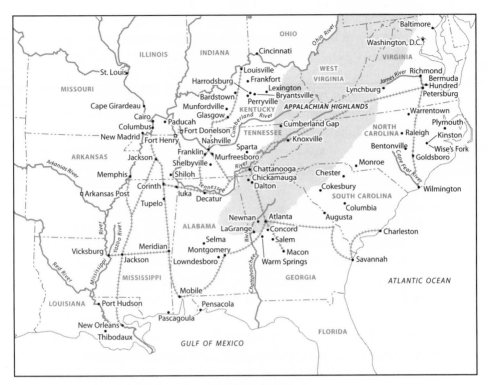

Bragg's Civil War

would be strong elements of success," but reported that only a few of his officers could handle their men well. Bragg also communicated directly with Davis on this matter, admitting that a siege of the fort was impossible for many reasons. Walker informed Bragg that the Confederate government wanted possession of Fort Pickens, but Bragg had to make his own decision as to whether an attack was likely to succeed. Bragg decided to act with caution, readying his troops and requesting more equipment and material for his ill-supplied regiments. When the men became unruly because of the availability of liquor in town, Bragg declared martial law and closed the grog shops. "I captured enough to have kept the Army drunk two months," he told Elise.[5]

Bragg continued to handle affairs at Pensacola so as not to provoke violence. When informed by the Federal naval commander that he had imposed a blockade of the coast near Pensacola, Bragg told him he considered that "an act of aggressive war" and even "a virtual acknowledgment of our national existence and independence." He received well-meaning advice from a variety of civilians who thought they had a good idea for

taking Pickens with minimal loss, or who warned Bragg of some imminent Yankee move they detected from reading newspaper reports. He
filed these messages but of course never acted on them. The firing on Fort
Sumter in mid-April and the consequent start of open hostilities between
the Confederate and Federal governments did not change the situation
at Pensacola. Bragg continued to act cautiously. When Davis requested
reinforcements to protect Richmond, however, Bragg quickly sent 2,500
of his own troops, one-third of his available manpower. Davis also was
pleased that Bragg praised the work of his nephew, Joseph R. Davis, at
Pensacola. "He/Genl. B./is not inclined to praise," Davis told Joseph, "and
is in no degree a courtier."[6]

The shortage of competent officers at Pensacola made Bragg even more
pleased than usual to see Richard Taylor in late May 1861. Taylor yet held
no position in the Confederate army but agreed to serve as a volunteer aide
on Bragg's staff until he was elected colonel of a Louisiana regiment early
in July. Bragg regretted his departure. "He had become almost a necessity
to me," he told Elise. "He is cool, sagacious and devoted to the cause & to
me." Bragg relied on former U.S. Army officers who had joined the Confederates to instill a high degree of training and discipline among the state
volunteers who made up his command. He also complained to Richmond
when many of his best subordinates were passed up for promotion in favor
of other, less qualified candidates. Bragg specifically noted that Mansfield
Lovell was named to command the area around New Orleans rather than
Daniel Ruggles. "That command includes my home and fireside," he told
the new secretary of war, Judah B. Benjamin, "and all that is dear to me in
life. I can appreciate the feeling of sullen dissatisfaction which pervades
my neighbors."[7]

Elise visited her husband in early July to find Bragg in good health. The
officers of the 1st Louisiana Regulars, a regiment Bragg had organized,
hosted a ball in honor of Elise on July 23 in the Navy Yard. It so happened
that a message from Davis relating to the Confederate victory at First
Manassas arrived in time for Bragg to read it to the assembled partygoers,
capping the festivities.[8]

Bragg was promoted major general in the Confederate army to date
from September 12, 1861, an appointment that was confirmed by the Senate in November. September also brought warlike activity to Pensacola.
The Federals raided the Navy Yard with three boats and burned an armed
patrol boat on the night of September 13. Bragg authorized a retaliatory
strike against Santa Rosa Island that took place on the night of October

Braxton Bragg as a Confederate general. Bragg appears in this photograph, apparently taken early in the Civil War, with a full beard and mustache. (Bragg Family Photographs, ADAH)

8–9. The raid included 1,000 Confederates who landed on the island by boat, surprised and captured a camp occupied by a portion of the 6th New York, but did not directly attack Fort Pickens. In fact, the Confederates had to retreat for fear of being cut off by a Union force sent from the fort. Bragg praised the commanders, but they lost eighty-seven men, while the Federals suffered only sixty-seven casualties.[9]

In the wake of this raid on Santa Rosa Island, the Richmond authorities more properly defined Bragg's command. They extended his area of responsibility to include the entire state of Alabama and named it the Department of Alabama and Western Florida. His staff members included many officers who would follow him through the war. Brother-in-law Towson Ellis served as an aide-de-camp, Hypolite Oladowski as Bragg's chief of ordnance, Surgeon A. J. Foard as his medical director, and Harvey W. Walter as his judge advocate. Bragg conducted an inspection tour of his enlarged department by visiting Mobile, a vital port city on the Alabama coast in need of enormous resources for its defense. Jones Withers commanded 4,200 men there, and Bragg decided to send him a handful of his own competent subordinates because too many of Withers's officers were "sadly addicted to drinking." By mid-November 1861, Bragg could count on 7,000 troops around Pensacola, 9,000 at Mobile, and the completion of a rail link between the two cities.[10]

Bragg's ability to administer a sizable department was evident to Davis

JEFFERSON DAVIS. Bragg had a long and shifting relationship with Davis. He fought alongside him at Buena Vista, resigned from the U.S. Army because of him, held a grudge against him for many years after, but gradually realized that Davis had always respected and admired his talents. Davis, in fact, relied heavily on Bragg throughout the Civil War, supporting him in numerous confrontations with subordinates, and the two developed a friendship by the end of the conflict that lasted the rest of their lives. (Library of Congress, LC-DIG-ppmsca-26716)

and his advisers. That is why they seriously considered sending him to the Trans-Mississippi, where Confederate forces were outnumbered, ill-led, and undersupplied. The fiery leader of Missouri's State Guard, Sterling Price, was constantly at odds with the regional commander of Confederate forces, Benjamin McCulloch. Cooperation between the two neared the breaking point, and the Federals who controlled key areas of central and eastern Missouri were determined to strengthen their tenuous hold on this border slave state. The pro-Confederate governor of Missouri, Claiborne F. Jackson, suggested that Bragg come west to take command and settle the squabbling between McCulloch and Price.[11]

Davis and Benjamin agreed that Bragg was the only high-ranking general they could send, but Benjamin made it clear that it was Bragg's decision. The secretary of war laid out the basic problem: Price's Missourians were brave but nearly a rabble as far as organization, training, and discipline were concerned. The cause needed a mastermind capable of shaping this rough material "into a real army." Davis and Benjamin could "find no one but yourself on whom we feel we could rely with confidence."[12]

More than a week later, Bragg responded to this offer with care and consideration. An ambitious and risk-taking man would have leaped at it, but Bragg had little desire to take such a chance. He admitted that his efforts had converted raw troops into good soldiers at Pensacola, but he also told Richmond that the situation in the Trans-Mississippi was "most gloomy" and far less promising of success than operations east of the river.

Yet he was willing to go if ordered, conceding that "[I would] offer myself (as a sacrifice, if necessary) to the great cause in which we are engaged." If he did so, Bragg insisted on taking a few of the best regiments and generals currently serving under him in Alabama.[13]

With a response like this, Davis decided not to order Bragg west. Instead, he chose Earl Van Dorn, a division commander in the Army of the Potomac which protected Richmond. Van Dorn eagerly accepted this chance for glory in the field. Meanwhile, rumors flew about that Bragg would be assigned to command the Army of the Potomac, headquartered at Centreville. Those rumors, of course, proved untrue.[14]

Another outbreak of violence at Pensacola continued to imply that Bragg's leadership was needed in the Department of Alabama and Western Florida. In retaliation for the raid on Santa Rosa Island, Federal artillery opened a massive bombardment on November 22, 1861, and the Confederate guns replied to it. The nearly daylong exchange resulted in a handful of Confederates killed and wounded, and it resumed the next day without injuring anyone. But the damage to Fort McRee was extensive, indicating the Northern guns had the advantage over this target. Some Federal rounds landed in residential areas on the mainland and set the village of Warrington on fire. The Federals fired a total of 5,000 rounds and the Confederates only 1,000. Yet, in reporting the two-day artillery combat, Bragg praised "my gallant little army" and key officers in it, especially Adley H. Gladden of South Carolina.[15]

News of the little affair shocked Elise when she heard about it back in Louisiana. "I was entirely alone when your first dispatch reached me," she admitted in a letter to her husband, "& I fear was too badly frightened to have that composure which a soldier's wife should now possess, but it was *my first experience under fire*. I will do better another time."[16]

Bragg's pride in the Army of Pensacola soared as he praised it for steadiness under fire during the artillery bombardment. He excelled at the tedious process of turning raw troops into effective soldiers, and upon arriving at Pensacola in March 1861 he had found the roughest material imaginable. The volunteers were "without discipline," he had told Elise when he reached the area, "each man with an idea that he can whip the world, and believing that nothing is necessary but go it and take Fort Pickens." Engineer officer Samuel Henry Lockett served with Bragg and later confirmed this impression of the rank and file. The men "were totally regardless of the ordinary rules of good conduct and propriety." It was impossible for any man riding a horse, or dressed "in a decent suit of clothes" to appear before them without eliciting "crude jokes and coarse witticisms." One day Bragg and Lockett rode through the camps, Bragg wearing a cocked hat. One man saw him and shouted, "Come out of that turtle-shell, General. I see your legs a dangling out." The cry was taken up by hundreds of other enlisted men who raised such a din that Bragg could only spur his horse and escape. "What a people!" he complained to Lockett, "What a people!"[17]

Yet, in later months, Lockett recalled that Bragg told him these very same enlisted men were "magnificent fighters." To a large degree, that was so because Bragg had succeeded in molding them into good soldiers. By mid-December 1861, he reported to Benjamin that "they are the best troops I have ever known, all inferior men having been culled out." Supply problems continued to plague him; the infusion of four new regiments of 3,000 men in late November was hampered by the fact that Bragg had only 600 weapons to arm them. Newspaper reports complaining about the quality of medical care under Bragg's command brought a deluge of letters written by his men and defending Dr. Foard and other medical officers. A woman volunteer nurse who worked in the hospitals later described the "beautifully organized little army at Pensacola" as a fit example for other Confederate forces to emulate.[18]

Generally, the men at Pensacola trusted Bragg. To some of them, at least, he looked the part of a commander, and he certainly took care of them. Thomas Butler, a relative of Elise and a lieutenant in the 1st Louisiana Regulars, described the general while he reviewed his troops riding "on a fine charger." Bragg "looked every inch a commander in chief or as a Sec. Lieut expressed it[,] just like a Gen'l you see in pictures!"[19]

With a small but good command that he had carefully fashioned over several months, it is not surprising that Bragg declined abandoning the Army of Pensacola in favor of the long odds to be faced in the Trans-Mississippi. Another outbreak of long-range combat at Pensacola offered him an opportunity to show that his guiding hand was still needed at that place. While on his way back from an inspection trip to Mobile on January 1, 1862, the Federals once again bombarded Confederate mainland targets. A privately owned steamer was allowed to go to the docks at the Navy Yard, and when the Federals saw this, they began firing at it and other targets. Richard Heron Anderson was in charge at Pensacola while Bragg was away, and he authorized return fire. The Federals stopped rather soon, but the Confederates continued firing long after it was necessary to do so. Many blamed Anderson, who reportedly was inebriated at the time.[20]

When Bragg returned, he was determined to investigate and bring Anderson to trial. He told the Confederate adjutant general of his intention and expressed it bluntly in a private letter to staff member Harvey Walter. "Having held subordinates to a rigid account I should deserve the contempt of my army would I ever fail in doing my duty towards a General." But Bragg doubted he could succeed because Davis would not act to support him. Nathan Evans had reportedly been drunk during the battle of Leesburg in Virginia the past October, and rather than punishment he received Davis's praise for the successful engagement. "Anderson may be commended and myself punished, but I shall try it," Bragg told Walter. In the end Anderson evaded the lash and received a brigade command in the Army of the Potomac early in 1862.[21]

The problem of inept subordinates continued to plague Bragg at Pensacola. After Leroy P. Walker left his post as secretary of war and received a commission in the army, he was assigned a brigade in Alabama. Walker had no notion of how to fulfill his important duties. Bragg complained that his brigade had "no organization, no system, and no instruction. Each regimental and battalion commander was independent of all the rest." Walker did not even stay with his command but lived in Mobile while his troops endured squalid conditions, one-third of them sick. Bragg ordered Walker to join his men but did not think it would help as he was totally over his head as a military officer. The only solution was to shift him to Montgomery to take charge of unarmed men. Walker "can do less harm there," Bragg told Samuel Cooper, the Confederate adjutant general. He put Gladden in charge of Walker's brigade.[22]

Bragg was pleased that his tenure at Pensacola produced a strong and supportive relationship with Jefferson Davis. "You will be surprised to hear of the very cordial message I have received from our old friend President Davis," he told Elise in March 1861. "He says with such men as Beauregard & Bragg at Charleston & Pensacola he feels easy." The relation strengthened when Davis, his wife, and several other Confederate leaders visited Pensacola in mid-May 1861 to inspect the defenses. Bragg complained to Davis that many inferior officers received promotion over his subordinates. "He said he never knew of it & would correct it on his return and did so," Bragg told his wife.[23]

Bragg's attitude toward war issues hardened considerably during his stay at Pensacola. When he realized that his old army friend, Henry Jackson Hunt, was stationed in Fort Pickens late in April 1861, he sent a message to him across the lines. It was "a scorching letter," as Bragg told Elise, because he now realized that Hunt was "lost to us having married into an abolition family." Accusing Hunt of allowing himself to "be the instrument of oppression in the hands of a Black Repub[lica]n," Bragg tried to tell his old friend that the common people of the South deeply supported the new nation. "We feel that we cannot live with the North in peace and we desire to be left alone to pursue the even tenor of our way," he assured Hunt. "You may destroy us, but cannot conquer." In his return letter, Hunt ignored the politics and focused on the friendship, musing on how strange it felt to be arrayed against one with whom he had shared close relations for years.[24]

English journalist William Howard Russell visited Pensacola a month later, in May 1861, and recorded an interesting exchange of views with the Confederate commander. He found Bragg "a tall, elderly man, in a blue frock coat with a gold star on the shoulder, trousers with a gold stripe and gilt buttons." Bragg talked freely about slavery, telling Russell that only black laborers could cultivate cash crops in the South, and the only way to make them work was by forcing them into a condition of servitude. Then, with no sense of irony, Bragg told Russell that the "North was bent on subjugating the South," as Bragg summarized the conflict in Russell's words, and he would resist it "as long as he had a drop of blood in his body."[25]

When Bragg reached Pensacola, he was appalled at the lack of suitable lodging for his wife. The place was "worse than Thibodaux." But he found a house to rent for Elise and other members of her family when they visited. Bragg encouraged Thomas Butler's father to visit the army camps and extended the invitation to other members of Butler's family, including an unmarried aunt. "The Gen'l also orders me to give you a very impertinent message," Thomas wrote to the aunt, "That he wishes to get a body guard of *old maids* and then he knows they will all be taken." Such a coarse joke probably was ill-received, and it indicates Bragg's rather crass sense of humor.[26]

While the general was cordial with his wife's family, the primary focus of his personal time was directed toward Elise. Even before leaving New Orleans in March 1861, after receiving the call for Pensacola, Bragg hurriedly made many arrangements to ease her management of Bivouac. He left a good deal of money with the Urquhart family so she could draw on that sum for expenses, and he ordered fifty-nine barrels of pork for the larder at the plantation. But he did not have enough time to arrange a supply of clothes for the slaves at Bivouac. Bragg also called on a photographer to pick up the "likeness of my old Father" that the man had worked on, and the photographer insisted on taking Bragg's photograph too, agreeing to send a copy to Elise.[27]

Once settled into his duties, Bragg began writing frequently to Bivouac. He urged Elise to "bear it all with the fortitude of a soldier, and pray for protection to our country and those who are dear to you." He assured her "that the last and most fervent prayers of your husband will be for you." After her first visit to Bragg in the summer of 1861, Elise made several subsequent trips, one of the few times during the war she had the luxury of seeing her husband in the field on a regular basis. She normally went alone and found it difficult. "I miss you so much in travelling, you were so full of thoughtfulness & kind attentions. Your arm your shoulder were at my disposal. You have spoilt your wife & it is hard to awake from it. I dare say I shall get accustomed to it." For her part, Elise tried to caution Bragg about exposing himself when the inevitable battle took place. "I know you are brave without being rash, & while you will shrink at no personal danger *if it be necessary*, you will bear in mind, that on *your safety* depends that of your brave little army, no one there can supply your place." Not only Bragg but Elise also won a place in the hearts of many in that "brave little army." She donated "a barrel of golden syrup" for the officers' larder of the 9th Mississippi, for which the men were grateful.[28]

An important topic of discussion between Bragg and Elise was the general's health. She did not want him to live in a tent during the winter of 1861–62, fearing a recurrence of rheumatism. Grady McWhiney listed the other conditions that had previously afflicted Bragg, including "dyspepsia, nervousness, and severe migraine headaches." By mid-December, carbuncles once again appeared on his left leg and left hand, "greatly troubling him," in the words of his brother Thomas Bragg. Just before that time, John Bragg suffered "a partial apoplectic attack" at his home near Montgomery and had to recover the full use of his eyesight. By late January, Thomas was heartened when one of Bragg's staff officers, who visited Richmond, told him the general was in much better health and "in good spirits."[29]

When word spread of the effective job Bragg did in administering his various duties at Pensacola, many other officials around the Confederacy began to copy his methods. Samuel Cooper adopted Bragg's order suppressing liquor and mandated that its details be followed by all Confederate commanders in January 1862. In fact, drinking came up as a topic in one of Davis's cabinet meetings. Thomas Bragg, who now served as the Confederate attorney general, was thrilled when the president of the Confederacy lavished praise on Braxton's handling of the issue. He "said he had put down drinking," Thomas recorded in his diary, "and that his had been the only well disciplined and managed Army in the field. That he set a proper example to his men. In speaking of the other Generals, their qualities, & c, he ranked him with Sidney Johnston and some others." On another occasion, Davis told Thomas that he thought Bragg was "the only General in command of an Army who had shewn himself equal to the management of Volunteers and at the same time commanded their love and respect." Thomas wrote a long letter telling Braxton of this, because his brother was "of the impression that the Pres't & Sec'y of War are not over well inclined towards him."[30]

But Braxton's assumption could not have been more wrong. In fact, Davis and Benjamin placed him among the very best generals available to the Confederacy. Few if any others had Bragg's administrative abilities. Therein lay the true source of Davis's faith in Bragg as a commander, a faith that would sustain the general through numerous, bitter controversies to come. That faith was not based on friendship, for Bragg and Davis did not develop a personal relationship until the general became Davis's military adviser in Richmond early in 1864. Davis supported Bragg because he sincerely believed him to be a reliable and effective commander.[31]

In the fall of 1861, when James R. Chalmers delivered a message that Bragg was willing to let his well-drilled troops move to Kentucky while taking in more raw units at Pensacola, Davis was heartened by his patriotism. "I remember the earnestness with which you said to me," wrote Chalmers to Davis more than twenty years later, "'That is like Bragg, he thinks more of the cause than of himself. But few Generals would give up without complaining an army they had drilled and made ready for service.'"[32]

In early January 1862, when Bragg declined to go to the Trans-Mississippi, there was talk in Richmond of enlarging his present command to include New Orleans. Bragg was eager for that change. New Orleans was at the heart of his home country, only forty miles from Bivouac, and there were signs of a Federal buildup on Ship Island, which could only mean a move against the Confederacy's largest commercial city. Judah Benjamin, however, talked Davis out of the idea of giving New Orleans to Bragg, and thus Mansfield Lovell received the command. On one level, Thomas was relieved, for he thought his brother had his hands full already. But when the city fell with little resistance in April 1862, Thomas regretted that Braxton had not been given responsibility for holding it.[33]

The fall of New Orleans came soon after a series of events that cracked open the Confederate defense line across Kentucky, which protected the entire western theater of the struggling nation. The fall of Fort Henry and

Fort Donelson in February 1862 altered the war for both belligerents and catapulted Bragg into active operations in the field. He had commanded at Pensacola for eleven months and had carried on a conservative policy so as not to antagonize the Federal garrison of Fort Pickens or the sizable fleet of blockading vessels near the harbor. For a few weeks in March and April 1861, it was not impossible that the opening guns of the Civil War could have been fired at Santa Rosa Island rather than at Charleston, South Carolina, but Bragg made certain that did not happen. In contrast to Beauregard at Charleston, Bragg was under no pressure from the state of Alabama or from the Confederate authorities in Montgomery to act, and he chose a wise and calm way of managing the situation.

That meant Bragg could concentrate on discipline, drill, and molding his officer corps as much as possible. He was in his element as a commander at Pensacola, responsible for a small enough army so that his personal stamp could be put on the men under his tutelage. Although a few of Bragg's subordinates resented his methods, most of them understood that they were necessary and became firm supporters of their commander. The same methods would be far more difficult to apply to a larger force, as Bragg would soon discover, but the Confederates had to work with incredibly raw material in forming a volunteer army at short notice, and Bragg's methods worked well.

The only thing missing so far was combat. Bragg had experience only in commanding a single battery under fire, and that was in the Mexican War thirteen years before. He did not personally direct any of the small actions that took place at Pensacola. Ironically, this old war hero still had to face a new experience commanding large numbers of troops under fire, and the turn of events with the fall of Fort Donelson provided him the opportunity.

3

Shiloh

On February 15, 1862, when the garrison of Fort Donelson tried to break through the encircling Union army, Bragg wrote a thoughtful letter to Judah P. Benjamin from his quarters at Pensacola. In his view, the Confederates had scattered their limited manpower in the West far too much. Responding to news of the fall of Fort Henry a few days before, he advised giving up fringe areas such as Pensacola, New Orleans, and Mobile in order to concentrate on holding the forward line in Kentucky and Tennessee. Bragg also deplored what he thought was a prevailing attitude among the green volunteers who filled Southern ranks. "Unfortunately, many of our higher officers and a larger proportion of our men consider there is no duty to be done in this contest but to fight. Gallant to a fault, they ignore preparation, and exhaust their energies and time in clamoring for this fight. Calamitous results teach them too late the unfortunate error."[1]

After Fort Donelson fell, Benjamin fully agreed with Bragg's views. Orders went out for thousands of men around the fringes of the Confederacy to report to Gen. Albert Sidney Johnston, commander of Confederate forces between the Appalachians and the Mississippi River. By then Johnston was already planning to give up his forward base at Bowling Green, Kentucky, and retire to Nashville. Bragg acted quickly, with an additional spur by Alabama governor John Gill Shorter, who told him that the entire Mississippi Valley would fall if something was not done to meet Union columns coming from the North. When Bragg learned that P. G. T. Beauregard, who held a subordinate command under Johnston at Jackson, Tennessee, had called on Shorter for more troops, he decided to send some of his men to him as well. "I am acting on my own responsibility, and doing what it seems to us ought to had been done long ago—concentrating our limited means at some important point to resist a vital blow." Bragg decided to go personally to help in this concentration, telling Samuel Jones "our fate may depend on two weeks in the valley of the Mississippi." He left Mobile on February 27 and arrived at Jackson on March 2.[2]

Davis was pleased that Bragg became part of the new team to defend Tennessee, telling Johnston that he would bring well-disciplined troops and "the highest administrative capacity" to the new field army Johnston was trying to assemble. Davis's nephew, Jefferson D. Bradford, assured his uncle that Bragg's appointment to replace Benjamin as secretary of war, a move widely circulated in the wake of Fort Donelson's fall, would give universal satisfaction.[3]

Upon arrival at Jackson, Bragg had to adjust his command style to co-operate with other officers of equal and superior rank to his own. Sherman had contended that Bragg was jealous the year before when Beauregard had been made a brigadier general in the Confederate service before him. If so, Bragg did not display any evidence of it in March 1862. He cooperated freely with Beauregard to organize the troops at Jackson into the Army of the Mississippi. It was expected that Johnston would soon bring his Army of Kentucky to make a junction with Beauregard at the important rail center of Corinth, Mississippi.[4]

When that juncture was made, after Johnston abandoned Nashville and all of Middle Tennessee, the two forces were joined to make one field army. Johnston decided to retain Beauregard's name for it and to command the whole, but he relied heavily on his chief subordinates to organize an administrative structure for the Army of the Mississippi. Bragg told his family friend and staff member David Urquhart that Johnston confided to him his misgivings about the failure of Confederate strategy thus far in the West. Johnston felt he had lost the confidence of his men because of the fall of Fort Henry and Fort Donelson; he wanted Beauregard to organize the army and Bragg to act as his chief of staff. But Bragg had already been designated commander of the Second Corps in the Army of the Missis-sippi, the largest command thus far in his military career, and he was loath to give it up. Johnston understood and allowed Bragg to fill both roles as corps commander and as army chief of staff. Urquhart recalled that Beau-regard did most of the work to organize the army, but Bragg claimed after the war that Beauregard did little as second in command and most of the organizing and administering fell into his area of responsibility.[5]

Whoever deserves most of the credit for organizing the Army of the Mississippi, Bragg was energized by his new duties and encouraged that he was accepted as a full partner by his more famous colleagues. "I find my opinions have some weight with both Johnston & Beauregard," he proudly told Elise, "and I shall not cease to urge my point. Johnston almost embraced me when I met him, saying, 'Your prompt and decisive move, Sir, has saved me, and saved the country. But for your arrival, the enemy would have been between us.'" Bragg's commissary was delighted that his chief had an opportunity to exercise his known talents for organization among the mass of raw material assembling under Johnston. "He is infusing new life and energy in the movements of the army," asserted John Walker. The purpose of organizing the Army of the Mississippi was to protect the river that lent its name to the new force. Bragg was convinced that the Mississippi Valley was "of more importance to us than all the country together." Losing it would be "almost fatal to us," he told Elise.[6]

The first problem Bragg had to deal with was a free-for-all spirit among the regiments assembling at Corinth, which had never known his discipline. The town was a madhouse, Bragg reported home. He arrested a colonel for not keeping control of his men and managed to stop the tendency to plunder private homes and shops. "It is my fixed purpose to execute the first one caught in such acts." Bragg also issued an order for the post commander at Memphis to declare martial law in that city in order to stop the sale of liquor to the troops. Sensitive to any disaster along the Mississippi, Bragg became angry when the Federals captured New Madrid, Missouri, thus putting the Confederate artillery batteries lining the shore of Island Number Ten in jeopardy. He was convinced that a combination of liquor and incompetency among the Rebel officers had caused this disaster and thought John P. McCown, the commander in the area, should be arrested. "Stern, dictatorial measures are necessary and as far as any influence goes will be adopted."[7]

Meanwhile, Bragg efficiently put his own house in order. On March 4, 1862, he issued general orders assuming command of the Second Grand Division of Beauregard's Army of the Mississippi and naming his staff members. All of them were men who had served him at Pensacola, and one of them was his brother-in-law, Towson Ellis. Fiercely loyal to his staff, Bragg endeavored to keep as many of these men with him as possible throughout the long trials to come. On March 29, when Johnston formally took command of the combined forces and retained its name as the Army of the Mississippi, Bragg's Grand Division was renamed the Second Corps. Leonidas Polk commanded the First Corps, and William J. Hardee the Third Corps. Bragg also was officially named Johnston's chief of staff and Beauregard named second in command on March 29.[8]

Thus was formed the major Confederate field army in the vast theater of the West. Thrown together haphazardly under great stress, there simply was no time to hone the units into a coherent whole before meeting the Federals in battle. Bragg was simply appalled at the condition of the army in its first few weeks of existence. While the regiments he had brought from Pensacola were in good shape, the others under Johnston, Beauregard, Polk, and Hardee seemed to be little more than armed mobs, despite the fact that they had been in service for several months. Among other transgressions they stole food from civilians. "Polk & Johnston do nothing to correct this. Indeed the good Bishop sets the example by taking whatever he wishes—requiring it to be paid for its true." Jefferson Davis put it well in his history of the Confederacy when he characterized the Army of the Mississippi, based on Bragg's description of it, as "a heterogeneous mass, in which there was more enthusiasm than discipline, more capacity than knowledge, and more valor than instruction."[9]

While her husband was working himself to the bone to impose some degree of order on the troops at Corinth, Elise worried about him. "It seems I never before realized how dear you were to me, & how hard it is to live without you. The past year was a blank except when I was with you; & I shudder when I think another, perhaps to be even more trying, is before me." She could console herself only in corresponding. "I hate to have to say 'good night' dearest—while I write, I am with you. . . . Your hard soldier's couch with you was far pleasanter to your wife, than her soft bed without you."[10]

Elise was a smart, alert person, who paid close attention to national events. She was appalled at the loss of Fort Henry and Fort Donelson and blamed Johnston whose "supineness has allowed him to be out-generalled." She feared that the entire Mississippi River, including New Orleans, would soon fall into Union hands. Elise had little faith in Beauregard, who was "an egotist," and Polk seemed to be "a wild enthusiast." She had faith only in her husband to extract some good out of the chaos at Corinth. Now, for the first time, Elise felt certain that Davis was a strong supporter of Bragg and hoped that someday soon he would elevate him to command the entire Army of the Mississippi. She fully understood the fearful responsibilities resting on the shoulders of anyone in that position and did not wish them on him for vanity or glory, but because she really was convinced he alone could bring victory.[11]

But Elise also informed Bragg of personal and family matters in those hectic days before Shiloh. She commiserated with him over the reappearance of carbuncles "in so sensitive a place" and was worried that more would appear as well. Dr. Foard had promised her to look after the general and tell her if anything serious was troubling him. Elise did not hesitate to inform her husband of the extremely high cost of clothing for his slaves at Bivouac or the difficulties she had in provisioning the work force on the plantation. She urged Bragg not to let his prejudice against the Creoles of southern Louisiana blind him to the fact that they probably would make very good soldiers. In general, she thought, they were not addicted to liquor, which was "the besotting sin of our Confederacy."[12]

Bragg squeezed some time from his arduous duties to inform Elise that he had anticipated her problems with provisions by purchasing 23,000 pounds of bacon in Mississippi, offered him by an acquaintance. He ordered half of it to be sent to Bivouac and the rest to family and friends. Bragg also wanted to have his nephew with him, Thomas's son John Bragg, who was a telegraph operator. An exchange of telegrams prompted John to move from Goldsboro, where he apparently worked for the army, and join his uncle at Corinth by late March.[13]

Johnston was determined to strike the Federals at their forward position near Pittsburg Landing, only twenty-two miles northeast of Corinth. Ulysses S. Grant had moved his Army of the Tennessee there during the month of March and was waiting for the arrival of Don Carlos Buell's Army of the Ohio, which was expected sometime early in April. If Johnston could attack Grant's 30,000 men before Buell's arrival, he would stand a good chance of success with the 30,000 men in the Army of the Mississippi. But when the Confederates left Corinth on April 3, the raw troops straggled, broke ranks to forage for additional food, and generally made a good deal of unmilitary noise along the way. In addition, the march was delayed by bad roads. Bragg's Second Corps made slower progress than expected, forcing some delay in Johnston's plans.[14]

"My troops moved this evening," Bragg told Elise just before setting out from Corinth. "I go to join them at day light to give the enemy battle." Approaching his first Civil War engagement, Bragg felt the awful consequences to his wife if he should fall. "All you hold dear in life is at stake," he told her, "but your suspense will not be long for before this reaches you the telegraph will have reported the result. Whatever it may be I hope to share the fate of my Army and my country."[15]

Johnston took Grant by surprise when he attacked early on the morning of Sunday, April 6, scattering several Federal units, capturing vast camps loaded with food, and throwing many regiments into confusion. But stubborn resistance soon developed along the battlefront. Following Beauregard's suggestion, Johnston arrayed his Army of the Mississippi into an unusual formation, assigning each of the three corps the task of covering the entire front of the army, one behind the other. The more normal method was to assign each corps a separate sector of the total frontage so that one man could command all successive lines in that area. Bragg's Second Corps was assigned the middle position. Beauregard's scheme produced a great deal of confusion in Confederate ranks as the troops of one corps tended to move forward and merge with troops of a different corps in their front. Command and control became much more difficult, and each corps commander made the best of it, throwing any units that were available into action even if they were not part of his own command. The battle of Shiloh became a much more confusing, chaotic, and ill-coordinated affair than most Civil War battles tended to be.[16]

Bragg's handling of his command became the focus of much criticism by some subordinates and modern-day historians. Some of it is justified, but most of the criticism is unfair. There can be no doubt that Bragg exerted himself personally to make the best of a bad situation on April 6, rushing about from one point of the line to another to push brigade and regimental commanders forward and keep up the pressure on the enemy. He freely exposed himself to fire all day long.

Giles Buckner Cooke had just joined Bragg's staff only a few days before the battle after coming west from Virginia. He wrote a report detailing his movements and that of his commander during the battle of Shiloh, sending a copy of it to his mother. Cooke quoted Bragg's orders to him, demonstrating that the general had a knack for clearly explaining what he wanted of his staff. Bragg sent Cooke off on numerous errands: to find Hardee's flank and communicate with him; to place Gladden's brigade in its proper position; to help Oladowski locate the ammunition wagons; to "find out what Regmt that was, that was standing still at ordered arms," to find and push forward any idle troops he could find; and to rally stragglers. At one point Bragg told Cooke, "Captain rush in there and see if our troops are not firing on each other." Cooke started "with the expectation of never coming out again," but he survived the mission. At times during the day, when finishing one task and reporting back to corps headquarters, Cooke could not find Bragg because the general had already gone forward to a new location. Cooke found his general under fire more than once during the day and at one point was given a new assignment only five seconds after reporting that the previous task had been accomplished.[17]

Although driving the Federals back to a point near the landing on the west bank of the Tennessee River, the Confederates were unable to break Grant's army on April 6. Buell arrived that night and added 25,000 fresh troops to the Federal position. On Monday, April 7, they took the tactical offensive against the outnumbered and tired Rebels. Bragg sent Cooke out to rally the faltering troops and went himself to do the same; "entreating them by everything they held dear 'to advance and drive the invader back,' they responded but feebly to the appeal." Bragg wound up that day exposed to "a very dangerous fire of bullets," and sent Cooke with a message to Beauregard, who now commanded the Army of the Mississippi after Johnston was mortally wounded on April 6. Bragg told Cooke "to say to Genl. Beauregard, if he don't send me reinforcements, my left will have to fall back."[18]

Cooke found Beauregard near Shiloh Church and was told to take whatever troops were nearby and send them to Bragg. When the men hesitated, Beauregard helped Cooke by grabbing their flag and urging them to move. As Cooke brought them to Bragg's position, his general seemed to cheer up but then the reinforcements moved forward only a short distance before retiring. As the Confederate position crumbled, Bragg and his staff raced from one end of the line to another "invoking our men to make a stand," and usually had little success. At one point Bragg "addressed a certain Regmt. and implored it to move forward, it hesitated [but] quick as thought the General snatched its banner from the standard-bearer, and said follow me." As long as Bragg personally led the unidentified regiment, it did well. As soon as Bragg gave the flag to its assigned color bearer and left for another part of the field, "it seemed to prefer being in the rear."[19]

Bragg had several horses shot under him at Shiloh, another sign that the general exposed himself fearlessly. At 10 A.M. on April 6, a bullet smashed into the forehead of his "noble and gallant charger," saving him because the ball would surely have smashed into his body instead. When the horse fell, it pinned Bragg's right leg to the ground, and the general had some difficulty getting away. A member of his bodyguard gave him his own horse, "an inferior animal," in Bragg's view. Canister balls from a Union artillery piece killed this horse at 11 A.M., only an hour after the first was shot, and another horse was found for the general. This mount was wounded later in the day but managed to carry Bragg through the rest of the battle. Throughout all this Bragg was untouched by enemy fire, although his right leg was considerably bruised by the horse's fall.[20]

Many soldiers saw Bragg on the battlefield and reported glowingly of his efforts to keep the Confederate attack rolling forward. Thomas Chinn Robertson recalled that Bragg stopped his 4th Louisiana, changed its direction of advance to more squarely hit the Union position, and pulled it out after a few minutes when it was clear that the regiment was making no headway. James Cooper of the 1st Louisiana (Regulars) called Bragg "the old hero." He sought the hottest spot on the battlefield and sent the regiment, which he had organized as commander of the state forces, into the fray by calling them "My old body guard," and urging them to do their best. "I think Generals Bragg and Beauregard are two of the greatest men living," declared Given Campbell of the 4th Kentucky Cavalry.[21]

There can be little doubt that Bragg rose to the occasion at Shiloh. Faced with a poor formation that created a great deal of confusion, his recourse was to personally oversee as much of the line as possible, exposing himself to danger, urging forward reluctant regiments, and trying to inspire the troops to keep pressing forward. He forgot himself in this endeavor, risking death and injury by the minute. Bragg fought the battle of Shiloh with passion, even with an air of desperation.

But there were black spots in his record as well. Randall Lee Gibson commanded a brigade of Louisiana troops that had been assigned to Bragg's corps. Gibson and Bragg had known each other for years but their relationship before the war had not been without problems. For reasons never explained, Bragg distrusted Gibson's father, Tobias Gibson, and did not like Gibson's younger brother Claude. A recent biography of Randall describes Claude as lacking in self-discipline, extravagant in his expenses, and negligent of his responsibilities. This would have been enough to earn Bragg's ill favor, and perhaps it was also enough to earn Bragg's distrust of Randall as well. When Randall purchased Lackland, a sugar plantation adjacent to Bivouac, in 1858, he occasionally dined at the Bragg house but never became a true friend of the retired army officer, even though Elise's brother, Towson Ellis, had attended Yale University with Randall. Lackland never proved to be profitable; when crevasses inundated his fields, Randall Gibson sold it in 1860. He never understood why Bragg remained cold to him and regretted the assignment of his brigade to Bragg's corps.[22]

Gibson's problems with Bragg began on the approach march to Shiloh. His men were performing outpost duty at Monterey, Tennessee, when suddenly the Army of the Mississippi marched past. In the presence of both Johnston and Bragg, Gibson mentioned that he had received no orders alerting him to the move. Johnston asked Bragg how that happened, and Bragg became flustered, according to Gibson. Relations between the brigade and corps commander worsened after that incident. Johnston treated Gibson kindly, which only made Bragg even more angry.[23]

In his report of Shiloh, Bragg singled Gibson out for severe criticism. He noted that after ordering Gibson's Brigade forward, it actually fell back "in considerable disorder." Bragg and his staff members had to rally the men and send them back two more times. "This result was due entirely to want of proper handling," Bragg noted. In his own report, Gibson made no mention of this. He merely stated that his troops attacked four times on April 6 and were repulsed each time by the Federals who held a strong position in what came to be known as the Hornet's Nest. Gibson claimed his men retired in order each time and that he lost one-third of his command in these fruitless assaults.[24]

By August 1863, extracts of Bragg's Shiloh report appeared in the newspapers, and Gibson was livid with anger. He requested a court of inquiry to erase the slur against his name and that of his regimental commanders. He fully described the tactical and terrain difficulties that inhibited success in his assaults, claimed the men fell back in good order, and denied that Bragg or any of his staff members rallied his men. Both the adjutant general and the assistant secretary of war in Richmond denied Gibson's request for a court as unjustified, but Gibson nevertheless assembled written testimony from his officers about the matter. While they agreed that Bragg had urged forward the 4th Louisiana and the 13th Louisiana after the second repulse, all regimental commanders denied that anyone had to rally broken regiments in Gibson's brigade.[25]

To give Bragg some benefit of the doubt, he did have to grab the flag of an errant regiment in the desperate defensive fighting of April 7, as evidenced by Cooke's report to his mother. Bragg might have mixed up incidents in this confusing battle, which continued for a total of some 18 hours over two days. But in a letter to Elise, written the day after the engagement, Bragg explicitly identified Gibson's Brigade as a problem and Gibson himself as the cause of it. After the first repulse, Bragg and his staff had to intervene to get the brigade back into action. "I gave them a talk, took their flag and led them in, but it was no use, they were demoralized and nothing would induce them to go. A want of confidence in their leaders, Gibson, destroyed them. *Entre Nous* he is an *arrant coward* and *claude* is the cause."[26]

Gibson's co-biographers find it "almost impossible to fathom" why Bragg hated Gibson so much. They speculate that he was jealous of Gibson's good relations with powerful men like Albert Sidney Johnston,

Leonidas Polk, and John C. Breckinridge. They also note that Towson Ellis did not graduate from Yale as Gibson had done, but Gibson always treated Towson with respect and friendship. It is true that the vindictive feelings Bragg harbored toward Gibson were unnecessary and created a vicious relationship between the two men. Gibson grew to hate Bragg with a passion that never ceased during his long life.[27]

It was unfortunate that Bragg tended to take a strong dislike to some people and become blinded to their good qualities. It was worse that he allowed himself to act on those feelings. The fact is Gibson commanded a brigade for years and did so consistently well. Moreover, in contrast to his harsh and unwarranted criticism of Gibson, Bragg could offer nothing but praise for the Pensacola men he had brought with him to Tennessee. Adley H. Gladden was mortally wounded on April 6, and Bragg eulogized him whenever possible. Referring to Gladden as "my best and truest friend," he sent Gladden's sword to the fallen officer's daughter after his death.[28]

Aside from unnecessarily creating a feud between himself and Gibson, Bragg became a player in a raging controversy regarding Beauregard's handling of the fight on the evening of April 6. Beauregard called off further attacks a bit early, when there was still some daylight available, because he believed the offensive action could be continued with more prospect of success the next day. Of course, Beauregard had no idea that Buell would show up that night and alter the tactical situation dramatically on April 7. After Shiloh, many critical voices were raised condemning this decision to halt early on the evening of the first day.[29]

Bragg's view of this controversy is not easy to pin down. Dr. Josiah C. Nott of Mobile, who served briefly on Bragg's staff at this time, recalled seven years later that Bragg's view coincided with Beauregard's about whether it was wise to continue advancing on the evening of April 6. The troops seemed "much demoralized, and indisposed to advance" because of heavy shelling from Union gunboats on the Tennessee River. Nott agreed with Bragg "that our troops had done all that they would do and had better be withdrawn."[30]

But there is convincing evidence coming from other men close to Bragg at Shiloh that the general thought it was a mistake to call off the assaults so early on April 6. Samuel H. Lockett claimed that Bragg agonized mightily over Beauregard's decision to call off the fighting too early that day. "I heard him say over and over again, 'One more charge, my men, and we shall capture them all.'" When word of Beauregard's decision arrived, stating that "the victory is sufficiently complete; it is needless to expose our men to the fire of the gun-boats," Bragg broke down. "My God, was a victory ever sufficiently complete?" he asked Lockett. He considered ignoring the order, but then word arrived that all other commands were falling back. "My God, my god, it is too late!" Bragg concluded. A month after Shiloh, St. John R. Liddell recalled hearing Bragg state "very regretfully that our successes had not been pushed at all hazards without a moment's delay."[31]

T. Harry Williams, Beauregard's biographer, categorically states that Bragg agreed with his superior's decision to call off the assaults on April 6 but later "Bragg remembered more and more about the episode, until finally he thought that he had threatened to disobey the order." It should be borne in mind that the only evidence for this lies in Nott's letter, written to Beauregard's friend and staff officer Thomas Jordan after the war and included in Jordan's adulatory book about Beauregard. In contrast, not only Lockett but another member of Bragg's staff, volunteer aide-de-camp C. L. Le Baron, argued firmly that Bragg had contemplated disobeying the order. "These are facts" he told Jefferson Davis more than twenty years later. When Le Baron repeated the story to Bragg sometime after the war, the former general confirmed his memory by saying, "That is so."[32]

Whether the Army of the Mississippi actually could have crushed the Federals if it had continued attacking is far from certain. Grant had already assembled a strong defense line covering Pittsburg Landing, studded with artillery, and he had the support of the gunboats. But the evidence indicates that Bragg was in favor of pressing the advantage until dark on April 6, in contrast to the views of Beauregard.[33]

The need to admit failure and retire from the field of Shiloh depressed Bragg and most of his men. "It was sad beyond measure," he told Elise the next day. The retreat to Corinth was awful; the roads were deep with mud, regiments were disorganized, the troops were demoralized, and food for man and forage for animals almost gone. "Myself and my staff are utterly exhausted and our horses barely able to walk," Bragg reported to Beauregard at midafternoon of April 8. Fortunately for the Confederates, Grant and Buell failed to mount an effective pursuit.[34]

Immediately following his first Civil War battle, and his first effort at large command in combat, Bragg struggled to explain his feelings to Elise. "So much has been crowded in a small space of time that the mind becomes confused and unable to compass it all at once." Of one thing he was certain: lack of discipline among the men and lack of training and competency among the officers were the chief causes of failure at Shiloh. "Universal

sufferage, furloughs & whiskey, have ruined us. If we fall it is our own fault."
While his old Pensacola troops performed magnificently, all others fled the
ranks or were reluctant to go into heavy action. Bragg repeated these same
points in official reports.[35]

Elise was stunned by the death of Albert Sidney Johnston. She did not
hold him in high regard, but his fall shocked her into the realization that
even generals were vulnerable on the battlefield. "I had taught myself to
believe *you could not* be hurt, danger had so often surrounded you, your
high rank in a measure protected you." But Johnston held an even higher
position than her husband, "his poor wife has probably thought the same
with me." In addition to a heightened degree of worry for her husband's
life, Elise continued to fret about his health. "My great anxiety is that you
have been overtaxed," she told him, "tried to the utmost. The reaction
may prostrate & overpower you. Dont give up dearest—not for *my sake*,
alas—not a feeble woman alone depends on you—but *a nation* in her tear-
ful agony, looks to you for help." She urged Bragg to make an arrangement
so that if he was wounded, he would be sent to Louisiana for recovery.
"I *must be with you* in that sad event," she told him. "Johnston's death has
frightened & unnerved me. . . . The fearful deaths of those we knew have
made great cowards of us."[36]

Bragg's first missive to her, a penciled note written on April 7, arrived
by April 16. The note was "almost rendered illegible by the handling &
perusal of anxious relatives." Still Elise saw no mention of her husband in
newspaper accounts while all public reports praised Beauregard. This did
not please her. "Your wife is too proud of you to consent to it—as a compensation to her for having so freely . . . given you to your country, I must
insist *that country* shall sometimes hear of you." Bragg's judge advocate,
Harvey Walter, could write well. Why not encourage him to send personal
letters to the newspapers? "You can curb his disposition to exaggerate,"
she told Braxton.[37]

"Truly troubles are upon us in earnest," Elise told Bragg after hearing
further news from him about the battle. "Your letter dearest, breathes a tone
of the deepest despair. We are sadly disappointed in our soldiers. I thought
Southern men were at least *brave*." Elise gamely tried to encourage her husband to do his best despite his many troubles. "Rouse & be yourself again. If
we are to have a S. Confederacy you will be spared, for it cannot be without
you. If we are not, you will not wish to live, nor I either."[38]

While absorbing news of Shiloh, Elise also had to deal with the fall of
New Orleans to a Union naval and land force moving up the Mississippi

River on April 29. One of Elise's relatives brought the sad news to Bivouac by early May. Thibodeaux, only forty miles west of the captured city, was adrift with rumors about the Yankees visiting the Lafourche area, and all expected to see blue-coated soldiers any day. Elise despaired of ever retrieving the misfortune; New Orleans seemed lost forever.[39]

As important as New Orleans was to the Confederacy, Bragg was fighting in a more important sector of the war against a much larger military threat to Southern hopes of independence. The fighting at Shiloh failed to turn back the Northern invasion of the Mississippi Valley, despite the enormous casualties. Bragg's role in the engagement has been treated by historians in a mostly critical way. Grady McWhiney roundly condemned Bragg's criticism of Gibson as unfounded and "impulsive." One can hardly disagree with that. But McWhiney faulted Bragg further for throwing individual regiments and brigades piecemeal into many attacks on the Hornet's Nest. In fact, McWhiney faulted Bragg for relying on frontal attacks at all to deal with this strong Union position.[40]

Most historians who followed McWhiney also followed his line of interpretation. Wiley Sword concluded that Bragg's "blundering tactics and piecemeal frontal assaults cost the Confederates severely. Although an adept organizer and administrator, as a combat general there were few worse." Larry Daniel blames Bragg for most of the failed assaults on the Hornet's Nest, although he admits that other commanders were responsible for some of the eight Confederate attacks on the position. "Flanking movements would probably have produced the desired results," Daniel has concluded, "but once again the Confederate command relied upon brute strength rather than finesse." As a result, 2,400 men were lost out of a total of 10,000 engaged against the Hornet's Nest on April 6.[41]

Much of McWhiney's interpretation (which is essentially the interpretation of the historians who followed him) was based on the assumption that the widespread use of rifle muskets allowed defenders to dominate Civil War battlefields with long-range rifle fire. In fact, many years after the publication of his biography of Bragg, McWhiney coauthored the main study promoting this interpretation of the impact of rifles on Civil War operations. Bragg therefore became an early victim to this view of the rifle musket and its effect on warfare in the 1860s. James Lee McDonough, in echoing McWhiney's interpretation of Bragg at Shiloh, wrote of what he termed an outdated offensive doctrine of frontal attacks and targeted Bragg as foolishly employing it in the face of rifled musketry.[42]

The old interpretation of the rifle musket—that it dominated Civil

War battlefields with long-range fire, made frontal attacks prohibitively costly, and gave more power to the side that acted on the defensive—has been thoroughly questioned and debunked by a number of historians. The difficulties of seeing targets at 500 yards in rolling, wooded terrain, the parabolic trajectory of the bullet, and the fact that Civil War officers and men overwhelming preferred to fire at short ranges consistent with the range of the older smoothbore musket meant that the rifle had little impact on Civil War military operations. A comparison of casualty rates between smoothbore battles of the eighteenth century and those of the rifle battles of the Civil War clearly show that the smoothbore musket produced as many (often more) casualties than the new weapon. The rifle musket did not produce a tactical revolution on the battlefield.[43]

Bragg certainly is open to criticism for throwing his units piecemeal into the fighting at the Hornet's Nest, but in fairness it must be pointed out that this was a common failing among all Union and Confederate commanders, especially during the first half of the Civil War. It was common because of a lack of experience at handling large formations of troops on the battlefield. One can see this problem lessening with experience by the midpoint of the conflict. It is wrong to single out Bragg as if he was the only officer guilty of this error. To criticize him for not finding a way to flank the enemy out of the Hornet's Nest also is unfair. The Hornet's Nest was but one sector in an extended Union line. As long as that line remained intact, there was no possibility of flanking one part of it. Oftentimes Civil War commanders had little choice but to hope that frontal attacks could work, even if uncoordinated, because there were precious few viable options available to them, a point historian Albert Castel has made in response to the McWhiney thesis.[44]

Samuel Martin, the most recent biographer of Braxton Bragg, also criticizes him on the basis of the old interpretation of the rifle musket. But he thinks historians ought to treat Bragg more fairly for what he did (and failed to do) at Shiloh. He implies that the general did not realize frontal attacks were failing at the Hornet's Nest. "It seems obvious that Bragg's current critics are biased," Martin has written, "looking in every instance to find fault with his actions."[45]

The best way to achieve some degree of balance in the historical view of Bragg and Shiloh is to point out that his experiences mimicked that of all Civil War commanders, blue and gray. Bragg was by no means alone in his reliance on piecemeal frontal attacks to get the job done. The improvised nature of Civil War armies inhibited attempts to use more precise and controlled efforts to achieve tactical goals. Only repeated experience on the battlefield could alter that situation. It was unfair to expect it of Bragg, Johnston, Beauregard, Polk, or Hardee at Shiloh.

It is true that Bragg was to a large extent responsible for the uncoordinated assaults against the Hornet's Nest that resulted in 2,400 casualties with nothing to show for it. But Robert E. Lee ended his highly praised Seven Days campaign with his army conducting equally uncoordinated, piecemeal attacks against a strong Union position at Malvern Hill that was protected by dozens of artillery pieces. The Army of Northern Virginia lost 5,650 men on July 1, 1862, with even less to show for the slaughter than Bragg could produce. Yet Lee was never criticized for this costly exhibition of ineptness in the Army of Northern Virginia.[46]

4

Corinth and High Command

The Army of the Mississippi recuperated for several weeks at Corinth as the Federals were reinforced to the strength of 100,000 men at Pittsburg Landing. Then the blue host began a ponderous advance under Henry W. Halleck. Union troops constructed field fortifications nearly every day of the campaign toward Corinth to prevent the kind of surprise that had afflicted Grant's army at Shiloh. With barely half his opponent's strength, Beauregard dug in and waited for an opportunity to strike at Halleck, but the cautious advance offered him no chance to deal a significant blow.[1]

Bragg continued to command the Second Corps but no longer acted as the army's chief of staff. Beauregard filled that office with a trusted subordinate, Thomas Jordan. But Bragg was ready to weigh in with advice. When the Southern Telegraph Company asked for government help to construct a new line, Bragg informed Beauregard that he was convinced its president, Dr. William S. Morris, was "a yankee." Bragg had experienced difficulties with Morris in 1861 about the construction of a telegraph line linking Mobile with Meridian, and he still did not trust the doctor.[2]

Bragg tried to encourage his troops after Shiloh. In an address to them on May 3, he pointed out that the Federals were leaving their gunboat protection to approach Corinth. He noted that another Confederate force, Earl Van Dorn's Army of the West, was on its way from the Trans-Mississippi to reinforce Beauregard. "We have, then, but to strike and destroy," Bragg concluded, "and . . . we shall not only redeem Tennessee, Kentucky, and Missouri at one blow, but open the portals of the whole Northwest."[3]

Three days later, when Van Dorn's army reached Corinth, Beauregard shifted command of the Army of the Mississippi to Bragg. He continued to control Department No. 2, the name that had been given to Johnston's territorial command. Bragg assumed the position on May 7 "with unfeigned diffidence," he told the men in his first general order, "but with a confidence inspired by the justice of our cause, which nothing can shake." He was not an independent commander: Beauregard was still his superior and responsible for making strategic decisions. But Bragg now commanded a force of some 50,000 men, the largest responsibility of his life thus far.[4]

Bragg settled into his new authority well. In a penciled note to his brother John, he assured the family of his well-being. He was "cheerful and seems pretty confident of success," as his brother Thomas put it when John informed him of the news. Bragg announced his staff with mostly familiar names on the roster, and he received his promotion to full general to date from April 12, skipping the grade of lieutenant general.[5]

Beauregard evacuated Corinth without a battle in late May, having found no opportunity to strike at Halleck. Bragg was so concerned about the process of pulling out that he personally took charge. It was impossible to haul away everything, so he ordered excess personal baggage of officers to be burned. "It is the first time I have played chief quartermaster," he told Beauregard, "but it is no difficult task." Bragg and his staff left Corinth at 9 P.M. of May 29 and camped for the night more than three miles from town. The Army of the Mississippi was hampered by bad roads and severe shortages of food and water during the retreat. Half a dozen railroad trains loaded with material had to be destroyed because guards prematurely burned bridges before the engineers could cross them. Stragglers lined the roads as the columns made their way south. "The more I see of the condition of our troops, moral and physical," Bragg told Beauregard, "the better satisfied I am with our move."[6]

An incident happened on the march that marred Bragg's reputation forever. Beauregard issued strict orders not to fire a gun during the evacuation, and in his determination to stop violations of it Bragg went too far. Because several rumors took the place of accurate reports, exactly what happened has long remained obscure. According to some versions, a Rebel soldier shot at a chicken and instead hit a black child, but another version identified the victim as a man rather than a child. In some stories Bragg executed the soldier for killing an innocent civilian rather than for shooting an animal. Another variation had it that the man tried to steal roasting ears of corn. As rumors circulated through the army and made their way into civilian society, Bragg's name became a household word associated with executing Confederate soldiers for trivial reasons in the perspective of many Southerners.[7]

Fortunately Giles Buckner Cooke provided reliable evidence to lay bare these stories. As a member of Bragg's staff during the retreat from Corinth, he was well placed to see and hear everything that happened at army head-quarters. On May 30, the day after pulling away from the town, a guard brought a soldier he had arrested to Bragg's headquarters and accused him of shooting a hog. The man, whom Cooke refused to identify by name in his diary, belonged to Charles L. Lumsden's Alabama Battery, attached to James R. Chalmers's Brigade of Jones Withers's Division. The accused said his battery had joined the army only a couple of weeks before, and he knew nothing of the order that prohibited the firing of weapons. "Gen. Bragg—after hearing all he had to say—decided that it was stealing be-sides disobeying orders, and ordered the man who brought the accusation against him—to take him out and shoot him." The accused understandably became desperate. "I didn't know that it was [against orders]—Have mercy on me—Oh: Gen. please don't shoot me!" he cried.[8]

Cooke overheard everything and was shocked. He made arrangements for Withers to see Bragg and intercede for the man, but Withers did not make a strong case for clemency even though, according to Cooke's inter-pretation of what Withers said, the division commander favored the killing of the hog. So Cooke had to think of something else to save the man. He persuaded Bragg to postpone the execution until the battery commander could be located. Cooke delivered the message personally, "got there in time to save him and delivered the order." Then Cooke found and took an officer of the battery to see Bragg. The general questioned him minutely concerning the accused man's character. Once the officer promised to take charge of him and make sure he obeyed orders, Bragg released the accused to the officer's custody. Cooke assumed he would be tried by a court-martial and probably acquitted. The staff officer understandably concluded that he had saved the poor man's life.[9]

Cooke wrote a brief, unpublished memoir of his service in the West that provided a slightly different version of the details in this story. He recalled that Bragg was "sitting up against a tree in the woods" when the man was brought to him and that the accused was "almost in a state of collapse" as he was led away to be executed. Cooke saw that the soldiers who were within hearing of the proceedings were reacting very badly. He said to another staff member, "if this man is shot it is the uprooting of Christianity." Cooke was not certain if Bragg heard this remark, but the general called Cooke immediately after and told him to countermand his order.[10]

Cooke was a careful and reliable witness. We can conclude that, even though Bragg initially made a terrible decision to execute the man with-out due process of military law, he reversed that order. Given the various rumors that circulated, one wonders if there was more than one incident during the retreat from Corinth. But Cooke was with Bragg during the entire movement and surely would have recorded any other cases if they had occurred. We can be reasonably certain that this was the only case brought to Bragg's attention and that the general did not execute the man. Nevertheless, Bragg was hounded by the accusation that he wantonly killed his own men for trivial reasons for the rest of his life. Moreover, these rumors began the process of breaking down public confidence in his generalship, especially among the civilian population, which was even more enraged by the rumors than his own army.

It took some time for the rumors to have their effect on the Confederacy, and in the meantime Bragg's star continued to rise. As Beauregard's health weakened following the retreat to Tupelo, Bragg became ever more important to Confederate fortunes in the West. Governor Thomas Moore of Louisiana urged Davis to replace Beauregard as commander of the western department with Bragg as early as May 8. Governor Francis W. Pickens of South Carolina argued that Bragg should replace John C. Pemberton in charge of the defenses of Charleston, but Davis informed him Beauregard relied very heavily on Bragg to run the Army of the Mississippi.[11]

However, when combined Union army and naval forces ascended the Mississippi River in an attempt to capture Vicksburg, Davis was compelled to act. On June 14, he ordered Bragg to Jackson, Mississippi, to take command of Department No. 1 from Mansfield Lovell and coordinate the meager resources to defend the important river town. Beauregard, however, refused to let him go. He told Bragg that his doctors insisted he take a leave of absence for his health. In fact, they had just written a medical certificate to support a two-week leave for Beauregard that day. Bragg telegraphed this information to Davis and waited for a response. Meanwhile, without going through proper channels, Beauregard left Tupelo to begin his leave. When Davis responded to Bragg's telegram by insisting that the original order be implemented, Bragg decided it was impossible to do so. That would have left both the Army of the Mississippi and Department No. 2 without a commander.[12]

For several days Bragg filled in as temporary commander of the department while continuing to lead the Army of the Mississippi. Davis was greatly irritated that Beauregard left before receiving permission. Meanwhile, Davis sent Earl Van Dorn to take charge in Jackson. Bragg fully explained the circumstances in a telegram dated June 19 and made a case that his disobedience of orders was justified. Davis agreed. The next day,

P. G. T. BEAUREGARD. A strong
supporter of Bragg in 1862–63,
Beauregard came to distance
himself from his testy colleague
by 1864. After the war, Bragg's
deep friendship with Jefferson
Davis placed him in the camp of
Beauregard's enemies. (Library of
Congress, LC-DIG-cwpb-05515)

he decided to name Bragg permanent commander of Department No. 2.
This irritated Beauregard, who now was angry at Davis for maneuvering
him out of his command, but he really had no one to blame but himself.[13]

Bragg endured public controversy concerning the way in which he assumed command of both the army and the department. "The papers seem
to be groping in the dark as to the reasons which influenced the change
here," Bragg told Beauregard, "and attributing motives to each of us never
entertained by either. Fortunately we know each other too well and have
this cause too much at heart to be influenced by these things." Beauregard
agreed. From the resort at Cullum's Springs near Bladen, Alabama, he
wrote a letter to the *Mobile Evening News* proclaiming Bragg his personal
friend who had "not a superior in the service. If untrammelled, rest assured
he will leave his mark on the enemy."[14]

Demonstrating that their trust was real, Bragg shared with Beauregard
his plans for shifting most of the army to Chattanooga, where it could take
the offensive and perhaps drive into Kentucky. He went into much detail
and explanation, knowing that "the cordial and sincere relations we have
ever maintained" justified his confidence in Beauregard's advice.[15]

Beauregard, however, could not forgive Davis for depriving him of his
command. When he was well enough, Davis assigned him to command
at Charleston. But, even as late as August 1863, Beauregard was eager to
resume command of the army he had largely created in the spring of 1862.

He learned that a group of congressmen had tried to make that happen but that Davis refused to concede. Beauregard and his supporters made such a stir about the way in which he lost the command that Davis wanted support from Bragg. When he visited Richmond following his Kentucky campaign in the fall of 1862, Bragg scribbled a memorandum stating that Beauregard "was not deprived of his command—But voluntarily surrendered it." He also noted that Beauregard had failed to properly inform the government of his need for a leave of absence. Resolution of the situation was delayed several days because there was no telegraph line to Cullum's Springs and mail delivery was irregular. Finally, Bragg pointed out that Davis did not directly inform Beauregard he had been permanently superseded because it was not proper to funnel orders through a commander who was on sick leave.[16]

Bragg was caught between three forces in this controversy: his friendship with Beauregard, his duty to the commander in chief, and his commitment to the truth. In the end, he supported Davis and the truth. It did not damage his friendship with Beauregard, who consistently referred to Bragg in warm terms at least until 1864.[17]

But the real story about how Bragg became the most important Confederate commander in the West was a minor issue compared to the problems he now faced. Never before had he such an opportunity to shape the course of the Southern war effort. For the first time he acted as an independent commander, answerable directly to the president of the Confederacy and the secretary of war.

The first problem Bragg addressed was the condition of the Army of the Mississippi. Reports circulated that the troops were demoralized and the army was in a state of crisis during its retreat from Corinth. Politician J. L. M. Curry witnessed the retreat and thought the cause was "incompetency or shameful neglect on the part of Division, Brigade and Regimental commanders." Davis took these reports seriously. "I wish to aid and sustain you in every practicable manner," he assured the general in July.[18]

Bragg rejuvenated the army and began to plan grand strategy at the same time. Only a few days after taking command of the department, he assured Samuel Cooper that the Army of the Mississippi was "rapidly improving in health and spirits." Bragg wanted to take it on the offensive soon and received the "full authority" of the War Department "to attempt the movement you indicate or any others which in your judgment promises success." Many observers thought Bragg was working wonders with the tone of the army. It was "getting to be well drilled & organized," thought William C. D. Vaught of the Fifth Company, Washington Artillery.[19]

Bragg's staff now grew to include twenty-seven officers, four of whom constituted his personal staff while the rest were assigned to the headquarters of Department No. 2. When his men did something well, he publicized the achievement in general orders. Col. W. H. Jackson's 1st Tennessee Cavalry captured more than fifty Federals and destroyed Union railroad equipment in a raid on Fayette Station, Mississippi. When a subordinate arrested a civilian named Asa Hodges for talking publicly of defeat, Bragg ordered him released but wanted Hodges to know that "it is an unbecoming, discreditable weakness in any one to give way to despondency at this time because the enemy have possession of a portion of our soil and have had successes against us in this quarter. . . . Such language may do as much hurt with the ignorant, weak and hesitating as downright disloyalty." Hodges had apparently tried "to discredit the capacity, conduct and policy of the public authorities, the military especially."[20]

Bragg chafed at a policy that allowed regiments to elect their own officers, which had been written into the Conscription Act of April 16, 1862. The law mandated that all Confederate units that had enlisted for one year at the start of the war would automatically be held in service for the duration of the conflict. To ease the discontent with the law, they were given the opportunity to "re-organize" by electing new officers. This resulted in ousting some good company and regimental commanders who had not gained the favor of the rank and file. Bragg tried to circumvent it by refusing to let some regiments hold elections and making selections of officers himself.[21]

George Knox Miller was surprised to be told that, on Bragg's order, he would now command his company of the 8th Confederate Cavalry. He was promoted over the head of the only lieutenant currently on duty with the company. "Gen. Bragg has taken things in his own hands generally," Miller told his fiancée, "has seen fit to appoint officers to fill vacancies . . . frequently taking men from the ranks. . . . I don't know how he finds the men out, but it seems that he knows every one & his standing."[22]

When J. L. M. Curry complained to Davis that Bragg was not obeying the Conscription Act, Davis asked Bragg to explain his views. The general tried to argue that he enforced the letter of the law "however much I may regret the injury resulting to our discipline and efficiency." But there is no doubt that he tried whenever possible to mitigate the negative results of the policy and hide the fact from the Richmond authorities.[23]

Bragg was beginning to amass a national reputation in the summer of 1862, due to his elevation to high command and the controversial things he did as a commander. Stanley Horn selected this time period to offer his most damning criticism of the general. "His severity had gained for him the name of tyrant throughout the army. No wonder morale slumped when he was raised to the high command." Horn provided no primary evidence to support that assertion. "There was complete absence of that devotion and blind confidence which characterized the feeling of Robert E. Lee's men for him and which later was shown by this Army of Tennessee for Joe Johnston." Horn agreed that the Army of the Mississippi needed a heavy dose of discipline, but thought Bragg should have applied it with "tact and diplomacy." Horn condemned Bragg for exacting a brand of discipline that "verged on brutality" yet he contradicted his assertions by claiming that the men's morale picked up soon after Bragg took charge of the department.[24]

Actually there is ample material upon which to gauge soldier reaction to Bragg in the summer of 1862. Many of the troops were fully aware of the rumors circulating about his tendency to shoot men for firing at chickens, but they still thought he was an effective leader. David Pierson of the 3rd Louisiana, in the Army of the West, admitted that Bragg "handles things without gloves, and it is . . . so as to do the country some good. He will be an unpopular man, but no good soldier who does his duty as disinterested[ly] as a Genl should can be otherwise." Arthur M. Manigault, who served in the Army of the Mississippi, thought disciplinary actions during the retreat from Corinth and thereafter "had a most excellent effect, and were percep-tible throughout [the army's] after career." George Knox Miller was not blinded by the ominous nature of Bragg's reputation. "He has instituted an extremely rigid if not terrible discipline. . . . But still it has all had its good effects—we have a splendid army, finely drilled, & effectively organized."[25]

C. Irvine Walker of the 10th South Carolina was a fervent supporter of Bragg throughout his army career. He believed rumors that the general had executed a soldier for aiming at a chicken and shooting a Negro. The army felt, as a result, "that it has at its head a man who would do what he said, and whose orders were to be obeyed." Walker blamed newspaper correspondents banished from army lines for slanting the story in a nega-tive way, claiming that "they all went for him as a tyrant, a despot, without heart, etc." Philip B. Spence, a member of Polk's staff, also admired Bragg's sense of discipline. He believed the general rejuvenated the Army of the Mississippi from its defeat at Shiloh and the loss of Corinth. "Officers and men at this time had the utmost confidence in Gen. Bragg." It is worth noting that Spence wrote this assessment many decades after the war, when Bragg's reputation as an unlucky loser had been firmly planted in Southern minds.[26]

Of course, some Confederates in Department No. 2 did not like Bragg from the beginning. James C. Bates of the 9th Texas Cavalry thought he was fit to command regular troops but not volunteers. He noted that Bragg seemed "haughty" and could "only be approached by officers of superior rank—and his army will obey him through *fear*." Bates described the general as having "square shoulders & a full deep chest & is so straight that he leans *backward* a little." The Texan thought Bragg seemed to weigh about 140 pounds and sported "tolerably gray" hair with "eyebrows which are completely united over his nose." He had a "large mouth—thin lips always seeming to be tightly compressed." William Preston also found Bragg "secluded & inaccessible," but he criticized the general's sense of discipline as well. Preston was the brother-in-law of Albert Sidney Johnston and as yet had no personal reason to dislike Bragg (although he would find many reasons to do so in a few months). In June 1862, right after arriving at Tupelo, Preston told Johnston's son, William Preston Johnston, that the Army of the Mississippi had straggled and plundered a great deal during the retreat. "Bragg had them shot for it by order, but it did not mend matters," Preston concluded. "Bragg is a stern & imperious soldier and is endeavoring by excessive severity to establish discipline, but the men are indignant, and I fear trouble."[27]

While Bragg had many supporters and some critics among the soldiers, his reputation among civilians worsened considerably. When word of his disciplinary measures reached the citizens of Richmond, Mary Chesnut was stunned by the news. One of her acquaintances, a man named Halcott Green, was equally stunned. "'For a chicken!' said Green. 'A Confederate soldier for a chicken!'" Nurse Kate Cumming decided not to believe half of the stories then circulating about Bragg. To accept them would compel her to "think him a perfect monster of cruelty. It is said he makes a perfect pastime of shooting the men." Cumming conversed with a soldier who had participated in the retreat from Corinth. He stated that several men were executed but all by due process of military courts and that the man shot for killing a pig had also killed a Negro. Cumming noted that everyone seemed to be "discussing the merits of our respective commanders, Bragg and Beauregard" in the summer of 1862. The tenor of opinion, in her view, was that the "tide is running in favor of Bragg. It is now said, if he had had his way at Shiloh, we would have gained a complete victory."[28]

As Cumming demonstrated, many Southerners heard the stories of cruelty, discounted some of them, and came to the same conclusion as many of Bragg's soldiers, that their new leader was an effective commander. Other civilians, as indicated by Mary Chesnut's comments, easily believed everything they heard and concluded that Bragg was a monster. Others could joke about the furor over the new head of affairs in the West. When Kentuckian Lizzie Hardin and her mother visited Bragg to confer about returning across the lines to their home, a friend later "asked us if we were not afraid when he got us in the parlor he would say we had taken a chicken from a citizen and execute military law on us."[29]

Southern newspapers had no room for joking. They took decided stands pro or con on Bragg. A correspondent calling himself "Justice" wrote to the *Mobile Advertiser and Register*, edited by a supporter of Bragg named John Forsyth, about the general's disciplinary measures. Justice claimed that five men were found guilty of desertion and spying and Bragg approved the death penalty for the two of them who fell under his jurisdiction. He wanted to correct an erroneous impression about Bragg, "one of our greatest Generals, and as pure and Christian a patriot as we have in our Confederacy." Without naming names, however, it is impossible to verify the cases Justice mentioned. Thomas Bragg kept close watch on newspaper reports throughout the summer of 1862 and also believed, with Kate Cumming, that the tenor of opinion was swaying in Bragg's favor compared to that of Beauregard.[30]

But some newspaper correspondents began to assail Bragg with venom-dipped pens that summer, attempting to stir up a sense of jealousy between him and Beauregard over the manner in which the former supplanted the latter. John Forsyth squarely attacked them in his newspaper and defended Bragg, prompting the general to write him a letter of thanks. Bragg asserted that he maintained the best of relations with Beauregard. "No two men living ever served together more harmoniously or parted with more regret.... Our intercourse was daily, free, unrestrained and as harmonious as if we had been brothers."[31]

Harmful rumors of Bragg's disciplinary measures inspired a reaction in the Confederate Congress. Senator James L. Orr of South Carolina initiated a resolution on September 8 to inquire whether Bragg was shooting soldiers without due process of military law. Four days later the committee on military affairs recommended Congress drop the resolution from consideration. Then Orr tried another strategy: creating a special committee to investigate the rumors. Thomas Bragg, who kept careful watch on all this, listed not only Orr but John B. Clark of Missouri and William L. Yancey of Alabama, "all 'sore heads,'" as supporters of this strategy. Orr "denounced Gen'l B. as a tyrant, assassin, murderer," but Clement C. Clay Jr. of Alabama, James Phelan of Mississippi, Louis T. Wigfall of Texas, and Henry C. Burnett of Kentucky defended Bragg in the heated discussion. The Senate voted 13 to 8 to create a select committee on September 13, but Orr was compelled to compromise by letting Davis select the three members. Davis never made a move to set up this committee.[32]

Bragg had indeed stirred up a good deal of indignation among some congressmen, but the rest either supported him or found the furor unimportant. Andrew G. McGrath, who served as a Confederate district judge, well explained the situation in a letter to an acquaintance. Accepting the fact that Bragg executed several men, McGrath noted that "nothing but the conviction of his valuable, if not indispensable service," prevented the senate from investigating the charges. "Should his good fortune in the field desert him, he would be greatly exposed to proceedings against him, for murder." McGrath thought Bragg was "a most excellent officer, but carried his opinion of the necessity for vigorous discipline so far that he does not suffer any law of any kind to interfere with him."[33]

Bragg was not yet aware of the threat from Congress and paid only modest attention to the newspaper reports about him. He was absorbed with army duties during the summer of 1862 but managed to write short letters to Elise. After the fall of New Orleans he was heartened to learn that she remained safe at Bivouac "and the country still free of Yankees." He admitted to her that taking command of the department "has well nigh overburdened me, but thanks for good health, I am bearing it well, and hope yet to mark the enemy before I break down."[34]

Bragg was thinking of taking the offensive as early as mid-June. He issued an address to his men hinting that he would assume an aggressive policy and called on them to recognize that obedience to orders was "a sacred duty, an act of patriotism. . . . A few more days of needful preparation and organization and I shall give your banners to the breeze," he told the troops.[35]

Of course, Bragg did not divulge exactly how, when, or where he would take the offensive, but the strategic situation was just then turning in favor of such a move. Rather than advance south from Corinth, Halleck turned his attention to the necessity of consolidating Union control of the huge area Federal forces had conquered since February. Guerrillas were even then beginning to attack his rail supply lines, and vast stretches of Middle

Tennessee were not controlled by either army. Halleck had concentrated heavily after Shiloh, bringing Union troops from all corners of the West; in fact, he had overconcentrated to the point that there were no resources to secure much of the territory won. Dispersion of his large army at Corinth was a necessity. In fact, he could not have supplied 100,000 men in a southward advance from the town in the summer of 1862 even if he had wanted to do so. When Grant tried it with only 30,000 men in December 1862, he found it impossible as well. Bragg also was aware that, in the summer months, the northeastern quarter of Mississippi suffered from scant water and bitter heat, another impediment to the movement of large numbers of troops.[36]

Climate, geography, and Halleck's strategic needs allowed Bragg to seize the initiative. Halleck had detached Don C. Buell's Army of the Ohio on a mission to take Chattanooga, and little stood in the way. Edmund Kirby Smith commanded the Department of East Tennessee but most of his men were scattered around Knoxville in occupation duties. The Federals already held Cumberland Gap, at the junction of the state lines of Kentucky, Tennessee, and Virginia. Kirby Smith seemed to have little chance of holding on to Chattanooga in the face of Buell's advance.[37]

Bragg sent a division under John P. McCown from Mississippi to Chattanooga, but he did not trust McCown to handle the situation. "New Madrid fell by his errors and want of decision and firmness," he told Kirby Smith on July 20. Bragg had to send him, however, as he "had no alternative at the time." Two days later, Bragg informed Davis that he had decided to shift most of the Army of the Mississippi to Chattanooga. The difficulties of advancing northward against Corinth were too great, and Chattanooga was too important to lose. Moreover, two cavalry columns under John Hunt Morgan and Nathan Bedford Forrest were just then raiding Buell's rail network with great success. An invasion of Union-occupied Tennessee by way of Chattanooga could completely reverse the strategic environment in the West and lend itself to an invasion of Kentucky. Bragg spelled out the details to Beauregard. He planned to go to Chattanooga with 34,000 men and act in concert with Kirby Smith's 20,000 troops. The Richmond authorities expected the two generals to cooperate, refusing to place one over the other. It was an unpleasant situation, but one Bragg could not alter. Meanwhile, he would leave 16,000 men in northeast Mississippi under Sterling Price. Earl Van Dorn already had 20,000 troops near Vicksburg. Together, Price and Van Dorn could hold the state and maybe help with the new offensive by advancing northward.[38]

Bragg's first independent campaign of the war was a bold venture designed to reverse Confederate fortunes in a single stroke. He deserves great credit for it, especially considering the meager resources to be employed. Albert Sidney Johnston had initially devised a frontier defense scheme, holding several points along a 400-mile line from the mountains to the Mississippi River. That policy ended in disaster with the fall of Fort Henry and Fort Donelson in February. Then Johnston and Beauregard concentrated Rebel strength to defend the Mississippi Valley, abandoning the interior of the Western theater. That strategy resulted in failure at Shiloh and the loss of Corinth and Memphis. Now Bragg reversed his earlier view and felt the Mississippi Valley was "infinitely less important" than securing the rail lines that penetrated the Deep South from Nashville to Chattanooga. The main Confederate army in the West continued to operate along that system of rail lines for the rest of the war.[39]

There was also a distinct possibility of invading Kentucky. Much pressure to do so came from a variety of people in and out of the army. Thomas L. Connelly has identified a large Kentucky clique in the Confederacy, men who were convinced the sentiments of that border slave state favored the South and were suppressed only by the presence of Union troops on its soil. Ironically, Bragg had been urged by Col. W. P. Buckner to send help to the state as early as September 20, 1861, when he commanded at Pensacola. At that time he refused, telling Buckner "that what I did offer was for the cause at large, not for Kentucky, which deserved no consideration at our hands." Bragg was disgusted by the fact that Kentucky governor Beriah Magoffin had declared the state neutral in May 1861, a position supported by many Kentuckians. After Leonidas Polk violated that neutrality by occupying Columbus in early September, Kentucky secessionists held a meeting at Russellville and voted the state out of the Union. It was not a legal proceeding, but Davis admitted Kentucky into the Confederacy anyway. The force of public opinion now tended to push Bragg into an incursion of the state.[40]

Bragg started his army from Tupelo on July 22 and began to move department headquarters two days later. By July 30, he personally reached Chattanooga after a long rail journey by way of Mobile and Atlanta. The day after his arrival, Bragg took time to deal with the most irritating newspaper attack yet to appear. Someone had written a vicious piece that wound up in Forsyth's newspaper, the *Mobile Advertiser and Register*. It slurred both Bragg and Davis for wrongly depriving Beauregard of his department command. Bragg sent the clipping and several letters concerning the article to Davis. He was irritated that it attacked not only him but Davis as well. Who wrote it was the important question, and John Bragg, who also was incensed at the letter, believed the culprit was Thomas H. Watts.[41]

Watts had been an Alabama state legislator before the war and had organized the 17th Alabama, serving as its colonel. When assigned to the Army of Pensacola, Watts and Bragg could not get along. The reasons are unclear. In fact, Thomas Bragg heard that Braxton had placed Watts under arrest after the troops moved to Corinth. For whatever reason, Watts developed an intense hatred for Bragg. Ironically, Davis nominated Watts to replace Thomas Bragg as Confederate attorney general, and he was confirmed by the Senate. If Watts was the author of the letter, it represented a telling commentary on the man that he would carry on his personal grudge against Bragg as a member of Davis's cabinet.[42]

While John Bragg believed that Watts had authored the piece, he also heard from someone else who thought William L. Yancey had written it. John decided to send a copy of the piece directly to Davis without knowing that Braxton intended to do the same. Meanwhile, Thomas Bragg, who still retained Davis's trust and confidence, hinted to him that he believed Watts had written the offensive article.[43]

Davis did not have time to burrow to the root of this controversy. He reassured John that "malignments cannot disturb the confidence of the Govt. in [Braxton's] capacity and unselfish devotion to the cause of his country." Braxton also complained to Davis that some newspapers were revealing the current movements of his army. He assured the Confederate president that he would not take mere personal abuse too seriously, but giving the enemy information about his army's course of action could "frustrate the whole object of a campaign."[44]

When he had more time to attend to this matter, Davis wrote reassuringly to Bragg. "You have the misfortune of being regarded as my personal friend," he told the general, "and are pursued therefore with malignant censure, by men regardless of truth and whose want of principle to guide their conduct renders them incapable of conceiving that you are trusted because of your known fitness for command, & not because of friendly regard." Davis also did not believe that Watts authored the article because he had shown the piece to Watts who failed to give any signs that he had been found out. According to Davis, Yancey had written it.[45]

Of course, Bragg was extremely busy with preparations for his offensive throughout the month of August and could not devote time to root out the truth in this matter. He consulted with Kirby Smith and agreed on a rough plan of cooperation. Kirby Smith would move against Cumberland Gap while Bragg waited for the rest of his army to arrive at Chattanooga. Then the Army of the Mississippi would invade Middle Tennessee and cut Buell's supply line. The plan was based on loose coordination of forces too far apart to offer mutual assistance, but Bragg entered the campaign with hope. Morgan and Forrest assured him that the residents of Middle Tennessee and Kentucky were intensely hostile to the Federals "and nothing is wanted but arms and support to bring the people into our ranks." Bragg received further encouragement from J. Stoddard Johnston, a Kentucky blueblood who made his way to Chattanooga in early August and pleaded for an opportunity to serve on Bragg's staff.[46]

August was a month of busy preparation. When Lizzie Hardin, her mother, and brother obtained an interview with Bragg at Chattanooga, they were impressed by his appearance. He was "a tall, soldierly-looking man, dressed in plain grey pants and hunting shirt, without any mark of rank but a sword. Ma was particularly pleased with the kind expression of his face, but a peculiar way he had of showing his lower teeth when he laughed or talked gave to him rather a grim look. His manner delighted all of us. Very far from having us 'shot to death with musketry,' he told us that hearing of our arrival he would not leave without first coming to welcome us within his lines. The visit was short and when he left we begged him if he entered Kentucky never to give it up. Jimmie [Lizzie's brother] insisted they should rather stand until the last man was killed, but Gen. Bragg said there was a good lady in Mississippi who might object to that."[47]

Braxton barely had time to write to that "good lady" and was too busy to correspond with his extended family. His brother Thomas kept track of Bragg's movements through letters from friends in Montgomery that indicated the general had been "in good health and spirits" when he passed through that city. In mid-August, Thomas prayed that his brother was "getting his force in position and that he will be heard from soon."[48]

5

Kentucky

Following a month of preparation, Bragg ordered the Army of the Mississippi to leave Chattanooga and cross Walden's Ridge on August 28, 1862. Thus began the first and only strategic offensive of his Civil War career—a bold move to recover Tennessee and secure the border state of Kentucky for the Confederate government. After six months of suffering one defeat after another, the main Rebel army in the West grabbed the strategic initiative and threatened to do more than just recover its losses.[1]

After a few days of marching across the rugged terrain, Bragg found time at Pikeville, Tennessee, to inform Elise that "mountain air[,] fine water & bathing" had greatly improved his health. But he also told her of another newspaper attack. The long period of preparation for the campaign had led some commentators to describe the Army of the Mississippi as "hard to move as an ox." "What can Gen. Bragg be waiting for?" complained Edmund Ruffin in Virginia after reading the newspapers on August 26. Bragg hoped that his new campaign would disabuse anyone of the impression that he was slow. "We expect . . . to redeem Tenn. and Ky. in less than Sixty days," he predicted on September 2. "We propose taking Cincinnati & Ohio to *Swap* for New Orleans & Louisiana. A sort of Yankee plan, but the most feasible now." Bragg was so elated at his prospects that he gently kidded Elise. "If you have any further use for an old grey headed, grey bearded, slow general for a husband you had better be following up, for he has innumerable messages from the pretty women of Nashville that he will be literally consumed if he reaches there safe."[2]

Moving from Pikeville, Bragg paused at Sparta on September 5 to issue General Order No. 128 to his army. News had arrived of Robert E. Lee's victory over John Pope at Second Manassas and of Edmund Kirby Smith's defeat of a small Union force at Richmond, Kentucky. His own army's progress thus far was commendable. "Comrades, our campaign opens most auspiciously and promises complete success," he told the men. Bragg also praised their restraint. "Your general is happy and proud to witness the tone and conduct of his army. Contented and cheerful under privations and strictly regardful of the rights of citizens, you have achieved a victory over yourselves which insures success against every foe."[3]

With an army filled with men from the states affected by his campaign, Bragg sought to encourage their hopes. For the Alabama regiments he pointed out that "your State is redeemed. An arrogant foe no longer treads her soil." He promised the Tennesseeans that their state capital would be redeemed. "You return to your invaded homes conquerors and heroes." For those men from Kentucky, "the first great blow has been struck for your freedom." He encouraged Southern sympathizers to rise against the Federals who occupied their state. Bragg was proud of General Orders No. 128. He sent a printed copy of it to Pierce Butler in Louisiana and scribbled on its back a note that Thomas Butler was well. "Tommy marched yesterday—due north—for Kentucky."[4]

Moving on from Sparta, the Army of the Mississippi crossed the state line and neared Glasgow, Kentucky, by September 12. Bragg now placed his army between Buell and Kirby Smith, a major objective of the campaign. "From Glasgow we can examine [Buell] and decide on the future," he reported.[5]

Upon reaching Glasgow on September 13, Bragg rested his army a few days and gathered provisions from the area. He reported his progress to Adj. Gen. Samuel Cooper and expressed confidence in achieving much more. Just as Bragg was conscious of shoring up the spirits of his men, he was keen to tell the citizens of Kentucky what he intended. "We come not as conquerors or as despoilers," he informed them in a proclamation issued on September 14, "but to restore to you the liberties of which you have been deprived by a cruel and relentless foe." He promised to discipline his men so as not to harm their property and assured the residents of the border state that his cause and theirs were the same. It was "our great struggle for constitutional freedom." But Bragg injected a realistic tone in the proclamation. "Kentuckians, we have come with joyous hopes. Let us not depart in sorrow, as we shall if we find you wedded in your choice to your present lot. If you prefer Federal rule, show it by your frowns and we shall return whence we came."[6]

Bragg stated the case succinctly in his proclamation. Although the Confederate government had accepted a rump convention that took Kentucky out of the Union in the fall of 1861, no one outside the Confederacy considered it a legal process. For all practical purposes, Kentucky was still a

JAMES R. CHALMERS. An officer in Bragg's Army of Pensacola, Chalmers later attacked the Union garrison at Munfordville and compelled Bragg to divert his army to that place early in the Kentucky campaign. Chalmers remained a staunch but quiet supporter of the general throughout the war. (Library of Congress, LC-DIG-cwpb-07598)

state within the Union, and only a portion of its residents chafed under that condition. Bragg had always harbored doubts about the popular mood in Kentucky and now made it clear that he had no intention of risking his army to destruction in an effort to "free" people who did not want to be liberated.

Confederate forces east and west, more by coincidence than design, were taking the offensive at approximately the same time. By September 14, when Bragg rested at Glasgow, Lee had already penetrated western Maryland in an effort to secure that border state for the Confederacy. The Army of the Potomac was on the move against him, fighting a heavy battle for control of the passes in South Mountain that day.[7]

Also on September 14, a small battle took place close to Bragg's position at Glasgow, a battle he did not authorize. Bragg had dispatched James Chalmers with his Mississippi brigade to cut the Louisville and Nashville Railroad, which crossed the Green River at Munfordville, Kentucky. Chalmers attacked the Union garrison protecting the bridge. The Federals, aided by earthworks, repelled the assault and inflicted 288 casualties. Chalmers admitted defeat and reported the result.[8]

Bragg decided to take the event seriously. "Unwilling to allow the impression of a disaster to rest on the minds of my men," he moved the Army of the Mississippi thirty miles to Munfordville. Bragg disapproved of Chalmers's action, calling it "unauthorized and injudicious," but he felt the damage to morale was important enough to change his strategic plan by capturing the garrison of Munfordville.[9]

In a tactical sense, the move was entirely successful. Bragg greatly outnumbered the garrison even though the Federals received some reinforcements and now numbered 3,500 men. He compelled their surrender on September 17 after nearly surrounding the place and engaging in some negotiation with the commander, John T. Wilder. The very day that Wilder's men lay down their arms, Lee's Army of Northern Virginia struggled for its existence in the terrible battle of Antietam and barely survived.[10]

The tone of Bragg's written communications in the wake of his victory at Munfordville helps to explain why he diverted his troops to that place. "My admiration of and love for my army cannot be expressed," he told Cooper. "To its patient toil and admirable discipline am I indebted for all the success which has attended this perilous undertaking." Bragg placed the morale of his men above nearly all else and worried excessively about the effect of Chalmers's defeat. After erasing the sting of that event by capturing 3,500 Yankees, Bragg asked the men to continue exhibiting "the same confidence and regard for discipline in order to insure the most complete success." He honored Davis's proclamation of a day of prayer and thanksgiving on September 18 by releasing Confederate soldiers held in arrest and returning them to their regiments.[11]

Bragg's emphasis on discipline stemmed not only from his own view of life but from the chaotic manner in which his troops had marched during the Shiloh and Corinth campaigns. But he allowed this concern to divert his strategic purpose in Kentucky. Many options were open to him at Glasgow, and it was not wise to allow Chalmers's rash attack at Munfordville to shape the course of the campaign. That diversion allowed Buell to catch up with Bragg and close in on the Army of the Mississippi. Prior to this point, the opposing armies had operated many miles apart and with the Confederates shaping the contours of the campaign according to their own needs. Now that the two forces were within striking distance, Buell had much more opportunity to influence the campaign. Bragg had already lost an important advantage.[12]

Of course, Bragg did not interpret the campaign in this way. Writing from Munfordville on September 17, he informed Cooper that the situation "must be exceedingly embarrassing to Buell and his army. They dare not attack me, and yet no other escape seems to be open to them." But Buell played the confrontation at Munfordville conservatively by refusing to assault the Confederates. For several hours the two armies remained immobile within striking distance of each other. Bragg lost his patience and called a conference with Polk and Hardee wherein he told them of his intention to break away and march toward Louisville, Buell's base of supply. Polk and Hardee approved. Before the move began, Bragg came close to changing his mind in favor of attacking Buell. If he could defeat the Army of the Ohio at Munfordville he could descend on Nashville and reclaim it. But Bragg considered this option only briefly during the early morning hours of September 18 before deciding against it. "This campaign must be won by marching," he told staff officer David Urquhart, "not by fighting." The Army of the Mississippi moved north on September 19, and Buell moved north too, bypassing Bragg's army to the west and moving swiftly toward Louisville.[13]

Urquhart claimed after the war that Bragg did not regret his decision to avoid battle at Munfordville, but the incident became the first controversy surrounding the Kentucky campaign. Many began to see it as a turning point, a test, and Bragg had failed to pass it. Such criticism compelled explanation, and Bragg provided it when he filed his official report of the campaign in May 1863. His army had too few provisions on September 17–18 to risk a major battle at Munfordville, and Buell outnumbered him two to one. Even if he had won an engagement at Munfordville, his army would have been hampered by thousands of casualties, and there would have been no guarantee that Buell was crippled to the same degree. Food and reinforcements were to be found in north central Kentucky, where he could make contact with Kirby Smith. In short, Bragg was not ready for a major battle that could decide the campaign in one stroke.[14]

Having reached north central Kentucky, Bragg decided not to make a play for Louisville. Occupation of that large city would have gained him little, for Buell was already near the place, and could have compelled Bragg to evacuate it or risk being trapped with the Ohio River to his back. It made more sense to take up a position at Bardstown, twenty miles southeast of Louisville. There he could recruit troops, find food, and coordinate efforts with Kirby Smith. After tramping sixty miles from Munfordville, the Army of the Mississippi entered Bardstown on September 22, the day that Lincoln issued his preliminary Emancipation Proclamation.[15]

Bragg explained the course of his campaign thus far by noting that he had "secured" Kirby Smith's position in the Bluegrass. He expressed some regret that Buell had been able to reach Louisville but asserted that supply problems dictated his course of action. While the area around Munfordville was "nearly all hostile" to the Confederate cause and offered scant provisions, the region south of Louisville seemed to welcome the Rebels, and there was much more to be secured in the way of supplies. But hopes of a union between Bragg and Kirby Smith remained fleeting. Kirby Smith seemed to grasp at any opportunity to operate independently, too far away for immediate support.[16]

Jefferson Davis began to worry about the lack of coordinated movement in the West. He was concerned that there was no master plan, no high degree of cooperation between independent commanders in Kentucky and between those commanders and other generals left behind in Mississippi. Sterling Price and Earl Van Dorn only hesitatingly cooperated with each other to pool their forces in Mississippi and decide on a course of action that could draw Federal attention from Kentucky and prevent the Yankees from sending reinforcements to confront Bragg. But the lack of swift, united action by Bragg and Kirby Smith was even more ominous in the face of Buell's resting army, bulging with fresh troops recently organized under Lincoln's July call for 300,000 more men. It was becoming more apparent that the Confederates had embarked on a risky venture with minimal manpower and a lack of coordination, not to mention the absence of a secure line of supply linking Bragg and Kirby Smith with their home base. Both commanders were compelled to rely on local resources for their provisions and wagon trains to bring up whatever else they needed from the South.[17]

With the benefit of hindsight, some historians have criticized Bragg for avoiding battle at Munfordville. Stanley Horn exaggerated the Munfordville incident as "one of the great crises of the whole war—probably its greatest moral crisis," and believed Bragg was responsible for "a major disaster of the conflict." Horn found Bragg's explanation for breaking away from Buell to be little more than "an excuse—a feeble excuse." Other historians accept Bragg's explanation, but Thomas Connelly, Grady McWhiney, and Steven Woodworth blame him for going to Munfordville in the first place. Up to September 14, he "had conducted a brilliant campaign" in Woodworth's estimation.[18]

The Army of the Mississippi rested at Bardstown as Bragg tried to deal with the enlarged problems his drive north had created. While his health had been good during the early phase of the march from Chattanooga, the pressure of events around Munfordville imposed a severe strain. He managed to sleep no more than four hours a night before reaching Bardstown.[19]

Bragg felt compelled to issue another proclamation explaining the purpose of his campaign. Written by John Forsyth and issued over Bragg's name on September 20, it was addressed to the people living in the northwestern states. Forsyth was a friend of Bragg's, a newspaperman who edited the *Mobile Advertiser and Register*. He acted as a volunteer member of Bragg's staff and now tried to calm the fears of people living in the upper Mississippi Valley about the near presence of a Confederate army.[20]

In the proclamation, Forsyth and Bragg tried to convince Northwesterners that the Confederacy wanted only to defend itself. Southerners fought "to vindicate a great principle. . . . that no people can be rightly governed except by their own consent." The Confederate government desired peace with the North. Forsyth and Bragg assured Northerners that the Confederate government would guarantee them the free navigation of the Mississippi River. They argued that the northeastern states started the war and believed the Emancipation Proclamation would destroy the Southern plantation economy and erase the best market for grain the northwestern states ever enjoyed.[21]

Bragg endorsed everything Forsyth wrote and penned another proclamation of his own, addressed to the people of Kentucky, on September 29. This document was a call to arms. Bragg needed troops and tried to rouse Kentuckians to the cause. He warned that the Conscription Act would be applied to Confederate occupied areas of the state and this was the last chance for Rebel sympathizers to enter service voluntarily. "As you value your rights of person and property and your exemption from tyranny and oppression you will now rally to the standard."[22]

But Bragg already was becoming disappointed at the response to his presence in Kentucky. While his men witnessed a joyous welcome when they reached Bardstown, few Kentuckians committed themselves to military service. This was a critical issue in the fate of the campaign.[23]

"We have 15,000 stand of arms and no one to use them," Bragg complained to Samuel Cooper. Kirby Smith received the equivalent of half a brigade of recruits while Bragg received no appreciable number at all. With Buell refitting and enlarging his army at Louisville, Bragg needed at least 50,000 men, nearly a 100 percent increase in his troop strength. "Unless a change occurs soon we must abandon the garden spot of Kentucky to its cupidity. The love of ease and fear of pecuniary loss are the fruitful sources of this evil." Without that popular uprising, there was no possibility of staying. "Should we have to retire, much in the way of supplies and *morale* will be lost, and the redemption of Kentucky will be indefinitely postponed, if not rendered impossible."[24]

Bragg had been undone by his own success. The initial stages of the campaign were brilliantly conceived and effectively managed. The Confederates seized the strategic initiative, stole a march on Buell, and were in a position to direct the flow of events. Bragg could have made it a short campaign by aiming to cut Buell's line of communications with Louisville and engaging in a major battle in Middle Tennessee. But instead he chose to move into Kentucky in favor of the possibilities inherent in securing that rich state. He also felt compelled to offer support to Kirby Smith, whose actions more than anything else compelled Bragg to move north or risk defeat in detail. In essence, the option of offering battle to Buell in Tennessee was taken away from Bragg by Kirby Smith's ambitious drive.

Deep in Kentucky, the two Confederate forces still were not closely cooperating with each other. Both were at the end of a tenuous communications link that could not supply them with the reinforcements they needed. Both were dangerously exposed to Union military power, and neither received much help from the local population. Very quickly, Confederate success had created more problems than beneficial results.

Bragg tried to establish a sympathetic state government in Frankfort as soon as possible to encourage friends in the state to rise. It made sense; the inauguration of Richard Hawes as the new Confederate governor would stand as a symbol that the Rebel army intended to stay in Kentucky.[25]

The Army of the Mississippi rested at Bardstown as Bragg established a supply depot at Bryantsville sixty miles east. He also opened a line of communication with the South by way of Cumberland Gap, located at the junction of the Kentucky, Tennessee, and Virginia state lines. His only link with home would be wagons and dispatch riders making their way along rugged mountain roads.[26]

Bragg left Bardstown on September 28, assigning Leonidas Polk to command the army in his absence. He told Polk to fall back toward Bryantsville if confronted by a large force of the enemy. Bragg intended to concentrate there to meet Buell, but he hoped he could install Hawes before that became necessary. Reaching Lexington on October 1, Bragg met Hawes and planned an installation ceremony and celebration for October 4 in Frankfort, thirty miles northwest of Lexington. Kirby Smith agreed to shift most of his available troops to the Frankfort area.[27]

"Our prospects here, my dear Sir, are not what I expected," Bragg ruefully informed Davis on October 2. "Enthusiasm runs high, but exhausts itself in words." He still had thousands of muskets ready to arm recruits but no more than 1,500 Kentuckians had joined Confederate ranks.[28]

On October 2, Bragg's plans began to unravel. Polk informed him of reports from cavalry pickets that the Federals were on the move out of

LEONIDAS POLK. Bragg and Polk, one of Bragg's most persistent enemies, never developed cordial or respectful relations, although they served together from March 1862 until Bragg relieved him of corps command in October 1863. Polk's willful tendency to ignore orders, his slackness in discharging responsible duties, and his bitter criticism of Bragg expressed in correspondence with his longtime personal friend, the president of the Confederacy, severely hampered Bragg's effectiveness as a commander. Before the war, Polk served as bishop of the Episcopal Diocese of Louisiana. (Library of Congress, LC-DIG-cwpb-06715)

Louisville, approaching Bardstown by way of Shepherdsville, Mount Washington, and Taylorsville. Polk intended to hit them if possible and retire by way of Harrodsburg and Danville to Bryantsville if that proved to be unfeasible.[29]

At 1 P.M. on October 2, Bragg dispatched Polk with news of his own. A Federal column was approaching Frankfort directly from Louisville by way of Bloomfield. Bragg wanted Polk to move north from Bardstown and attack that column while Kirby Smith approached it from the east. "If we can combine our movements he is certainly lost," Bragg assured his subordinate.[30]

Polk received this dispatch but took several hours to respond to it. At 3 P.M. on October 3, he finally informed Bragg that it was not possible to obey his instructions. Developments taking place during the past twenty-four hours had changed the situation. Polk indicated that the Federal approach toward Bardstown was too threatening to ignore. Polk called a council of his subordinates and most of them agreed the army should follow Bragg's first instruction and retire toward Bryantsville. He informed Bragg of this course of action and then set out on his way. Polk felt "assured that when facts are submitted to you you will justify my decision."[31]

By 8 P.M. on October 3, it was clear to Bragg that the Union column approaching Frankfort from the west was "only a feint and has ceased." That relieved much pressure and he gave Polk the latitude to act according to his discretion. Not until the morning of October 4 did Bragg receive Polk's message indicating that the Army of the Mississippi was already on its way to join Kirby Smith. Bragg accepted that decision and told Polk to concentrate at Harrodsburg until Federal moves became clear. "Keep the men in heart by assuring them it is not a retreat, but a concentration for a fight. We can and must defeat them," he assured Polk. "We shall put our governor in power soon and then I propose to seek the enemy." Bragg wanted to concentrate and offer battle "wherever the enemy may be." He assumed Buell would head toward Frankfort, the shortest route to interrupt Confederate efforts to accumulate supplies at Lexington.[32]

But the Federals marched faster than Bragg expected and were in close pursuit of Polk rather than moving toward Frankfort. Bragg misread his enemy's intentions and would pay dearly for the mistake. Buell dominated the strategic context of operations in Kentucky, and Bragg never realized he was no longer in control of events.

Meanwhile, thousands of citizens gathered to attend the installation of Hawes as the new governor of their state. Bragg, Kirby Smith, and other high-ranking officers were there to lend support. An elaborate dinner followed, but soon after it ended, the sound of artillery drifting in from the west electrified the assemblage. The Union column heading toward Frankfort had arrived and was skirmishing with Confederate cavalry. "Enemy in heavy force advancing on us," Bragg informed Polk, "only 12 miles out. Shall destroy bridges and retire on Harrodsburg for concentration and then strike. Reach that point as soon as possible."[33]

But events prevented Bragg from concentrating and that proved to be a key factor in the campaign. Kirby Smith began to remove supplies from Lexington to Bryantsville, but he balked at the thought of losing his independence. Instead of moving toward Harrodsburg, Kirby Smith suggested that his troops remain north of the Kentucky River to protect the area around Lexington as long as possible. He could quickly move south to join Bragg when needed. Bragg agreed to this arrangement; given that he had no power to command Kirby Smith, he had little choice. Both men underestimated how long it would take for Kirby Smith to join Polk, and neither had accurate information about Buell's location and intent. The only thing that could save Confederate fortunes at this point was rapid concentration at a central location, and it did not happen.[34]

WILLIAM J. HARDEE. A far more capable corps commander than Polk, Hardee nevertheless became tainted by Polk's corrosive attitude toward Bragg and often ill-served his army commander as a result. Bragg respected Hardee's talents but realized they were limited; he did not think the general could effectively command the Army of Tennessee. (Library of Congress, LC-USZC4-7972)

The period October 5 to 8 was the most confused phase of the campaign. The Army of the Mississippi was essentially on its own to deal with Buell, even though Kirby Smith was in the region. After lending Jones Withers's Division to Kirby Smith, Bragg had only three other divisions under Polk's command. In its retreat from Bardstown, Polk's Corps (which now consisted only of Benjamin Cheatham's Division) reached Harrodsburg. But Hardee and his two divisions followed behind, harassed by Buell's vanguard.[35]

Bragg rode to Harrodsburg on October 6 where he met Polk. Hardee stopped near Perryville, about fifteen miles southwest of Harrodsburg, to confront the Federals. By October 7, it became apparent to Bragg that a battle at Perryville was the best option. At 5:40 P.M. that day, he ordered Polk to move Cheatham's division back to that town, take charge of Hardee's Corps, and attack the enemy. He intended the strike to be preemptive, to give Polk time to join Kirby Smith. The battle at Perryville therefore was never intended to be a fight for possession of Kentucky. If Kirby Smith was unwilling to join Bragg, all Bragg could do was to join him.[36]

Polk continued to think for himself rather than obey orders. In fact, he wrongly considered Bragg's order to attack as merely a suggestion. "Give the enemy battle immediately," Bragg wrote, "rout him, and then move to our support at Versailles." Upon arrival at Perryville on the night of October 7, Polk decided not to strike at all but to act on what he called "the defensive-offensive." Such a term made no sense within the context of the campaign. Polk reported that he had 15,000 men at Perryville and believed Buell confronted him with two to three times more troops. Nevertheless, his course of action played to Buell's advantage.[37]

Bragg received intelligence during the night of October 7 that convinced him the Federals were not making a major move against Kirby Smith. He therefore decided to personally superintend operations at Perryville. Bragg and his staff left Harrodsburg early on the morning of October 8 and reached Perryville by 9:30 A.M. He was surprised to find that Polk had not yet attacked. Bragg refused to resume command of the Army of the Mississippi, but he did take charge of the situation. He quickly examined the ground to see if an attack was feasible and then issued another direct order. This time Polk obeyed and the battle at Perryville opened at about 12:30 P.M.[38]

The Confederate attack fell on the left wing of Buell's army, principally Alexander McDowell McCook's corps. The Army of the Mississippi took the Federals by surprise, launched repeated assaults across mostly open, rolling terrain, and came close to crushing McCook's command. The Federals were battered and forced to fall back in stages until Buell's left wing was crunched together in a tight defensive posture several hundred yards from its starting point. Buell was not even aware that a major battle had erupted until quite late and sent McCook few reinforcements. By the end of the day, the Army of the Mississippi achieved a clear tactical victory over a portion of the opposing army. Bragg exercised little control over the movements that day; neither did Polk. The engagement at Perryville was carried primarily by division and brigade leaders.[39]

"For the time engaged, it was the severest and most desperately contested engagement within my knowledge," Bragg wrote a few days later. According to his own count, the Confederates drove the Federals two miles, captured fifteen guns, and inflicted 4,000 casualties. Polk's losses amounted to 2,500 men according to Bragg. A more objective estimate of the butcher's bill at Perryville places it at 4,276 out of 55,261 Federals engaged while the Confederates lost 3,401 out of 16,800 men who took part in the fighting.[40]

But what had this tactical success achieved? In the end, McCook's command survived, and Buell had two other mostly fresh corps available on the field. Bragg was badly outnumbered. That night, reports filtered in concerning enemy strength, and Bragg realized he had to leave. At 9 P.M. he issued orders for the dead to be buried, the wounded to be gathered and transported, and the Army of the Mississippi to evacuate the hard-won field.[41]

The Confederates were gone by dawn of October 9, leaving Perryville in Buell's hands. Polk's men trudged to Harrodsburg where Kirby Smith finally joined the Army of the Mississippi on October 10, too late for what could have been the climactic battle for Kentucky. After resting two days at Harrodsburg, a welcome treat offered by Buell's slow follow-up, the combined Confederate armies moved to Bryantsville on October 11. "My future movements cannot be indicated," Bragg informed Samuel Cooper the next day, "as they will depend in a great measure on those of the enemy."[42]

The course of the campaign certainly had gone against all Bragg's expectations. In part it was due to his inability to gain accurate information about Buell's intentions. Bragg and Kirby Smith had too few cavalrymen to screen their movements and gather information. Buell devised a very effective plan of approaching the Confederates along several lines of advance. The column sent toward Frankfort especially confused Bragg, who continued to be uncertain where Buell's main force was located until the realization that it was at Perryville dawned on him during the evening of October 8.[43]

But another source of Bragg's woes lay in two recalcitrant generals. Kirby Smith contributed greatly to Confederate failure in Kentucky by his persistent refusal to cooperate with Bragg. In fact, only after the terrible bloodletting at Perryville did Kirby Smith finally join the Army of the Mississippi. This could have and should have been done much earlier. Jefferson Davis deserves primary blame for the fact that neither Bragg nor Kirby Smith had the authority to command the other.

But Bragg certainly had the authority to command Leonidas Polk. Unfortunately, Polk failed to live up to his duty as a subordinate. His decision to retire from Bardstown toward Harrodsburg rather than move northward to strike the Union column heading for Frankfort was justified by the circumstances. But his refusal to carry out Bragg's order to attack at Perryville early on October 8 was not justified. A few more hours of daylight might have allowed Polk's brigade commanders to punish McCook further, but it also could have allowed Buell to shift more reinforcements to his battered left wing as well. The delay in attacking probably made little difference in the outcome of the fight, but it demonstrated that Polk did not understand the purpose of Bragg's order or how it fit into the context

EDMUND KIRBY SMITH. Bragg was compelled to cooperate with Kirby Smith during the Kentucky campaign but found him only a reluctant partner in this risky endeavor. Davis refused to place one man over the other, and therefore the Confederate effort was severely hampered by a lack of close support; two major Rebel forces never combined their strength in an effective way to deal with Don Carlos Buell's large Federal army. There were many other factors affecting the outcome of the Kentucky campaign, but Kirby Smith contributed his share of blame for Confederate failure. (Library of Congress, LC-DIG-cwpb-06082)

of the campaign. As Polk's most recent biographer has put it, the general tended to be "overly deliberate" and consistently displayed "a lack of aggressiveness" during his Civil War career that poorly served his superior. In disregarding a direct order, Polk exhibited an unusual attitude of disobedience that would hamper Bragg's ability to command the army for a year to come.[44]

Although some writers criticize Bragg for installing a Confederate governor in Frankfort instead of tending to military duties, other historians point out that Jefferson Davis wanted Hawes in office so he could extend conscription in the state. Bragg was aware that the Federals were on the move, but he hoped Polk could delay those moves until the installation was over. Buell maneuvered too quickly, and Polk failed to satisfy Bragg in these hopes. Steven Woodworth criticizes the bishop for "hating to take orders," and being in the long run "a basically incompetent general."[45]

In short, Bragg was not well served by either his colleague or his subordinate. Although taking an aggressive stance upon receiving word of Buell's advance from Louisville, the result at Perryville was not a decisive battle for possession of Kentucky. After retiring from the field, the two forces were finally united at Bryantsville, but it did not take long for Bragg to lose his confidence. With Buell carefully approaching, he weighed Confederate strengths and weaknesses. Bragg was surprised to learn that only four days of food had been accumulated at Bryantsville. A report arrived that Earl Van Dorn had been badly defeated in an attempt to recapture Corinth on October 3–4 and that Bragg could expect no help from the South. He was outnumbered nearly two to one, and hope for a popular uprising by the Kentuckians had become a cruel joke. There seemed no point in sacrificing his army to "redeem" the state.[46]

Staff officer George Brent recorded the tenor of discussions at Bryantsville on October 12. While Kirby Smith opposed giving up Kentucky, Brent accurately wrote that "our position is a critical one." Bragg's counsel prevailed, and the discussion then turned to the method of getting both armies back to the Confederacy. "The campaign here was predicated on a belief and the most positive assurances that the people of this country would rise in mass to assert their independence," Bragg wrote Samuel Cooper on October 12. "Willing perhaps to accept their independence, they are neither disposed nor willing to risk their lives or their property in its achievement."[47]

Many years later, Simon B. Buckner and Edmund Kirby Smith portrayed Bragg as uninformed and overly sanguine before the battle of Perryville. Polk told Buckner that Bragg felt no sense of hurry in concentrating his forces against Buell. "Why, General, the enemy are divided, and we can afford to divide, too, instead of concentrating," Bragg reportedly told Polk. Kirby Smith recalled that he tried to persuade Bragg to postpone Hawes's installation and fight the Yankees. Bragg told him, in Kirby Smith's words, that "he could crush Buell with his own command alone and that he should carry out his intention of inaugurating Gov. Hawes at Frankfort."[48]

But, according to his critics, Bragg's mood changed completely after the battle of Perryville. Buckner thought the general was "overwhelmed, didn't know what to do" on the night of October 8 after he learned of Buell's superior numbers on the battlefield. He "made some expression which showed his hesitancy and almost despair." Polk suggested he could pull the Army of the Mississippi away with safety, and Bragg told him, as Buckner remembered, "General, I wish you would do it." By October 11, Buckner conceded that the campaign was lost and advised Bragg to retreat South. "The Army had lost confidence in Gen'l Bragg and there was left no other course to pursue," he told Thomas Claiborne.[49]

The many problems of the Kentucky campaign would have taxed the mental abilities and emotional stamina even of Robert E. Lee, and Bragg did not deal well with them. The Confederates pulled away from Bryantsville before Buell reached within striking distance on October 13. Marching in two columns, the men suffered terribly from lack of food while crossing the rugged mountains. Bragg's headquarters reached Cumberland Gap at midafternoon of October 18, followed by the head of his army the next day. For five days the weary troops moved through the gap and into Tennessee, returning to Confederate territory and wondering why the campaign had resulted as it did.[50]

6

Controversy and Recovery

By the time Bragg reached Cumberland Gap on October 18 he had already begun to formulate ideas about future strategy. Davis wanted to know his views, prompting Samuel Cooper to telegraph Bragg on October 20 to dispatch a reliable officer to Richmond so he could question him about the army's plans. The next day, Bragg sent Harvey Washington Walter, his assistant adjutant general, and briefly telegraphed Cooper about his views on October 22. "Shall press into Middle Tennessee and hold the country south of Cumberland [River]," he wrote. That curt statement did not seem adequate to Bragg so he telegraphed Davis on October 23 that he was sending a brigade commander named Preston Smith to Richmond. Smith had full authority to answer any questions posed by Davis. Bragg further explained in his telegram that he hoped to secure provisions for the Army of the Mississippi in the area between the Cumberland and Tennessee Rivers. The Federals still held Nashville but no points farther south. "It will be an exposed and hazardous position," Bragg admitted, "but with caution I hope it may be maintained."[1]

Walter arrived in Richmond on October 23, the day that Bragg sent his latest telegram to the authorities. But Davis suddenly felt the need to consult directly with the army commander on this important issue. Cooper told Bragg that, if he felt comfortable leaving his command "for a few days," he should come immediately. The general wasted no time. He reached Knoxville by October 23 and took the first train east the next day, arriving at Richmond on the evening of Saturday, October 25.[2]

After the failure of his first campaign as commander of the main Confederate department in the West, Bragg's career was at stake. He fully anticipated criticism and sought to firm up his support among the authorities in Richmond. Bragg engaged in lengthy meetings with Davis and Secretary of War George W. Randolph, explaining the details of his foray into Kentucky and the reasons for retreating. He put the best spin on results, stressing the fact that his army had taken a large amount of material out of the state for Confederate use. Ironically, the cattle and cloth that were hauled south were turned over to commissaries for general distribution rather than issued to the starving, ill-clad troops of the Army of the Mississippi, who suffered more material deprivation on the march out of Kentucky than they had yet endured in the war. "His retreat from Kentucky was made without loss," Randolph told another general about Bragg's conference, "and he brought away an immense amount of material." According to Randolph, Bragg hauled 1 million yards of cloth, a number of horses, beef cattle, and the 15,000 guns and ammunition that he had taken into Kentucky to arm recruits. "His expedition, therefore, has not been without its fruits." Randolph had suspected since at least October 20 that Bragg would position his army in Middle Tennessee to secure territory not yet held by the enemy, and Bragg confirmed that objective during his visit to Richmond.[3]

This proved to be Bragg's first major conference with Davis, and he effectively presented his case. It has to be noted, however, that Davis was ready to be convinced. As early as October 17, absorbing the distressing news from Kentucky, Davis admitted that the Confederate cause had little chance of succeeding in his native state even though many of its residents were sympathetic. "Without the aid of Kentuckians, we could not long occupy the state and should have no sufficient motive for doing so," he wrote Bragg. It was relatively easy to persuade Davis that the retreat was necessary and that something had been gained from the campaign. Randolph fully believed both points as well.[4]

Bragg seems to have spent more time in Richmond than necessary to convince his superiors of his spin on circumstances because Davis was not entirely convinced that occupying Middle Tennessee was the best course of action. Having arrived on October 25, Bragg was still in Richmond four days later when Davis finally accepted the plan. "To recover from the depression produced by the failure in Ky. no move seems better than to advance into Middle Tenn.," he informed Kirby Smith. Ironically, Bragg telegraphed orders for Polk to move the Army of the Mississippi to Middle Tennessee the day before, October 28. Cooper approved the move and authorized Bragg to draw men from Kirby Smith's department to Middle Tennessee on November 1.[5]

Bragg visited his family while in the capital. Brother Thomas had resigned as Confederate attorney general and lived in a rented house in Petersburg only thirty miles south of Richmond. Thomas used the rail link between the two cities and visited Braxton on October 27. "I found him

THOMAS BRAGG JR. Sympathetic brother of Braxton, Thomas practiced law, served in the North Carolina legislature, and was governor of the state from 1855 to 1859. He then served in the U.S. Senate until the secession of North Carolina led him to resign in 1861. Davis appointed him Confederate attorney general but also accepted his resignation in 1862. For the last few years of his life, Thomas continued to practice law. (Bragg Family Photographs, ADAH)

looking well & in good spirits. He was in daily conference from 10 A.M. to 4 P.M. with the Pres. & Sec'y of War." It was obvious to Thomas that Davis and Randolph approved Bragg's course, but he worried about his brother's apparent lack of interest in public opinion. "Some of the newspapers are attacking Gen'l B. but he seems indifferent, too indifferent it may be to all such assailants."[6]

Braxton finally left Richmond on October 31, stopping briefly in Petersburg on the way to have dinner with Thomas's family. He visited his brother from 11 A.M. to 5 P.M. before departing for Tennessee. The pair most likely discussed the administration and Bragg's relationship with Davis. Thomas had been a member of the cabinet for several months and was well regarded by the president of the Confederacy. But Thomas did not indicate that anything of moment was exchanged between them. These two brief visits apparently were the only times the two met in many years.[7]

Bragg returned to his headquarters at Knoxville on November 2. George Brent found him "in good spirits. He brought the gratifying fact that his conduct in Kentucky had been approved by the President. That the President had expressed his delight at the safe return of the Army." Bragg threw himself into the task of rejuvenating his command and getting it ready for battle. On November 3, he sent a long telegram to Cooper deploring the shortage of manpower in the Army of the Mississippi, warning Richmond that it was "gradually, but certainly, melting away." Some of his regiments had no more than 100 men on duty and he received no draftees since the Conscription Act had been implemented last spring. The Federals increased their army by almost 100 percent due to Lincoln's call for an additional 300,000 troops the previous July. The Confederate government did nothing to match that increase. It was "the most serious question to be solved," in Bragg's view. He actually had more guns than men at present.[8]

Bragg now learned from Elise of disaster at their Louisiana home. Bivouac, whose sugar industry had been developed by Bragg, was devastated and taken over by the Federals. Benjamin Butler, commander of the Union Department of the Gulf, sent a brigade under Godfrey Weitzel into the Bayou Lafourche area in late October. Weitzel expected to meet resistance at Thibodeaux. His brigade fought a small but hard battle at Georgia Landing near that town on October 27, driving the Confederate force away and occupying Thibodeaux the next day.[9]

Federal troops spread out into the area, arriving at Bivouac on October 28. Bragg's plantation manager, Alvin N. Gardner, testified that there were 250 hogsheads of sugar in store on the property. He had been unable to sell them because of the fall of New Orleans the previous April. A buyer from the Union-occupied city recently negotiated with Elise, but Federal troops came before the deal could be finalized. She had sold more than 300 hogsheads of sugar in New Orleans before the fall of the city, representing more than half of the 550 hogsheads produced at Bivouac in 1861.[10]

Elise told the full story of what happened when the Yankees arrived, confiding to the wife of Confederate general Ben Hardin Helm long after the war. A Federal warned her that he could not restrain his men, that she should expect pillaging. Elise left before the worst was done leaving behind 120 to 130 slaves on the plantation. A few days later Elise returned to find the place devastated. The "house was pillaged and everything broken up, even the feather beds cut open and carpets torn from the floors and every animal that was not killed was carried away." The Federals were using the house to shelter "the poor oppressed negroes in my service," she sarcastically remembered. The destruction of Bivouac caused Elise to stay with her husband as far as possible. She made plans for the trip to Middle Tennessee.[11]

"Oh! my wife, how much I suffer to think of your trials and tribulations," Bragg wrote from Knoxville after hearing about the overrunning of the Lafourche country. The news distressed him terribly. "I often think myself wrong in sacrificing all to a sense of duty," but he was committed to his course and could not change it now. "Could I but hear you were all safe this side of the Miss. I should be grateful and happy. Suspense is torture, yet there is no help."[12]

Bragg occupied his troubled mind by explaining to Elise why he left Kentucky. The women there supported the Confederacy, he argued, but the men were afraid to commit themselves. "Why then should I stay with my handful of brave Southern men to fight for cowards who skulked about in the dark to say to us, 'we are with you,' 'only whip these fellows out of our country, and let us see you can protect us, and we will join you.'" Bragg was disgusted. He had no intention of keeping his "noble army to be *ice-bound* in a northern clime *without tents or shoes* & *obliged to forage daily for bread*."[13]

Elise obviously had more pressing problems to deal with than her husband's need to be vindicated at this moment. The rumor that black troops had participated in the incursion into the Lafourche country was true. Butler had organized a few regiments from the African American population around New Orleans and sent a brigade of them to cooperate with Weitzel's New England troops. Weitzel, however, did not want to command the black men. He did not believe they could be made into reliable soldiers and was afraid their presence would incite formerly docile slaves to rebel, and the result might be a race war in Louisiana. Many civilians expressed their fears on this score, and Weitzel did not want to assume the responsibility for such results.[14]

Through George C. Strong, his assistant adjutant general, Butler tried to convince Weitzel that the time had come for sterner measures to defeat the South. "Consider this case," Strong wrote to the brigade commander, "General Bragg is at liberty to ravage the homes of our brethren in Kentucky because the Union army of Louisiana is protecting his wife and his home against his negroes. Without that protection he would have to come back to take care of his wife, his home, and his negroes. It is understood that Mrs. Bragg is one of those terrified women of whom you speak in your report."[15]

Of course, the expected black uprising never took place, but the emotional strain of what happened at Bivouac continued to weigh on Bragg's mind. In late November he unburdened himself to Davis in an early expression of private matters by the general to his commander in chief. "My own home has been pillaged," he confessed, "my wife driven forth destitute, and my negroes, stock, and all movables carried off. It has been so long anticipated that the reality is a sort of mental relief, when I learn that my wife, at least, is safe." Davis's plantation in Mississippi would undergo the same experience in 1863.[16]

Bragg had to subdue his private worries while managing the difficulties of moving the army to Middle Tennessee. He shifted his headquarters from Knoxville on the morning of November 10, arriving at Chattanooga late that night. Three days later he left Chattanooga and reached Tullahoma by midnight. Staff officer George Brent did not like the place. "Tullahoma a miserable dirty village," he wrote in his journal, "Our office a mere stye." Fortunately for Brent the general moved his staff on November 16 and reached Murfreesboro that night. There were many substantial families and a strong Confederate spirit among the residents. Mr. Maney and his family welcomed Bragg as the staff settled into comfortable quarters.[17]

Many of Bragg's troops were still moving forward to Murfreesboro, which was located about thirty miles southeast of Nashville. It was in some ways an exposed position. William S. Rosecrans replaced Buell in late October, due to Buell's hesitating follow-up to his victory at Perryville. The army was renamed the Fourteenth Corps because uniform corps designations were only then being instituted in the Federal armies in the West. Early in 1863 it became known as the Army of the Cumberland. After merging many units from Kirby Smith's Army of Kentucky into his own, Bragg also renamed the Army of the Mississippi as the Army of Tennessee. His Department No. 2 was renamed the Department of Tennessee. After the fall of Fort Donelson, the force of circumstances shifted the main Confederate force in the West toward defending the Mississippi Valley. Now, that shift had been corrected. Bragg firmly planted his command in the path of a Union offensive down the rail line linking Louisville with Nashville, Murfreesboro, Chattanooga, and Atlanta. He prepared to defend the heartland of the Confederacy and Middle Tennessee would be the next battleground.[18]

Bragg was determined to put up a heavy fight. His combative spirit was remarkable considering the grueling and disappointing campaign in Kentucky. While meeting a Union advance with his infantry, Bragg planned to employ his cavalry force to cut Rosecrans's supply line. He considered taking the offensive himself, although warning Cooper that Nashville was fortified and would be very difficult to capture. "I have troops ready to dare anything their leaders may order," he assured the adjutant general. But he clearly preferred a defensive strategy. His army boasted 40,000 men available for duty, after taking 11,000 from Kirby Smith, who took charge of the Trans-Mississippi Department. Rosecrans reportedly could field 60,000 men. Nevertheless, "we will meet him with confidence," Bragg wrote, and "hope thus to force him to fight or fall back."[19]

While the manpower shortage was worrisome, Bragg had other troubles to deal with in the fall of 1862. The public tended to be less generous than Davis in evaluating the results of his Kentucky campaign. Some of his enemies, such as the newspaper correspondent Samuel Chester Reid, declared that "Bragg [was] universally anathematized" within his own army. Artillery officer William C. D. Vaught noted that the "outcry against Genl. Bragg for this unsuccessful Campaign is great. He made several very obvious blunders, let slip opportunities that every common soldier saw & wondered at." Members of the Kentucky clique roundly criticized Bragg. William Preston, the brother-in-law of Albert Sidney Johnston, admitted that the Army of the Mississippi would obey and fight no matter who commanded it, "but the General inspires no enthusiasm." Corps and division commanders were "united in their censures and complaints." Tennessee senator Gustavus A. Henry, who observed the Army of the Mississippi as it passed through Knoxville in October, argued that everyone in it was disgusted with their leader. "They don't object to Bragg on account of his discipline . . . but because of the failure of his campaign." Henry had defended Bragg in Senate debate but now was convinced he should be replaced. "I do not say anybody else could do any better but I can say no one can do any worse."[20]

By November and December, the full weight of public opinion about the Kentucky campaign came crashing down on Bragg. Both in and out of the army, however, he became the subject of carefully measured leniency as well. Some observers were willing to give him the benefit of the doubt. Others immediately seized the opportunity to declare that Confederate fortunes needed a new man at the helm in the West.

Bragg's personal composure became the subject of speculation. Randall Gibson, certainly no friend of the general, recalled years later that everyone in the Army of the Mississippi heard "that Genl Bragg had become demoralized & sick & had broken down utterly & turned the Command of the Army over to Genl Polk." Of course, there was no foundation for this rumor. All indications are that Bragg's health held up well throughout the campaign despite the almost insurmountable problems he faced. All accounts agree that, once out of Kentucky and vindicated by Davis, Bragg was in a buoyant, optimistic mood. Maj. John Walker, his chief commissary, found the general "in fine health & spirits" at Tullahoma in late November. At this stage in his career, Bragg's health cannot be counted as a major factor in his performance in the field.[21]

What exactly led so many people to criticize the Kentucky campaign and Bragg's handling of it? Irving Buck, a member of Patrick R. Cleburne's staff, pinpointed the basic reason. The initial success achieved by Kirby Smith and Bragg in driving into the state had created expectations of ultimate success that were unrealistic, given the severe limitations on Confederate ability to secure Kentucky. The authorities in Richmond were well advised concerning those limitations and accepted the result with understanding, but the public either did not gain access to the facts or ignored them in its passionate response to the results of the campaign.[22]

The editor of the *Richmond Examiner* was among those who held strong, single-minded opinions on the subject. He argued that the sole cause of the Kentucky failure was poor generalship and blamed Bragg for everything that went wrong. "Something more than the qualities of a drill officer and disciplinarian is needed in the West," he asserted, "public sentiment is now in favor of placing some general of larger brain and more active talents" in that important region. The editor of the *Mobile Tribune* wondered why the public had placed so much confidence in him.[23]

While key figures in Richmond supported Bragg, other men who were well placed in the Confederacy disagreed. Governor Francis W. Pickens of South Carolina believed that Bragg should have stayed longer in Kentucky in order to foster negotiations between the Confederacy and the northwestern states of the Union. He placed an inordinate amount of faith in the willingness of those states to form some sort of alliance with the Confederacy and had seen Bragg's campaign as instrumental in that hope.[24]

Politicians viewed the Kentucky adventure through their own, politically focused lens, while military men saw it in a different light. Truthfully, there were many episodes in the campaign wherein Bragg was open to second-guessing. Richard Taylor, his acquaintance from Louisiana, argued that Bragg should have compelled Buell to do battle somewhere from Middle Tennessee to Louisville. If that was not possible, then Bragg should have concentrated his force with Kirby Smith's and fought Buell as the Federals advanced from Louisville. With the benefit of hindsight, these were obvious points to make, but they do not take into account what Bragg knew at the moment of decision. They also do not take into account the most fundamental problem Bragg faced; he had to cooperate with an uncooperative colleague who in essence robbed him of an opportunity to control the course of the campaign. Kirby Smith, even though holding an independent command, was never subjected to the criticism that was directed on Bragg. He escaped censure almost completely.[25]

One of the most extreme criticisms of Bragg came from the pen of Seth

Barton, a brigade commander in the West who did not participate in the Kentucky incursion. "Bragg is either a madman or a coward," he asserted in a private letter, "if he is not removed from his command great disasters must unmistakably ensue." The general's "disgraceful retreat" lost to the Confederacy the state and its resources.[26]

News of the campaign filtered through the civilian population and mostly portrayed it in a negative light. Catherine Ann Devereux Edmondston in North Carolina, a niece of Leonidas Polk, heard that Bragg won decisively at Perryville but then retreated to Cumberland Gap. "Sad indeed does it seem that even tho' we gain victory after victory they are barren of results!" A few days later, Edmondston noted that the "country rings with complaints" of Bragg. Newspapers spread the news that the Confederates brought out much-needed supplies from Kentucky, and soon Edmondston realized a key reason for the retreat had been the reluctance of its citizens to support the Rebel cause. But she could not shake off the notion that Bragg had "mismanaged shamefully." She also was struck by the "storm of abuse" sent his way by late November. "He is pronounced incapable of making the combinations necessary for the management of an Army—'a good Artillery officer but no general,'—& many other flattering speeches all of which are generally believed to be *true*."[27]

Despite the growing public reaction, Davis remained steadfast in his support of Bragg. This was not based on personal friendship, for at this stage of their relationship the two men enjoyed only a professional trust. Davis explained his views on the controversial general in a letter to Kirby Smith. He felt, of course, a sense of "bitter disappointment" about the results of the Kentucky campaign, but Bragg "has explained in a direct and frank manner" why he had to leave the state. Davis also felt Bragg "evinced the most self denying temper in relation to his future position. That another Genl. might excite more enthusiasm is probable, but as all have their defects I have not seen how to make a change with advantage to the public service. His administrative capacity has been felt by the Army of Missi. His knowledge of the troops is intimate and a new man would not probably for a time with even greater ability be equally useful." This pragmatic assessment remained Davis's view of Bragg for the rest of the war, and it sustained his faith in the general through thick and thin.[28]

It is important to keep in mind that, despite the torrent of abuse hurled toward Bragg, many members of the Confederate public agreed with Davis. They accepted the results of the Kentucky campaign and recognized that Bragg was not solely to blame for its outcome. An anonymous captain in the Army of the Mississippi wrote a letter exonerating his commander that was published in several newspapers. This officer admitted he was "no special admirer of General Bragg," but he participated in the campaign and pointed out that Kentucky was "utterly subjugated" and "we may hope for nothing from her in our present great struggle." Bragg had also proved that "the idea of invasion by our army is absurd," and he ought to be given credit for saving the army, bringing out supplies, and making the best of a bad situation.[29]

A woman who signed herself Ada wrote an indignant letter to the newspapers to protest the criticism heaped on Bragg. She had nursed his troops for many months early in the war at Pensacola and offered a balanced analysis of the Kentucky campaign that laid out the basic problems Bragg faced. Another nurse named Kate Cumming also saw Bragg's viewpoint in this controversy.[30]

Within the Army of the Mississippi, Bragg had considerable support for his actions. Brig. Gen. St. John R. Liddell, who commanded a brigade at Perryville, argued that Bragg could not have fought a major battle with Buell at Munfordville because of logistical problems. "There was nothing in that section in the way of provisions at that time," and Bragg "could not wait without starving" there. The general took the best course open to him, and "I believe he was right." Hardee said in Liddell's hearing that Polk deserved the credit "for saving Bragg's army," and the remark "proved to me what I suspected[;] Bragg was not well supported by his generals, on whom he had every reason to rely." Liddell partly blamed Bragg for caving in to the opinions of his chief subordinates, an action caused in part by Bragg's "own apprehensions." This combination of internal doubts and outside pressure, in Liddell's view, caused many of Bragg's problems and points to a certain lack of stamina in following his own course of action. Liddell pinpointed a significant factor in Bragg's Civil War career, a willingness to accede too readily to the opinion of subordinates when his own resolve wavered. Unfortunately, Polk and Hardee often failed to serve Bragg well in this regard.[31]

A South Carolina officer in Arthur M. Manigault's brigade supported Bragg in the controversy about the campaign. C. Irvine Walker gave his chief the benefit of the doubt. "We must suppose that he did not come into Kentucky merely to be driven out or to run whenever the enemy showed himself," he wrote home. While Walker faulted Bragg for not fighting at Munfordville, he pinpointed lack of support in the state as the key to the campaign's failure. By mid-December, Walker was surprised that "the Army has not lost so much confidence [in Bragg] as I first expected they would." Everyone seemed to "admit that Genl. Bragg did well to retreat" from the state.[32]

No one in the army was a more vigorous defender than brigade commander John K. Jackson. "The opinion of the army sustains Genl Bragg," Jackson assured a friend, "he is an idol with them notwithstanding the censure of newspapers." Jackson accepted all the points put forth by Bragg to explain the retreat from Kentucky and blamed most of the problem on "newspaper and street-corner warriors" who "abuse every body in relation to the conduct of the war, about which they know nothing."[33]

Bragg made efforts to mollify key subordinates in the wake of the Kentucky failure, but with only limited success. Edmund Kirby Smith had written his wife as early as October 20 to blame his colleague for the turn of events. "Bragg's movements . . . have been most singular and unfortunately, the campaign which opened so gloriously has since . . . proved a failure." He also conferred with Davis after returning from the state and agreed to join most of his troops permanently with Bragg's army even though the "men are dissatisfied, and tis told me are almost mutinous and will desert if placed under Bragg." When he returned to Knoxville, Kirby Smith accidently met his colleague on the cars. Even though "every one prognosticated a stormy meeting," Bragg surprised the general by speaking very kindly and "in the highest terms of praise and admiration of 'my personal character & soldierly qualities.' I was astonished but believe he is honest & means me" no harm, Kirby Smith assured his wife.[34]

But Bragg could not mollify the Kentuckians in his army. Although he had strongly supported John C. Breckinridge's promotion to major general after Shiloh and desperately wanted his division with him in the Kentucky foray (a wish that was impossible to fulfill), relations soured dramatically when Bragg insisted on executing a Kentucky soldier for desertion. Corp. Asa Lewis of the 6th Kentucky had left the army without permission to tend to family problems early that month. When he returned, Bragg meant to make an example of his case and insisted on fulfilling the death sentence handed down by Lewis's court-martial. Breckinridge and other officers tried to intercede, but Bragg would not relent. Lewis was executed on December 26 even though he had left to attend to family problems and returned to the army of his own accord.[35]

The death of Asa Lewis understandably soured many Kentucky soldiers against Bragg. However, Breckinridge's biographer ties it too closely to the bad relations existing between the two generals. William C. Davis argues that Bragg blamed Breckinridge for the failure of the Kentucky campaign (because his division could not join him there) and believes Lewis's death sealed a mortal antagonism between division leader and army commander. Actually there is no evidence that Bragg made a whipping boy of Breckinridge following the campaign. As discussed in the following chapter, it was the battle of Stones River that developed a feud between Bragg and Breckinridge. While their relationship certainly was strained before that engagement because of the Lewis execution, it was by no means irreparable.[36]

Outside the Army of the Mississippi, John Forsyth came forth as a public champion of Bragg. He had served only a short time as volunteer aide on the general's staff during the campaign before resuming his editorial duties with the *Mobile Advertiser and Register*. Forsyth wrote for the *Atlanta Confederacy*, citing the lack of public support in the state and Van Dorn's failure to come north as chief causes for the campaign's failure. The *Memphis Daily Appeal* reprinted Forsyth's testimony.[37]

With the public clamor rising, Forsyth took another step toward helping his friend. He wrote a memoir of the Kentucky campaign to give more breadth to his explanation for its outcome. His plan was to publish it in the newspapers of several cities, including Charleston, Augusta, Atlanta, and Mobile. "The true policy & history of the campaign are greatly misapprehended by the newspapers," he told Bragg. "I hope it shall be instrumental in correcting their errors." Forsyth drafted the memoir in late October and published it in his own newspaper on November 11 and 16. He also wrote to Davis alerting the Confederate president to the memoir's appearance.[38]

Entitled "Gen. Bragg's Kentucky Campaign," Forsyth explained the contours, expectations, and results of the incursion, writing a piece that must have greatly pleased Bragg. He correctly noted that many Southerners developed "absurdly exaggerated expectations" and unfairly castigated the general for not fulfilling them. He spread blame for the outcome of the campaign among many factors and pointed out that nearly all high-ranking officers agreed at Bryantsville that retreat was the only option left the Confederates. Bragg gained quite a bit from the campaign, including the recovery of much of Middle Tennessee, Cumberland Gap, thousands of prisoners, a huge amount of cloth, and he "paid a debt of honor" by allowing Kentucky a chance to rise up and join the Confederate cause. Forsyth concluded that the campaign "was the grand conception of a master mind" and that it was "boldly and vigorously executed."[39]

Forsyth followed up his two-part newspaper piece by printing an expanded version of his memoir as a pamphlet. Entitled *Memoranda of Facts Bearing on the Kentucky Campaign*, it fully explained every phase of the incursion into the border state. Forsyth pointed out that many people believed Bragg harbored vindictive feelings toward the citizens of Kentucky. He apologized for giving that impression in his first newspaper testimony in the *Atlanta Confederacy* and explained that his views were his own, not Bragg's. In fact, Forsyth admitted that he had served as a volunteer aide on the general's staff only about ten days before being captured, exchanged, and sent back to Mobile. But he was deeply conversant with the facts of the campaign and produced a pamphlet that delved more deeply into its details than Bragg would have written.[40]

Forsyth exaggerated, however, when he argued that Bragg felt keenly for the suffering of Kentucky. His own state of Louisiana was but recently overrun and his family sent into exile. The general knew what occupation by a hostile army meant, in Forsyth's view. There is no evidence in Bragg's correspondence to support such hyperbole. But Forsyth correctly pinpointed the basic problem by stating that Bragg "conceived, organized, and executed the campaign. He is responsible for its results, and should be equally credited with its success, as censured for its reverses."[41]

The *Memoranda of Facts* produced a reaction. Richard Hawes had been simmering with anger ever since he was forced to abandon Frankfort only hours after taking the oath as Confederate governor of Kentucky. Upon reading Forsyth's defense of Bragg, he unloaded his frustration in a long letter published in the *Richmond Enquirer* and reprinted in the *Charleston Mercury*. Forsyth reprinted it in his *Mobile Advertiser and Register* on December 5 as well in order to deal with its points.[42]

Hawes systematically criticized Bragg regarding every phase of the Kentucky campaign. He believed the general should have engaged Buell in a major battle before the Federals fell back to Louisville. He should have marshaled more troops to fight a decisive engagement at Perryville. Hawes admitted that many prosperous men of Kentucky refused to offer aid to the Confederate army but argued that others were willing to do so. Progress was being made within the areas that Bragg controlled in terms of fostering support and raising troops. In Hawes's view, Bragg retreated from the state too early.[43]

Forsyth carefully refuted Hawes's arguments. He consulted Bragg's ordnance officer to find that 2,300 small arms had been issued to Kentucky recruits, and half of them were lost when the men refused to stay with the army on its retreat from the state. "Kentucky did not rise," Forsyth repeated. "My interest in Gen. Bragg is limited by my desire to see justice done to a brave soldier who has not taken off his harness for an hour since the war began." The newspaper editor held "high admiration for some of the very extraordinary characteristics of Gen. Bragg" and wanted to help anyone against "*fashionable clamor*."[44]

No one stood up in public view to defend Bragg like John Forsyth. Even his sympathetic brother Thomas did nothing except to bemoan the vicious attacks he read in the newspapers. "I see the Raleigh Standard in every number is swearing at Gen'l Bragg as extremely tardy, cautious & c." He blamed this stance on editor William W. Holden who was a political and personal enemy of Thomas. "He is the meanest, basest man alive—that is & has been for a long time my deliberate opinion."[45]

Thomas pinpointed a key component of the arguments against his brother when he perused the pages of the *Richmond Examiner* and the *Richmond Whig*. Both newspapers attacked Braxton "for want of activity & skill in the conduct of the Campaign in Kentucky." But, as Thomas noted, while Braxton had "the smallest means & the hardest task of all our Generals, he seems to be held to a stricter account than any."[46]

Ironically Robert E. Lee's invasion of the border state of Maryland was a bloody failure as well. He suffered 10,300 casualties in one day of fighting at Antietam compared to Bragg's 3,400 losses at Perryville. Yet nothing resembling the criticism heaped on Bragg descended on Lee. Most Southerners assumed Lee had done all he could; he had won spectacular victories in the Seven Days campaign of June and at Second Manassas in August. In the eyes of the public, Lee had proved his worth. It was Bragg's misfortune to fail in his first campaign and many refused to forgive him for it.[47]

It is ironic that Bragg's opponents gave him more respect than his own people. Federal officers were impressed by the fact that Bragg risked logistical catastrophe in driving his army northward without a full line of communications. Buell was subjected to a long court of inquiry for his handling of the Kentucky campaign. Division commander Gordon Granger testified before the court that Bragg's march "was certainly a very extraordinary one. After he found he could not force the evacuation of Nashville he certainly did violate, to a certain extent, some of the fundamental rules of war." It was justified, Granger thought, by the fact that Bragg was heading toward friendly troops under Kirby Smith and a region of Kentucky that could provide supplies. In the end, the bold move failed to pay rich dividends but at least there were elements of brilliance in its early phase in Granger's view.[48]

Henry Halleck, now general-in-chief of the U.S. Army, read the testimony collected by the Buell court and penned an assessment of Bragg's generalship. "History of military campaigns affords no parallel to this of an army throwing aside its transportation, paying no regard to its supplies, but cutting loose from its base, marching 200 miles in the face of and really victorious over an army double its size."[49]

William T. Sherman, busy with occupation duties in southwestern Tennessee, kept himself informed of his old friend's activities. Two years after the campaign began he referred to the significance of Bragg's swift movement in the late summer of 1862 when urging Federal officers to penetrate enemy territory by living off the land. "When Buell had to move at a snail's pace with his vast wagon trains, Bragg moved rapidly, living on the country. No military mind could endure this long, and we are forced in self-defense to imitate their example." In other words, Sherman targeted Bragg's Kentucky campaign as the start of a major trend in the Civil War toward foraging off the countryside, a precursor to Sherman's March to the Sea and through the Carolinas in 1864–65.[50]

Of course, Bragg could not have known how the enemy viewed his campaign, but he exercised remarkable restraint in the face of criticism leveled by Southerners. Restraint had not been his strong point when fuming about the newspaper criticism of his disciplinary methods or the way in which he obtained command of Department No. 2. Now, instead of reacting to criticism, Bragg remained above the fray during the fallout of his campaign into Kentucky. As Thomas suggested, perhaps his brother was too disinterested for his own good.

In fact, Bragg waited until he wrote his report of the Kentucky incursion in May 1863 before he addressed the criticisms. Taylor Beatty and Thomas Butler visited Bragg at his headquarters one day early that month and were treated to three hours of conversation with the general, most of it revolving around Kentucky. Bragg told the pair that logistics were a key factor in the retreat, and he severely criticized Polk for not obeying orders to attack the Federals early on October 8 at Perryville, exaggerating when he stated that he "had to ride up and lead the lines into action himself." Bragg gave a full account in his official report, dated May 20, and it coincided with Forsyth's earlier pamphlet on the subject.[51]

Many Bragg supporters waited until after the war before they defended him in print. David Urquhart, a staff member and family friend, rode with the general throughout the campaign and noted that it was Bragg's "habit to confide to me his hopes and fears." Prominent Kentuckians had visited

Bragg before the start of the campaign to convince him the state was ripe for revolution. Even before the troops left Chattanooga, however, the general began to doubt these reports, but he was determined to go on. "At the same time he was resolved to do nothing to imperil the safety of his army, whose loss, he felt, would be a crushing blow to the Confederacy," Urquhart noted.[52]

Once deep in the state, it became apparent that Bragg's fears were well founded. "The people here have too many fat cattle and are too well off to fight," he remarked to Urquhart. Bragg now felt he had made a mistake in deviating from his original idea to seek a decision with Buell in Middle Tennessee. The fundamental goal of saving his small, exposed army now drove strategy. This was one reason that Perryville was not a general battle, but an intermediate measure to facilitate the delayed concentration of Confederate forces in the state. Unfortunately for Bragg, it was the beginning of a persistent phenomenon in his military career—winning tactical victories from which his men and the public expected great things that never materialized.[53]

Nevertheless, the campaign could have resulted far more disastrously than it did. "So well satisfied was General Bragg at having extricated his army from its perilous position in Kentucky," wrote Urquhart, "that he was not affected by the attacks upon him by the press for the failure of the campaign. He was cheerful, and would frequently join the staff about the camp-fire, and relate with zest incidents of his services under General Taylor in Mexico."[54]

Another Bragg supporter, Joseph Wheeler, offered his views of the campaign in a postwar article. Although Bragg was irritated that political pull had led to Wheeler's promotion from lieutenant to lieutenant colonel in 1861, he came to appreciate Wheeler's worth as a cavalry officer, praised his performance at Shiloh, and supported his further rise in rank. Wheeler pinpointed the same reasons for failure that others had already indicated. Unfortunately, only "thoughtful people" were well informed of these reasons and understood them. "The censure which fell upon Bragg was therefore severe and almost universal. It somewhat abated after the prompt advance of the army to Murfreesboro; but to this day there are many who contend that Bragg should have defeated Buell and maintained himself in the rich and productive plains of Kentucky."[55]

Leonidas Polk did not survive the war, but his son embarked on a crusade to vindicate his father's career in a two-volume book published long after the conflict. William M. Polk bypassed no opportunity to portray

JOSEPH WHEELER. Bragg supported Wheeler's rise in rank, trusting him to command cavalry in conjunction with the operations of his army. Wheeler conducted his mounted men well during the Stones River campaign and became a quiet supporter of Bragg, assessing his campaigns fairly in postwar articles. (Library of Congress, LC-DIG-cwpb-05987)

Bragg negatively in the campaign, arguing that he was indecisive when confronted with complicated problems and unwilling to listen to the sound advice of Polk and Hardee.[56]

Jefferson Davis did not share these negative views of Bragg. In his two volume work, *The Rise and Fall of the Confederate Government*, the ex-president of the Confederacy called the Kentucky adventure "a brilliant piece of strategy on the part of General Bragg, by which he manoeuvered the foe out of a large and to us important territory."[57]

Bragg has been vilified and exonerated by historians. Thomas Robson Hay, writing in 1925, critiqued his handling of Buell's approach before the battle of Perryville. Stanley Horn, writing in 1941, had nothing kind to say about him either. But twenty years later, historians began to treat Bragg more gently. Ralph Wooster argued that Perryville was a Confederate victory in that Bragg achieved the limited goals he set for the engagement. The tenor of subsequent analysis by historians echoes that view—tactical success on the local level at Perryville but strategic failure on the theater level in the state. As Grady McWhiney points out, Buell nullified his tactical defeat at Perryville by outgeneraling Bragg in subsequent movements. McWhiney, however, does not really see Perryville as a Confederate victory. "The battle proved that Bragg was no better at commanding an army in combat than he had been at leading a corps." The primary reason for this assessment is the same that McWhiney used to criticize Bragg's effort at Shiloh, the erroneous assumption that rifle muskets doomed frontal attacks to bloody failure. McWhiney, however, correctly points out that only two of Bragg's twenty generals openly expressed dissatisfaction with his handling of the campaign.[58]

In the end, McWhiney cited other reasons for Bragg's failure. He had inadequate staff to handle matters such as overseeing the accumulation of supplies, and he suffered from a paucity of information about enemy movements. "Outguessed by Buell, upset by Polk's disobedience of orders, and confused by conflicting reports, Bragg had fought blindly at Perryville with only a fragment of his force." Ultimately, Davis's refusal to assign a supreme commander in Kentucky doomed hope of unitary action with Kirby Smith. McWhiney asserts that Bragg had performed better in his first campaign as the army commander than Albert Sidney Johnston had fared in the Shiloh campaign. McWhiney also believed Bragg performed better than either Polk or Hardee if those two subordinates had been in charge of the army. "Bragg might have been more successful if Polk and Hardee had given him the support he needed and had a right to expect, or if Kirby Smith had cooperated fully."[59]

Kenneth Noe sees a real change in Bragg during the campaign. The general acted with energy and optimism after taking over Department No. 2 in June and strengthening the Army of the Mississippi. "The history of the Confederacy would have been much shorter had he been half the incompetent some claimed him to be." During the first phase of the campaign, those characteristics continued to shine. Bragg "had shown initiative, determination, self-confidence (occasionally too much), and real ability."[60]

But on realizing that Kentucky residents would not rise, his mood changed. As Noe correctly points out, there was no larger vision in conducting the campaign than the need to go north and support Kirby Smith. For that, Bragg could not be blamed, for he was not in full control of events that compelled him forward. The only saving for the Confederates would have been if the people welcomed them and flocked to the colors, and when that failed to happen, Bragg was burdened with more problems than he could solve. "Abrupt mood swings, barely restrained anger, and a total inability to act decisively without second-guessing himself would characterize his generalship from then on. Just when his army needed a clear-headed commander most, Braxton Bragg began breaking under the strain."[61]

The Kentucky campaign spawned a host of judgments by Bragg's contemporaries and a string of historians well into the twenty-first century. The nature of those judgments range from the terribly misinformed to the most thoughtful imaginable, and yet no real consensus has ever developed. It is important to keep in mind that Bragg had many supporters in this controversy. In fact, it is fair to say that for every criticism to appear in the newspapers or the personal accounts of his contemporaries, at least one supportive voice was raised in his defense. That would change in 1863 as Bragg continued his controversial Civil War career.[62]

7

Stones River

Whatever had been his mistakes and deficiencies during the Kentucky campaign, Bragg got over that dismal episode of his career while approaching Middle Tennessee in November. He took up a position only thirty miles from the forward Union post in the region and counted on his army, rejuvenated by rest and experienced by the flames of Shiloh and Perryville, to maintain that position. Bragg was entering upon the most successful phase of his Civil War career. If the enemy ventured from Nashville, the Confederates would "soon fight him," Bragg told Beauregard. "He will outnumber us, as usual, but our hopes are strong and our troops very confident."[1]

Davis visited the Army of Tennessee, reaching Chattanooga from Richmond on December 11 and traveling to Murfreesboro the next day. The troops "were in fine spirits and well supplied," he told his wife. "Much confidence was expressed in our ability to beat them if they advance." Joseph E. Johnston, who traveled with the Confederate president, also was impressed by the condition of the Army of Tennessee. "I see no evidence of the want of confidence & dissatisfaction of which we heard so much in Richmond," he informed Texas senator Louis T. Wigfall. After spending two days with the army, Davis and his party left on December 14 for Chattanooga and then proceeded to Mississippi.[2]

While at Murfreesboro, Davis persuaded Bragg to send Carter L. Stevenson's Division to Mississippi, a depletion of his army he could ill afford. But Bragg continued to plan for an obstinate stand at Murfreesboro. He sent cavalry units toward Nashville to constrict Union foraging. Bragg also sent John Hunt Morgan to raid the Federal line of communications between Nashville and Louisville. Morgan defeated the garrison of Hartsville, Tennessee, and captured hundreds of troops. To help John C. Pemberton's forces holding Mississippi in the face of Grant's drive down the Mississippi Central Railroad, Bragg also ordered Nathan Bedford Forrest to raid Union railroads in west Tennessee. He retained four brigades of cavalry to operate closely with his own army.[3]

In the middle of these concerns, Bragg was reunited with his wife. Elise joined her husband at Murfreesboro in late December. She later told her friend Mrs. Ben Hardin Helm that she had not seen Braxton in a year and a half, ever since her visit to Pensacola in the summer of 1861.[4]

Bragg involved himself in a heated exchange of dispatches with Federal authorities in December 1862. He wrote a long complaint to Horatio G. Wright, the Union commander in Kentucky, about the treatment of civilians in that state. Prompted by reports that Wright condoned the arrest and imprisonment of citizens for acts committed by Confederate soldiers, Bragg told Wright that he had often been urged to arrest Kentucky Unionists and hold them for the ransom of civilians incarcerated by Federal authorities. But he had always resisted that course of action.[5]

Bragg saved most of his venom for a number of letters to the new Federal commander in Middle Tennessee, William S. Rosecrans. After taking over from Buell in late October, Rosecrans brought the Army of the Ohio to Nashville in stages and repaired the Louisville and Nashville Railroad. Under pressure from Washington, he restored his line of communications and rebuilt the army before setting out toward Murfreesboro. Caught in the middle of renumbering Union corps across the nation, the Army of the Ohio was renamed the Fourteenth Corps and divided into three wings. But while preparing for his onward push, Rosecrans received a letter from Bragg dated December 3. It included documents to protest Federal violation of the laws of war, mostly centering on reports from Confederate surgeons of bad treatment accorded captured and injured Rebels in Union hands. Bragg referred to an "extended and uniform system of unparalleled and savage warfare" waged by Union authorities.[6]

When word arrived that Rosecrans was arresting civilians for expressing pro-Confederate sympathy and holding them in the state penitentiary at Nashville, Bragg became angry once again. "I shall enforce rigid and unyielding retaliation against the commissioned officers who fall into my hands," he warned Rosecrans, "until this violation of good faith be corrected in deeds as well as words." Bragg warned Rosecrans that Federal mistreatment of Rebel soldiers and civilians alike must stop, "and until it does I shall retaliate in kind for every violation of humanity and justice."[7]

Several weeks of rest at Murfreesboro offered an opportunity for extended housekeeping in the Army of Tennessee. Bragg issued a general order urging his subordinate officers to honor Sunday as a day of rest and hold divine services if possible. He continued to pursue his vendetta against alcohol by approving the dismissal of a lieutenant in the 12th Tennessee for drunkenness.[8]

When reviewing court-martial proceedings, Bragg held officers to a higher standard of conduct than enlisted men. Two lieutenants of the 26th Alabama left their company during the movement toward Murfreesboro and rode in wagons at the rear of their regiment. They were found guilty and sentenced to suspension of rank for one month, forfeiture of pay, and a public reprimand by the colonel before the men. Bragg only reluctantly approved the sentence, noting the two had "reason to congratulate themselves on the leniency of their Judges." He also noted what he considered excessive leniency in the case of a lieutenant in the 6th Kentucky who was absent during a roll call of the regiment. His only punishment was a public reprimand before the men. While Bragg approved everything in this case, he could not refrain from noting that the infraction deserved a harsher sentence.[9]

These cases involved minor problems of discipline within the army, but desertion remained one of the most serious issues. Bragg approved the court-martial sentence of death for two men in the 28th Alabama and 60th North Carolina, but he also approved the court's recommendation for leniency for another man in the latter unit. Nine members of the 32nd Mississippi left the regiment under "aggravated circumstances" and were caught twenty miles away. The court, with Bragg's approval, sentenced them to only sixty days of hard labor. As long as the court complied with regulations, Bragg was willing to support its conclusions in his review of each case no matter what the members decided was fit punishment.[10]

The image of a man too ready to kill his soldiers in the name of discipline has to be tempered by his actual conduct in reviewing court-martial cases such as these. Bragg's handling of capital cases was in line with most other generals in blue and gray. Yet the image of a man killer continued to haunt Bragg. It was reinforced by the occasional order, such as the one issued in November, declaring "All soldiers who continue absent will be treated as deserters and punished as such."[11]

The day after Christmas, the Federals started their long awaited move toward Murfreesboro. Rosecrans approached Bragg by dividing his Fourteenth Corps into three columns heading south and southeast from Nashville. Bragg was compelled to concentrate his forces and assume a position covering all these roads as close to Murfreesboro as possible. With only about 35,000 men, he believed Rosecrans had 60,000 troops to oppose him.

On December 28, the Army of Tennessee took position a mile or two from town straddling the Nashville and Chattanooga Railroad and the Nashville Pike. It was the only feasible position for the army, even though Stones River bisected the line. As long as the water level was low enough to expose several fords, this would not pose a problem. Bragg placed Polk's Corps west of the river, with Jones M. Withers's Division in front and Benjamin F. Cheatham's Division behind it. He placed Hardee's Corps, consisting of John P. McCown's Division, John C. Breckinridge's Division, and Patrick R. Cleburne's Division, east of the river.[12]

Rosecrans brought his army together opposite this line by December 30, skirmishing heavily along the way. Before that was accomplished, Bragg sent McCown's Division from his right across Stones River to extend his left wing. By the evening of December 30, noting that the Federals seemed disinclined to attack soon, Bragg saw an opportunity to seize the tactical initiative. He shifted Cleburne's Division from right to left and assigned Hardee to direct the operations of McCown and Cleburne as those two divisions led an attack on the Federals at dawn the next day. The move necessitated much shifting during the night, but it proved advantageous. Despite evidence of the shift, Federal commanders remained unaware that they were soon to be treated with an attack on their right.[13]

Bragg not only displayed a great deal of pugnacity but stole a march on his opponent. In many ways it was his best move on the tactical chessboard. Bragg framed his strategy as an aggressive-defensive stand close to Nashville, dared the enemy to approach him, and then struck on the tactical level to punish him as much as possible. It is true that the position he assumed outside the town was not the ideal place for a battle—level land cluttered with cedar brakes, limestone outcroppings, and bisected by a river. But strategically Murfreesboro was a good spot to stand, and it was a strongly pro-Confederate town. Believing himself outnumbered two to one, Bragg sought an advantage by striking first where the enemy least expected it. The night march placed some of his best troops in position to deal a heavy blow at the enemy.

Bragg had displayed a good deal of tactical aggressiveness at Perryville, but he had not been in charge of the details of that attack. Stones River was a different scenario. The decision and execution were solely his responsibility, and the battle of Murfreesboro, as Confederates called it, would be Bragg's battle. He has rarely received the credit due him. What Bragg did on the evening of December 30 was consistent with the aggressive rhetoric of his dispatches to Richmond.

But Bragg was not yet finished with his preparation. He retained four brigades of cavalry, assigning John A. Wharton's Brigade to screen Hardee's left flank and cooperate with the infantry during the attack. John Pegram's Brigade was assigned to screen the right flank, now held east of Stones River only by Breckinridge's Division. Joseph Wheeler took the remaining two brigades on a daring raid around the Federal army. Starting on the evening of December 29, Wheeler devastated Rosecrans's supply line with Nashville. The Confederate troopers ran into large wagon trains lightly guarded. They captured or burned hundreds of wagons, captured many mules, and escaped before the Federals could arrive. Even before Bragg's assault began, Rosecrans's men began to suffer logistical problems.[14]

Bragg wrote clear instructions for Hardee's attack. McCown supported by Cleburne was to start at dawn, "the move to be made by a constant wheel to the right, on Polk's right flank as a pivot, the object being to force the enemy back on Stone's River, . . . cut him off from his base of operations and supplies by the Nashville pike." Polk's two divisions were to start after Hardee began the movement. Bragg imposed a difficult task on his army, conducting a wheeling movement of four divisions across cluttered terrain, but it held the promise of flanking the Federal line.[15]

In many ways, Bragg's plan worked admirably. The Confederates started their advance about 6 or 7 A.M., before Rosecrans's planned attack east of Stones River got underway. Therefore one key element fell into Bragg's favor, the element of surprise. Federal plans were completely disrupted, and Rosecrans was forced to scramble all day to counter the Confederate attack west of the river.[16]

What followed was one of the best days of fighting by the Army of Tennessee. Four divisions moved forward and began to batter their opponents. McCown flanked the Union line and shattered Richard W. Johnson's division of Alexander McCook's Right Wing, Fourteenth Corps. While the Federals to the left of Johnson often held firm against frontal attacks, they had to retire when units to their right collapsed. As the battle progressed, it developed into a series of fights that gradually pressed blue-clad troops farther back toward the Nashville Pike. Hundreds of Yankees broke and scattered on the far right, chased by Wharton's horsemen who also nearly captured McCook's ordnance train.[17]

"The enemy was taken completely by surprise," Bragg reported two months later. When the attack began, some Union gunners were watering their horses while breakfast was cooking on campfires. It was reminiscent of the first day at Shiloh, and Bragg made the most of it in his report to

Richmond. He revealed a vicious and vengeful streak when boasting that his men enjoyed the sight of "upturned artillery, fleeing battalions, and hosts of craven prisoners begging for the lives they had forfeited by their acts of brutality and atrocity."[18]

By 10 A.M., Bragg felt the need for fresh troops west of the river. He called on Breckinridge to send one brigade and a bit later ordered him to send a second, intending both as a reserve for Hardee. But Breckinridge responded to the first call by telling Bragg that the Federals were crossing Stones River. In response to the second call, Breckinridge reported the enemy was advancing on his position. Bragg rescinded his orders and told Breckinridge to advance and meet them. He then received a report that Federal troops were advancing along the Lebanon Road toward Breckinridge's right flank, but a little later a reconnaissance by Pegram's cavalrymen confirmed that the report was false. It was not all Breckinridge's fault. The Federals had indeed crossed the river that morning, but they retired to meet the developing emergency west of the stream. Bragg, however, was right to blame Breckinridge for not clarifying the situation early enough to prevent "these unfortunate misapprehensions." Federal moves east of Stones River should have become clear to Breckinridge by late morning.[19]

By the time all this was settled, Bragg felt it was too late in the day to help Hardee. Instead he ordered Breckinridge to send three of his brigades west of the river, leaving only two brigades to hold the position east of the stream. Those three brigades splashed across Stones River in stages and reported to Polk, who threw them into piecemeal attacks against the Federal center. Polk's own people had previously failed to drive the enemy away from where the Union line crossed the Nashville Pike. A cluster of trees called the Round Forest sheltered stout Yankee defenders who repelled every attack, including Breckinridge's men.[20]

Only through desperate fighting and the shifting of heavy reinforcements to the right could the Federals survive Bragg's attack on December 31. The far left of the Confederate line—McCown's and Cleburne's men—advanced three miles in a semicircular arc, captured several Union field hospitals, and drove the enemy to the Nashville Pike and the Nashville and Chattanooga Railroad. By evening the Federals stabilized their position along these two important lines of communication. The Confederates failed to secure the pike and the railroad, but they won an impressive tactical victory. As many as 10,000 Federal troops were killed, wounded, or captured. Rosecrans's logistical support was severely damaged by the loss of some 300 wagons, more than 2,100 horses and mules, and 25 tons of provisions. Most importantly, his plan to advance into Murfreesboro had been wrecked. Even if the ultimate goal of the Confederate attack failed, Bragg's army achieved a great deal on December 31.[21]

Given the magnitude of Confederate success, Bragg assumed the Federals would retreat on January 1. But as the cold day continued its course, all signs indicated that Rosecrans had no intention of leaving. Ironically, this was the day that Lincoln's Emancipation Proclamation went into effect, inaugurating a bold new phase in American history, but the guns were largely silent near Murfreesboro. While skirmishing took place, no major moves developed on either side.[22]

The status quo did not change on January 2, but the Federals quietly made a move that alarmed Bragg. They shifted a division of infantry across Stones River, which took post on a rise of ground near the river. From the new Union line, the terrain sloped gradually southward toward Murfreesboro, and much of it was open field. Rosecrans seemed to have begun the first phase of an advance on the town, and only two Confederate brigades stood in the way. The new Federal position also allowed Yankee artillery to enfilade Polk's line west of Stones River.[23]

On detecting signs of this movement, Bragg decided to drive the enemy from the east side of the stream. "The dislodgment of this force or the withdrawal of Polk's line was an evident necessity," he explained in his report. "The latter involved consequences not to be entertained." By 11 A.M., the general issued orders for Breckinridge to shift his brigades from the west of Stones River to the east so as to reform his division. Bragg arranged for ten Napoleon guns to support the attack and sent Wharton's cavalry brigade to reinforce Pegram on the far right. His instructions to Breckinridge were to drive the Federals across the river and then hold the high ground.[24]

The result was one of the most controversial episodes of Bragg's career. Breckinridge questioned the wisdom of the move, for he would be unsupported and place his men close to the main Federal position on the other side of the river. Bragg insisted on the attack, and the division commander had no choice but to obey. His men started across the open ground at 4 P.M. and moved swiftly northward. They engaged in a fierce, close-range firefight with Samuel Beatty's division of Thomas L. Crittenden's Left Wing, which held the high ground. The Confederates gained the upper hand in this exchange as the Federal line crumbled and retreated in haste.

But then Breckinridge's men exceeded their original instructions. They pursued the Federals across Stones River as heavy fire began to descend from a concentration of forty-five guns John Mendenhall assembled on high ground north of the battlefield. Whether that artillery fire turned the tide in this fight is open to question, for Breckinridge also ran into a heavy concentration of Union infantry hastily assembled west of Stones River. The Federal reinforcements counterattacked just as the Confederates began to cross the stream, and they rolled Breckinridge's Division back. This was the true turning point of the assault. Union troops drove the Confederates south, capturing guns and prisoners, until darkness and confusion put an end to the battle. Breckinridge lost 1,700 men out of 5,000 engaged in the fight.[25]

Worried about the repulse, Bragg sent James Patton Anderson's Brigade to support Breckinridge that evening. Anderson reported that he could not find a line to support, that Breckinridge apparently had not re-formed his division properly. Later that night, Bragg sent for the assistant adjutant general on Anderson's staff to clarify this disturbing intelligence. E. T. Sykes therefore had an opportunity to meet the commanding general in his headquarters, "one of the finest mansions in Murfreesboro." An aide escorted Sykes into "a large double-roomed folding parlor, elegantly furnished," where Bragg was in consultation with his corps and many division commanders. Sykes answered all of Bragg's "pertinent and laconic questions" to the general's satisfaction and left. One of the seeds constituting a rift between Bragg and Breckinridge was planted.[26]

The weather, which had been difficult throughout the campaign, worsened on January 3 with almost continuous cold rain. Despite severe food shortages, the Federals gave no signs of retiring from the field. McCook's papers had fallen into Confederate hands on December 31 and by the evening of January 2 made their way to Bragg's headquarters. They seemed to indicate that Rosecrans commanded 70,000 men, even larger than Bragg's earlier estimate. Before noon of January 3, Wheeler reported that even more Federal troops were on their way to Rosecrans. "Prospects forbidding," commented J. Stoddard Johnston, one of Bragg's aides, in his diary.[27]

Even more ominous was a dispatch written at 12:15 A.M. of January 3 by Benjamin Cheatham and Jones Withers. It urged Bragg to order a retreat from Murfreesboro as there were no more than three brigades in the Army of Tennessee that could be relied on to continue operations. Nearly three months later, Cheatham and Withers corrected their original dispatch to say that they meant to indicate there were no more than three reliable divisions, rather than brigades, but on January 3 Bragg knew only of their stunning evaluation that seventeen out of twenty infantry brigades in his army were in no shape to continue fighting. "We do fear great disaster from the condition of things now existing, and think it should be averted if possible," wrote Cheatham and Withers. Polk endorsed their view. "I greatly fear the consequences of another engagement at this place in the ensuing day," he added.[28]

Bragg's initial reaction to the dispatch reflected a stubborn desire to stay and fight. W. B. Richmond, one of Polk's aides, delivered the document while Bragg was asleep. He awoke and read it while still lying in bed at 2 A.M. After hastily going through the dispatch, Bragg told Richmond, "Say to the general we shall maintain our position at every hazard." Polk was miffed by this offhand rejection of his endorsement. At 3 A.M. he wrote a note to Hardee telling his colleague the news. "I think the decision of the general unwise, and, am compelled to add, in a high degree."[29]

During the course of the morning on January 3, Bragg's determination to fight began to weaken. By noon, he decided to order a retreat to take place that night. When brigade commander St. John R. Liddell visited the general at the Maney House that evening, he found him "thoughtful and hesitating." Bragg told Liddell some of the reasons that seemed to compel a retreat—the men were tired and exposed to bad weather, and the Federals were receiving reinforcements. Liddell argued that Wheeler's report could not be relied on and that he would support Bragg. "General, I know that you will fight it out, but others will not," the harried commander replied without revealing the full story about Cheatham, Withers, and Polk. He then informed Liddell that the army would retire that night. Liddell was deeply disappointed. Upon returning to his command, the men wondered what to expect. "Ask General Bragg," Liddell told them. The men "saw the hidden meaning and said, 'Well, boys, retreat again. All our hard fighting thrown away, as usual.'"[30]

"Common prudence and the safety of my army," Bragg argued, "upon which even the safety of our cause depended, left no doubt on my mind as to the necessity of my withdrawal from so unequal a contest." He pointed to the fact that Rosecrans was receiving reinforcements and his men were exhausted and exposed to inclement weather with no hope of relief as the chief causes for his withdrawal. For the time, Bragg did not mention the dispatch by Cheatham, Withers, and Polk, but it is obvious the document played a key role in his decision. Once again, Polk demonstrated that he could not be relied on, and his pessimism was infecting division commanders as well.[31]

But Bragg hesitated just before the planned retirement began. His concern centered on some 1,200 wounded Confederates who filled every available building in Murfreesboro, many of them badly injured. He thought of postponing the withdrawal twenty-four hours to offer surgeons an opportunity to remove them. But the delay would increase the level of illness among his men generally and more than compensate for any good achieved by retrieving the wounded troops. When the army began to pull away, it left behind 1,200 wounded comrades, 300 sick Confederates, and 200 attendants and medical officers to take care of them.[32]

The weather continued to be horrible when Bragg, Elise, and the staff left Murfreesboro at 11:30 on the night of January 3. "We had an awful ride," wrote J. Stoddard Johnston, "amid darkness, wind and rain." The party reached Shelbyville twenty-five miles to the southeast by 7:30 A.M. of January 4. Bragg stayed there only a few hours, leaving with Elise and the staff at 3 P.M. for Winchester eleven miles away. There a Mr. Carr allowed Bragg to use his house as army headquarters. The troops also suffered during their march to assigned positions.[33]

When Bragg filed his report of the campaign in late February, he claimed to have damaged Rosecrans a good deal despite his retreat. He estimated that his army captured 6,000 Federals, took more than 30 artillery pieces and 6,000 small arms, destroyed 800 wagons, and captured at least 9 Federal flags. Confederate losses amounted to 10,000 men out of 35,000 engaged. Bragg's estimate of Union loss was consistently higher than that reported by Rosecrans.[34]

By January 8, Bragg settled into his new positions and reported that he intended to hold the line of the Duck River "and operate on enemy's flanks and rear with cavalry." He sent Wheeler's command on a productive raid against Rosecrans's supply line near Nashville and Murfreesboro, worsening the Federals' already strained logistical system even further.[35]

But Bragg had to reckon with public reaction to his handling of the campaign. Unfortunately, that reaction was shaped by a glowing report Bragg sent to Richmond announcing the stunning success of his army on December 31. "We assailed the enemy at 7 o'clock this morning, and after ten hours' hard fighting have driven him from every position except his extreme left, [where] he has successfully resisted us. With the exception of this point, we occupy the whole field." At that early stage of the engagement Bragg claimed the capture of 4,000 prisoners, 31 guns, and 200 wagons. "Our loss is heavy; that of the enemy much greater."[36]

Not surprisingly, this telegram sparked enormous joy across the Confederacy when it became known. The authorities spread the word and praised Bragg. From Jackson, Mississippi, Joseph E. Johnston telegraphed,

"I congratulate you upon the success which has attended all your opera-tions. Press them vigorously." At Charleston, South Carolina, Beauregard informed a colleague that "Bragg has gained brilliant victory; driven enemy at all points." Lee told the secretary of war the "glorious victory obtained by General Bragg will, I think, produce a pause in the military operations of the Federal Army everywhere." Details of Bragg's telegram became known to soldiers of all ranks across the Confederacy.[37]

Members of the Butler family of Louisiana, related to Bragg by marriage, were thrilled by the news coming from Murfreesboro. Edward G. Butler, a captain in the 1st Louisiana Heavy Artillery at Vicksburg, told his mother that Bragg "completely whipped Rosecrans" and captured 14,000 prisoners and fifty guns. "I think our prospects now look more cheering than they have at any time since the commencement of the war. The wise heads here predict an armistice in less than thirty days and peace before the 1st of June." Butler was further delighted that the much-maligned general now could reap the credit for his skill. "I think he has suffered enough already for the faults of others and others have too often obtained the praise for *his* actions."[38]

Civilian response to the first news of the battle was ecstatic. Bragg's dispatch of December 31 "put us almost 'beside' ourselves with joy" exulted War Department clerk John B. Jones. It "caused even enemies to pause and shake hands in the street. I think we will get Nashville now," Jones pre-dicted. Catherine Ann Devereux Edmondston also rejoiced when she read the initial reports. They led her to praise Bragg for his "great judgment and heroism. There is no doubt but that we have gained a splendid victory."[39]

This may have been the peak of Bragg's public reputation, but of course it did not last long. Soon the newspapers conveyed the melancholy in-telligence that the Army of Tennessee evacuated Murfreesboro. For Ed-mondston, that news arrived on January 6. It filtered through the Confed-eracy at varied rates of speed until the entire South knew of it. The reaction was inevitable. Edmondston now criticized Bragg for want of capacity. He was "a good Division Commander, nothing more, & it is wrong to place him in a position for which he has no capacities." What was needed was a general who had the ability "to combine, to manoevre an Army."[40]

The retreat from Murfreesboro, following the extensive bloodletting at Stones River, led many people in the South to question Bragg's conduct of the campaign. That trend continued into the modern era. Grady Mc-Whiney argued that the position Bragg selected for his troops outside Mur-freesboro was not the best ground for 35,000 men to hold. Yet McWhiney admitted that Bragg had legitimate reasons for staying at Murfreesboro and had chosen as good a position as was available to him. But McWhiney believed he committed "a serious tactical error" in not fortifying his line.[41]

McWhiney also faulted Bragg for adopting a complicated attack plan and misusing Breckinridge's Division, his only reserve, on the afternoon of December 31. Instead of reinforcing Hardee, who was in charge of the most extended part of the wheeling movement, he sent Breckinridge's men against the Union center, leaving it up to Polk to determine how to use them. McWhiney also argued that even if Jefferson Davis had not insisted on detaching Stevenson's Division to Mississippi before the campaign started, Bragg would not have used that division in the right way and at the right time to insure Rebel victory at Stones River.[42]

McWhiney assessed Bragg's conduct of the attack on December 31 in a way that resonated among other historians. "Bragg's tactical plan lacked that subtlety and flexibility so necessary for success; it had within itself all the elements of failure." Even if successful, it would push the Federals into a more compact defensive position while forcing his own army to extend in a less concentrated posture. But McWhiney censured Bragg even more for ordering Breckinridge to attack on January 2.[43]

Thomas Connelly's treatment of Bragg at Stones River is thoroughly negative. He faulted Bragg for wanting to hold Murfreesboro, arguing that supplies had already been gleaned from the area and the position could be outflanked by a system of good roads extending from the Nashville area. Connelly spared no invective when criticizing Bragg's attack plan. It asked too much of his troops, and he did not provide for a reserve to aid Hardee when the latter needed it. In detailing the conduct of the right wheel attack on December 31, Connelly focused on the problems rather than the accomplishments, and he virtually ignored the effect of this attack on the Federal army. He also criticized Bragg for not having a contingency plan in case the assault of December 31 failed to force Rosecrans to retreat. Connelly wrote of Bragg's "inability to adjust to a new situation," and referred to his "apparently confused state" after the vicious fighting of December 31. Connelly also condemned Bragg for Breckinridge's attack on January 2 but agreed with his reasons for retreating from Murfreesboro.[44]

Subsequent historians followed the line of McWhiney and Connelly in assessing Bragg's handling of the campaign. James Lee McDonough, in his general history of the battle, echoed virtually all the major criticisms offered by the previous historians. "With the exception of the devastating opening flank attack on the morning of December 31," McDonough concluded, "Bragg fought the battle of Stones River badly."[45]

Peter Cozzens authored the standard history of Stones River for the past twenty years, and he also largely followed the lead established by Mc-Whiney and Connelly. On all major points of interpretation and analysis, Cozzens believes these previous historians were right. The recent biography of Bragg by Samuel J. Martin takes a more sympathetic view of the general by simply accepting Bragg's version of controversial events without question. Larry Daniel, author of the most recent study of the battle, criticizes Bragg's selection of a position for his army on December 28 and his decision to strike at the Round Forest with Breckinridge's men on December 31, although Daniel recognizes that Bragg had few other options.[46]

Only Steven Woodworth has supported Bragg's actions with analysis. He thought Bragg's strategic plan was sound and his selection of a line judicious. Woodworth points out that Bragg was not well served by his subordinates. Polk was responsible for throwing Breckinridge's men piecemeal at the Round Forest on December 31, not Bragg, and Cheatham was obviously drunk. Breckinridge failed to gather accurate intelligence of Federal moves against the Confederate right wing and derailed Bragg's plan to use his men to help Hardee. Woodworth accurately notes that Rosecrans's stubbornness was the key to Union victory. Bragg had nothing with which to counter it and was compelled to give up the field.[47]

Except for Woodworth and Martin, most historians have crafted a view of Bragg at Stones River that emphasizes mistakes, oversights, and setting impossible goals for his men. It is a picture of failure because Bragg retreated from the field and rendered Stones River yet another episode of Confederate defeat in the Civil War.

But it is possible to craft a more favorable view of Bragg, as Woodworth has done, which highlights legitimate aims and careful efforts to achieve those aims. It is a story of clear vision and partial success, with failure largely coming about through circumstances beyond his control. This interpretation is based on four avenues of approach: breaking away from the old assumption that Bragg was a miserable failure in everything he touched; looking at the effect of Bragg's actions on his Federal opponents; looking at the views of Bragg's own men; and comparing Stones River to other campaigns in the Civil War.

Taking up a position close to Nashville in November made strategic sense as a way to limit Federal control of Middle Tennessee. Lee also tried to keep Federal forces as far from Richmond as possible. He pushed the theater of operations from the capital some sixty miles north in the summer of 1862 and maintained it along the line of the Rappahannock and Rapidan Rivers (except to invade Maryland and Pennsylvania) for nearly two years. In essence, Bragg attempted something similar when he concentrated the Army of Tennessee at Murfreesboro.[48]

"I hope thus to force him to fight or fall back," Bragg wrote of his opponent. In general orders issued to his troops, Bragg envisioned the next confrontation as "the great struggle which must soon settle the question of supremacy in Middle Tennessee." Lee's victory over Burnside at Fredericksburg on December 13 was an inspiration. George W. Brent hoped the Federal defeat would teach Northerners "how idle & foolish their efforts [are] to subdue us." If Bragg could punish Rosecrans only thirty miles outside Nashville as Lee punished Burnside at Fredericksburg, Confederate forces in both theaters might exhaust Northern will to continue fighting.[49]

Bragg was aware that Murfreesboro offered a poor defensive position and that provisions were scarce in the vicinity. "Our position not very secure. Supplies short," Brent noted as early as November 28. "If enemy were to press us vigorously, disaster would befall us." But the strategic opportunities at Murfreesboro seemed bright enough to risk those problems, justifying a view of Bragg as a more daring commander than is generally acceded.[50]

The prevailing mood among Rosecrans's men played into Bragg's strategy. The Federals were full of confidence in "old Rosy." "You may expect to hear that the rebels are soundly whipped down here," Col. Hans Christian Heg of the 15th Wisconsin told his wife, "I do not think there will be another such affair as at Fredericksburg." Brigade commander Edward Needles Kirk assured his wife that "we are all anxious to get as far South as the Tennessee River before winter sets in."[51]

Self-confidence is an important factor but it can go too far. The confidence in Rosecrans created a negative view of Confederate fighting power; many Federals believed that Bragg's troops could not stand up to Rosecrans's men. The army's chief of staff, Lieut. Col. Julius P. Garesche, reflected and reinforced this confidence at army headquarters. "Rosecrans has never yet lost a battle," he informed his wife. "He has now a magnificent Army. It is not now, that he would allow himself to be beaten by an Army like that of Bragg." Garesche went further when he told his wife, "I don't think they will dare accept battle from him." The chief of staff worried that Bragg would lure Rosecrans deep into the heart of the Confederacy rather than fight at Murfreesboro. When headquarters learned by Christmas Day that Bragg had sent Stevenson's division to Mississippi, Garesche was even more convinced. "All of our principal officers have finished by sharing my opinion, that we will have no battle."[52]

Garesche can be forgiven his optimistic view for he had not served in the field since the war began, but all of Rosecrans's commanders seemed to agree with him. The strange idea that the Confederates would run rather than fight at Murfreesboro gave Bragg an opportunity to offer battle with an emotional edge, often important in military operations.[53]

Historians have criticized Bragg's selection of ground because it offered no defensive advantage to the Confederates; but the Federals were positioned on the same ground and had no defensive advantage either. In that case, Bragg's move to seize the tactical offensive was a brilliant way to turn this problem into an advantage.

The fighting on December 31 was a tactical success for the Confederates. They drove back two-thirds of Rosecrans's army, inflicted heavy casualties on the Federals, and came close to crushing the Fourteenth Corps. The scholarly literature often fails to appreciate that tactical achievement. Bragg accurately reflected it in his initial reports of the battle, and his soldiers uniformly viewed the results of December 31 as a victory. "It is enough to say that we gave the miserable abolition invaders one of the worst whipings they have ever had," exulted John Kennedy Street of the 9th Texas.[54]

The Federals admitted they had been outgeneraled and came dangerously close to disaster. Many Yankees came away from the fighting of December 31 with deep admiration for their enemy's ability. Regimental commander Benjamin Scribner referred to "the snap and vim" of Bragg's assault, while John Brandon Guthrie of the 1st Kentucky told his aunt that "it is wonderful to me the bravery with which his men fight. I believe that if we had half the Discipline in our Army that he has in his we could whip him anytime." Struggling with the rules of spelling, Willis Jones of the 84th Illinois assured his family, "when you here folks sa that the rebbles wont fite[,] tel them to cum an try them[,] I tel you tha fite like Tigers."[55]

Bragg's attempt to crush the Union center with Breckinridge's three brigades on the afternoon of December 31 made sense at the time; if the Union right was being steadily driven back and the center was holding firm around the area of the Round Forest and the Nashville Pike, then collapsing the center could have forced the entire Federal army to abandon the field. It is less easy to justify Bragg's decision to attack the Federal left on January 2. Such an assault made much more sense on December 31, as a support to Polk's and Hardee's attacks west of the river, than it did two days later. A more carefully prepared plan to outflank the Union line east of Stones River on the morning of January 3 might have had more chances of success.

Bragg's decision to retreat from Murfreesboro on the night of January 3 muddled the perception of his conduct at Stones River. Confederate cavalrymen who were involved in the supporting operations on Hardee's flank during the advance on December 31 bitterly denounced their general for retreating. But Bragg's infantry reacted to the fall back from Murfreesboro in different ways. Some of them joined the cavalrymen in condemning their commander. Charles George of the 5th Georgia argued that Bragg "was the only one the Yanks whipped[,] his men were all right and expected to be let at the yanks any moment but [he] insisted we had to *skedaddle*." An Arkansas captain moaned that Bragg "had the independence of the Confederacy and a glorious peace in his grasp, but . . . by bad management, he has opened his hands and let the prize fly."[56]

A misunderstanding contributed to frustration over the army's retreat. Due to heavy rains that raised the water level of Stones River, Rosecrans ordered his troops to evacuate the east side of the stream on the night of January 3 just when the Confederates began their withdrawal from the field. Reports filtered in that erroneously portrayed the Yankees as retreating to Nashville. The rumor that they found out about Bragg's retreat and then returned to the field floated freely through the Army of Tennessee, angering many soldiers.[57]

Other Confederates were puzzled by the decision to retreat, or they tempered their frustration over it with an understanding of why Bragg gave up the field. James Patton Anderson found it difficult to understand why the army pulled away after its success on December 31, but admitted that the troops were exhausted and suffering from exposure. "It may be strategic," wrote the chaplain of the 8th Texas Cavalry for a hometown newspaper. "It may be a needful change of base—time will decide the wisdom of our withdrawal from the battle-field after holding it three days."[58]

But there were many Confederates who fully supported Bragg's decision to retire. John Kennedy Street told his family everyone believed "Bragg knew what he was doing and were willing to do his bidding sadisfied that all would work out right in the end." These men cited the arrival of Union reinforcements, an advantage Bragg could not counter, as the primary reason for pulling away. "We had everything to lose and nothing to gain by risking another battle," wrote Arkansas surgeon W. L. Gammage. A member of Vaughan's Brigade stated in the *Memphis Daily Appeal* that "it would have been the policy only of a suicidal general to have done otherwise than to retire when General Bragg did." A soldier in Stanford's Mississippi Battery put it well. "Like a good General he wants to save his men. If the 'Army of Tennessee' were annihilated, we have no new troops to fill its place." C. Irvine Walker, a member of Arthur M. Manigault's staff, grew tired of newspaper criticism of his commanding general. "I tell you, if Genl. Bragg had not fought the battle as he did, surprising the enemy by the desperate charges of our men, he would have been compelled to leave the field, if not beaten, at any rate ten times worse off than we were."[59]

After Stones River, Bragg reassured everyone that he intended to hold what was left of Tennessee. "I have saved my Army, in good condition," he told Davis, "and shall be able to meet the Vandals again when they advance." Southerners often referred to Unionists as Vandals or invaders to impugn a different motive to the latter other than freeing the slaves. John Kennedy Street heard Bragg assure troops at Winchester that he "had no idea of abandoning Tenn but would defend the state against the invader to the last extremity." Bragg also told them "he did not feel disposed to sacrifice his men to no purpose."[60]

Dabney H. Maury, commander of Confederate forces at Mobile, was well satisfied with Bragg's "partial success in Tennessee." He viewed it within the context of more strident Confederate victories in Mississippi and Virginia that winter. All of those actions "have contributed to restore confidence" among Southerners, in Maury's estimation.[61]

Among the Federals, soldier morale soared after the battle of Stones River, but many general officers were stunned by the battle. Not long after the engagement, Thomas L. Crittenden accompanied Rosecrans on a ride through Crittenden's camps. Rosecrans responded to the cheers of his men by telling them, "All right, boys, all right; Bragg's a good dog, but Hold Fast's a better." Crittenden wrote after the war that this "well expressed my feeling as to the kind of victory we had won." In short, he thought that all the Federals had accomplished was survival, with a small gain of territory as a bonus.[62]

Higher-ranking officers had a wider perspective on the scale of damage the enemy inflicted at Stones River and more responsibility to bear for failure on the field. Although a limited strategic victory, Stones River "was fought according to the plan of General Bragg," as Crittenden sarcastically put it. "Indeed, our uniform experience was—at Perryville, at Stone's River, at Chickamauga—-that whenever we went to attack Bragg we were attacked by him, and so our plan had to be extemporized."[63]

Confederate assessment of the battle's outcome was mixed. Bragg himself proclaimed in a message to his troops that their accomplishments had been "unparalleled." He boasted of a "moral" victory over the Federals. "In retiring to a stronger position without molestation from a superior force, you have left him a barren field in which to bury his hosts of slain and to rally and recuperate his shattered ranks." Moreover, "we shall yet teach him a severe lesson for the rashness of penetrating a country so hostile to his cause."[64]

Most Confederate soldiers and their officers agreed that the Army of Tennessee had been successful on December 31, even if the retreat reduced the strategic benefits of their achievement. James Patton Anderson told his wife in one letter that the cost of the victory was not worth the results, but in the next letter argued that Rosecrans's command was so damaged it could not continue advancing for a long time to come. Many Confederate soldiers, perhaps prompted by Bragg's own message to his troops, concluded that Bragg had taught Rosecrans a lesson. A. T. Gay of the 31st Tennessee argued that another such "victory" by the Federals "will soon force them to recognize us as an independent nation." Hannibal Paine of the 26th Tennessee put it bluntly when he wrote, "All of the soil that Rosencrans gains now is going to cost him blood." The policy of wearing down the enemy through bitter fighting struck the right note with quite a few Rebels. In fact, Surgeon W. L. Gammage argued that it was "our true policy."[65]

Many Confederates hoped to exhaust Union willpower. Alfred Tyler Fielder prayed that the Yankees would "learn from this that they cannot conquer us and go home and let us enjoy our rights as they wish to enjoy theirs." C. Irvine Walker cited the rise of Copperhead sentiment, the increasing financial burden of prosecuting the war, and the imminent collapse of Northern currency as factors in his hope that Lincoln's war effort would soon fail. Dunbar Affleck of the 8th Texas Cavalry thought neither side would win the military struggle, for "the Yankeys cant whip us and we can never whip them, and I see no prospect of peace unless the Yankees themselves throw down their arms, and refuse to fight any longer."[66]

The Confederates could not know that morale among the Union troops was very high after Stones River, but the same was not true of Rosecrans and his generals. The Federal commander boasted of his intention "to push them to the wall" on January 6, but soon found many excuses for not resuming his winter offensive. By March, the Army of the Cumberland seemed committed to winter quarters at Murfreesboro indefinitely. The Confederates interpreted this long delay as a lack of willpower on Rosecrans's part to resume the offensive they had bluntly stopped at Murfreesboro.[67]

They may have been right. When Rosecrans requested the views of his subordinates on the next stage in the struggle for Middle Tennessee, division commander Thomas J. Wood replied that the army needed to have an overwhelming numerical advantage over Bragg. To engage in another battle when the opponents were of equal strength, as at Stones River, "is simply a prize fight," Wood contended, "yielding the victor little more than the ground he stands on, and by no means compensating for the expenditure of human life necessary to obtain the results." To approach the Army of Tennessee with insufficient force, Wood continued, was to "expose ourselves to defeat."[68]

Bragg deserves more credit for his handling of the Army of Tennessee than historians have normally given him. He had a coherent and viable strategy—to hold a forward position and punish the enemy as much as possible, striking for a psychological victory as much as a military one. He seized the tactical initiative, held it for the length of a bloody day of fighting during which his army drove the Federals back three miles, inflicted stunning losses, and shattered the complacent notion that the conquest of Middle Tennessee would be easy. So far, this description could easily be applied to Lee's operations in Virginia as well.

Historians have criticized Bragg for adopting an attack plan on December 31 that forced the Federals into a compact defensive position, but the same was true of Stonewall Jackson's attack at Chancellorsville on May 2, 1863. Historians praise Lee for the success of that attack, but in reality it merely blunted the Federal right flank before stalling in the darkness of the Wilderness. Moreover, Lee's army remained disunited after the attack stalled, and only fierce attacks by the Confederates on the morning of May 3 pushed the Federals back and reunited the Army of Northern Virginia, representing the true turning point of Lee's tactical success at Chancellorsville.[69]

Bragg's attack on December 31 was more successful than Jackson's. Hardee and Polk conducted that difficult advance while maintaining connection with other parts of the army. Of course, Bragg's course of action after December 31 left him open to legitimate criticism—the attack of January 2 was an awful failure, but the decision to disengage and retire was at least partly justified. Joseph Hooker had not the stamina of Rosecrans and retreated from Chancellorsville even though much of his available manpower had not been engaged. Lee outlasted his opponent and gained not only the battlefield victory but almost legendary status as a tenacious fighter.

Bragg was severely criticized for retreating from Murfreesboro, but Joseph E. Johnston retreated nearly 100 miles in more than two months while commanding the Army of Tennessee during the Atlanta campaign. Privates and officers alike trusted and loved Johnston. They rarely criticized him for this abdication of territory without fighting a major battle. Moreover, Lee and Johnston tended to keep themselves above personal squabbles and conducted themselves with a dignity that inspired respect. They retained the affection and goodwill of their subordinates.[70]

An assessment of Bragg's generalship should not be clouded or influenced by the personality troubles he generated off the field. His conduct of the Stones River campaign came close to the strategy adopted by Lee in Virginia, an apparently winning strategy at least for a time in keeping the Army of the Potomac far from Richmond and straining Northern will to continue the war. Bragg at least attempted and partially succeeded in doing the same in Tennessee.

8

Turning Point

In many ways, the campaign that led up to the battle of Stones River was Bragg's golden hour as a commander. Up to January 1, 1863, he embarked on a clear strategic and tactical plan to deal with Rosecrans, executed that plan with skill, and won a tactical success on December 31. When that success failed to result in a Federal retreat, few options seemed open to the Confederates. Pelted by bad weather, lacking fresh troops, and throwing Breckinridge's Division into a futile assault on January 2, Bragg was faced with subordinates who had no faith in his decision to remain on the battlefield. The Federals could outlast Bragg in this standoff, and Bragg came to realize it. The retreat depressed public morale as much as Bragg's initial reports of success had inflated it. Now, as far as many Southerners saw it, all that resulted was further loss of territory combined with heavy loss of life. How Bragg handled these problems in the wake of Stones River proved to be the turning point in his Civil War career.

Unlike the period following the Kentucky campaign, Bragg took more active measures to explain his actions and shore up his reputation with the public, starting with high-level politicians. Senator James Phelan of Mississippi and Representative James Pugh of Alabama were consistent supporters of Bragg, but others wavered. On January 10, a week after retreating from Murfreesboro, Bragg wrote Senator Clement Claiborne Clay of Alabama to explain why he fell back from the battlefield. He regretted the newspaper attacks on him because they impaired his "usefulness" as commander of the army. "When all else was lost, I had hoped my fair name would be left me, but I fear even in that I am really to bow to the decree of Fate and await the sober judgment of history."[1]

Bragg also tried to shore up his support within the Confederate army and the civilian leaders of the Rebel war effort. He started with his immediate superior, Joseph E. Johnston, who had been appointed commander of Confederate forces in the West the previous November. Within days of the

JOSEPH E. JOHNSTON. As his superior, Johnston admired Bragg's handling of the Stones River campaign and played a large role in helping the embattled general retain his command of the Army of Tennessee. Later, as Davis's military adviser, Bragg played an important role in Johnston's removal from command of that army in the middle of the Atlanta campaign. By handling that incident badly, Bragg unnecessarily made Johnston his enemy as he tried to faithfully support Davis's views. (Library of Congress, LC-DIG-cwpb-06280)

retreat from Murfreesboro, Bragg addressed a nagging logistical problem that involved divided authority. Chattanooga was now his primary supply depot but it lay within the neighboring Department of East Tennessee. That led to struggles between staff officers to use the town's facilities.[2]

The issue gave Bragg an opportunity to write a long letter to Johnston on January 11. He took some credit for Johnston's appointment to the western command, having recommended it to Davis the previous fall. Bragg admitted feeling vulnerable after Murfreesboro. Upon hearing a rumor that Kirby Smith was on his way to Richmond, perhaps to replace him, Bragg was ready to accept dismissal. "I shall be content. Whenever and wherever I am in the way of a better man, let me be put aside. I only ask to serve the cause where I can do it most good, even should that be in the ranks."[3]

Bragg offered one of the more compelling explanations for his defeat. He blamed it partially on Davis's order to send Stevenson's Division to Mississippi before the battle. "Five thousand fresh troops, as a reserve on the first day's battle, would have finished the glorious work," he assured Johnston. "I told the President Grant's campaign would be broken up by our cavalry expeditions in his rear before Stevenson's command could meet him in front, but he was inexorable, and induced me to the defensive, or, as he expressed it, 'Fight if you can, and fall back beyond the Tennessee.'"

Bragg had done just that at Murfreesboro. To have remained longer on the battlefield while Rosecrans received reinforcements would have been "suicidal." Bragg currently estimated his losses at Murfreesboro at 12,000 men, and now had only 20,000 infantry and 1,500 artillerymen to defend the rest of Middle Tennessee. But Bragg was ready to "fight him again at every hazard if he advances and harass him daily if he does not." He ended his dispatch by assuring Johnston of his gratitude "for the support, personal and official, you have given me." Johnston quickly issued an order giving him control of Chattanooga.[4]

Bragg had the support of Davis, and he made certain he had the support of Johnston. But it was clear he did not have the support of many newspaper editors. Pieces critical of his action at Murfreesboro appeared in the *Richmond Examiner*, which was an anti-Davis paper, and in the *Augusta Chronicle*. Ironically, they also appeared in the *Mobile Advertiser and Register* even though it was edited by his friend John Forsyth. When the *Chattanooga Rebel* published an article claiming that Bragg retreated from Murfreesboro against the advice of his generals, however, Bragg had enough of these newspaper attacks. A fundamental fact of history was at stake in this issue.[5]

"Finding myself assailed in private and public by the press," Bragg wrote in a round-robin letter to Polk, Hardee, Breckinridge, Cleburne, and Cheatham, he noted the erroneous assertion that his subordinates did not want to retreat from the battlefield. Bragg reminded the generals that he had resisted their advice to retreat until word of Federal reinforcements compelled it. He felt under pressure "to save my fair name" even if he could do nothing about "the deluge of abuse, which will destroy my usefulness and demoralize this army." In this letter, dated January 11, Bragg also noted that rumors indicated a few staff officers in the army were spreading the idea that the generals did not favor a retreat. He now called on his subordinates to openly state whether they had advised a withdrawal or not. "If I have misunderstood your advice, and acted against your opinions, let me know it, in justice to yourself. If, on the contrary, I am the victim of unjust accusations, say so, and unite with me in staying the malignant slanders being propagated by men who have felt the sting of discipline."[6]

So far Bragg was on firm ground in his endeavor to secure the truth. But then he overstepped himself. Hardee had earlier indicated in a note written to Bragg's assistant inspector general that there was a general want of confidence in their army leader. In the first draft of his January 11 letter, Bragg requested his subordinates to state whether that was true. He showed the draft to staff members who argued that it was unwise to send it. Bragg therefore changed the wording. He told his generals the same thing he told Johnston, that Kirby Smith was currently in Richmond and probably trying to replace him as commander of the army. "I shall retire without regret if I find I have lost the good opinion of my generals, upon whom I have ever relied as upon a foundation of rock," Bragg wrote. Strictly reading the language of this sentence, it is clear that he simply expressed his personal view, but the sentence could also be interpreted as implying that he was asking his subordinates' opinion about whether he should remain in command. It was only a slight alteration of the original draft. After sleeping on the matter, Bragg decided to send the letter on January 12.[7]

Hardee, whose subordinates were not involved in the effort to coax Bragg from Murfreesboro, responded quickly to this letter. He consulted staff officers and confidently reported that none of them had spread any rumors. But Hardee assumed the letter called for his opinion about Bragg's suitability for the command, and he expressed it in frank but professional terms. All of his subordinates agreed "that a change in the command of this army is necessary." Everyone had "the highest respect for the purity of your motives," he told Bragg, "your energy, and your personal character; but they are convinced, as you must feel, that the peril of the country is superior to all personal considerations." Cleburne consulted his brigade leaders and joined them in praising Bragg's "great capacity for organization." But they also agreed "that you do not possess the confidence of the army in other respects in that degree necessary to secure success." Breckinridge wrote in the same way.[8]

Bragg initially reacted to these responses with ambivalence. He expressed his feelings to Benjamin Stoddert Ewell, Johnston's staff officer and an old friend. Ewell had written a note expressing concern that Bragg seemed willing to give up the Army of Tennessee command, having heard somehow of the January 11 letter. Bragg assured him he would take "no hasty and unadvised action." He went on to complain of trouble from a few officers who "did not meet my expectations, and to their short comings I am indebted for the failures of Wednesday evening and Friday evening on the enemy's left flank." This was a pointed reference to Breckinridge. "Finding themselves responsible for serious failures they and their friends are moving all power to saddle me with the responsibility, before official reports can put the matter right." Bragg felt that he had helped these men in their careers and now they were turning on him. "But such is human gratitude," he told Ewell.[9]

Yet the frank admissions of Hardee and Cleburne had something of an effect on Bragg. He seriously contemplated asking to be relieved if more fallout from the round-robin letter seemed to justify it. But, he told Ewell, there was no one competent to replace him. Hardee was "a good drill master but no more, except that he is gallant. He has no ability to organize and supply an army and no confidence in himself when approached by the enemy."[10]

Meanwhile, word of the January 11 letter spread rapidly through the army. Stouten Hubert Dent, an officer of Robertson's Florida Battery in Polk's Corps, told his wife that there was "a good deal of dissatisfaction here with Genl Bragg among some of the prominent officers of the Army while the remainder are satisfied." He also accurately reported that the generals had advised retreat twenty-four hours before Bragg finally left Murfreesboro. "I am afraid some trouble will grow up yet out of this thing." Dent's battery commander, Felix Robertson, was a staunch supporter of Bragg.[11]

Hardee created more mischief by sending copies of Bragg's letter to William Preston Johnston. The son of the first commander of the army, Johnston now was serving as aide-de-camp to Jefferson Davis. William Preston, the brother-in-law of Albert Sidney Johnston and nephew of William Preston Johnston, had by now become a bitter foe of Bragg largely because of the Kentucky campaign. Preston assumed Bragg meant to identify his opponents among the officer corps and "crush out the opposition." It was almost natural to see the round-robin letter in that way, except that it was not true. Bragg had not intended to solicit his subordinates' opinion on his fitness to command in that letter, but it was widely interpreted that way.[12]

Still holding a brigade command in the Army of Tennessee, William Preston severely criticized Bragg in a letter to his nephew. He dismissed his selection of a line on December 28 as foolish. Rather than attack with his entire army, the general had moved against the Union right first and then much later against the enemy left. "Bragg cannot hit with but one hand at a time, or follow up a blow," he told Will. He concluded that "the men were clumsily handled" at Murfreesboro. "We lost a fourth of the army & achieved nothing but a retreat." Preston went on to criticize Bragg's tenure as army commander, faulting him for not fighting Buell at Munfordville, for fighting with only a portion of his army at Perryville, then planting the Army of Tennessee "in a country as open as a chessboard, in thirty miles" of the Union stronghold at Nashville. "I cannot think or imagine what his motive was, unless the social influences of the people, his random promises

WILLIAM PRESTON. Brother-in-law of Albert Sidney Johnston, Preston became a virulent enemy of Bragg because of the Kentucky campaign and the retreat from Murfreesboro. He personally and professionally attacked the general in letters to his nephew, William Preston Johnston, who served on Davis's staff. (Robert E. Steiner Confederate Officers Photographs, Q3624, ADAH)

of resistance, and his irritated state of feeling about the criticisms on the Kentucky campaign warped his mind."[13]

Going from analysis to personal attacks, Preston told Will a fable to express his view of Bragg. He told the story of a Lion who had bad breath and, in order to maintain his good reputation, asked his chief councilors their opinion. The Ox stated bluntly that it smelled awful, so the Lion beheaded him. The Bear also said "funky smell," and he was killed. The Ape tried to calm the Lion by saying his breath smelled sweet, but the Lion forever distrusted him as a yes-man. Then the Fox slyly pleaded that he had a cold and could not smell anything, and the Lion made him his prime minister.[14]

The obvious intent of this fable was to show that Bragg had no personal qualities for judging men and acted as a potentate instead of a colleague. Preston felt his own career could not flower under him. "I am not in favour at this time with Boomerang Bragg," he told Will. "He has neither the love of the soldiers, nor the confidence of the officers. He is ... inconstant, impetuous ... and narrow minded." In Preston's view, the men were numbed by Bragg. "No cheer salutes him as he passes the lines, no terror of his discipline or executions is felt by the brave soldiers he leads. After all the carnage, he never has had a decent plan or a decided victory, but executions precede and retreats follow his battles. We obey but do not tremble, and into action without hope of honor or renown and retreat with sullen indifference and discontent."[15]

There is no doubt that Preston sincerely believed all he said to Will in this extraordinary letter, but his views were not typical of officers in the Army of Tennessee. As we have seen in the previous chapter, not all members of the rank and file agreed with Preston's sentiments. There were limits to dissatisfaction in the Army of Tennessee after Stones River, and there were limits to its spread outside the army as well. The problem was growing, but it was not yet out of control.

In the wake of the first round of responses to his January 11 letter, Bragg felt compelled to shore up his relations with Davis. This also was a sign that the embattled general was beginning to fight, once again, to save his job. On January 17, he wrote a long dispatch explaining his reasons for retreating. "For this I am again assailed, as no man ever was, probably, except yourself. But I have saved my Army, in good condition, and shall be able to meet the Vandals again when they advance." Bragg also sent David Urquhart to Richmond for personal conferences with the Confederate president.[16]

Bragg decided by January 17 not to resign as commander of the army but to let Davis choose if he should stay or go. "To disembarrass you, however, steadfast as you have been as my friend and supporter I must repeat that whenever policy may dictate any change for the public good, I ask, as a favor to myself and justice to the cause we both represent and ardently support, that you will disregard my personal feelings and interests for the time being and dispose all for the general good."[17]

Did Bragg feel confident Davis would keep him in command and write the January 17 letter as a way to obtain public reassurance of his worth as commander of the army? Or was he seriously willing to leave the army if Davis wished it? The answer probably lies closer to the former than the latter because in the same letter Bragg took the offensive against his detractors. He referred to "a temporary feeling of a great part of my Army— mostly new men under new officers—that is all subsiding and confidence and tone are again assuming sway. It had its origin in false reports and rumors circulated by newsmongers that the Enemy was falling back when we withdrew from Murfreesboro." Bragg targeted the *Chattanooga Rebel* as the chief problem and further argued the paper tended to offer "the enemy more information and says more to discourage our troops than all the spies of the enemy could accomplish."[18]

As the Richmond authorities absorbed the contents of his January 17 dispatch and listened to Urquhart, Bragg continued to worry in Tennessee. He could be more open in his feelings with friends than with the commander in chief. "With so little support," he told brigade commander

John K. Jackson on January 24, "my aching head rebels against the heart, and calls for relief, still I shall die in the traces."[19]

Before Davis could reply, Leonidas Polk weighed in on the issue. He had been on leave of absence and did not see Bragg's round-robin letter until late January. On the thirtieth of the month, Polk wanted to clarify the purpose of the letter. It seemed to contain two points: Did the generals counsel a retreat from Murfreesboro, and did they think Bragg was fit to command the army? Bragg responded by telling him the letter "contained but one point of inquiry," regarding the generals' support for retreat. The second point "was only an expression of the feeling with which I should receive your replies should they prove I had been misled in my construction of your opinion and advice." Polk quickly admitted he supported the retreat. It is interesting that Bragg's chief enemy in the army should be so scrupulous in charting the parameters of his response as to avoid an explosive result while Hardee, who now emerged as an open critic of Bragg, should assume he could speak his mind frankly on an issue that was sure to threaten his superior.[20]

Polk may have been reticent with Bragg, but he opened himself to Davis without reserve. "If he were Napoleon or the great Frederick he could serve our cause at some other points better than here," he wrote of Bragg. "My opinion is he had better be transferred." Davis had earlier told Polk "I can make good use of him here in Richmond." Polk believed that Bragg's administrative ability, "which has not been equaled among us," would serve the entire Confederacy well in Richmond. He urged the appointment of Joseph E. Johnston as Bragg's replacement.[21]

Davis did turn to Johnston but wanted him to serve the role of observer, not commander. Concerned about the unusual way Bragg was behaving with his generals, the Rebel president instructed Johnston on January 22 to visit the Army of Tennessee and send a report. Davis assured him his confidence in Bragg was "unshaken," but if the corps and division commanders were in revolt, it could be disastrous for the army. Johnston's arrival at Tullahoma on January 26 inspired hope among the Bragg dissidents. William Preston was among the first to report his arrival. "I met Bragg & was studiously cold[;] he was unusually civil. Johnston very kind." Preston told Will that Cheatham was "decidedly and emphatically with us." Those who were dissatisfied with Bragg hoped that Johnston would take personal command of the Army of Tennessee.[22]

But those hopes were quickly dashed. Johnston weighed in on the controversy in clear terms. His headquarters issued a general order praising

Bragg and the Army of Tennessee for "an exploit unparalleled in modern battles" at Murfreesboro. He also wrote a long telegram to Davis on February 3 supporting Bragg. Johnston talked with many officers and the Confederate governor of Tennessee, Isham G. Harris, while visiting Tullahoma. Bragg assured him the lack of trust in his generalship was caused by a disgruntled faction in the army and was "passing away." Polk and Hardee thought the feeling came from the sorry results of the Kentucky campaign, while Harris thought the feeling did not justify the removal of Bragg, whose value to the army outweighed the criticism. Cheatham, at least, pointedly told Johnston he would never fight under Bragg again, but Bragg felt he could "bring him to his senses." Moreover, Johnston managed to inspect about one quarter of the troops before February 3, and the rank and file appeared to be unaffected by the poisonous mood developing among the generals.[23]

Johnston concluded his report by strongly recommending Bragg retain his command, and he knew Davis shared that view. "I am very glad to find that your confidence in General Bragg is unshaken," he told Davis. "My own is confirmed by his recent operations, which in my opinion evince great vigor & skill. It would be very unfortunate to remove him at this juncture, when he has just earned if not won the gratitude of the country." In case Davis decided to fire Bragg anyway, Johnston cautioned him not to name himself or anyone associated with the controversy as the replacement.[24]

Having an opportunity to inspect most units in the Army of Tennessee, Johnston followed up his report with a strongly worded dispatch on February 12. The Army of Tennessee was in superb shape and reflected great credit on Bragg's skill as an administrator. "It is well clothed, healthy & in fine spirits." Johnston reiterated his view that Bragg had conducted the Stones River campaign with skill and daring. "I can find no record of more effective fighting in modern battles than that of this army in December, evincing skill in the commander & courage in the troops which fully entitled them to the thanks of the government." Bragg had no stronger supporter within the Confederate army than Johnston, who told Davis "the interest of the service *requires* that General Bragg should not be removed."[25]

Johnston also had the ear of a strong-minded congressman in Louis T. Wigfall of Texas. Believing the Army of Tennessee put out of commission 20,000 Federals at Stones River with only 30,000 men, Johnston thought it inflicted more damage "than any army of modern times." The man responsible for such a success had "made the best use of his troops of all arms" than almost any other commander in the South.[26]

Davis was relieved to read Johnston's reports. The president of the Confederacy had seen no evidence of dissatisfaction when he visited the Army of Tennessee in December and was sorry it had now cropped up. Moreover, if a change in commanders should become necessary, there were few choices to replace Bragg. Many of those who outranked the general had already run afoul of Davis, including Johnston. Moreover, Johnston automatically seemed out of the running because of his inspection visit to Tullahoma. In addition to his high opinion of Bragg, the Southern president found it easier to maintain the status quo than to contemplate a change in commanders.[27]

William Preston Johnston had an idea about Bragg's replacement. In a letter to his uncle, Will suggested that Davis take charge of the Army of Tennessee with Bragg as his second in command. "I feel satisfied that if he would, in sixty days we would be on the Ohio River," Will exulted. In fact, Will had already made this suggestion to Davis himself. To his wife, he reported the "imbroglio" in the Army of Tennessee and noted that Preston and Breckinridge were reportedly the ring leaders of the affair. "I think Bragg will have to go under," Will told Rosa. "He is not equal to his position, but the Prest is always loth to yield a General to the popular clamor or sacrifice one for failure. He always hopes for better luck next time. But Bragg is incompetent."[28]

Wigfall had another idea about Bragg's replacement. The Texas senator told Johnston he had long been pressing the secretary of war to remove him and send James Longstreet from Lee's Army of Northern Virginia to take his place. Wigfall thought Bragg should be assigned to Lee's army "where there had grown up no antagonism to him & where he would have a fair start & where he might be very useful as second in command." According to Wigfall, Davis had nearly agreed to this proposition but now, in February, 1863, backed away from it. Wigfall also urged Johnston not to take over the Army of Tennessee with Bragg as second in command or as chief of staff. The anger toward Bragg would then transfer to Johnston and destroy his usefulness. "Let Bragg go," he vainly urged Johnston. "He should not longer remain in command of that Army because he has not its confidence. If you do not want the command Longstreet should have it & Bragg come here to discharge Bureau duty as Lee did or take Longstreet's place in Lee's Army."[29]

None of the advice flowing from one officer to another caused Davis to change his mind; Bragg survived a major threat to his career. Not only Davis's support but Johnston's praise secured his place as commander.

Bragg gloated at his success in a letter to William Whann Mackall, a close friend of Johnston who also had been Bragg's West Point classmate and who now held a district command. Davis was influenced by "accounts of dissatisfaction as well as getting private letters from some vile scamps who writhe under the lash of my rigid discipline," and he had sent Johnston to visit the army. After two weeks spent at Tullahoma, Johnston was well pleased with everything he saw. "I find complaining against you," Johnston said, in Bragg's words, "but generally totally ungrounded. And had your generals given you proper support these complaints would have ceased at once. That they did not do this is no fault of yours, and they now regret it." When Bragg asked Johnston for advice, the senior general was happy to consult with him but refused to give Bragg any orders.[30]

Johnston admired the way Bragg handled his command in part because it offered such a contrast with his own command style. His record paled in comparison with Bragg's at Stones River. Acting mostly on the defensive, retreating some sixty miles to the gates of Richmond without a general battle during the Peninsula campaign, Johnston launched an uncoordinated attack at Seven Pines in late May 1862 that gained minimal ground and no important result. In contrast, Bragg's tactics at Murfreesboro and the toll it took on Rosecrans's army greatly impressed Johnston.[31]

The embattled general could also count on support from the small circle of subordinates who voiced their loyalty. John K. Jackson, who commanded the post of Chattanooga since Johnston had included the city within Bragg's Department of Tennessee, encouraged his commander with strong words. "You have risen in your stirrups and resolved to continue to be *our* General," he told Bragg on January 17. Jackson knew nothing of the "secret combination against you," but he suspected for quite a while that something was developing "which was intended to sweep you away. You may with confidence rely upon all the support that I can bring to your aid." Preston Smith believed the Army of Tennessee needed Bragg to function as an effective field force. "I sincerely hope for the discomfiture of the disorganizing schemes now at work for your disadvantage," he wrote him.[32]

Bragg began to relish the fight with his generals for it released his naturally combative spirit. In writing to Mackall, he blamed the trouble on officers who disliked his discipline and were jealous of his success at administering the army. By mid-February the Army of Tennessee was as strong and ready for battle as before Stones River. "My prowess for accomplishing this has been most distasteful to many of my senior generals, and they wince under the blows. Breckinridge, Polk & Hardee especially. The former failed most signally at Murfreesboro, and is very anxious to saddle me with the responsibility, but will be beautifully shown up."[33]

As commander of the army, Bragg was in a position to spin the story of Stones River through his official report. Writing the document in late February, he also penned a letter to Davis assuring him the report "tells the whole truth. Assailed, myself, for the blunders of others, and by them and their friends, my mind is made up to bear no sins in the future but my own."[34]

Bragg criticized McCown for starting the attack on December 31 later than planned, reducing the time available to reap the full benefits of his assault. He indirectly criticized Breckinridge for being fooled into believing the Federals were threatening the Confederate right wing on December 31, delaying the dispatch of reserves to the left. Bragg also noted that Breckinridge mishandled the attack of January 2, placing his second line too close to the first. The commander also implied that Breckinridge lost control of his men in the retreat from that assault. He credited James Patton Anderson with saving the position and stopping the Union counterattack. Bragg carefully ignored Breckinridge from his list of commendations, which included Polk and Hardee.[35]

The rank and file of his army received unusual praise in the report. Bragg recognized that the discipline of the regular army was impossible with volunteers, admitting one had to "trust to the individuality and self-reliance of the private soldier" who "justly judged that the cause was his own." The citizen went into the army "with a determination to conquer or die; to be free or not to be at all. No encomium is too high, no honor too great for such a soldiery." Bragg argued that the first monument erected after the war should honor the "unknown dead."[36]

These words were not mere hyperbole; Bragg always retained a higher regard for the common soldier than for most of his subordinate officers. But he also expressed admiration for the enemy, noting that Rosecrans skillfully maneuvered his troops on December 31 to stall the attacks and save his supply line.[37]

The official report would help Bragg's cause only if it were circulated generally and the public believed what he wrote. Meanwhile, the shadowy world of newspaper correspondents and their often venomous attitude toward the general continued to have its effects as well. One of the vilest critics of Bragg among newspaperman was Samuel Chester Reid, who developed a dislike of him dating to the onset of the Kentucky campaign. Reid requested permission to accompany the army on August 22, 1862.

Three days later, one of Bragg's staff members told Reid he was banned from the army. Reid became so angry he began to write "an expose of Braggs persecution & tryranny." When finished, he sent it to the *Charleston Mercury* for publication. Reid saw his position as an opportunity to seek revenge for personal insults.[38]

Reid continued his vendetta after Stones River. He had been in Murfreesboro during the battle and accompanied the army when it retreated, penning an account of the events. By January 21, Theodore O'Hara, who served on Breckinridge's staff, informed Reid that Bragg intended to arrest him so Reid left for Chattanooga later that night.[39]

O'Hara emerged as a major figure in the anti-Bragg coalition after Stones River. Born in Kentucky and a college student friend of Breckinridge, O'Hara had served in Mexico, engaged in filibuster activities in Cuba (where he wrote a famous poem titled "The Bivouac of the Dead"), and worked as a newspaperman before the Civil War. As colonel of the 12th Alabama, he developed a long-standing grudge with Bragg dating from the Pensacola days and was currently serving as Breckinridge's assistant adjutant general. Bragg was fully aware of O'Hara's feelings toward him. He told Mackall the man was "a drunken loafer from Mobile, who was discharged by me when I first assumed command at Pensacola in March '61, as a disgrace to the service." O'Hara had access to nearly all records in the Army of Tennessee. Josiah C. Nott also knew O'Hara and told Bragg he was "perhaps your most untiring enemy—he is a coarse, drunken, blackguard, & what St Paul calls a 'petulant fellow.'"[40]

Another figure in this imbroglio was an unidentified newspaper correspondent who signed himself Ora. Bragg was well aware of this man but never identified him by name. He had ordered Ora away from his headquarters at Corinth in April 1862 "as a nuisance, and my Staff officers and the sentinel at the gate directed to keep him out." Ora later attached himself to Beauregard's staff until Bragg informed Beauregard of the man's character, whereupon he was ordered away from the army. Ora turned up again right after the battle of Stones River and tried to attach himself to Joseph E. Johnston when the general visited Bragg. Johnston however would have none of him, so Ora attached himself to Breckinridge's headquarters, where O'Hara most likely supplied him with documents from the army's archives to feed his own hatred of Bragg.[41]

Ironically, Ora's chief outlet was the *Mobile Advertiser and Register*, edited by Bragg's friend John Forsyth. Repeatedly, articles denigrating Bragg appeared in that paper over Ora's name. Bragg was understandably frustrated.

He informed Forsyth four times of this embarrassing situation, and the editor apologized, "but I see no amendment," Bragg ruefully admitted. "Being considered as my special friend, his paper has done me more injustice and more real harm than all others in the country."[42]

Forsyth truly was Bragg's friend, but he also seems to have been a sloppy editor. According to Nott, Forsyth felt bad about Ora's comments and tried to restrain him. He gave orders for none of Ora's work to be published without his approval "but in the hurry of a daily paper some letters, greatly to his mortification, did get into print, unpurged." Forsyth then told Ora to leave the Army of Tennessee and go to Charleston as the only way to deal with the problem. "Forsyth is much mortified at what has happened," Nott assured Bragg, and "I am sure has none but kind feeling towards you."[43]

Nott advised Bragg to forebear these newspaper attacks as best he could. "Never . . . allude to these fellows, they will always beat you in controversy & your reputation is not worth having if you cannot live down such opposition." Bragg fully understood this advice. He tried to regard newspapers "with silent contempt."[44]

Despite the many threats to his career, Bragg won the first round of the post–Stones River controversy. But by early March, due to rising newspaper clamor and the opinions of many people in the Confederacy, Davis weakened in his resolve. Johnston felt the first wave of this renewed threat. He repeated his opinion in early March that it would be unwise to replace Bragg. Johnston was still impressed by the losses he had inflicted on Rosecrans. "In the great European battles of modern times there was no destruction equal to it, in proportion to the destroying force." If, however, the administration wanted to relieve him, Johnston thought Longstreet was the best replacement.[45]

Yet, Davis ordered Johnston on March 9 to Tullahoma in order to take charge of the Army of Tennessee. Bragg would go to Richmond "for conference." Whether this was meant to be a permanent replacement is unclear, but it certainly seemed to portend a change in command. Johnston was on his way to Mississippi, an important part of his large western command, when he received this order by telegram at Mobile on March 16. There is no explanation for the delay in its receipt except that perhaps Davis wrote the order and then held it while rethinking the wisdom of the move. Word of this development reached Bragg's headquarters on March 18 only a few hours before Johnston himself arrived at Tullahoma; Benjamin S. Ewell arrived the next day.[46]

Whatever plans Davis had in mind for Bragg were disrupted by an unexpected turn of events. Elise had been with her husband ever since a few days before the battle of Stones River, waiting out the engagement in Murfreesboro and retiring from the town when the army retreated. By mid-March she became seriously ill with typhoid fever. Bragg took her to a private house in Winchester on March 16 and was not at Tullahoma when Johnston and Ewell arrived. Johnston immediately telegraphed the news and told Seddon he could not order Bragg to Richmond. As Elise later recalled of that time, "my life was despaired of." Johnston assumed command of the army, but it lasted only a few days before he too became seriously ill. This was a good argument for keeping Bragg in Middle Tennessee, and all thought of replacing him evaporated. When Johnston recovered, he resumed his trip to Mississippi, and Bragg continued to shuttle between Winchester and Tullahoma, taking care of his wife and the army at the same time. Elise slowly recovered.[47]

Ironically, the man most often identified as Bragg's successor was his strongest supporter in the Confederate army. Even Johnston's wife Lydia spoke out in favor of Bragg. She met Varina Howell Davis, the wife of the Confederate president, in Montgomery sometime in March 1863 and asked Varina "if I ever heard of a man so ill treated as Bragg." Mrs. Davis played the situation coolly, responding "is there any thing the matter with him, you generals wives find out everything." Lydia was taken aback by this reaction, "blushed, and said no more."[48]

Bragg appreciated Johnston's support, but he also felt oppressed by the fact that Davis sent him to Tullahoma twice since the battle of Stones River. Dr. Charles Todd Quintard, the widely known chaplain of the 1st Tennessee, recalled Bragg's remark to him when Johnston finally left the Army of Tennessee for Mississippi. "Doctor, he was kept here too long to watch me!"[49]

The illness that struck Elise and Johnston saved Bragg from the latest attempt to deprive him of command, but as mentioned earlier, it is unclear exactly what Davis had in mind for the embattled general. Merely calling him to Richmond for a conference did not necessarily mean a permanent change. Bragg had traveled to Richmond for a conference after the Kentucky campaign, yet retained his position. Davis specifically placed Johnston in command of the West to supervise matters in Bragg's department and that of John C. Pemberton in Mississippi, with authority to personally take charge of either force if he felt the need to do so. It is quite possible that Davis wanted to gauge Bragg's temper face to face but did not have the opportunity to travel to Tullahoma (or felt it would send the wrong signal to go there). Johnston could have resumed his previous position upon Bragg's return to the Army of Tennessee.

With Johnston gone, Elise improving, and Rosecrans not yet on the move, Bragg turned his attention to dealing with subordinates whose conduct was problematic. Polk had played a quiet role thus far in the Stones River controversy, but Bragg always harbored resentment against him. When Polk's report of the battle of Pittsburg Landing was published in March 1863, Bragg sarcastically referred to it as "the 'Romance of Shiloh.'" Bragg had no opportunity to review or correct that report because he was not Polk's superior at the battle, but he tried to privately correct errors in it. Writing to the president of the Mobile and Ohio Railroad, the general did his best to disabuse Milton Brown of the notion that Polk had handled his troops well on the second day of that battle.[50]

But, as commander of the Army of the Mississippi, Bragg was well placed to deal with Polk's report of the Kentucky campaign. He was shocked to learn, for the first time, that Polk called a council of war at Bardstown on October 3 and at Perryville on October 8 that led to Polk's disobedience of direct orders from Bragg. Hardee's report was highly critical of Bragg's handling of several aspects of the campaign as well.[51]

Bragg once again sought information from his subordinates concerning Polk's conference on October 3. Addressing a circular letter to at least half a dozen officers on April 13, he told them that Polk admitted disobeying orders. "I beg, if consistent with your sense of duty, you will inform me to what extent you sustained the general in his acknowledged disobedience." The response was entirely negative. Hardee endorsed his copy of the circular letter and sent it to Polk, fearing that Bragg had not informed his colleague what he was doing. Hardee made it clear to Polk that he had no intention of answering the letter. "If you choose to rip up the Kentucky campaign you can tear Bragg into tatters," Hardee wrote with a good deal of emotion. He explained his views in more detail to George W. Brent three days later. "Gen Hardee said that he did not mean to answer the circular," according to Brent. "Such matters he deemed injurious to the service, & as he supposed the circular would cause a Court of Inquiry, he would withhold any expression of what he said & advised at that time."[52]

The only officer to respond to the circular was Simon Buckner. He refused to answer Bragg's inquiry but advised him to forgive and forget. He was certain the generals were sincere in their efforts for success and simply viewed the Kentucky campaign differently than did Bragg. "I believe that a frank personal explanation with them will be the means of removing any cause of dissatisfaction which may naturally exist, will harmonize the discordant elements which may now be present in your army, and at the expense of little personal pride on either part result in great public good." Buckner felt he was "sufficiently your friend" to offer this advice.[53]

As historian Thomas Connelly put it, Bragg's circular was "poorly timed." The heat surrounding the Kentucky campaign had cooled; in fact, it had been supplanted by the heat surrounding Stones River. No one wanted to bring up those old issues. More importantly, in the wake of Bragg's round-robin letter of January 11, none of his subordinates felt comfortable being honest anymore. He had unnecessarily created an air of fear within the Army of Tennessee. "If Bragg hoped to divide his enemies," Connelly has written, "he was unsuccessful."[54]

The circulars of January 11 and April 13 were attempts to solicit information from his officers, but Bragg also pursued individuals in the Army of Tennessee. Breckinridge loomed as a major target after Stones River. Bragg blamed him for poor intelligence regarding Union threats against the Confederate right on December 31, which resulted in dribbling his division to Polk so late in the day as to make it difficult to use the army's only reserve force to win a decisive victory. He also blamed Breckinridge for mishandling the attack of January 2; there was no coordination between the infantry and the two cavalry brigades assigned to his area. Moreover, Breckinridge failed to rally his broken ranks after the failure of the assault.[55]

Bragg went out of his way to saddle Breckinridge with responsibility for the defeat. He collected letters supporting his view and sent them in with Breckinridge's report on March 11. As part of that effort, Bragg coerced Felix Robertson to rewrite his report. Robertson commanded several pieces of artillery temporarily assigned to Breckinridge's Division for the assault, and his first report, dated January 12, was not strong enough in Bragg's view. Robertson substantially rewrote it in mid-February. Gideon Pillow, one of Breckinridge's brigade commanders, also testified that he warned Breckinridge to coordinate his cavalry support before the attack began. David Urquhart wrote many of the orders Bragg issued to Breckinridge about how to conduct the attack; he was careful to get receipts upon delivering them to division headquarters. "General Bragg cordially said to me afterward that my preservation of those receipts had saved his reputation," Urquhart recalled.[56]

When Breckinridge became aware of the report, he naturally was incensed. The division commander requested a court of inquiry on April 2. He also asked William Preston Johnston to intercede with Davis about

JOHN C. BRECKINRIDGE. Bragg had a stormy relationship with this division and corps commander. He refused to pardon Kentucky soldier Asa Lewis, tried to blame Breckinridge for much of what went wrong at Stones River, and claimed he was beastly drunk during the Chattanooga battle. Yet Bragg cooperated with Breckinridge when the latter was named Confederate secretary of war late in the conflict and wrote at least one friendly letter to him after the war was over. (Library of Congress, LC-DIG-cwpb-04793)

getting the court underway. By May, Bragg's report of Stones River was published in the newspapers, and Breckinridge became even more angry. He wanted to have his letter requesting a court published as well. Bragg prepared for the official investigation.[57]

In targeting Breckinridge, Bragg aimed at the very heart of the Kentucky clique in the Army of Tennessee. The division leader certainly was responsible for much of what went wrong concerning his command's role in the December 31 and January 2 attacks, but Bragg exaggerated his case against him. Coercing a subordinate to rewrite an official report was unprofessional. As happened with Randall L. Gibson, Bragg's personal dislike of a subordinate led him to go beyond propriety in dealing with him. Breckinridge did not deserve to be made a scapegoat for the failure at Stones River, even though he was legitimately responsible for some of it.

Friends of the Kentucky clique felt Bragg's sting. An anonymous writer to the *Chattanooga Daily Rebel* was upset at the "studied effort" to criticize Breckinridge's Division when he read Bragg's report in the newspaper. Col. Robert P. Trabue, who took command of Roger Hanson's Kentucky Brigade in Breckinridge's Division upon Hanson's mortal wounding on January 2, also struggled with Bragg. Trabue was keen on receiving permanent command of the brigade and promotion to brigadier general. Bragg and Breckinridge recommended him but Bragg inserted a caveat to indicate that he had no brigade to give him after his promotion. Trabue tried to talk the army commander into rescinding that comment, but Bragg refused.

According to J. Stoddard Johnston, as told to William Preston, Bragg said he heard that Trabue thought the army had lost confidence in its leader. If that was true, his recommendation would mean nothing in Richmond. "Trabue assured him his opinion was otherwise," in Preston's words. "This Bragg construed into recantation." If Preston reported the incident correctly, it shows that Bragg was pressuring Trabue to break away from the Kentucky clique to obtain his favor. That also was a course of action as unsavory as it was unprofessional.[58]

In the end Breckinridge never received his court of inquiry. Many officers requested courts, and few received them because it was time-consuming and demanded the calling of officers from their duty to serve as witnesses and court members. There was even less opportunity for a court of inquiry after Breckinridge's Division was moved to Mississippi as Grant's Vicksburg campaign demanded an influx of reinforcements in May 1863. But Breckinridge's letter requesting a court was eventually published in the newspapers when a friend of his cajoled it from Adj. Gen. Samuel Cooper.[59]

Getting rid of the Kentucky clique was about the only victory Bragg could achieve. But he also had trouble with Benjamin Cheatham over an entirely different matter. He heard from several officers, including Hardee, that Cheatham had been drunk during the battle of December 31. Cheatham was generally a good division commander, and this obviously was a delicate matter, so Bragg consulted with Polk. The corps commander admitted it was true and assured him he had already spoken to Cheatham about it. Bragg told Polk to rebuke the division leader in writing as well, and Polk agreed to do so, but there was no mention of the incident in Polk's report. Instead, in Bragg's view, it seemed as if Polk praised Cheatham more than necessary. In his own report, Bragg also refrained from mentioning that Cheatham was drunk, but he blamed him for not properly supporting Cleburne's Division. Bragg also refrained from mentioning Cheatham in his list of officers deserving commendation.[60]

Bragg's effort to be understanding of Cheatham's faults and protective of his drinking backfired. The division commander became his instant enemy because of what he considered the slights contained in Bragg's report. The truth is, even before that report was written Cheatham expressed his distrust of Bragg to Johnston. That feeling originated from disgust with the outcome of the battle, but, ironically, it was Cheatham who played a large role in urging Bragg to retreat from Murfreesboro with his alarming report that most of the army was in no condition to continue fighting. Cheatham's contemptible actions toward Bragg, given how seriously he

BENJAMIN F. CHEATHAM.
Bragg became deeply concerned
that Cheatham, an effective and
popular division commander,
was intoxicated during the
battle of December 31, 1862.
Bragg's gentle efforts to
correct Cheatham's drinking
habit backfired as the insulted
Cheatham became a vicious
enemy of Bragg for the rest of
his life. (Library of Congress,
LC-DIG-cwpb-05991)

could have dealt with the division commander for being drunk on the field,
are astonishing.[61]

St. John R. Liddell correctly noted that Bragg's leniency toward
Cheatham was ill-advised. "An example of severity was needed. But when
the opportunity offered in high position, Bragg failed to apply the screws.
The disaffected generals of Bragg's Army had but small barriers to their
expression of dissatisfaction with him." Bragg's handling of an issue as
important to him as drunkenness can only be explained by his belief in
Cheatham's value as a division leader. He had told Johnston that he could
"control that officer, & bring him to his senses." But that proved to be impossible; Cheatham became one of Bragg's most vocal critics in the Army
of Tennessee.[62]

Bragg could handle John P. McCown more easily. He developed a
dislike for McCown ever since the general was compelled to surrender
Island Number 10 in the spring of 1862. Saddled with him as a division
commander from the summer of that year onward, Bragg waited for an opportunity to get rid of him. He thought he found it in McCown's handling
of the December 31 attack. Bragg blamed McCown for starting that assault
at 7 A.M., later than ordered, and limiting the time available to reap the full

benefits of success. Hardee also implied that McCown was at fault for the same thing. But the division leader was supported by his subordinates, who testified that the attack began earlier than 7 A.M. There was no reason to believe a later start of no more than one hour played any role in the army's ability to win its objectives that day.[63]

McCown further exposed himself to Bragg's agenda when he persisted in sending his staff members and other officers on detached duty outside the boundaries of the department. This was a direct violation of orders, and Bragg made it clear it should stop. Why McCown did this is obscure, but Bragg arrested him early in February 1863 and preferred charges. Alexander P. Stewart, one of the army's best officers, took over McCown's Division. The arrested man's political supporters urged Davis and Seddon to convene a court-martial. It was finally done in late March, with a number of Bragg supporters serving on the court. If McCown thought he could survive this ordeal he was wrong. The court found him guilty and sentenced him to suspension of rank for six months. McCown never again held a significant command after returning to duty.[64]

Bragg dealt with his enemies for five months after the battle of Stones River, but he also devoted attention to friends and supporters. He had developed a high opinion not only of James Patton Anderson but of brigade leader Edward C. Walthall. His favorites tended to be among the lower-ranking officers—the brigade and divisions leaders—rather than among the upper echelon of the army's command. Ironically, those he favored also tended to be quiet in the post–Stones River controversy.[65]

An opportunity to influence the Confederate Congress developed when Bragg sent his staff member John B. Sale to Richmond early in March 1863. Sale accompanied Felix Robertson as the two delivered Union flags captured at Murfreesboro, and Sale submitted Bragg's official report of the battle. Bragg gave Sale authority to answer points raised by the Confederate president, but Davis declined to ask any until subordinate reports were ready for his examination. Meanwhile, Sale waited in Richmond. He advised Bragg that Hardee should be more critical of McCown in his report and that Patton Anderson could write "distinct and full" criticisms of Breckinridge to make Bragg's case stronger.[66]

While waiting, Sale decided to see what he could do about congress. Without Bragg's authorization, he tried to help the Senate approve a House resolution of thanks to Bragg and the Army of Tennessee for what they accomplished at Murfreesboro. Sale personally knew Clement Claiborne Clay of Alabama and saw that James Phelan of Mississippi seemed to be leading the defense of Bragg in Senate debate over the resolution. When Bragg's report came back from the copyist, Davis invited Clay, Phelan, and Thomas Jenkins Semmes of Louisiana to study it closely with Sale offering advice. The staff officer gave Phelan a copy of Forsyth's pamphlet about the Kentucky campaign, and Davis promised to consult with the senator about its details.[67]

Senator Henry C. Burnett of Kentucky led the opposition to Bragg's resolution of thanks, but Sale believed most senators supported it. A few members of the upper house were swayed by anti-Bragg rhetoric in the newspapers, but Sale hoped to influence the rest. The staff officer viewed this as an important battle. "Your vindication will be *triumphant*. It will be regarded as a semi-official trial of the truth or falsehood of all the malicious slanders of non-combatant croakers and mal-contents, and will authoritatively settle and silence them forever."[68]

James L. Pugh, an Alabama member of the House of Representatives, introduced Felix Robertson to several senators so he could lobby on Bragg's behalf. "There has been an organized effort to break you down," Pugh told Bragg, "and it is not to be denied that your enemies have harmed you to an extent, but a reaction is taking place." Pugh believed that only five senators would vote against Bragg's resolution of thanks, which passed the House by a vote of 76 to 4 on February 26.[69]

But a month later it became obvious that enough senators opposed the resolution to block it. Jillson P. Johnson, aide-de-camp to Breckinridge, traveled to Richmond to deliver his commander's report of the battle of Baton Rouge. He stayed a while to observe developments in the capital. Johnson cited senators Burnett of Kentucky, Robert W. Johnson of Arkansas, Gustavus A. Henry of Tennessee, William E. Simms of Kentucky, Louis T. Wigfall of Texas, Clement C. Clay of Alabama, and Charles B. Mitchel of Arkansas as friends of Breckinridge and enemies of Bragg. Obviously Bragg's effort to influence Clay had utterly failed. The opposition of these senators prevented the joint resolution from passing.[70]

In addition to the failed resolution, Bragg faced a coalition of senators who worked to unseat him as commander of the Army of Tennessee. Wigfall, who was among them, told Johnston that these senators "believed Bragg utterly and wholly incompetent & wanted him removed for that reason and not because of personal dislike." Wigfall was convinced that Davis kept Bragg in place to avoid naming Johnston as his successor. "[The president] would rather sacrifice the Army and even the country than put you in command," he told Johnston. According to the senator, Seddon had worked Davis up to the point of removing Bragg until Johnston's glowing reports convinced him to retain the general. Wigfall criticized Johnston for his role in this episode. "Governed by generous feelings & sympathy for Bragg you have allowed the President to shuffle off the whole responsibility for continuing him in command. In protecting Bragg you have at the same time protected the President."[71]

Bragg's enemies in and out of the army worked openly against him, but many of his supporters only quietly voiced their concern for him. David Urquhart certainly exaggerated when he wrote that "corps commanders, as well as their subordinates down to the regimental rank and file, scarcely concealed their want of confidence." Writing of the public abuse of his commander, Isaac Alexander of the 10th South Carolina told his brother, "I must say that he does not deserve it." Alexander blamed the furor on callous newspapermen and a public that held unrealistic expectations. Brigade leader St. John R. Liddell both supported and criticized Bragg but he thought the general's handling of the army at Stones River was "admirable" and blamed lack of support from high-ranking generals for the retreat. "The best-laid plans must fail for lack of faithful cooperation," Liddell wrote. Arthur Manigault, another of Bragg's brigade leaders, read the general's report and liked it. "The censure that he bestows in one or two instances is generally believed to have been deserved."[72]

Staunch friends such as Josiah Nott were relieved at "the manly, just & generous course of Genl Johnston towards you." He correctly diagnosed at least part of the problem when noting that Bragg had few subordinates "competent to any thing beyond a Brigade, & you have been obliged to make enemies by constantly watching & making them perform duties, which they would not otherwise perform."[73]

Support for Bragg came from many quarters. Frank Campbell of Knoxville praised the general's actions at Murfreesboro and in Kentucky alike. Campbell stretched the point when he told Bragg that the nation was beginning to understand that both had been conducted "with masterly skill and correctness." He told Bragg that Davis and Lee "had the genius to see beyond the present moment and the moral courage to will down the frowning opposition" and urged him to do the same.[74]

When Bragg's Kentucky campaign report appeared in print, a correspondent for the *Knoxville Register* believed the general's explanation for its failure. "If Gen. Bragg committed a fault, Kentuckians cannot become prosecutors at the bar of public opinion. His failure arose from their own *lacks, and his crime was his confidence in them.* Beyond this the campaign was no failure." Josiah Gorgas, head of the Confederate Ordnance Bureau in Richmond, was persuaded by Bragg's version of affairs at Stones River when that report also was published. A. S. Lyon of Demopolis urged the general to endure all abuse because "truth & justice will prevail in the end." Lyon praised the "chastisement" Bragg had administered to Rosecrans and predicted that such "victories" as the Federals claimed at Murfreesboro would undo their war effort.[75]

From her plantation in northeast Louisiana, Kate Stone heard that Bragg had been replaced by Johnston and thought it a shame. Bettie Ridley Blackmore lived near Murfreesboro during the Stones River campaign and felt that Bragg had won a great victory. "When the history of this war is impartially written," Blackmore confided to her journal, "it is my deliberate opinion, that to *Bragg* will be awarded the praise of *having done more with his men and means, than any other Gen. of the War, with equal resources.*"[76]

But publication of the Bragg reports had a negative effect on some people. Robert Garlick Hill Kean saw in the Stones River document that "there are deep quarrels in that army, and that Bragg is cordially hated by a large number of his officers." Far away from Richmond, near the small community of Osyka near Baton Rouge, Louisiana, James Fulker Kent's family heard nothing but criticism of the general. "Every body down here speaks against Bragg," Kent's sister told him. "Tyrant & fool are mild words used to express their opinion of his character. You don't hear one speak in his favor."[77]

Did Bragg succeed in his effort to confront critics and defend himself after Stones River? Yes and no; he gained many points with members of the Confederacy, but other people turned against him too. Winning battles was probably the only thing that could have given Bragg a thoroughly good name with the public.

There is no doubt that Bragg erred badly when trying to determine which of his generals supported him after Stones River. The round-robin letter of January 11 was viewed as a challenge, a demand that they declare themselves openly. No other commander in the Civil War did anything like this, and for good reason. Ironically the real trouble emanated from Hardee and his subordinate Breckinridge rather than from Polk, who had been a longer and more vocal critic of Bragg before Stones River. The Kentucky clique was the origin of this trouble, and that clique was lodged in Hardee's Corps. In the words of biographer Nathaniel C. Hughes, "Hardee may have thought he was doing best for the army when he opened the gates of controversy, but he only weakened the army's command structure."[78]

Bragg wrote of his willingness to step aside if the good of the service demanded it. The response to the round-robin letter obviously demanded it, but Bragg refused. This is the most damning criticism of Bragg in the entire war. Faced with open expressions of distrust in his ability coming from his most important subordinates, he dug in his heels and fought back instead of gracefully leaving the Army of Tennessee. Bragg's native stubbornness colored his judgment. From now on the general fought increasingly for himself and not solely for the common good; it would ruin his war career. If Bragg had submitted a letter of resignation, Davis might have considered accepting it.

Davis played a large role in the troubles afflicting the Confederate army. Bragg counted on Davis's support to retain his job. Moreover, he manipulated that support for his own benefit by placing the onus of deciding whether he should stay or go squarely on Davis. In supporting Bragg, Polk, and Hardee at the same time, the Confederate president failed in his job as commander in chief. Lincoln would have relieved Bragg of command even before the battle of Stones River. The Union president readily experimented with many generals to see who could bring victory, laying many of them on the shelf to remain idle for months at a time. Davis never adopted that attitude. He lacked a commitment to change and experimentation in the field. Thus, he held on to Bragg even though he realized the man had serious limitations as a commander.

From Bragg's perspective, he was a victim of public opinion, of malicious attacks by the Kentucky clique, and of a lack of commitment to his views by officers who had no personal grudge against him. With a man who tended to be myopically focused, stubborn, and convinced that his way was the correct way, staying put and fighting back seemed to be the course to take. Moreover, Bragg had supporters inside and outside the Army of Tennessee, and they gave him some hope he could continue to lead the army with success.

In June, when Bragg sent papers to John Forsyth with the admonition to use them in his defense if needed, Forsyth responded with a plea for reconciliation. The editor urged his friend to make peace with his generals. Bragg did not know how to do that and never really tried. David Urquhart recalled that Bragg maintained good relations with a number of division and brigade commanders. Among them he named Joseph Wheeler, Jones Withers, James Patton Anderson, John C. Brown, John K. Jackson, William B. Bate, and Edward C. Walthall. These men were either neutral in the anti-Bragg controversy or quietly supportive of their commander.[79]

A cold war developed between Bragg and his chief subordinates. David Urquhart and Irving Buck, one of Cleburne's staff members, recalled that Polk and Hardee never interacted with Bragg except when necessary. Feelings of alienation also seeped down unevenly into lower levels of command and into the rank and file.[80]

The post–Stones River controversy, with its unusual exchange of letters between commander and subordinates, marked the beginning of Bragg's decline as an effective leader. The boldness that impelled him to invade Kentucky and to stand defiantly at Murfreesboro became a thing of the past. He acted strictly on the defensive and worried rather than planned boldly. His health also deteriorated in the coming months, contributing to his decline as an effective field officer. Most of all, the round-robin letter flushed out a good deal of distrust in him. Bragg felt he could not fully count on many of his key subordinates and that crushing realization contributed to the stress that worsened his health. It was largely because of Bragg's stubborn refusal to give up his position in the face of problems partially created by himself that the Army of Tennessee's prospects worsened with each passing month.[81]

9

Tullahoma

An unusual hiatus in military operations took place following the battle of Stones River. For six months Rosecrans remained idle at Murfreesboro, rebuilding his army and planning the next move. The pause gave Bragg an opportunity to rebuild the Army of Tennessee until it was about as strong as it had been before the Murfreesboro campaign. It also gave Bragg an opportunity to deal with his subordinates.

But as spring arrived, Bragg's appearance sometimes indicated an aggressive spirit toward the enemy. When John H. Marshall of the 41st Mississippi saw the general at Shelbyville in mid-April, he was impressed by his commander. "The old fellow look[ed] devilish. I was glad to see him[;] we will move now somewhere but I hope we won't fall back." Bragg further gave the impression that the army would soon be engaged in another campaign when he announced Lee's impressive victory at Chancellorsville in early May. "Let us emulate the deeds of the Army of Virginia," he wrote. "We cannot surpass them. Let us make them proud to call us brothers. Let us make the Cumberland and the Ohio classic as the Rappahannock and the Potomac." It was mere rhetoric, for Bragg had no intention of taking the offensive anytime soon.[1]

Bragg even felt able to treat a newspaperman with civility. Samuel Chester Reid returned to the Army of Tennessee on June 8 but was placed under arrest for not having proper papers allowing him within army lines. The provost marshal ordered him to leave by June 9, but Joseph Wheeler interceded with Bragg on his behalf "and procured permission for me to remain." Reid happened to meet Bragg at a religious service at Shelbyville on June 14. Much to his surprise, the general "bowed to me!"[2]

Apparently Bragg was beginning to try a softer approach to newspapermen, but he continued to have an acerbic attitude in general toward the public sheets. They tended to give too much information, which the enemy was able to use. "This element is a great weakness with us," he told Elise, "and I fear leads to many of our small disasters. Nothing transpires but what it is paraded before the public, and where the truth is not sufficiently exciting, falsehood is substituted."[3]

Arthur Fremantle was no newspaperman, but Bragg readily gave him all the information he could about the battle of Stones River. Fremantle, an officer in the Coldstream Guards, was touring the Southern states. Bragg talked to him for "a long time" about the recent campaign, Fremantle reported, and emphasized the damage inflicted on the Federal army. Bragg "allowed that Rosecrans had displayed much firmness, and was *the only man in the Yankee army who was not badly beaten.*" Bragg was once again bothered by a boil on his hand in late May that limited his opportunity to show Fremantle the army's outposts. When Fremantle's book appeared, it contained a largely positive view of Bragg. The English officer knew of Bragg's reputation as "a rigid disciplinarian, and of shooting freely for insubordination. . . . I understand he is rather unpopular on this account, and also by reason of his occasional acerbity of manner."[4]

Years after the war, one of Bragg's veterans recalled the execution of three men at Shelbyville, two of them young and the other middle-aged. Bragg rejected strong appeals for clemency; he was worried about the effect of rampant desertion on the army's morale. The two young men asked that family photographs in their possession be forwarded to their homes, and Bragg agreed to do so. "The execution cast a shadow of gloom over the army," the anonymous soldier recalled, "as well as over the citizens."[5]

Bragg's public image of an austere, grim officer hid the fact that with small groups and selected individuals he was warm and friendly. His staff became his military family, and he was devoted to its members. The Confederate government had to maintain a small army in feeding the animals at Bragg's headquarters. A total of 187 horses and 26 mules served the escort, requiring 25,500 pounds of corn, 10,400 pounds of oats, and 15,100 pounds of hay during the last week of January 1863 alone. From all accounts, Bragg managed this military family well, closely supervising its work on a daily basis.[6]

When George W. Brent joined Bragg's staff on October 2, 1862, he heard the general was "difficult to please" but "tried to be just." After seven months' service with him, Bragg admired Brent's "intelligent discharge" of his duties and found that the staff officer had "endeared himself to me personally." Bragg also developed good personal relations with Harvey Washington Walter, a Mississippi lawyer who had opposed secession but supported the Confederacy when war came. Walter's daughter sent a sewing kit to Bragg, which touched the general's sympathy. Engineer John M. Wampler also had a daughter who liked Bragg and sent the general a wreath made of bergamot. He also developed close relations with commissary John Walker. When Walker decided to resign from the staff and accept appointment as chief commissary for the state of Alabama, Bragg regretted the move. "Our relations, official and personal, have ever been so pleasant, indeed cordial, that no separation could be less than painful." David Urquhart recalled that Bragg regularly told the staff stories about his Mexican War experiences while relaxing in the evening. The atmosphere at army headquarters was by all accounts pleasant, the relations among staff members cordial and supportive. The staff reciprocated Bragg's high esteem; Kinloch Falconer called him "the paen, in my opinion, of any officer of the late war."[7]

Bragg not only developed family relationships with staff officers but maintained brother-in-law Towson Ellis on his staff for the duration of the war. He arranged for the state of Louisiana to appoint Towson his aide-de-camp on February 15, 1861, as well as obtained for him a lieutenancy in the 1st Louisiana Artillery in the state forces. Soon after becoming a Confederate brigadier general, Bragg appointed Ellis as his aide on March 16, 1861. Ellis admitted to the adjutant general of the Confederacy that "my knowledge of military matters is very limited," but he served his brother-in-law with extreme faithfulness for four years.[8]

When visiting Richmond some of Bragg's staff members jokingly told William Preston Johnston in hearing of Mary Chesnut that they simply destroyed nine out of ten letters written to him by civilians. Johnston countered by telling them Jefferson Davis wanted to hear from the public, but he admitted he showed only one out of sixty letters to the Confederate president. It is clear that Bragg's staff showed the general the best civilian letters that arrived at headquarters. Mrs. C. J. Pope of Eufaula, Alabama, sent a box of food to him in exchange for some "kindness" he had shown her in the past.[9]

Bragg continued to rely heavily on his staff not only for military duties but as a substitute family. He resisted letting George Garner go with Simon B. Buckner when the general was sent to Mobile. Bragg finally consented to part with Garner, who was eager to be reunited with his wife and children in that city. William Whann Mackall became Bragg's chief of staff in April and served him for nearly the rest of the year. Bragg offered his friend Taylor Beatty a position on his staff when Beatty lost his commission due to a consolidation of his Louisiana regiment's companies.

Later Beatty asked his advice when offered a promotion in rank and a position on Hardee's staff, and Bragg encouraged him to take advantage of the opportunity.[10]

John J. Walker was a stalwart of Bragg's staff, keeping the army fed as his chief commissary. When Walker traveled to Richmond on business, Bragg expressed to Walker's wife how much her husband meant to him. "He has instructions to return as soon as possible, as he has become a necessity to me officially and socially. You ladies must prepare yourselves to win us back again when the war is over for really we have become so wedded by long association under dangers mutually encountered that it will be difficult to sunder the ties."[11]

David Urquhart remembered Bragg in a good mood one day while riding through the country near Tullahoma. The general came upon a citizen and asked him for information regarding the roads. Urquhart characterized the man as "one of those rough, independent citizens of the mountain district of Tennessee." After pumping him for information, Bragg asked if he belonged to his army. "'Bragg's Army?' was the reply. 'He's got none; he shot half of them in Kentucky, and the other got killed up at Murfreesboro.' The general laughed and rode on."[12]

Like many other high-ranking Confederates, Bragg "got religion" during the war. Bishop Stephen Elliott visited the Army of Tennessee in late May 1863. After the many trials he had gone through, Bragg urged all his men to prepare for baptism but gave no indication of his personal views about religion. Charles Todd Quintard, chaplain of the 1st Tennessee, wanted to help him but felt afraid to try because of his "reputation of being so stern and so sharp in his sarcasm." Quintard tried to approach the austere general, entering his headquarters tent one day only to be told by the sentry that Bragg saw no one except on life and death matters. Quintard lost his nerve and went away.[13]

But the chaplain returned the next day and insisted on being admitted. He interrupted Bragg's dictation to two secretaries, but the general agreed to hear him. Fixing his eyes on a knot hole in the pine wood flooring of the headquarters tent, Quintard told Bragg that a man in his position should consider his spiritual needs. "When I looked up after a while I saw tears in the General's eyes and took courage to ask him to be confirmed." To Quintard's surprise, Bragg agreed. "I have been waiting for twenty years to have some one say this to me, and I thank you from my heart."[14]

Elliott's arrival sparked a good deal of interest in the Army of Tennessee. Officiating at Sunday services in the Episcopal Church of Shelbyville on

May 31, Bragg, Hardee, and Polk came to listen to him. The sermon was "full of deep piety & lofty patriotism," thought Capt. Daniel Coleman in the 15th Mississippi Battalion of Sharpshooters. Elliott baptized Bragg on the evening of June 2 at the same Episcopal Church.[15]

Bragg's conversion fit a pattern evident by the midpoint of the war. The number of religious revivals and high-level professions of faith blossomed by the spring of 1863 in the Confederate army and, to a more limited degree, in the Union military as well. It is estimated that as many as 150,000 Rebel soldiers openly converted to a high degree of religious fervency during the war. Later commanders of Bragg's army, Joseph E. Johnston and John Bell Hood, were among the number. Bragg's worries increased in the early months of 1863, helping to explain the motive and timing of his conversion. But it certainly was not all due to religious feeling. Historians have noted that religious conviction often shaded off into politics to create a kind of civic religion in the Confederacy that linked God's favor with the political and national aspirations of the Southern cause. It lent a conviction of morality, virtue, and divine purpose to the war effort, and Bragg certainly fell into this mode of thinking about the cause he so fervently espoused.[16]

Elise remained with her husband during the time from mid-December until June, although she spent much of that period recovering from her serious bout of typhoid fever. Bragg visited her frequently at Winchester. As soon as well enough to travel, he planned to send Elise to his brother John's plantation near Montgomery but later considered a place for her in the mountains. "How would you like the top of Lookout Mt. at Chattanooga?" he asked her. Elise was gone from Winchester by late June, although it is unclear exactly where she went, but Bragg was lonely without her. He felt anxious about her comfort and safety now that she was a refugee from their confiscated home in Louisiana and reliant on friends. Bragg received mail from Nashville, smuggled through the enemy lines, and could obtain some articles of comfort for her from that city. "What kind & Sizes of Shoes and gloves, Handkf &c &c &c shall I send for. Of course they can only be had in very small quantities, and at much risk; as my friend Rosecrans is exceedingly rigid, but we do manage to elude him." Bragg could afford a few luxuries for his wife. Pay accounts in his service record indicated that he earned an extra $100 for commanding the Department of Tennessee, taking home a total of $401 per month.[17]

There were signs of uplifting spirits. Bragg heard from Elise's family that all but five of his slaves were yet living at Bivouac. Bragg also wrote a lengthy conundrum, a sort of word puzzle that was popular in Civil War era culture. It mixed elements of love for Elise with his pride at being a soldier, fighting for Southern causes.[18]

Bragg further cemented his relationship with Davis when the president of the Confederacy asked him to send troops to Mississippi in May. Grant's campaign to seal up Vicksburg prompted this shift, and Bragg responded quickly and enthusiastically. He agreed to send Breckinridge's Division and 2,000 cavalrymen, getting rid of a negative element in the Army of Tennessee. Davis was thrilled. "Your answer is in the spirit of patriotism heretofore manifested by you." In fact, the Confederate president told Lee, Bragg was so eager to send the troops that he had "to warn him to be mindful of his own necessities." When Johnston suggested that the department of East Tennessee be merged with Bragg's for better administration, Davis sought Bragg's advice on the idea. "I will be glad to have a full expression of your views," he assured him.[19]

By June 1863 Johnston was faced with a major crisis in Mississippi. Davis had shifted some 20,000 men his way and expected him to move west from Jackson and raise Grant's siege of Vicksburg. Johnston knew he was badly outnumbered and took his time preparing the scratch force he now commanded. Bragg commiserated with him, offering the kind of emotional support Johnston had given him in previous months.[20]

But Bragg admitted to Johnston that his health was getting worse. "Since parting with you I have at no time been well enough until now to say I was fit for duty, though I have not given up. The annoyances of those boils, instead of indicating returning health, was only the precursor of a general breakdown." The twin stresses of public criticism and Elise's health had "well nigh prostrated me." Mackall's arrival took much of the daily work from his shoulders, and when Elise was well enough to travel, another load was lifted from his burden. But then Bragg suffered a severe illness, having kept it at bay only through force of will up to that time.[21]

Bragg certainly appeared "sad and careworn" to observers. Arthur J. L. Fremantle described his appearance in May 1863: "He is very thin; he stoops, and has a sickly, cadaverous, haggard appearance, rather plain features, bushy black eyebrows which unite in a tuft on the top of his nose, and a stubby iron-gray beard." But Fremantle noted that despite his physical infirmities, Bragg possessed "bright and piercing" eyes. When reviewing troops the general could drum up enough energy to honor the common soldier he loved, doffing his cap in a touching way at the passing of regimental colors. By late June, he was beginning to feel much better.[22]

BRAXTON BRAGG. This is the most widely published photograph of Bragg, exemplifying the grim general with iron self-discipline gazing into an uncertain future. (Library of Congress, LC-USZC4-7984)

The coming campaign would stress Bragg's health once more. Ironically, despite the six-month hiatus, the Army of Tennessee and its commander were not ready for Rosecrans's next move. While the Army of the Cumberland had been increased in size until it contained something like 56,000 men, Bragg had only been able to recoup the losses suffered at Stones River. He still had only about 38,000 troops, and they suffered for want of food. Bragg could not draw supplies from the Atlanta depot because the War Department had reserved that for Lee's Army of Northern Virginia. The Army of Tennessee had to forage from the region it held, and it had too few wagons to do so effectively. This was one reason that Bragg adopted a defensive strategy, spreading his troops across a front of seventy miles. It was similar to the defensive stance he had adopted before Rosecrans advanced from Nashville in December. When the Federals came out in three columns, Bragg pulled in outlying units and concentrated them before Murfreesboro, skirmishing to delay the enemy along the way. He then mounted an energetic attack on Rosecrans that nearly won the battle.[23]

But the same scenario did not play out when Rosecrans finally resumed his offensive. The Federals set out on June 24 with a plan to bypass the fortified towns of Tullahoma and Shelbyville by pushing through a series of gaps in a range of hills called the Highland Rim along the frontier between the two armies. Bragg's troops were poorly positioned and unaware of what was happening, and there is no real explanation for their failure to serve him well. When Federal troops approached Hoover's Gap, they chased away the one Confederate cavalry regiment guarding the place. The troops ran so fast they did not even give information to their infantry supports, and those infantrymen, for some reason, were camped five miles south of the gap. Later in the day, Hardee rushed William Bate's brigade to the scene. Bate attacked and was repulsed, so Hardee fell back as more Unionists came forward to secure Hoover's Gap. Five miles west, other Federal units captured Liberty Gap in a similar way.[24]

On June 26, Bragg planned an attack to regain the gaps. He wanted to push Polk's Corps north of the Highland Rim to strike the Federals from behind at Liberty Gap. Polk complained so much about the difficulties of doing so, and Hardee seemed reluctant as well, that Bragg was compelled to cancel the strike. Bragg gave up the Highland Rim entirely and fell back to Tullahoma on June 27. Moreover, the Confederate cavalry continued to disappoint Bragg. Without authorization, John Hunt Morgan took his brigade on a raid into Kentucky, across the Ohio River, and into Indiana and Ohio. The raid stripped Bragg's right front of its cavalry screen and 20 percent of his army's mounted men. Joseph Wheeler and Nathan Bedford Forrest failed to impede the Federal approach to Tullahoma. Rosecrans came forward aggressively and full of confidence with a well-oiled military machine that outnumbered the Army of Tennessee. In the apt words of historian Steven Woodworth, "Bragg had suffered a remarkable series of reverses despite good strategy and tactics." In fact, Woodworth states that Bragg "had failed to get the behavior he needed out of the officers he had to work with."[25]

What transpired thus far was only the beginning of the Tullahoma campaign. As Rosecrans approached, he sent a brigade of mounted infantry to strike the Rebel supply line at Decherd. Confederate troops chased them away, and Bragg continued firm in his resolve to stay put, but Polk was alarmed by the raid and told Hardee of his fears. When the two met Bragg on June 29 for consultation, Polk vehemently expressed his worries to the commander, arguing that Confederate cavalry was incapable of protecting the railroad. Hardee agreed with Polk but hesitated to advise a retreat, although Polk had no qualms about insisting that the army fall back. Once again harried by Polk, Bragg stood his ground for the time. He adopted Hardee's suggestion that infantry be dispatched to guard the railroad, and the conference broke up on that decision.[26]

But over the next twenty-four hours reports filtered in of another Union thrust at the railroad. Although these reports were not fully confirmed, they seem to have unnerved Bragg. His resolve to stay and fight was shaken by Polk's fears and Hardee's lack of faith in Bragg's plan; now these new rumors tipped the scale. Bragg ordered the army to pull back on the afternoon of June 30.[27]

Rosecrans entered Tullahoma without a battle on the morning of July 1 as the Confederates pondered what to do. The most alarming discussion took place between Hardee and Polk. The former wrote to his colleague at 8:30 that night expressing concern about the fate of the army. "I deeply regret to see General Bragg in his present enfeebled state of health," wrote Hardee. "If we have a fight, he is evidently unable either to examine or determine his line of battle or to take command on the field. What shall we do? What is best to be done to save this army and its honor? I think we ought to counsel together." Although short, Hardee's note to Polk was an extraordinary document. After doing a good deal to undermine both Bragg's health and his opportunity to command effectively, Hardee now acted as if he was surprised the army leader was feeble and indecisive. Bragg had had no difficulty deciding where and how to fight until his two subordinates undercut that determination and intensified the natural doubts that any commander harbors about his course of action. If Hardee and Polk had supported Bragg in his decision to fight for Tullahoma, there would have been no enfeeblement or indecision.[28]

Could Bragg have ignored his subordinates' fears and compelled them to attack against their better judgment? That was possible, but Bragg was not prepared to take such a course of action. It would have opened him up to bitter criticism if the attack had failed. It is also true that by this point in the campaign, Bragg truly was becoming more indecisive, questioning his every decision, and that was mostly because he had no support from his chief subordinates. His willpower and self-confidence were weakening and his persistently poor health only made the situation worse.

In falling back from Tullahoma, Bragg wondered where the army should take up its next position. He sent a message to both Hardee and Polk late on the night of July 1 asking their opinion as to whether it should stop at the Elk River or farther on at Cowan near the foot of the Cumberland Plateau. Hardee was delighted to receive the note and informed Polk that he favored retreating all the way to the mountains. Polk agreed with Hardee, so Bragg consented to their advice by pulling the army to Cowan.[29]

It was a mistake to give up so much territory without a major battle. The

Army of Tennessee could have taken up a good position at the Elk River, falling away from it only when necessity demanded that action. Bragg was losing his power to make hard decisions on his own, relying too much on men who had demonstrated that they did not have his best interests in mind.

Gauging his situation at Cowan, Bragg now came to the conclusion that there was no option except further retreat to Chattanooga. "We were now back against the mountains," Bragg explained to Johnston, "in a country affording us nothing, with a long line of railroad to protect, and half a dozen passes on the right and left by which our rear could be gained. In this position it was perfectly practicable for the enemy to destroy our means of crossing the Tennessee, and thus secure our ultimate destruction without a battle. Having failed to bring him to that issue, so much desired by myself and troops, I reluctantly yielded." Bragg refrained from telling Johnston that the reason he could not bring Rosecrans to battle lay mostly in the recalcitrance of Hardee and Polk.[30]

The Tullahoma campaign was a disastrous episode for the Army of Tennessee. Rosecrans brilliantly planned and deftly executed his strategic plan, but a major factor in Federal success lay within the worsening command relations inside the Confederate army. For the first time Bragg's ability to communicate with and trust the men who he most relied on had worsened to the point of collapse. The Army of Tennessee staggered from one position to another and lost much territory with nothing to show for it. At Murfreesboro the army at least had exacted a heavy price for victory on Rosecrans; now the Tullahoma campaign seemed an easy success for the Federals. The campaign demonstrates an important fact: either Bragg should have resigned or Davis should have replaced both Hardee and Polk before it started. The results of their attacks on Bragg, and of Bragg's unwise counterattacks, were ruining the field effectiveness of the Confederacy's main army in the West.

On a personal level, Bragg was sorely pressed by the campaign. Quintard happened to meet him at Cowan when the army reached that town and felt free to say to his commander, "'My dear General, I am afraid you are thoroughly outdone.' 'Yes,' he said, 'I am utterly broken down.' And then leaning over his saddle he spoke of the loss of Middle Tennessee and whispered: 'This is a great disaster.'"[31]

The Tullahoma campaign left Bragg depressed and worried about the future. Rosecrans took a month to consolidate his gains before striking out across the Cumberland Plateau, offering the Confederates a much-needed break. "For two months my health has been anything but good," Bragg confided to Johnston on July 22. "Long continued and excessive labor of mind and body have produced its natural result on a frame not robust at best. Were it possible, I should seek some repose, but at present I see no hope." He envisioned spending some time at Cherokee Springs near Ringgold, twenty miles south of Chattanooga, where mineral waters were available for the infirm. It was "highly recommended for me."[32]

Many factors contributed to Bragg's failure in Middle Tennessee, but as the commander he bore the weight of responsibility. Woodworth has correctly summarized this point by noting that Bragg's overall strategy was sound and his willingness to accept battle at Tullahoma commendable. But then it all unraveled. "He had somehow failed in communicating to his subordinates precisely what he wanted them to do and motivating them to do it, and he had allowed his subordinates' carping, obstructionism, and lack of nerve to break down his own force of will."[33]

Thinking of the strategic situation, Bragg saw only problems. The question of moving Johnston's force of 25,000 men from Mississippi to the Army of Tennessee came up. Could Bragg take the offensive with a combined force such as that? His answer was decidedly in the negative. "To 'fight the enemy' is a very simple operation when you have the means and can get at him," he told Johnston. "But with less than half his strength, and a large river and 50 to 100 miles of rugged, sterile mountain, destitute even of vegetation, between you and him, with our limited commissariat, the simple fighting would be a refreshing recreation." With limited resources, "the defensive seems to be our only alternative, and that is a sad one."[34]

Bragg sent a similar message to Samuel Cooper, arguing that Rosecrans had 60,000 men and another 30,000 who could quickly reinforce him. "With this disparity of numbers, it would be rashness to place ourselves on the farther side of a country rugged and sterile, with a few mountain roads only by which to reach a river difficult of passage. Thus situated, the enemy need only avoid battle for a short time to starve us out. Whenever he shall present himself on this side of the mountains the problem will be changed." He inserted a bit of optimism by assuring Cooper that "I should look for success if a fight can be had on equal terms."[35]

An odd recommendation found its way from Bragg's pen to Richmond in August. Isham G. Harris, who had been a strong supporter of the Army of Tennessee since its creation, would soon end his term as the state's governor. Bragg was willing to give him a brigade, but he had no vacancies at the moment. Seddon and Davis liked the idea, but one wonders why Bragg made the offer. Harris had no military training or experience. Given Bragg's dislike of military amateurs, one can only conclude he saw Harris as a possible supporter within the ranks of the Army of Tennessee.[36]

While Bragg refused to countenance a strategic offensive and lost faith in his highest-ranking generals, he never gave up on his men. Headquarters issued a general order early in August encouraging them to be ready for a confrontation with the enemy. "Heretofore you have never failed to respond to your general when he has asked sacrifices at your hands," Bragg told the rank and file. "Our cause is in your keeping. Your general will lead you, you have but to respond to insure us a glorious victory."[37]

Polk contacted Davis to warn him that the situation at Chattanooga had reached a state of crisis. He recommended the infusion of reinforcements before it worsened. Troops from Buckner's command in East Tennessee and Johnston's in Mississippi should be rushed to Bragg's assistance. The Richmond authorities already were working on it. Plans were underway to consolidate Buckner's department with Bragg's and to send two divisions of James Longstreet's Corps from Virginia.[38]

Davis also wanted to send a new general but he picked one of the worst options. Daniel Harvey Hill had known Bragg in the pre–Civil War army and was currently uninvolved in a major command. Davis sent him west on July 13, and Hill reached Chattanooga six days later. "My interview with General Bragg at Chattanooga was not satisfactory," Hill later wrote of the colleague he had not seen since 1845. "He was silent and reserved and seemed gloomy and despondent. He had grown prematurely old since I saw him last, and showed much nervousness." Hardee had secured a transfer to Mississippi, so Bragg gave Hill his corps to command.[39]

Bragg saw the mountains as no barrier to Rosecrans. "It is said to be easy to defend a mountainous country," he told Hill, "but mountains hide your foe from you, while they are full of gaps through which he can pounce upon you at any time. A mountain is like the wall of a house full of rat-holes. The rat lies hidden at his hole, ready to pop out when no one is watching. Who can tell what lies hidden behind that wall?"[40]

To Hill, the mountains posed an opportunity to hit one Federal column while crossing them before the others could intervene. But he noticed that Bragg had no good scouts, relying in vain on cavalry for information. "The truth is, General Bragg was bewildered by 'the popping out of the rats from so many holes,'" Hill later concluded. He had seen how Lee operated, always with full information about enemy movements and a chain of command devoted to him. "I was most painfully impressed with the feeling that it was to be a hap-hazard campaign on our part."[41]

Hill's pessimism was shared by many in the Army of Tennessee but Bragg still possessed the loyalty of others. The Bolling Hall family of Alabama sent several sons to war, and all of them were fervent supporters. "You would be surprised to go into Bragg's army to find really how much his men like him," Lieut. Col. Bolling Hall Jr. of the Second Battalion, Hilliard Legion, assured his father. "The confidence they have in his ability even surpasses their friendship for him." Bolling argued that "the best officers of his army like him while the poorest ones dislike him. Whenever you find an officer who never attends to his duty or who is incompetent he abuses Bragg." Three other brothers served under the general. Thomas B. Hall of the 24th Alabama assured his father that Bragg still had fight left in him. Crenshaw Hall believed he "was getting popular" with a wider circle of his men, and John E. Hall called him "the Hero of the War."[42]

With the Federals still preparing, Bragg took a short vacation. He visited Elise at Cherokee Springs from August 12 to 16. Elise had already been there for some time before. A military hospital was located at the springs, which were near Ringgold only a short distance south of Chattanooga by rail. Confederate nurse Kate Cumming was well aware of his presence. "General Bragg is in this hospital sick," she confided to her journal. "He has his head-quarters at Dr. Gamble's house, which is near here. Mrs. Bragg is with the General." Dr. Cary B. Gamble served as the post surgeon at Ringgold.[43]

Cumming often saw Elise and believed she had "the appearance of being a very modest, lady-like person, as I am told she is. She is also in bad health," apparently still recovering from her bout with typhoid fever several months before. But Elise bore other concerns as well. "It is said she worries a good deal whenever she hears of the necessity of shooting any of the men, and pleads for them when she can."[44]

On Sunday, August 16, Bragg left his sick room to attend worship services. Gamble's wife, Elise, and Kate Cumming sang hymns, but Cumming saw that Bragg did not seem healthy. She did not wonder that he suffered, for "he is so much harassed. He is a member of the church, and, I am told, a sincere Christian. He has done his utmost to have Christianity diffused in the army."[45]

Bragg probably left Cherokee Springs no better than when he arrived. The problems confronting the Army of Tennessee also did not improve in the interim. Elise continued to worry about her husband. Her health was tolerably good, although she still suffered from "those pains in my limbs." She missed her husband very much. On August 28 Elise told him that he should plan another visit to Cherokee Springs if the Federals allowed it. Or, if that were not feasible, she was ready to visit him at Chattanooga. "You are out of the range of the enemy's guns, & at a very nice place."[46]

Back with the army, Bragg continued to view his strategic role as waiting until enemy columns appeared across the mountains. At that point, in Mackall's words, he would "neglect all smaller affairs and fall on him with our whole force." This really was the best policy to follow given the circumstances. Hill, however, worried that the Confederate reaction might be too late. "If we wait until the meshes be thrown around," he warned Bragg, "we may find it hard to break through." If the army could take the offensive it "would thereby as effectively frustrate Rosecrans as you did at Murfreesborough by the same course."[47]

But Bragg insisted on striking the enemy as the Federals emerged from the mountain barrier, while at the same time protecting his own supply line. The railroad was located quite close to the area where the Federals would likely cross the mountains. Historian Peter Cozzens portrays Bragg as in a state of near collapse, exhibiting "nothing less than the frenzied excitement of a man nearing his breaking point." That is not a truly convincing portrayal. Bragg expressed in dispatches to Hill and Cooper, and through his chief of staff Mackall, a calculating and feasible strategy to deal with the enemy approach to Chattanooga. Cozzens does credit Bragg for having the devious idea to send volunteers toward the Federals who acted as deserters in order to feed Rosecrans false information about demoralization in Confederate ranks. This apparently had some effect in making the Yankee commander overconfident.[48]

Despite his poor health and the sorry state of personal relations with his generals, Bragg was ready for a fight. "With our present disposition we are prepared to meet the enemy at any point he may assail," he assured Cooper on September 4. "Should he present an opportunity we shall not fail to strike him."[49]

10

Chickamauga

Rosecrans put together an effective plan for crossing the Tennessee River and approaching Chattanooga. While Thomas L. Crittenden's Twenty-first Corps marched directly toward the city from the northwest, George H. Thomas's Fourteenth Corps moved from the Decherd and Cowan area toward the mouth of Battle Creek to find a crossing twenty miles southwest of Chattanooga. Alexander M. McCook's Twentieth Corps crossed near Stevenson, Alabama, about thirty miles from the city. The Federals started to move on August 16 when Bragg was still at Cherokee Springs.[1]

Bragg's army was not ready for the enemy. It included about 12,000 mounted troops, roughly the same number as Rosecrans, but the Rebel horsemen were poorly positioned to guard the river crossings. Nathan B. Forrest's division was upstream from Chattanooga in East Tennessee and facing no Union advance at all. Joseph Wheeler's division was strung out in driblets all the way from Chattanooga southwest to Gadsden, Alabama. There was no appreciable concentration of Confederate troops at the crossing points Rosecrans intended to use, and Bragg had left only one brigade of infantry in Chattanooga. The rest of the Army of Tennessee was located at various points south of the town. By August 28 the Federals were crossing the Tennessee River and having an easier time of it than Rosecrans expected.[2]

The river proved to be only one natural obstacle to the Union advance. Two massive ridges (called mountains in this part of Appalachia) stood along the border between Alabama and Georgia. Sand Mountain was the first and Lookout Mountain the second, both stretching from northeast to southwest. It was difficult to move columns of infantrymen, artillery, and wagon trains up and down their steep sides. The valley of Wills Creek and Lookout Creek drained the lowland between Sand Mountain and Lookout Mountain. By September 8, Thomas's corps led the way across Lookout by sending James Negley's division over the mountain at Stevens' Gap

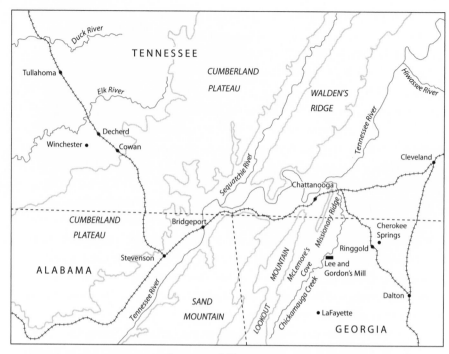

Area around Chattanooga

eighteen miles from Chattanooga. Negley crossed the eminence and entered McLemore's Cove on the east side of the mountain by September 9.[3]

In Bragg's metaphor, the rat had popped its head out of the hole in the wall. For several days Negley occupied McLemore's Cove unsupported and was vulnerable. Bragg began to move. He and his staff left Chattanooga at 8 A.M. on September 8, and the Confederate infantry evacuated the town the next day as Crittenden's command neared the place. The Army of Tennessee took position from Lee and Gordon's Mill about thirteen miles south of Chattanooga and stretched along a general line thirteen miles farther to LaFayette, Georgia. By now Bragg received Simon B. Buckner's 8,000 men from East Tennessee, but Longstreet's two divisions were still moving from Virginia. If Bragg could concentrate overwhelming superiority on Negley's 6,000 troops, he could win a significant victory.[4]

The two divisions closest to Negley were commanded by one good officer and another whose record was mixed. Unfortunately, Bragg felt compelled to rely on the latter to play the primary role in the attack simply because his command was already in a good position to do so. He instructed Thomas C. Hindman to move his division toward McLemore's

Cove from the north, approaching Negley's left flank. Some Confederate cavalrymen were already skirmishing to keep the Federals in place. Bragg then instructed Patrick R. Cleburne to move his division directly toward Negley's front from the east. If all went well, the Confederates would outnumber Negley at least two to one on the morning of September 11.[5]

Problems developed, but Bragg responded to them effectively. Hill informed him that Dug Gap, which Cleburne needed to approach Negley, was filled with trees the Confederates had cut to obstruct Union movement. Bragg therefore ordered Buckner to lead two divisions from Lee and Gordon's Mill behind Hindman and support him as Cleburne's men worked to clear the gap. Buckner caught up with Hindman by 5 P.M. on September 10. Bragg moved his headquarters to LaFayette and ordered two more divisions under W. H. T. Walker to support Cleburne. All told, Negley would be outnumbered six to one, and the Federals still were unaware of approaching danger. Never before had the Army of Tennessee enjoyed such prospects on the field of battle, and it was due to Bragg's conception, planning, and execution.[6]

But then the bitter command relations of the army came into play to wreck this scenario. As soon as Buckner obtained Hindman's ear, he convinced him the entire plan was too dangerous. Hindman had acted with vigor and an aggressive spirit while commanding in Arkansas the previous year, but he was new to the Army of Tennessee and became infected with Buckner's pessimism. Calling a council of officers at 8 P.M. on September 10, Hindman worried that Crittenden could move south from Chattanooga to assault his rear areas. He decided not to attack and sent a suggestion to Bragg that the whole operation be called off.[7]

Hindman sent his suggestion with engineer officer James Nocquet, who reached Bragg's headquarters at LaFayette sometime during the night of September 10–11. A stormy confrontation took place with several officers present. David Urquhart recalled that Nocquet urged Bragg to call off the operation and talked of enemy forces moving "in a particular direction." Bragg did not believe such reports. Taking a map he told Nocquet, "Major, I wish you to tell me nothing but what you know as a fact." The engineer had to admit that it was based only on hearsay. "General Bragg then turned to him and said his information amounted to nothing, and he would not modify his orders to General Hindman." W. T. Martin, whose cavalry division supported Hindman, also was present at the meeting and argued that Nocquet's map was inaccurate. Bragg lost his composure as he told Nocquet and everyone else at the conference that the attack had to proceed.

"I was so greatly vexed," he recalled after the war, "that my deportment . . . was observed by my staff and intimations given me of some harshness."[8]

Bragg retained full confidence in his plan. After all, he had other divisions under Polk positioned near Chattanooga to deal with Crittenden and knew how foolish it was to alter operations on mere rumors. Cleburne had orders to strike when he heard the sound of Hindman's guns and had only to advance three miles from Dug Gap to do so. By now part of Absalom Baird's division reinforced Negley, but the Federals were still badly outnumbered in the region. Both Hindman and Buckner had no faith in Bragg's handling of the affair, even though that handling had been nothing less than brilliant.[9]

Three years later, Martin reminded Bragg what was said at the end of the conference. "You then stated that the three corps of Rosecrans's army were so far separated by distance and mountains as to make a concentration impossible in time to save his army, if he were struck in his centre in the Cove and that you having your army well in hand could hurl the whole of it in succession upon the detached corps of the enemy."[10]

On the morning of September 11, Hindman advanced slowly, allowing one Union regiment to delay his division. He claimed that a dispatch arrived from William Whann Mackall at 11 A.M. that gave him the option of calling off the attack if needed. Later, Hindman claimed to receive another dispatch indicating Federal troops were approaching Dug Gap. He took this opportunity to stop and do nothing, but copies of the dispatches cannot be found today. Not long after, word arrived that the Federals had become aware of their vulnerability and were retiring from McLemore's Cove toward Stevens' Gap. Hindman followed up their retreat with minor skirmishing.[11]

Hindman destroyed one of Bragg's most promising operations. Bragg sent Taylor Beatty to urge the division leader forward on the morning of September 11, but Beatty found him so reluctant to move that it was impossible to push him. "He gave as a reason for not attacking in morning—that discretion was left with him & that his information was of so various a character that he had *vacillated*." Beatty thought Bragg was right in assessing the situation—"the facts show his sagacity." In his report, Hindman listed no less than seven reasons for his failure to strike Negley, none of which he argued were his own fault. Steven Woodworth has correctly noted that Negley began to sniff trouble early enough to extricate his command from the trap, and Hindman's slowness in executing Bragg's orders gave him much-needed time to do so.[12]

Bragg was understandably angry at the turn of events. Martin met him after the failure of this operation and reminded Bragg that "[you were] indignant and excited at what you called the utter disregard of your orders." Martin also was present when Hindman rode up to meet Bragg and recalled that his "greeting was by no means cordial." Bragg narrated the affair in McLemore's Cove with much detail in his official report.[13]

Bragg also found he could not rely on Polk to support his plans. When Crittenden's corps moved south from Chattanooga, Bragg ordered Polk to attack one Federal column moving along Peavine Road at dawn on September 13. Polk hesitated and complained that he did not have enough men to do the job. In the end, no attack took place, and Bragg had to endure a second instance of outright insubordination among key players in his operational plans. Ironically, Polk's attitude toward Bragg brightened a bit during this time period. On September 10 he informed his daughter that "General B['s] health is now very good and he is in good spirits also." But Polk had an almost instinctive fear of taking responsibility for battle on his own hook. He could fight only when directly under the eye of a commander he liked, and there was too much distance between him and Bragg on September 13 to bring about that effect.[14]

The combinations Bragg put together to deal with the Federal crossing of Lookout Mountain were the best of his Civil War career, yet they fizzled just as readily as did several of his other plans. Historians have presented mixed conclusions to explain why this occurred. Stanley Horn not surprisingly placed all the blame on Bragg, arguing the commander issued confusing orders to Hindman at the critical moment of the McLemore's Cove incident. Steven Woodworth largely exonerates Bragg for the failures of early September 1863, squarely placing the blame on Hindman and Polk. Peter Cozzens mostly blames those subordinates as well, but he accepts Hindman's contention that Bragg gave him the discretion to call off the attack at McLemore's Cove. One cannot verify the existence of those orders for no copies have been preserved. Therein lies the only way to saddle the blame for the failure at McLemore's Cove on Bragg. It would have been a mistake to give Hindman discretionary orders, but if Bragg did so, it was only because Hindman himself quailed at the thought of risking an attack. Any commander has to take something like this into account. An assault launched by a subordinate who has no faith in the operation could turn out to be worse than no assault at all. Even if Bragg did issue that discretionary order, it represents a more severe failure of Hindman than of Bragg. Historians such as Thomas Robson Hay have used that discretionary order to slam Bragg as "slow and uncertain." Hay even went so far as to state that if Lee and Jackson had been at McLemore's Cove, Rosecrans's army would have been destroyed.[15]

There is no doubt that Bragg performed well in laying a trap for the head of any column emerging from the height of Lookout Mountain, and he caught Rosecrans at a disadvantage. The failure to achieve anything from that arrangement was attributable to Hindman and Polk. But Bragg can be blamed for helping to create a poisonous atmosphere in the Army of Tennessee due to his ill-advised attempts to manipulate its generals after Stones River. He also should not have given discretionary orders to Hindman (if he did), but even that action is explainable given the situation Bragg found himself in because of Hindman's lack of fortitude.

What would likely have resulted if Hindman had attacked as ordered? There is no doubt that "destroying" Rosecrans's army was a fantasy that could never have happened. Only one and a half divisions of that army were exposed in McLemore's Cove. It is even doubtful that this small contingent could have been destroyed. Most likely, the Confederates would have inflicted heavy losses on Negley, but the majority of the Federals could have retreated up the mountain and taken refuge in Stevens' Gap. Even so, that would have given Bragg's army a much-needed boost in morale and perhaps raised the confidence of the officers in his handling of affairs. If Polk could have stopped Crittenden and other Confederates had stymied McCook's column, Bragg might have penned up the Federals on Lookout Mountain in very difficult terrain with no possibility for foraging. Even a delay of a few days in conditions such as this would have presented enormous problems for Rosecrans and might have altered the nature of the campaign. Military operations rarely turn on a single event; they normally are the result of many small and incremental episodes. But even a limited success at McLemore's Cove could have started a chain of such events that might have imperiled the Army of the Cumberland's ability to survive in the mountainous terrain of northwest Georgia.

Hindman's and Polk's failure to support their general destroyed all these possibilities. The missed opportunities were beginning to wear him down. "Gen. Bragg seems sick and feeble," George W. Brent confided to his journal on September 15. "The responsibilities of the trust weighs heavily upon him." Thomas Connelly and Peter Cozzens recognize that lack of trust in his subordinates lay at the heart of Bragg's problems. "He has responsibilities and care enough to break down a hearty man," W. H. T. Walker told his wife.[16]

In the immediate aftermath of the incident at McLemore's Cove, the Federals were still vulnerable. Rosecrans understood the need to concentrate the army, reporting later that it was "a matter of life and death." He issued the necessary orders, but it took some time for his troops, who were arrayed across a front of forty miles, to execute them. Alexander McCook's corps had the farthest to march and a mix-up of instructions caused him to take the wrong route. As a consequence it was not until September 17, four days after the near-defeat at McLemore's Cove, that Rosecrans's units were within supporting distance of each other with Crittenden holding the left at Lee and Gordon's Mill.[17]

Rosecrans screened his moves with aggressive cavalry skirmishing that led Bragg to take up a defensive position on September 14. This gave the Federals a decisive opportunity to concentrate. Peter Cozzens, however, argues that the fundamental reason for Bragg's defensive-mindedness stemmed from the shock of realizing that he could not count on Hindman or Buckner to execute his directives, and perhaps even more division commanders might be added to the list.[18]

Faced with the prospect of his army losing all responsiveness, Bragg narrowed his tactical plans to ever simpler and limited objectives, but those objectives had to be of an aggressive nature to deal with the threat posed by Rosecrans. On September 15, a council of officers agreed to move toward Chattanooga, and Bragg continued to favor that course the next day. For once Polk offered a sound plan; his corps would hold Federal attention opposite Lee and Gordon's Mill as other units crossed Chickamauga Creek farther to the right and then swung around to crush Rosecrans's left flank. Daniel Harvey Hill later praised Bragg for "superior boldness" in adopting an aggressive plan.[19]

Bragg issued marching orders on September 16 for the following day, but they encompassed only short movements along the line proposed rather than a sweeping and aggressive move to implement the plan. Rather than crossing Chickamauga Creek in force, he intended only to secure the crossings. Moreover, at 3 A.M. on September 17, Bragg suspended the marching orders. He further instructed Polk to keep his command ready to move at a moment's notice and to meet him at his headquarters for further consultation.[20]

The cause of Bragg's hesitancy is unclear. He officially reported that it stemmed from uncertainty as to the exact positions of Rosecrans's units, and that is certainly believable. After all, the Federal army was almost constantly moving during this period. But William Whann Mackall reported that Bragg neared the breaking point of his stamina on September 17. "He asked me to go and examine the condition of his Army that he was not well enough." When Mackall returned to headquarters, word arrived that the Federals had retired. In the wake of this news, "I suggested a movement. He replied shortly & positively it would do no good, & only fatigue his troops. After keeping them in the Sun till past noon he could think of nothing better and then ordered the movement of the morning. It really was then useless."[21]

Mackall, who was fast developing a critical attitude toward his chief, ascribed Bragg's problems to his personal health and lack of decisive thinking. But one wonders how anyone could act confidently with the knowledge that key subordinates were likely to disobey orders and ruin well-laid plans. In any case, Bragg's hesitancy lasted less than a day. He shifted army headquarters from LaFayette to Leet's Tanyard on the afternoon of September 17 and issued orders for several units to cross Chickamauga Creek the next day. Bragg also planned to move army headquarters to Thedford's Ford on September 18.[22]

Events moved more slowly than anticipated on the 18th. Rather than a crushing force, only five Confederate brigades managed to cross Chickamauga Creek in the face of surprisingly stiff resistance by Federal infantry and cavalry. Rosecrans had more opportunity to shift his army northward so that his left and center now confronted the crossing points. There was no option to call off the move; Bragg was committed to a confrontation and arranged for more units to cross the creek and engage the enemy on September 19.[23]

The Confederates were forcing an early collision, but Thomas Robson Hay has suggested that it might have been better for Bragg to wait a while. Only one of Longstreet's divisions was about to join the Army of Tennessee; it was enough to give Bragg a numerical superiority over his opponent. The other division was some few days behind. If Bragg had acted purely on the defensive until that second division arrived, he could have taken on Rosecrans with an even greater advantage in numbers. In Bragg's view, however, there was no time to waste.[24]

Events were pressing Bragg toward the biggest battle of his career, with the fate of the western Confederacy hanging in the balance. Unknown to him, rumors floated around Richmond that he was soon to be replaced. Henry S. Foote, a member of the Confederate House of Representatives from Tennessee, urged Bragg's relief in a letter published in the *Richmond Whig* in late August. Davis received a letter from a citizen named J. Preston

Williams of Eden, Georgia, who informed the Confederate president early in September that he would not permit his son, who was home on leave, to return to Bragg's army. He did not want his offspring to become "a bloody sacrifice to the vain conceit and heinous imbecility of the most incompetent General who ever commanded an Army, unless I may make an exception of Genl Pemberton." Davis coolly passed the letter to the War Department on September 19 as evidence of desertion by the son. On the eve of the battle at Chickamauga, war department clerk John B. Jones seemed convinced that Joseph E. Johnston would soon replace Bragg in command of the Army of Tennessee, "for Bragg is becoming unpopular. But Bragg will fight!"[25]

Elise was aware that her husband was nearing the most severe test of his career, even though she was quite busy with moving from Cherokee Springs near Resaca to a suitable place farther south. The move was prompted by the near approach of the enemy. Elise had stopped for a time at Newnan, Georgia, to be near the railroad but was compelled to move on to Warm Springs near LaGrange by September 8. At Newnan she stayed in "a large uncomfortable dilapidated building, filled with refugees, officers & families, loafers." But Col. John L. Mustian, the proprietor of Warm Springs, took special care of Elise. Born in North Carolina, Mustian had worked as a carpenter's apprentice under the guidance of Bragg's father before making Georgia his home. He provided transportation for Elise to travel from the railroad at LaGrange to his establishment twenty-eight miles away and put her up in a room of his own cottage. She had a servant named Sarah to attend to her wants.[26]

Upon arrival, Elise was stunned to see that Warm Springs was alive with people enjoying rich clothes and plenty of good food. The spa was filled with many refugees from New Orleans and elsewhere, playing billiards, cards, and whiling away their time with dances. "The ladies appear at night in ball or opera costumes, the refugees having saved their fine clothes & jewelry." Elise stayed away from the gaiety but indulged in the hot baths, even though the temperature was quite high. "The water is ninety degrees instead of seventy five as at the Trout Springs," she told her husband. "Salamander as I am, I even shiver at the first plunge. I trust they may benefit me for my hands are still painful & my feet badly swollen." Elise allowed herself a game of ten pins now and then, but mostly concentrated on her health. She proudly reported that her weight had nearly returned to normal after the severe bout with typhoid fever but her hands and feet continued to trouble her. Despite that, "I am *perfectly well*," she assured her husband.[27]

Elise kept abreast of developments as best she could. If reinforcements had reached Bragg earlier, she felt assured he could have saved Chattanooga. She expressed great concern about Bragg's health in a letter dated September 17 in which she recalled the last time she saw him. "You were so feeble, looked so ill, "it was so hard to give you up. You needed all the tender care of a wife—the delicate comforts of a home, & you were so unfit to encounter the stern realities of your present position[.] You are more than human to bear up under them, *if you have*. You remember you told me you must be very ill indeed before you would yield up your present command. I have hardly thought of our army movements, except in connection [with] my restless fears about you." Isolated from the harsh realities facing the Confederacy, Elise continued to worry as her husband maneuvered the Army of Tennessee 150 miles north of Warm Springs toward battle.[28]

After several days of worried movement, the two armies clashed twelve miles south of Chattanooga near Chickamauga Creek. The first day, September 19, witnessed uncoordinated lunges through the tangled vegetation of the field. Heavy fighting and equally heavy losses resulted, but the Confederates were unable to coordinate their strength for a decisive showdown.[29]

Longstreet and his staff reached the Army of Tennessee at 11 P.M. on the night of September 19, and Bragg made a controversial decision to reorganize his army into two wings, placing Polk in charge of the right and Longstreet in command of the left. Historians have debated the wisdom of this move ever since and have wondered why Bragg placed Daniel Harvey Hill under Polk's command. Hill's son later believed Longstreet schemed to have this arrangement made in order to promote his career, but Bragg displayed a consistent distrust of Hill during the subordinate's short tenure with the Army of Tennessee. It must be remembered that Bragg had not requested Hill's assignment; Davis decided to send him to the Army of Tennessee. Even though Bragg held a high opinion of him in the 1840s, Hill had made a nuisance of himself to his superiors while serving in the Army of Northern Virginia early in the war. It is also interesting to note that at McLemore's Cove, Bragg refrained from giving Hill the responsibility of taking charge of the planned attack against Negley even though at least half of the assault force was part of his corps. Hill had not pushed Cleburne forward with much urgency or determination, confirming Bragg's wisdom in not trusting him.[30]

Bragg's plan for September 20 was simple. Polk was to attack "at daydawn" in succession from right to left, and Longstreet was to attack soon after Polk. It would be a general assault but in successive waves rather than simultaneously, and Polk would hit a Federal position strengthened by crude breastworks. Bragg pinpointed no weak spot in the enemy position for special effort. Moreover, Longstreet was a complete stranger to everyone in his wing except the men of Hood's division. He took command only minutes before the planned start of the assault.[31]

The arrangement Bragg made on the night of September 19 was admittedly not ideal, but it did not produce unwarranted confusion in the army's operations the next day. Longstreet assumed command and organized his troops effectively for action. Bragg had every reason at this point to trust Longstreet. He had a sterling reputation for success under Lee's tutelage, and Bragg probably was delighted to have him. With Longstreet there, Bragg hoped to avoid untrustworthy officers such as Hill and even more untrustworthy old hands in the Army of Tennessee.

Ironically, the most serious trouble with the start of the September 20 fighting at Chickamauga came from an old hand and a new but unreliable man. Both Polk and Hill complicated and frustrated Bragg's plans through lack of attention to their duties rather than through a deliberate effort to wreck their commander's timetable.

At 5:30 P.M. on September 19, Polk asked his chief engineer to find a central location for his headquarters. The engineer selected a site near Alexander's Bridge that was half to three quarters of a mile from the structure and 100 yards inside the woods. Polk told Bragg where his headquarters were located, according to the general's son William M. Polk, and rode back to the site near Alexander's Bridge to write attack orders for his division commanders and Hill's Corps. He sent copies of these orders by courier to Cheatham and Walker, but the courier could not find Hill. William Polk admitted his father should have sent a second courier to Hill, but the general reasoned that word would filter through to him somehow. Polk had spoken to two of Hill's staff members regarding the order and had posted sentinels near Alexander's Bridge to guide anyone seeking his headquarters.[32]

But Hill failed to fulfill Polk's expectations. One of his staff officers told him about midnight that his command was now under Polk's orders and that Polk wanted to see him, but Hill felt too exhausted to go immediately. He had been riding from dawn to midnight that day and rested three hours. By the time Hill rode to Alexander's Bridge the sentinels stationed there had left, and Polk had gone to sleep. As a result Hill never consulted with his superior that night.[33]

At 5 A.M. on September 20, Polk learned that no one on his staff had seen or heard of Hill. He dispatched orders directly to Hill's division commanders and prepared to find him himself. Just before leaving, Maj. Pollock Lee of Bragg's staff brought a message asking why the battle had not yet started. Polk went forth to investigate. Meanwhile, Hill found out about Polk's attack orders to his division commanders and wrote a hasty note to his superior explaining that he could not find his headquarters the night before. Moreover, his men were not ready; they needed something to eat before the strenuous work ahead. Hill seemed in no hurry, and nearly everyone later testified that even Polk had not been clear about Bragg's wish to start the fight at dawn that day. Polk accepted everything calmly and passed on word to Bragg's chief of staff that the attack would begin as soon as the men had eaten.[34]

What had happened was bad enough, but Bragg exaggerated the story to make Polk and Hill more culpable. He could hear no sound of firing at dawn so sent Pollock Lee to find out the problem. Lee concocted a wild story: he found Polk two miles behind the line staying at a comfortable house. The general was "sitting in a rocking chair . . . waiting his breakfast, and did not know why the action was not commenced, 'as he had ordered it.'" Bragg told Elise that he had to personally intervene and push both Polk and Hill into attacking by 11 A.M.[35]

It was unfortunate that Lee made up the story about Polk placing more importance on his breakfast than in starting the attack, a story that Bragg readily believed, but the truth was bad enough. Polk let Bragg down in a major way on the night of September 19 and through no deliberate ill-will toward his old enemy. Polk simply was a poor corps commander ill-suited for his important position within the Army of Tennessee.

If anything, Hill deserves more blame than Polk. Exhausted or not, he had no business waiting three hours before consulting with his superior about operations so soon to begin. As Thomas Robson Hay has pointed out, regardless of orders, Hill also deserves censure for not readying his command for action at dawn. It was obvious the battle would recommence as early as possible on September 20, and his divisions were unprepared for it. Hill's problem is difficult to explain. Whether he was sulky because of his "demotion" to Polk's authority, or simply uninterested in his duties, or disgusted with Bragg, it really made no difference. His duty demanded better performance than he gave. Hill spent the rest of his life trying to explain away his shortcomings in this affair by shifting the blame to Polk.[36]

Peter Cozzens believes that "one of the sorriest nights and mornings in the annals of the high command of the Army of Tennessee" took place just before the opening of the second day's battle at Chickamauga. Cozzens thoroughly blames Polk and concludes the general had "no faith in Bragg's plan of battle, [and] was doing his best to subvert it through malignant neglect." Cozzens believes it would have been better for Bragg to divide the army into three wings and give Hill more responsibility because the general sulked at being placed under Polk. Thomas Connelly places the blame for what happened on Bragg and Polk, although Polk was more at fault. Connelly unfairly censures Bragg for not taking a more personal interest in affairs, writing that "something in his personality gave him an unwillingness to become closely involved on the field. His habit of being almost withdrawn from the field seemed more acute at Chickamauga." There is no reason to wonder at this; with a large field army operating in heavily wooded terrain, it was normal for commanders to rely on corps leaders to manage their sector effectively according to the general plan established by army headquarters. Bragg was doing just that, and every other commander of a large field army, even Robert E. Lee, did the same in the Civil War. The problem lay not in being disengaged from events but in the fact that Bragg had unreliable officers in important positions.[37]

Thomas Robson Hay has pointed out another problem Bragg struggled to overcome in the middle of the engagement at Chickamauga. The infusion of new troops and commanders in a short space of time created administrative and logistical problems. Longstreet's men came as fast as possible without their wagon trains or artillery. Bragg had to devise some way to merge them into the administrative structure of the army without the luxury of time. It was necessary for him to reorganize the army on the night of September 19, and it must be pointed out that the true cause of the confusion that started the fight late on the morning of September 20 was Polk's poor administration and Hill's poutiness. Longstreet had far more problems to deal with in assuming his own wing command and did it efficiently. "At no time after about September 1, was Bragg's army tactically cohesive," Hay has written. "It was rather an accretion of miscellaneous forces, all strangers to each other." That is true, but the problems arising from that situation were surmountable by able officers.[38]

Bragg was not entirely blameless for the problems plaguing the Army of Tennessee during the Chickamauga battle. His long-term anger at Polk boiled in the aftermath of the delayed attack on the morning of September 20. "I found Polk after sunrise sitting down reading a newspaper at Alexander's Bridge, two miles from the line of battle, where he ought to have been fighting," Bragg told Hill that morning. He also believed Lee's story about finding Polk at a comfortable house even earlier than that, although there was no foundation for that report. Even as late as 1873, Bragg continued to bandy about the story concerning Polk waiting for his breakfast at a private house well after dawn of that important day. The evidence is overwhelming that Polk did not stay at a house and that he tried his best to rectify the breakdown of communications which he was partly responsible for creating. Cozzens has characterized Lee as a sycophant who fed what he knew would be appetizing fare to his commander.[39]

Historians have generally criticized Bragg's attack plan for September 20 as uninspired, but it was as good as any that could have been devised. Polk was to flank Rosecrans's left in order to drive the Federals from their line of retreat to Chattanooga and into the scrub-timbered wilderness of the area. Breckinridge's Division nearly accomplished that goal. The rest of Polk's wing spent itself in piecemeal attacks that failed to drive the Federals from their breastworks. Polk more than Bragg was responsible for the uncoordinated assaults.[40]

Cozzens also criticizes Bragg for a "lackadaisical approach" to implementing his plan, relying on verbal orders to Polk and counting on the unreliable corps commander to inform Hill of the new arrangement. In Cozzens's view, Bragg's poor health accounts for this less-than-active approach to managing unreliable officers. There is some foundation for criticism such as this. Knowing both men as he did, Bragg would have been well advised to keep closer tabs on them by dispatching a trusted staff officer to help Polk that evening. No one would have been able to locate Hill that night (many men tried), but more effective communication directly with Hill's division commanders would have helped.[41]

If Bragg hoped that newcomer Longstreet would become the reliable subordinate he craved, events soon dispelled that notion. It is true that in many ways Longstreet performed well. Few other commanders had to take charge of half a major field army and prepare it for an important attack with only a few hours to spare. When that attack began about noon, Longstreet cashed in on a huge bit of luck by exploiting a gap inadvertently created in the Union line directly in his path. About one-third of Rosecrans's army collapsed on the field and fled its position. Rosecrans and two of his three corps leaders escaped to Chattanooga along with thousands of their troops. The Army of the Cumberland was saved only because the other refugees made a stand on Snodgrass Hill, where they held out under repeated hammering from Longstreet for the rest of the afternoon. Nevertheless September 20 became a black day in Union military history, and it was accomplished by a combination of troops from the Army of Northern Virginia, along with elements of the Army of Tennessee, guided by a complete stranger to the western Confederates and aided by Dame Fortune.[42]

Longstreet had no reason to distrust or hate Bragg on September 20. But by the time he wrote his memoirs the general accumulated plenty of reasons for both attitudes toward his superior. About 3 P.M. on that day, after the breakthrough and while hammering away at Snodgrass Hill, Bragg sent for Longstreet, who rode to meet the army commander near Jay's Mill. Longstreet suggested that Bragg draw troops from Polk to help him against the outnumbered Federals on the hill. "He was disturbed by the failure of his plan and the severe repulse of his right wing," Longstreet wrote in his memoirs, "and was little prepared to hear suggestions from subordinates for other moves or progressive work. His words, as I recall them, were: 'There is not a man in the right wing who has any fight in him.'" Longstreet was taken aback by this statement but decided not to press the issue. In a postwar letter to Hill, Longstreet went further and argued that it was apparent Bragg believed "the battle was lost, though he did not say so positively." Longstreet further argued in his memoirs that Bragg was disengaged from the flow of events yet claimed the success as his, "failing to mention that other hands were there."[43]

It is quite possible that Longstreet evaluated Bragg's mood correctly at midafternoon on September 20, although it surely was an exaggeration to say that the army commander believed the battle was lost. Bragg's perspective covered the entire field, not just the success enjoyed by Longstreet's left wing. In contrast, Polk's right wing was badly rebuffed with heavy losses. Bragg's efforts to encourage Polk to renew his assaults at midafternoon failed. Bragg was very frustrated with Polk and naturally came to the conclusion that half his army was immobilized for the rest of the battle. That was the true reason why Bragg told Longstreet that he could not expect help. What Longstreet described as Bragg's belief that the battle was lost and his supposed lack of interest in pressing home the advantage on the left were not signs of ill health or depression; they were the natural results of problems transpiring in the army's right wing.[44]

As Bragg left Longstreet after their 3 P.M. meeting, he told his subordinate to communicate with him at Reed's Bridge. Correctly assuming that he was on his own, Longstreet failed to keep in touch with Bragg for the rest of the day. After futilely pounding Snodgrass Hill until dusk, the battle sputtered out with approaching darkness. The Federals evacuated the entire field that evening. "It did not occur to me on the night of the 20th to send Bragg word of our complete success," Longstreet admitted in a post-war letter to Hill. "I thought that the loud huzzas that spread over the field just at dark were a sufficient assurance and notice to any one within five miles of us." This astonishing lack of interest in one of the more important aspects of command—informing your superior of vital developments on the battlefield—kept Bragg in the dark concerning what transpired on the left. An army commander should not have to rely on the sound of his troops cheering to know what was going on in his army.[45]

The sad truth was that all three of Bragg's corps commanders in the Army of Tennessee—Polk, Longstreet, and Hill—were willful, unreliable subordinates who could not be counted on to obey orders or to cooperate with their commander. The Army of Tennessee was at the peak of its strength thus far in the war and had won its biggest tactical victory on a bloody field, and yet its command structure was so fragile that the possibilities of the future—that it could take the strategic offensive in order to reap the full benefits of Chickamauga—would be very difficult if not impossible to meet.

11

Revolt of the Generals

Bragg spent the night of September 20 in woeful ignorance of the tactical situation at Chickamauga. Neither Polk nor Longstreet fed him updates, and the result was that Bragg did not even know the enemy had evacuated the field during the night. He had to assume Rosecrans was still in fighting trim and instructed Polk to advance his skirmishers and see what lay ahead. Thomas Robson Hay blamed Bragg's "absence from the battlefield" and the general's "incredulity at the success of his troops" for the fog in which he operated early on the morning of September 21. But Peter Cozzens has correctly identified the cause as a breakdown of communication between the army commander and his chief subordinates.[1]

After realizing the enemy had evacuated the field, Bragg conferred a bit with Polk and met Longstreet at dawn to ask his advice concerning the next step. The newcomer suggested crossing the Tennessee River north of Chattanooga to turn the Federals out of the city. If that failed, Bragg could send at least part of the Army of Tennessee to recapture Knoxville, which had been evacuated when Buckner shifted his troops to Chattanooga. Ambrose E. Burnside soon after occupied the city and established himself in the heart of East Tennessee.[2]

Longstreet believed Bragg agreed with him and fully expected to see the army move along the suggested line of advance. But as the day wore on, the Confederates conducted short, halting movements aimed at Chattanooga instead of a rapid flanking march. According to James N. Goggin, a staff officer with Lafayette McLaws's Division, Longstreet became frustrated as early as 10:45 that morning. "'General Bragg has changed his mind for some reason or other. I know not what,'" he confided to Goggin.[3]

In truth, Bragg decided to take position opposite the town at least on a temporary basis. Polk received orders to move the right wing at 2 P.M. that day so as to touch the Tennessee River above Chattanooga with his right flank, and Longstreet would move the left wing so as to extend Polk's line to the left. Bragg established his headquarters at a house on the east side of Chickamauga Creek. "Our troops have accomplished great results against largely superior numbers," he telegraphed Samuel Cooper.[4]

Bragg was more open in letters to his wife as he slowly contemplated the significance of his bloody victory. "I trust in God the tide is at last turned in our favor," he told her on September 22. He admitted to Elise that he had suffered more personally during the recent campaign than at any previous time of his career. "My mind and body taxed to the utmost. Thank God, the latter has not failed me, and I feel that my disease is entirely removed."[5]

Bragg had not completely abandoned Longstreet's suggestion to flank the Federals out of Chattanooga, but he also wanted to explore other, less risky options. Further movements brought the army closer to the town that day and onto Missionary Ridge by noon of September 23. Bragg established his headquarters at Nail's House on the ridge. "Our troops are arriving and deploying," he told Cooper that day, "but our policy can only be determined after developing him more fully. He is in very heavy force."[6]

It became increasingly clear that Bragg's conception of the strategic situation that followed Chickamauga differed from that held by Longstreet and other officers. To the generals, it was a smashing victory that opened opportunities to turn the tide of war in the West. To Bragg, it was a middling victory (despite the glowing rhetoric in his message to Cooper) that failed to achieve all that the Confederacy needed, and Bragg's conception was correct.

The results of Chickamauga were far less advantageous for the Rebels than it seemed on the surface. The Army of the Cumberland responded well to its tactical failure on September 20. The stout defense on Snodgrass Hill not only saved the army from a terrible disaster but enabled Rosecrans to occupy Chattanooga. The Federal army was battered and dependent on a tenuous supply line, but holding the city presented a major roadblock to the Confederates. The mountainous terrain and the Tennessee River north and south of Chattanooga severely impeded the movement of a large army. Having to rely on rutted, steep roads and a countryside lacking farms, forage, and food, moving nearly 50,000 men across seventy-five miles of what Bragg considered a mountainous "desert" was a daunting task even for a rested, well-organized command. But Bragg had lost over 18,000 men, and his army suffered from the administrative difficulties associated with infusing additional units into its organization.

In Bragg's view, it would be better to move forward if he could get the Federals out of Chattanooga rather than bypass the city. Given the perspective he held in the days following Chickamauga, it was a legitimate decision. Longstreet claimed that when he asked Bragg why the army was moving toward Chattanooga, the commander told him it would boost public morale if the Confederate army could march through the streets of the contested city rather than move around it. But that story does not ring true.[7]

Bragg frankly told Davis about his situation on September 25. He admitted the need to flank the Federals out of the city but noted two important problems that inhibited his ability to do so. First, he had far too few wagons for such a move. As noted earlier, the new units reinforcing his army before Chickamauga had left their transportation behind. For that matter, Bragg had too few wagons even for the Army of Tennessee before the Chickamauga campaign. This problem severely impeded his mobility.[8]

The second problem involved his generals. "Our greatest evil is *inefficient commanders*," he told Davis. Hindman's and Hill's actions at McLemore's Cove and Polk's delay in starting the attack on September 20 haunted Bragg's thinking. He saw those incidents as golden opportunities thrown away by unreliable subordinates. Bragg concluded that Buckner, Cleburne, and Hood would probably prove to be better corps commanders than the current ones. Buckner's role in convincing Hindman that Bragg's attack plan at McLemore's Cove would fail apparently was not yet known to the army commander.[9]

Pressured by the serious problems associated with an offensive move around Chattanooga, Bragg was further enticed by signs that Rosecrans might be in the process of evacuating the city after all. Such signs became so evident on September 25 that he issued orders for all subordinates to press forward skirmishers at early light the next day to see if it was true. Longstreet contributed to these hopes by informing army headquarters he anticipated a Federal attack on the evening of September 25 to cover the retreat. Even many junior officers in the Army of Tennessee strongly believed that the Yankees would be compelled to give up the city any day due to logistical problems.[10]

But Rosecrans had no intention of leaving, as became evident on the morning of September 26. The patience of the generals now wore thin. Rather than cave in to their desire for action, Bragg opted for a safer, less risky course—finding some way to eject the enemy from Chattanooga. Ever since the Kentucky campaign Bragg had avoided strategic offensives. His limited resources, the fact that the Federals dominated the strategic situation in the West, and the growing distrust he felt toward his chief subordinates contributed to his unwillingness to risk his fragile army in another strike against the enemy. Bragg became defensive-minded by the middle and latter part of 1863. He also lost most of his tactical offensive spirit, which he had demonstrated so sharply at Stones River. Increasingly bad health was a factor in this as well. In many ways, he had burned out as an effective commander by the fall of 1863. He should have resigned long before, but many problems affecting his performance in the days following Chickamauga were beyond his control.

By September 26, the generals tried to reverse Bragg's wait-and-see policy. They were motivated by a desire to seize the opportunity for offensive action before it was too late, and in doing so they directly challenged Bragg's authority. Several officers approached Longstreet and asked him to write Jefferson Davis about the issue. Longstreet did not feel comfortable doing so, but he was willing to write Secretary of War James L. Seddon. Longstreet exaggerated when he characterized Chickamauga as "the most complete victory of the war, except, perhaps, the first Manassas." He then detailed the middling moves since September 20 and castigated Bragg's handling of the situation. "Our chief has done but one thing that he ought to have done since I joined his army. That was to order the attack upon the 20th. All other things that he has done he ought not to have done." In Longstreet's view, the Army of Tennessee was lacking in organization and its ability to move, and he doubted that Bragg could rectify those problems. "When I came here I hoped to find our commander willing and anxious to do all things that would aid us in our great cause, and ready to receive what aid he could get from his subordinates. It seems that I was greatly mistaken. It seems that he cannot adopt and adhere to any plan or course, whether of his own or of some one else." Longstreet suggested that the War Department send Lee to take charge of affairs.[11]

George W. Brent spoke with Polk on September 26, the same day that Longstreet penned his letter to Seddon. The corps commander was "very restive at the delay and inaction of the army, he deemed a rapid movement across the Tennessee proper and stated that Longstreet Hill & Buckner all concurred with him." All believed that "active pursuit would have been better" than waiting for developments outside Chattanooga.[12]

From Bragg's perspective, the idea of mounting an advance was still possible. He informed Elise on September 27 that the railroad bridges at Ringgold had finally been rebuilt and "we can again get supplies, and prepare for a movement. To assault in front would be destructive to my whole army, already badly crippled, and by no means as strong as represented."

But instead of preparing for a major move, Bragg continued to seek ways to pry the enemy out of the city. He ordered Longstreet "to open heavy batteries on the enemy" on September 27, but the next day it became apparent that the Federals were still "in force in Chattanooga," in Brent's words.[13]

As news of the victory filtered through the Confederacy, Bragg received applause from some high-ranking officers. Joseph E. Johnston telegraphed to congratulate him "upon your glorious achievement. The value of your success is inestimable." Lee was impressed by the victory too. "I hope [Bragg] will be able to follow it up, to concentrate his troops and operate on the enemy's rear."[14]

Many of Bragg's own men rejoiced in the victory and gave their general credit for it. Governor Joseph E. Brown visited the Georgia regiments in the Army of Tennessee on September 30 with Bragg in tow. The general "gave them a really stirring speech, very short, but very appropriate, which was loudly cheered," according to an observer.[15]

While dealing with the strategic possibilities that flowed from Chickamauga, Bragg also decided to force a showdown with Leonidas Polk. Ironically, he relied heavily on the Confederate president, who was most responsible for keeping Polk in his position, for help in this effort. "Genl Polk, though gallant and patriotic, is luxurious in his habits, rises late, moves slowly, and always concieves his plans the best," Bragg told Davis. "He has proved an injury to us on every field where I have been associated with him." Bragg was blunt in writing to Elise "I am resolved to bring the matter to an issue this time. One of us must stand or fall .... I am not responsible for it and will not bear it, if Providence will only give me strength to see the issue thro." Bragg saw the delay as critical in Confederate history. Despite the terrible loss of life, Chickamauga was only a partial victory because of the six hours lost by Polk. A "complete success" at Chickamauga would have won Confederate independence, Bragg argued in a letter to his wife, and the missed opportunity weighed "heavily on my mind. I shall say candidly to the President that he must relieve Genl Polk or my self."[16]

Bragg began the showdown with Polk by requiring him to explain the delay in starting the attack on September 20. His first message on September 22 failed to elicit a response, but his second demand on September 28 prompted Polk to reply. He probably felt bold enough to respond because on the same day he had participated in a conference with Hill and Longstreet to discuss Bragg. As noted earlier, Longstreet wrote to Seddon, and Polk agreed to write to Davis about their commander. "He is not the man for the Station he fills," the bishop told his friend. "He has had as I believe

Genl Rosecranz' army twice at his mercy, and has allowed it to escape both times." Polk pleaded with Davis to send Robert E. Lee to the army instead.[17]

When Polk wrote to Bragg on September 28, he cast all blame for the delayed attack on D. H. Hill. Bragg was not satisfied. That day, he instructed Col. J. P. Jones of his staff to deliver orders suspending both Polk and Hindman from their commands. When Brent showed these instructions to David Urquhart, the latter tried to convince Bragg to back down from this confrontation. "I was deeply pained," Urquhart later wrote. Bragg relented for a time but the next morning decided to do it. He "felt that the urgent exactions of discipline made General Polk's arrest absolutely requisite." In Urquhart's view it only worsened the poisonous atmosphere within the Army of Tennessee.[18]

Bragg explained his actions in a telegram to Samuel Cooper on September 29. Davis responded through Cooper that suspending Polk without preferring charges was tantamount to "Punishment without trial." Davis was deeply troubled by this turn of events in his friend's career. "I think it was unfortunate that the evil resulting from delay had not been pointed out to the lieutenant-general to prevent its recurrence, and confidence preserved by abstaining from further action." According to Brent, Polk also asked to be reinstated in his position, but Bragg refused unless the Confederate president directly ordered it. This Davis refused to do. "The case is flagrant," Bragg told Davis, "and but a repetition of the past. . . . My personal feelings have been yielded to what I know to be the public good, and I suffer self-reproach for not having acted earlier."[19]

In Davis's view, whatever joy the nation felt at the costly victory of Chickamauga was squandered by this internal fighting among the men who won the battle. "The opposition to you both in the army and out of it has been a public calamity in so far that it impairs your capacity for usefulness, and I had hoped the great victory which you have recently achieved would tend to harmonize the army and bring to you a more just appreciation of the country." Davis was afraid that pursuing Polk over a relatively small issue would ruin Bragg's opportunity to restore public confidence in his generalship.[20]

But, once set on his course, Bragg could not be deterred. He took part of Davis's advice and prepared charges against Polk. These charges included allegations that Polk failed to ready his command on time to fulfill orders early on September 20 and that he was resting two miles behind the line when he should have been active among his men.[21]

Polk was not idle. He traveled to Atlanta and awaited developments while writing letters to several people about his predicament. "It is a part of that long-cherished purpose to avenge himself on me for the relief and support I have given him in the past," Polk told his wife. In his mind, Bragg wanted a scapegoat for his own troubles. Polk told Davis he had expected to be relieved of his command for two years and thus was not surprised when it happened. He also argued that his actions on the night of September 19–20 were without blame and attacked Bragg as incompetent. "He let down as usual and allowed the fruits of this great but sanguinary victory to pass from him by the most criminal incapacity, for there are positions in which weakness is wickedness." Polk also spread these views in letters written to civilian acquaintances in North Carolina.[22]

Other than a vain attempt to dissuade Bragg from his course, Davis refused to intervene on Polk's behalf. This was the key to Bragg's success in getting rid of the troublesome bishop. The president of the Confederacy would see to it that his friend was let down easily, but Bragg had gambled rightly when he placed his trust in Davis. The reason, once again, lay not in any personal friendship Davis felt toward Bragg, for none existed between the two men at this point, but in Davis's view that no one better than Bragg was available to lead the Army of Tennessee. It is interesting that while Davis held a very high opinion of Polk as a man, he never considered him indispensable as a general. Davis also refused to transfer Lee to the Army of Tennessee but Polk wrote directly to Lee about the matter. "I wish I could be of any service in the west," Lee told Polk late in October, but he was suffering from rheumatism and could "hardly get about."[23]

As a division commander, Hindman was more easily dismissed than Polk. The general had conducted himself with energy at Chickamauga, but Bragg could not ignore the fact that he had been the chief cause of failure at McLemore's Cove. Bragg preferred charges against him and relieved him of command. Hindman immediately wrote to Richmond explaining his version of affairs at the cove and requested a court of inquiry to clear his name. Davis refused to sanction an inquiry, believing if Hindman had explained to Bragg the circumstances, the commander would not have suspended him. Like Polk, Hindman was never brought to trial; Bragg's strategy for the two men was merely to get them out of his army. He preferred charges against Polk and Hindman only because the Richmond authorities had suggested that their removal required it.[24]

Hindman was restored to division command in the Army of Tennessee by April 1864, after Bragg left the army, but he was not satisfied. He demanded from Cooper copies of all documents associated with his relief "to ascertain what action, if any, may be necessary to my complete vindi-cation against the censure passed upon me." The adjutant general's office in Richmond refused to do so. "It would give occasion to counter reports and unending disputation," as Samuel Cooper's assistant put it. Many years after the war, Bragg claimed that Col. P. B. Starke of Mississippi informed him Hindman came to recognize "his great error in this matter, and said he yielded his own judgment and followed the advice of Genl. Buckner, his second in command."[25]

Bragg had to deal with disciplining his generals at the same time that he wrestled with the problem posed by Rosecrans. By October 1, it became clear to Mackall that waiting for the Federals to leave would not work. "In my judgment the day has passed in which we could reap advantage." On that day, Bragg sent Joseph Wheeler's cavalry to raid Rosecrans's fragile supply line, consisting of wagon trains crossing the Cumberland Plateau and entering Chattanooga from the north. The Confederate horsemen destroyed a number of wagons but were chased away by Federal cavalry. It proved impossible to starve the Yankees out of Chattanooga this way. As late as September 29 Bragg informed Davis, "We can only dislodge him by a flank movement and are concentrating all our means," but he continued to pursue both courses of action—flanking and siege-like measures to pry the enemy from the city. He assembled guns to heavily bombard Chattanooga, but Mackall did not see that any "good results" could be accomplished because the Federals were well fortified.[26]

Bragg was befuddled about what to do. None of the options open to him seemed promising of success. "To attack him in front, strongly intrenched as he is, would be suicidal," he told Samuel Cooper on October 3. "To assail any other point requires us to cross the river." He needed more supplies than were currently available to do that. When the railroad link with At-lanta became operable, Bragg hoped he could mount a flanking move soon. "The Department will, I trust, appreciate the embarrassments of an army with inadequate means of transportation; largely and hastily re-enforced without the slightest addition to these means, and just at the time of a very large loss in battle, especially of artillery horses, which makes a drain upon other resources."[27]

Up to the middle of October, Bragg held open the possibility of con-ducting a flanking move around Chattanooga as the best way to reap the fruits of Chickamauga. In the end he decided against the move. In his of-ficial report, the general commented at length upon the reasons. "Such a move was utterly impossible for want of transportation. Nearly half of our army consisted of re-enforcements just before the battle without a wagon or an artillery horse, and nearly, if not quite, a third of the artillery horses on the field had been lost." He had no bridging material and could have crossed the Tennessee River only at a handful of fords, some of which were too deep for his artillery. Any sudden rise in the water level would cut him off from his base at Atlanta.[28]

There was a more important reason that Bragg chose not to bypass Chattanooga. Such a move would have opened up all of northwest Georgia to the Federals. "It abandoned to the enemy our entire line of communication and laid open to him our depots of supplies, while it placed us with a greatly inferior force beyond a difficult and at times impassable river, in a country affording no subsistence to men or animals. It also left open to the enemy, at a distance of only 10 miles, our battle-field, with thousands of our wounded and his own, and all the trophies and supplies we had won. All this was to be risked and given up for what? To gain the enemy's rear and cut him off from his depot of supplies by the route over the mountains, when the very movement abandoned to his unmolested use the better and more practicable route, of half the length, on the south side of the river." Bragg overstated his case when he told Cooper that it "is hardly necessary to say the proposition was not even entertained, whatever may have been the inferences drawn from subsequent movements."[29]

These were valid reasons for deciding not to flank Chattanooga, but of course the stakes were very high; many men could argue they were so high that it was worth taking the risks. But the Army of Tennessee was weighed down by logistical problems and in Bragg's view was incapable of executing a march across the mountains. Its mobility was curtailed so much that Bragg thought it capable only of short moves near its tenuous supply line. The general justified his decision to stay put outside Chattanooga and await events, even if that course of action was less promising than flanking the city.

Many observers could not understand why Bragg waited supinely on the heights outside Chattanooga rather than take the risk of a flank move. "We are still here," William Preston told his nephew. "Another victory and twelve thousand brave men dead & wounded—the result nothing. *All* are discontented. . . . We now lie here rotting before works we dare not attack." Preston had enough and wanted to get away from the Army of Tennessee.[30]

Long after the war, veterans continued to ponder the army's inactivity before Chattanooga. "Why Gen. Bragg did not press forward and reap the fruits of his victory is a matter of wonderment now as it was then," commented a member of Polk's staff. "Calmly we viewed from Missionary Ridge the enemy as they hastily threw up fortifications until securely intrenched as in a second Sevastopol."[31]

Thomas Connelly recognizes that great obstacles stood in the way of a flanking maneuver around Chattanooga. But he also correctly points out that there were equally daunting obstacles to the course of action Bragg adopted. The Army of Tennessee did not have enough men to lay siege to the place. While Bragg opted for the least risky course it also was the course that promised the fewest dividends. Bragg had been burned by the results of the Kentucky campaign, he had lost faith in his subordinates, and his health was far worse in the fall of 1863 than a year before. Another commander in his place might have opted for the flanking movement, but the chances of success were probably well below fifty-fifty given the circumstances.[32]

If one judged by the words of his subordinates, any number of Bragg's men would have been willing to take that risk even at low odds. On October 4 several disgruntled officers agreed to send a petition to Jefferson Davis. The document stated their opinion bluntly. "Whatever may have been accomplished heretofore, it is certain that the fruits of the victory at Chickamauga have now escaped our grasp. The Army of Tennessee, stricken with a complete paralysis, will in a few days' time be thrown strictly on the defensive, and may deem itself fortunate if it escapes from its present position without disaster." The generals admitted that the Federal occupation of Chattanooga was a choke point in any Confederate move, but they insisted that Bragg's wait-and-see policy would fail. The generals wanted reinforcements and the replacement of Bragg, on the basis of his failing health alone. Twelve officers signed the petition, but there is evidence that it was never sent to Davis.[33]

Who took the primary role in drafting this document is unclear. Bragg's headquarters staff assumed it was Buckner, although George Brent thought that Hill was "prominent in this movement." Longstreet argued in his memoirs that Hill admitted his authorship to him, but Hill actually told Longstreet that "Polk suggested it and Lieut. Gen. Buckner wrote it." Many people thought Hill was the author because the petition had been left at his headquarters for others to read and sign. Hill believed for the rest of his life that he had been made a scapegoat, "the cats-paw to rake out chestnuts for others" as he put it. Breckinridge refused to sign the petition because his views of Bragg were already known. John C. Brown, a signee, later argued that "great demoralization prevailed and the general desire was that General Bragg should be . . . superseded by someone else." But only twelve of the sixty-four corps, division, and brigade commanders, less than 19 percent, signed the petition. Upon becoming aware of the document, Bragg telegraphed Davis requesting him to visit the army and investigate.[34]

Davis set out for the Chattanooga area very soon after receiving news of the petition. In Atlanta, he invited Polk to confer with him on the evening of October 8. When Davis requested Polk's version of the affair, the general "gave it to him plainly and simply," he told his daughter. Davis "thought it very unfortunate in every way for the country and the cause, and that he did not see the necessity for the action." Polk, in his own way, took the high road in this sordid controversy with Bragg. "I certainly feel a lofty contempt for his puny effort to inflict injury upon a man who has dry-nursed him for the whole period of his connection with him, and has kept him from ruining the cause of the country by the sacrifice of its armies."[35]

According to William Preston Johnston, Davis greeted every crowd at station stops along the journey from Richmond to Ringgold, shaking hands and giving impromptu speeches. He brought not only Johnston but George Washington Custis Lee, another aide, and John C. Pemberton, the disgraced general who had lost Vicksburg to Grant the previous July. Davis and his party reached Bragg's headquarters on the evening of October 9. William Whann Mackall could not predict what the Southern president would do concerning the petition, but he noted that Bragg seemed "in fine humour" the next day, "evidently thinks he has the Prest. on his side."[36]

The first thing Bragg had to deal with was Pemberton, who desired a command in the Army of Tennessee. Davis believed in him despite the failure of his effort to hold Vicksburg. Given the relief of Polk and the uncertainty concerning Hill, it was logical for the Confederate president to think of giving him a corps under Bragg. But Pemberton was sensitive about public reaction to his campaign in Mississippi. "You are aware of the prejudice which has been arrayed against him," Samuel Cooper told Bragg, as he assured him that Davis retained complete trust in the unfortunate general.[37]

Bragg also thought Pemberton was "as true & gallant as any man in our service," but he was too keenly aware of how public opinion could impair a commander's usefulness. Bragg consulted several division and brigade commanders, and all of them gave assurances that their men would never accept Pemberton. When Bragg conveyed these views, Pemberton quietly withdrew from consideration. Demonstrating his commitment to the cause, even though born in the North, Pemberton later gave up his commission as lieutenant general and accepted the rank of lieutenant colonel. He offered useful service as an artillery officer in Virginia during the 1864–65 campaigns.[38]

Davis began the main work of his visit on October 10, holding a conference with Bragg and the generals nearly all day. According to Longstreet, Davis favored placing him in command of the Army of Tennessee. He further stated that this had been the plan ever since he had been sent to Tennessee. But by now Davis admitted that "the time had passed" for that option. Longstreet was not too keen on it by then either, perhaps because the army was not in a good condition to do anything other than wait outside Chattanooga. When Longstreet suggested that Joseph E. Johnston replace Bragg, the president of the Confederacy reacted coldly to the idea. When Longstreet offered to resign, Davis would not hear of it. None of this is supported by evidence coming from anyone else who participated in the talks that day.[39]

We know that the most famous moment of the conference on October 10 was an open expression of opinions about Bragg. Davis invited the officers to speak generally on "military conditions & future operations," and then opened the discussion to "other suggestions." Longstreet took the opportunity to urge the removal of Bragg. He was followed by several other generals who supported the idea. Buckner and Cheatham spoke up as did Cleburne. Not a single voice was raised on Bragg's behalf in this unusual moment in Civil War history. "My memory is that nothing was unkindly said by any one or received in unkind spirit by Genl Bragg," Davis recalled more than a month later. In fact, Buckner remembered that Bragg said nothing. "He seemed to be a little confused." Davis "received these suggestions perfectly cool and collected," probably because they were expressed "very frankly and freely, and without any temper whatever."[40]

According to Longstreet, Davis held another conference on October 12 or 13 in which the discussion centered on what the Army of Tennessee should do next. Bragg proposed crossing the river above Chattanooga, while Longstreet suggested crossing downstream. No other participant offered a plan, but no one supported either proposal already made. Davis consulted maps that were laid out on the table and finally agreed with Longstreet's plan, but of course no move was ordered. Whether any of this actually was discussed is questionable as no one other than Longstreet reported it.[41]

The Rebel president did show himself to the troops. The band of the 1st Tennessee serenaded Davis on the evening of October 12, and he returned the compliment with a speech praising the Tennessee men of the army. Bragg was called upon to speak. "He praised Tenn. Soldiers & citizens," reported Edwin Hansford Rennolds Sr., who witnessed the impromptu ceremony. Bragg "hoped soon to redeem the State and claim the call as a proof of the soldier trust in their leaders."[42]

By October 11, it seemed to George Brent that Davis would probably keep Bragg in command of the army. Davis made clear his views when he offered a speech to the Army of Tennessee atop Missionary Ridge. A reporter for the *Memphis Appeal* noted that the Southern president "complimented Gen. Bragg in the highest terms, and said that notwithstanding the shafts of malice that have been hurled against him, he has bravely borne it all, and the bloody field at Chickamauga plainly stamps him as a military commander of the first order."[43]

The arrival of Armand N. T. Beauregard, Pierre G. T. Beauregard's brother, offered Bragg a welcome chance to talk to a friend. Armand reached the Army of Tennessee at the same time as Davis's visit. His purpose was to consult with Bragg on one of his brother's many strategic plans for an offensive in the West. Rather than discuss those plans, Bragg talked with Armand about his many problems. He pined for the mutually supportive relationship he had enjoyed with Pierre in 1862. Bragg admitted he was becoming depressed and was afraid "that the load was getting too heavy for his shoulders." Despite many efforts to engineer victory, "the best matured plans had been frustrated from the want of united action on the part of those who had been called upon to execute them." Bragg knew his subordinates did not like him personally; those feelings had resulted in defeat or fruitless victories, "so much so, that he was becoming dejected and nearly despondent."[44]

Polk and Hill emerged as the chief sources of Bragg's problems. Beginning with Shiloh, Polk "had invariably delayed operations by modifying instructions given him and executing them too late," Armand told Pierre. Both Polk and Hill had muffed Bragg's chance to destroy Rosecrans's army on September 20.[45]

As for his career, Bragg told Armand he was ready, even anxious, to give up his demanding job. Davis talked him into staying, however, and Bragg felt compelled to honor his commander in chief's request. But if he was to retain the command, Bragg meant to do so with firmness. He "would never countenance disobedience of or non-compliance with orders from any officer, however high in position, regardless of consequences."[46]

Armand's letter revealed much about Bragg's mood during Davis's visit.

The general had responded well to Pierre's strategic plan for massing troops and invading Kentucky. Bragg told Armand he had attempted it with too few men in 1862 "and had always kept it in view to act on whenever the opportunity would present itself." Bragg was "convinced more than ever that it was and is the only plan which can save the Confederacy." The question really lay in the condition of the Army of Tennessee and whether trustworthy officers could be found to lead its corps and divisions. Tellingly, Bragg expressed no willingness to personally lead such an expedition.[47]

Bragg was so frank and confiding with Armand Beauregard because he had no one to talk to in the Army of Tennessee. A sense of isolation and friendlessness intensified his stubbornness, gloomy outlook, and poor health. The one person who understood and supported him was Elise, and his thoughts were of her comfort. "I have telegraphed you twice, to ease your mind," he told her on September 22. "Be cheerful and resolute. Act for yourself in all things. I cannot even advise situated as we are. My means are ample yet for all your expenses. Believe in the devotion of your Husband."[48]

Elise kept herself informed of events, but she also had to deal with her fragile health. "I was sick in bed the week of the fight," she told her husband. "It depressed me a good deal." A young doctor "gave me a good dose of *Calomel*, followed by Morphine, & the consequence is I am badly salivated." In fact, her mouth became so sore she could only consume soup and liquids.[49]

But Elise understood Braxton's situation following the bloody victory at Chickamauga. She hoped the ever fickle public would rejoice over the battlefield success of September 20. "Poor Confederates, they have had so much bad news to swallow, no wonder they get drunk now on what we hope, is at least a happy omen, 'that the tide has turned.'" But Elise feared that "our victory is like all we are ever permitted to gain, *undecisive* & with a fearful loss of men. We have the glory[,] some prisoners & cannon—Rosecrans still holds the points *he* aimed at, Chattanooga, East Tennessee, Cumberland Gap." Elise completely understood that "to *get him out of Chattanooga* without a Second Gettysburgh affair is a question not easily settled."[50]

Elise identified the fundamental problem facing the Army of Tennessee, how to eliminate the roadblock posed by Union occupation of Chattanooga. All solutions to the problem were laden with difficulties, and neither Bragg, the generals, nor their president could agree on a promising solution. Davis left Missionary Ridge on October 14 and took a roundabout journey to Richmond. Along the way he assured the public that Bragg was the man for his position, calling him "brave and able" while stopping in Selma, Alabama. Privately, Davis could be more frank. In writing to Hardee he said he was keenly aware that "there is a want . . . of that harmony among the highest officers which is essential to success." He implemented a suggestion of Bragg that Hardee be exchanged for Polk, ordering the former to leave his post in Mississippi as soon as possible. When St. John R. Liddell spoke with Davis during his visit to the army and suggested he issue an order to keep the generals in line, Davis reacted with feeling. "'No,' said he, 'there is something more needed, that orders will not reach. It is zealous, unreserved cooperation with the Commander.'"[51]

Of course, Davis did not know how to encourage the officers to offer that kind of cooperation, but he remained firm in his support of Bragg. "My conclusion was that more would be lost than gained by any change of commander." Davis felt it was more expedient to separate Polk and eventually Hill from the army as the best course of action. He continued to feel that way for the rest of his life, expressing those views in postwar letters. When writing his history of the Confederate government, Davis did not mention his visit to the Army of Tennessee but strongly supported Bragg's explanations for why it was impossible to take the offensive after Chickamauga.[52]

With the president of the Confederacy firmly behind him, and driven by his near obsession with discipline, Bragg moved against Hill after Davis returned to Richmond in October. His opinion of the man had changed dramatically since their days together in the 1840s. Bragg told Davis that Hill was "despondent, dull, slow, and tho' gallant personally, is always in a state of apprehension." Bragg went farther and concluded that Hill's "open and constant croaking would demoralize any command in the world." Several months later, Bragg commented further on Hill when the latter continued to press his grievances to the president. "From the moment he arrived he proved a sensationalist, and a cancer. He caused the failure at McLemore's Cove, by neglecting to obey orders."[53]

Bragg requested permission to remove Hill on October 11, and Davis gave it two days later. The order was issued, and Hill received it on October 15. Unlike Polk, who left quietly for Atlanta, Hill forced a confrontation with Bragg. Archer Anderson, his staff member, was a witness to the scene. Hill demanded to know why he was being relieved. According to James W. Ratchford, who heard it secondhand from Anderson, Bragg "finally admitted that he had no reason for complaint against General Hill except that Hill did not have the proper confidence in his commanding officer (Bragg)." Hill accepted this but insisted that Bragg write it out for the record. Bragg initially agreed to do so but then hesitated to send the statement to Hill's headquarters. When Hill sent Ratchford the next day to pick it up, Brent told him the commanding general had reconsidered. "General Bragg desires me to say that he does not think it prudent or necessary to give General Hill such a statement as he refers to."[54]

Hill's brief tenure with the Army of Tennessee had been inglorious, and it was all due to his personal shortcomings. Alexander Mendoza has correctly concluded that "Hill failed to take his responsibility as a corps commander in Bragg's army seriously, putting personal biases and animosity ahead of his duties. . . . Hill's comportment in Tennessee and northern Georgia was simply deplorable." When Hill issued his farewell to the corps, Capt. Daniel Coleman of the 15th Mississippi Battalion Sharpshooters made a pointed note in his diary. "It causes minimal regret."[55]

Trouble between Bragg and Buckner also loomed in the wake of Davis's visit. Buckner had always harbored reservations about Bragg's handling of the Kentucky campaign, but the real conflict between the two erupted over an administrative issue. Buckner's Department of East Tennessee had been merged with Bragg's Department of Tennessee in mid-July 1863, and Buckner took most of his men to reinforce Bragg in early September, yet for some reason Buckner assumed he retained administrative control over the parts of his department still in Confederate hands. In addition, Buckner was demoted from corps to division command in the Army of Tennessee, and William Preston went from division to brigade command. Bragg meant to diminish what was left of the Kentucky clique in his army.[56]

Buckner went on the offensive, complaining "in bold terms of the injustice which has been done him." Bragg refused to accept the dispatch. He returned it to Buckner "as unfit to place on file in this office." But Buckner penned a second dispatch on October 24 demanding an explanation of what happened to his department. When Bragg shared these messages with Davis, the Confederate president was greatly embarrassed by Buckner's tone and explained why the general was wrong to act this way. Bragg passed on a copy of the president's letter and hoped Buckner would "calmly review his course and withdraw it." But Buckner replied with a third letter, finally getting everything out of his system. He blamed the fact that he favored a new commander for the army (and told Bragg so) as the chief cause of his superior's persecution. Buckner ended by requesting to be relieved of his division command. Bragg informed Davis of this letter and

SIMON B. BUCKNER. A member of the troublesome Kentucky clique in the Army of Tennessee, Buckner initially tried to soothe Bragg's anger at Polk's disobedience of orders during the Kentucky campaign. He then turned into a vocal critic of Bragg, to a large degree because his Department of East Tennessee was merged into Bragg's Department of Tennessee. Buckner played a key role in derailing Bragg's promising plan to smash the Federals at McLemore's Cove and retained a critical attitude toward his former commander for the rest of his long life. (Library of Congress, LC-DIG-cwpb-07431)

told his staff that he suspected Buckner was angling for his own position as head of the army.[57]

Another confrontation with a subordinate developed in October. Nathan Bedford Forrest had been ordered to Bragg's army in the summer of 1863 and placed in command of a division. He had, with Joseph Wheeler, been unable to provide timely information about Rosecrans's movements, contributing to Bragg's problems. Forrest seemed more interested in getting back to an independent command in West Tennessee than in doing his duties. On August 9, he told Samuel Cooper of a plan to give up his division under Bragg and organize a small force designed to harass Northern steamboat traffic on the Mississippi River. Forrest believed he could accomplish more good in this way than in his current position. At this point, Bragg still relied on Forrest and claimed he could not spare him. Davis was willing to let Forrest have his way but deferred to Bragg's judgment for the time being. When Forrest realized Bragg was reluctant to let him go, he sent a copy of his proposal directly to Davis. The Rebel president, however, continued to defer to Bragg's judgment.[58]

Forrest served Bragg poorly after Chickamauga as well. The commander wanted to use his mounted arm to cut the Union supply line into Chattanooga, but he also had to contend with a move by Burnside's cavalry

NATHAN BEDFORD FORREST. Bragg's only period of working with Forrest, during the Chickamauga campaign and early in the confrontation at Chattanooga, was a failure. Bragg accurately characterized Forrest as an independent raider unsuited to commanding cavalry forces that closely cooperated with a large field army. Moreover, there is every reason to doubt the veracity of stories that Forrest personally insulted Bragg and told him he would refuse to obey any of his orders. (Library of Congress, LC-DIG-ppmscd-00082)

from Knoxville early in September. He ordered Forrest to leave a brigade to cover the army's right flank on September 25 and take the rest of his division to Cleveland, Tennessee. When Forrest exceeded his orders by pushing Burnside's cavalry north of Cleveland, Bragg became angry. Striking Rosecrans's supply line was more important, so he ordered Forrest to detach most of his division to Wheeler. Bragg knew Wheeler could be counted on to obey orders. Moreover, Wheeler had done very well in destroying Rosecrans's wagon trains at Stones River. His decision to favor Wheeler instead of Forrest was fully justified.[59]

But Forrest did not see things this way. Despite the fact that he was willing to give up his command in order to go west, the general reacted bitterly toward Bragg's order to give Wheeler most of his men. Army headquarters received a "strong protest" from Forrest on September 26. Two days later, Bragg reiterated the order before Forrest finally complied. Forrest hated Wheeler because of a disastrous decision by the latter to attack Union works at Dover, Tennessee, the previous February, which resulted in heavy losses. At that time Wheeler outranked Forrest and temporarily commanded their combined forces. Forrest meant to speak with Bragg personally about his views.[60]

By this time Bragg had enough of his erratic cavalry general. "Look at

Forrest!" he told St. John R. Liddell. "The man is ignorant and does not know anything of *cooperation*. He is nothing more than a good raider."[61]

Forrest also knew nothing about decorum and respect for rank. According to a story started by his chief surgeon, Dr. J. B. Cowan, the general's meeting with Bragg produced a stormy confrontation. Cowan accompanied Forrest and thus was a witness to the meeting. Although Bragg extended his hand, Forrest refused to shake it. He heatedly accused Bragg of persecuting him ever since the battle of Shiloh, compelled him to give up his command in Kentucky, and sent his second brigade to West Tennessee with inadequate arms. Now he was being forced to give up that second brigade to Wheeler, according to Cowan.[62]

"You have played the part of a damn scoundrel, and are a coward," Forrest told his superior officer, "and if you were any part of a man, I would slap your jaws and force you to resent it. You may as well not issue any more orders to me, for I will not obey them, and I will hold you personally responsible for any further indignities you endeavor to inflict upon me." Forrest went further and stated, "if you ever again try to interfere with me or cross my path it will be at the peril of your life." At that, Forrest stormed out of Bragg's presence.[63]

This is one of the most incredible stories to emerge from the Civil War, yet most contemporaries and historians have accepted it as fact. The incident appeared in John Wyeth's *Life of General Nathan Bedford Forrest* in 1899 (later reprinted as *That Devil Forrest*) and in John Harvey Mathes's *General Forrest* in 1902. John Watson Morton, one of Forrest's artillery officers, related the story in a book published in 1909. "The general consensus of opinion of those who knew both men [is] that the facts are about as here set down," he commented. When Maj. M. H. Clift asked Forrest after the war about the incident, Forrest "told him the facts were about as he had heard"—that Surgeon Cowan's story was essentially accurate. Andrew Lytle, in his pro-Forrest book published in 1931, firmly believes the story. Brian Steel Wills, Forrest's biographer, accepts it but adds a quote by a friend of the general. "The truth may as well be told—he was unfit to serve under a superior." Paul Ashdown and Edward Caudill, authors of a study of myths surrounding Forrest, do not question the validity of Cowan's story. Even the pro-Bragg biographer Samuel Martin accepts it as fact.[64]

But two other historians question Cowan's veracity. Judith Lee Hallock points out that the story only surfaced years after the war and Cowan is literally the sole authority for it. More recently, David A. Powell thoroughly examined the evidence and concluded that the incident did not happen.

Even Morton hesitated a bit, making a point of stating that other men who knew Forrest thought it was consistent with his personality.[65]

The details as set forth in Morton's book do not coincide with the sequence of events in other sources. He placed the stormy confrontation on September 30 and stated that Davis was with Bragg at the time. Actually Davis had not yet arrived, and there is no indication in Brent's journal that Forrest met Bragg that day. Brent does indicate that the cavalry general visited army headquarters on October 20. "Forrest is here and is much dissatisfied. Troubles are brewing in the command." If Forrest had insulted Bragg as Cowan asserts, one wonders why Brent did not write about it. Brent kept a careful record of Buckner's heated dispatches and many other signs of discontent from Bragg's generals. Such an occurrence as this incident, with its deeply personal and insubordinate tone, should have raised a response from Brent.[66]

It is also unusual for Bragg to have ignored the incident. His insistence on discipline, his readiness to enlist the aid of the president to enforce it, and his stubborn reaction to opposition were evident in far less serious incidents than the one Cowan claims to have taken place. It is inconceivable that Bragg would have completely ignored it. There is every possibility that Forrest expressed himself heatedly in his conversation with Bragg, and just as conceivable that Cowan embellished the story decades later. Forrest's vague assertion that "the facts were about as [Clift] had heard," seems to be another exaggeration, or a bit of postwar mythmaking on his part.[67]

Another telling problem with Cowan's story is that Forrest recited a long history of persecution by Bragg which makes no sense. One cannot understand what he meant by Bragg taking his first command away from him. As far as taking his current command away, Forrest had willingly offered to give it up two months before in favor of his plan to go to West Tennessee and raise new troops. Even more ironically, Bragg had already decided a week earlier, on October 13, to give Forrest permission to do so. As Bragg wryly put it, he could now grant permission "without injury to the public interests in this quarter." It is inconceivable that Bragg failed to tell Forrest about this in their meeting a week later. Davis endorsed Bragg's recommendation and authorized Forrest to go west on October 29. Forrest's friends and admirers portrayed the process differently. They argued that Forrest bypassed Bragg and interceded with Davis to obtain permission to leave, ignoring the fact that Bragg was responsible for it.[68]

George Brent mourned the loss of Forrest to the army. He recognized the man's troublesome nature but still thought him the best cavalry leader in the army. Bragg thoroughly disagreed. "General Forrest's requests are all granted," he told Davis on October 30, "and he has started for his new field apparently well satisfied." Bragg did well to eject the troublesome Forrest, who was out of his league as a cavalry leader cooperating closely with other elements of a major field army.[69]

Ironically, Bragg latched onto another outsider temporarily attached to the Army of Tennessee. John Bell Hood boasted a sterling record as a division commander in Lee's Army of Northern Virginia before ordered west with his men. He survived a shell wound on the second day at Gettysburg that lost him the use of an arm but reached Bragg's army in time for Chickamauga. Hood recalled in his memoirs riding to report at Army of Tennessee headquarters on the night of September 19 and being struck by the fact that no one "spoke in a sanguine tone regarding the result of the battle." Early the next morning, Longstreet proved to be "the first general I had met since my arrival who talked of victory." A minie ball so severely injured Hood's leg on September 20 that it was amputated very close to the body. A long period of recovery was in order.[70]

Despite the double injury, Bragg saw Hood as a vibrant and optimistic officer. He recommended Hood to take over Hill's Corps when recovered. "He is a true soldier," Bragg wrote of Hood, "and will cordially sustain me." Davis shared Bragg's high opinion of the injured man, promising to promote Hood to lieutenant general. Breckinridge could lead Hill's Corps until Hood was ready to take the field again. Bragg called the injured man a "model soldier[,] an inspiring leader. . . . That his valuable life should be spared to us is . . . a source for thankfulness and gratitude." Bragg was so desperate for good division and corps leaders that he overreached in his estimate of Hood. He was eager to see fresh blood infused into the poisonous atmosphere of the Army of Tennessee—fresh blood he could count on to support his tenure as its commander.[71]

Bragg would have to wait a long while before Hood was able to assume his new duties. Meanwhile, old hands in the Army of Tennessee drifted off. Chief of staff William Whann Mackall's letters to his wife offer much insight into Bragg the man and the commander. He told his chief that it would be counterproductive to move against Polk and Hindman, but Bragg felt he had enough clout after the victory at Chickamauga to make it work. "He is as much influenced by his enemies as by his friends, and does not know how to control the one or preserve the other," Mackall concluded. When news of the October 4 petition reached army headquarters, it "gave B. much distress, & mortification. I do believe he thought himself popular." Only when Davis arrived did Bragg become confident again, but Mackall continued to worry. Bragg seemed "as blind as a bat to the circumstances surrounding" him. "He ought not to command this army unless his enemies are taken away, for he is vindictive and cannot do justice."[72]

Mackall accurately judged important aspects of Bragg's character and personality, yet, like Davis, he saw no one better suited for the job. If Longstreet were to replace him, the army would say "we don't know him and we know that Bragg is careful of us, don't fight unless he has a good chance & he has never been beaten exactly and . . . has beaten Ros. badly." Mackall worried that none of Bragg's officers seemed to be content and frankly told his wife that "I am afraid of his Generalship & would think the cause of the country far better placed in other hands," if those better hands could be found. "He has not genius," Mackall concluded, "he will fail in our hour of need. . . . His mind is not fertile, nor is his judgement good." Bragg seemed less willing to listen to the advice of his staff members after Davis's visit. There seemed little point in staying, so Mackall requested transfer to Mississippi. It was granted on October 16.[73]

Hardee arrived from Mississippi in October to take over Polk's Corps, while Breckinridge continued to lead Hardee's Corps in place of Hill. Bragg shifted some brigades and divisions about in order to break up the troublesome Kentucky clique. But the Army of Tennessee failed to maintain its "siege" of Chattanooga after Ulysses S. Grant arrived to take charge of Federal operations. He replaced Rosecrans with George H. Thomas and authorized a plan to open a new supply route into the city. Longstreet was responsible for the area around Lookout Mountain, southwest of Chattanooga, but he had few troops to cover it adequately. The Federals wanted to secure roads that ran within striking distance of the mountain and move supplies more directly to Thomas's men, who had been on short rations for a long time.[74]

Federal troops began to create the Cracker Line on the night of October 26–27 and took the Confederates by surprise. They met scant resistance and established the line without much trouble. Longstreet failed to inform Bragg what happened, compelling the army leader to send a staff officer to find out the cause of the scattered firing. Bragg understandably was angry at Longstreet's failure to impede the enemy or even to keep him informed of events on the left flank.[75]

Bragg tried to goad his subordinate into snipping the new supply line. His order for an attack on October 27 resulted in no action. By the end of the day, Bragg repeated the order and urged Longstreet to use his entire

JAMES LONGSTREET. A controversial general, he came with two divisions from the Army of Northern Virginia to help Bragg win at Chickamauga and then became a major figure in opposition to Bragg's authority after the battle. The revolt of the generals fizzled, Longstreet utterly failed to prevent the Federals from opening a secure supply line into Chattanooga, and Davis suggested he be sent north to attempt the capture of Knoxville. Bragg heartily approved. (Library of Congress, LC-DIG-cwpbh-04697)

command in the effort on October 28. On the morning of that day, Bragg still heard no firing. He rode to the top of Lookout Mountain and found Longstreet apparently uninterested in doing anything. Bragg was able to talk his subordinate into making an effort that night. Longstreet wanted only to use one brigade but in the end agreed to use two. When the attack took place under cover of darkness, it resulted in some heavy fighting. But in the battle of Wauhatchie, as it came to be known, the Federals held their position and saved the Cracker Line. The Confederates did nothing more to meddle with the new supply route except deliver long-range artillery fire from Lookout Mountain.[76]

George Brent correctly reasoned that failure to stop the Cracker Line meant the tenuous siege of the city was now over. When Bragg met St. John Liddell soon after, he was "very incensed" and "complained with bitterness of Longstreet's inactivity and lack of ability, asserting him to be greatly overrated." Bragg blasted his subordinate in a dispatch sent to Jefferson Davis, who responded, "Such disobedience of orders and disastrous failure as you describe cannot consistently be overlooked." Finally Davis was beginning to realize just how serious were the personnel problems in the Army of Tennessee. He had hoped that his support of Bragg would engender a spirit of cooperation within the army, but that obviously had failed.[77]

Longstreet became almost useless to the Army of Tennessee, and Bragg was determined to get rid of him. On October 29, he telegraphed Davis asking him to come once again to the army for a personal conference. "He means to demand the removal of certain officers, or ask to be relieved," Brent noted. Davis did not want to make the situation worse by removing more generals. "My recollections of my military life do not enable me to regard as necessary that there should be kind personal relations between officers to secure their effective co-operation in all which is official," the Confederate president wrote. Davis relied on Bragg "to combat the difficulties arising from the disappointment or the discontent of officers by such gentle means as may turn them aside."[78]

Bragg seemed incapable of "gentle means" in dealing with recalcitrant officers, and the rebellious mood among them was so deep that it was well past mending. George Brent knew the situation had already gone too far. Bragg should have insisted on resigning as head of the army long ago because now it was impossible for him "to suppress the jealousies & discontents which exist."[79]

To Davis's credit, Bragg's telegram explaining Longstreet's dereliction of duty concerning the Cracker Line changed his mind a bit. He still did not want to relieve him of command but suggested a previous idea to send Longstreet away from the Army of Tennessee in an effort to seize Knoxville from Burnside. "This will be a great relief to me," Bragg admitted to the Rebel president on October 31. Longstreet received his orders on November 4. On the surface it made little sense for Bragg to decrease his troop strength outside Chattanooga. The Federals had already shifted two corps from the Army of the Potomac, which now were holding Thomas's supply line from Chattanooga to Nashville. The equivalent of two more corps was on its way from the Army of the Tennessee in Mississippi under William T. Sherman, but the troops had to march overland from near Memphis. The dispatch of Longstreet to Knoxville made sense only if he could defeat Burnside before the Federals took refuge behind fortifications in the city and then return to Bragg before Sherman reached Grant. Such a victory would boost morale and reopen the heart of East Tennessee to the Confederates.[80]

Longstreet warned Bragg that his 12,000 men were inadequate to do the job quickly before Grant moved against the Army of Tennessee. "His sardonic smile seemed to say that I knew little of his army or of himself in assuming such a possibility," Longstreet recalled after the war. "So confident was he of his position that I ventured to ask that my column should be increased" to 20,000 men, but Bragg declined to do so. Longstreet put the worst spin on his relations with Bragg during this period, portraying him as deliberately withholding troops, proper guides, or maps. Shifting his corps by rail to Sweetwater proved troublesome as the overtaxed railroad could barely handle the traffic. "It began to look more like a campaign against Longstreet than against Burnside," he commented in his memoirs. But Bragg had no good maps or guides and had given Longstreet authority to control the railroad on his own. Soon after the start of the Knoxville campaign, Bragg dispatched several brigades to help Longstreet make short work of his task. He cooperated fully with his subordinate.[81]

The Knoxville campaign was not initiated solely to get Longstreet out of Bragg's hair. It was based on valid military objectives that could be profitable only if Longstreet succeeded quickly. If Burnside avoided disaster and retired to the city, he could prolong the campaign indefinitely, separating Longstreet from the Army of Tennessee, which soon would be heavily outnumbered. Longstreet set out from Sweetwater on November 13 but failed to defeat the Federals before they retired to Knoxville. He could do little more than try to find a weak spot in the fortifications protecting the city, drawing the Knoxville campaign out in ways that benefited the Federals more than the Confederates. It was therefore easy for many Southern observers to conclude that the Knoxville campaign was a mistake and Bragg was to blame for it.[82]

Faulty or not, the Knoxville campaign removed the last important dissident from the army. By early November, Bragg had "won" his struggle against the generals but at a high cost. Importantly, he wanted to increase the efficiency of the army rather than ruin anyone's career. When Davis consented to his suggestion, exchanging Hardee for Polk and dropping charges against the latter, Bragg was quite happy. He urged that Hindman be treated leniently as well, admitting the officer had performed good service at Chickamauga. "Nothing but the necessity for uniform discipline prevented my overlooking the previous affair for which he was suspended." Hindman "possesses my fullest confidence as a most gallant soldier and excellent disciplinarian." Davis was encouraged by such words and ordered Hindman back to the Army of Tennessee, but the assignment took place after the battle of Chattanooga and Bragg's resignation.[83]

Hill refused to take his relief from command quietly. In mid-November, he requested a court of inquiry into the events transpiring on the night of September 19. Samuel Cooper refused to grant it. An inquiry would become "an investigation into the conduct of the general who gave the order, and not into the conduct of the officers who received the order." As Cooper explained, he was "simply relieved from duty at the request of the commanding general," which did not constitute grounds for an investigation. Bragg was content merely to separate Hill from the Army of Tennessee. Davis admitted that he had foisted Hill on Bragg without the latter's request and thus felt compelled to support Bragg's efforts to get rid of him. The Southern president continued to value Hill's services and used him in various commands in the East for the rest of the war.[84]

The revolt was over, but there were still generals deeply dissatisfied with Bragg. Benjamin Cheatham harbored a grudge against him ever since Stones River. He had spoken out against Bragg in the October 10 meeting on Missionary Ridge and asked to be relieved on November 1. No one acted on that request. Cheatham then sought the help of Andrew Ewing, former member of the U.S. House of Representatives from Tennessee and a judge in the Confederate military justice system. Ewing worried in a letter to Davis that Cheatham might "give way to despair and drown his troubles in indulgence." Despite his personal faults, Cheatham was one of the more effective division commanders, and he remained in the Army of Tennessee.[85]

By November key dissidents had been ejected from the army, and those who were left became resigned to their fate. Bragg retained his position, even though at times he would have preferred to leave. Davis's insistence that no one could better fill the place kept him in position. Accepting his fate, Bragg meant to command the army in his own way, through the same discipline he exacted on himself. In some ways, he was as much a victim of higher decisions as his dissident generals. Ultimately, Jefferson Davis was most responsible for failing to cure the poisonous mood in the Army of Tennessee.

Howell Cobb, commander of the District of Georgia and Florida, visited the Army of Tennessee early in November "expecting to find much discontent & serious embarassments." But Cobb found little to cause worry. After speaking with many officers he "was greatly gratified to find that Genl Bragg—had their good feeling & confidence, to a much greater extent than I had supposed." Cobb believed Bragg's plan for future operations was wise and would "be executed with energy & wisdom."[86]

Surgeon T. G. Richardson served temporarily at Bragg's headquarters after Chickamauga. Like many members of the medical staff, he respected and admired the commander. When Longstreet failed to prevent the opening of the Cracker Line, Richardson urged Bragg to resign, but the general said it was not possible. Davis told him "'to hold on,' that his place cannot be filled." Richardson believed the revolt had died out by early November, giving "a period of rest to the poor man."[87]

Bragg's motive in the revolt of the generals is complex. Largely it stemmed from Davis, who refused to let him resign. But his native stubbornness came into play as well, the two factors working hand in hand. When St. John R. Liddell tried to talk Bragg into making peace with the dissidents, he was shocked at the general's reaction. "But to my distress, *his* mettle was also up and beyond the control of dispassionate reason. He said with emphasis, 'General, I want to get rid of all such generals. I have better men now in subordinate stations to fill their places. Let them send in their resignations. I shall accept every one without hesitation.'" Liddell blamed this attitude in part on the victory at Chickamauga. "Bragg had been successful up to this time and asked nobody's advice now. . . . He was wrapped up in his own self-opinion, and at present was unapproachable. I gave it up for the time, at least until his pride and elation had subsided."[88]

In Liddell's view, the problem ran even deeper. He became alarmed by the degree to which Bragg isolated himself from the army. "He had no friendship for anybody except to serve his own purposes or to maintain his reputation," Liddell rather harshly judged. "His social and personal relations were, in consequence, affected by his ambition. I had seen enough to satisfy me that, able as he was, he was better fitted for high official place in the Government than in the field of active, offensive operations."[89]

"He is very earnest at his work his whole soul is in it," William Whann Mackall assured his wife, "but his manner is repulsive & he has no social life—Is easily flattered and fond of a seeming reverence for his high position." Bragg did not seem to be able to judge "a friend from a foe, and taking subserviency as evidence of friendship." Moreover, Mackall thought Bragg was also incapable of listening to the truth and could not deal with unpleasant reality.[90]

Simon Buckner also thought he had an accurate perception of Bragg's character flaws. When Davis asked his frank opinion of the commander while visiting the army in early October, Buckner complied. Bragg was "wanting in imagination. He cannot foresee what probably will occur. When he has formed his own opinions of what he proposes to do, no advice of all his officers put together can shake him; but when he meets the unexpected, it overwhelms him because he has not been able to foresee, and then he will lean upon the advice of a drummer boy."[91]

Bragg's oldest brother John provided further insight into the general's personality and problems. Although John rarely kept in touch with either Braxton or Elise, he keenly read the newspaper at his home near Montgomery. In writing to his sisters, John blamed the lack of resources and com-

JOHN BRAGG. Eldest son of Thomas Bragg Sr., John graduated from the University of North Carolina, served in the U.S. Congress, was a judge in Alabama as well as a member of the state legislature, and owned a large plantation near Lowndesboro, not far from Montgomery. Braxton and Elise lived on that plantation for more than a year after the war. (Bragg Family Photographs, ADAH)

petent generals for the failure to reap more benefits from Chickamauga. He partially blamed his brother for the critical newspaper editorials. "He has a way of announcing his successes which is very unfortunate & always re-acts against him. The public are led to believe that a great deal more has been effected than really has been." John knew his brother's personality well. "The whole trouble of B in this respect arises from his impulsive and sanguine temper. He ought to try to subdue this tendency. Even under the flush and excitement of victory calmness and moderation are always most becoming as well as most politic."[92]

John fully supported Braxton in relieving Polk. "He has always been a nuisance in the Army & always will be. His dream has been, by every sort of insinuation and intrigue, to get command of the Army in Tenn. . . . The truth is he ought to have been arrested a dozen times long ago. I sincerely trust this may be the last of him. Let him go back to preaching—his piety is sadly out of repair & requires all his care."[93]

Bragg, of course, did not see things as did Liddell or his brother. He believed he had achieved a signal success in his war with the generals. "It will be seen," he told his wife in mid-November, "my friends are aroused, and even the soldiers, and inferior officers are coming out. I shall be glad to see the war [with the generals] end, but it has done good, and I am infinitely stronger than ever with my Army."[94]

Now that the worst of the infighting was over, Bragg could relax a bit. He enjoyed the view from the top of Missionary Ridge. At night thousands of campfires lit by Union and Confederate soldiers could be seen from the door of the house he used as headquarters, and Bragg enjoyed the aesthetics of the scene. And with Harvey Washington Walter, his trusted staff officer, Bragg could joke about the war with his generals. Walter was away on duty but soon would return to army headquarters when, as Bragg put it, he could "share in the odium & abuse of being a Bragg man."[95]

12

Chattanooga

By mid-November many men in the Army of Tennessee had lost their patience with Bragg's wait-and-see policy outside Chattanooga. T. G. Richardson called it "this most incomprehensible position." Fall rains made the dirt roads linking one end of the line with the other almost impassable, and the army's constant problems with supply became worse. "Rations are scarce," George W. Brent noted in his journal, and "complaints great. The troops have been several days without meat. Want of transportation said to be the cause." After nearly two months of waiting on Missionary Ridge, the defensive policy pursued by Bragg seemed futile to everyone except Bragg. "It strikes me that it is high time to leave this place," concluded Brent. "I can see no use in persistently holding on here, when no good is to be gained, & much risk is to be run."[1]

Judging by Bragg's actions, the commander seemed content to stay indefinitely. Now that the war with his generals was at least in a recessive phase, Bragg busied himself with administrative issues. Gideon J. Pillow had earlier been assigned to conscript duty within Bragg's department and now requested permission to offer amnesty to deserters as a way to strengthen the army. "Gen Bragg instructed me to reply 'the only promise he could give deserters was to shoot them if caught,'" Brent noted with surprise. "Before it was sent it was modified, that no conditions could be promised."[2]

General orders coming from Bragg's headquarters dealt with a variety of issues relating to the army. They included instructions for daily parade inspections and how to fill out the paperwork reporting results in a proper manner. Bragg also warned Confederate soldiers that if captured they could not expect to return soon because the prisoner exchange system had broken down. "If their liberty and their lives must be lost," Bragg's order read, "the alternate of honorable death on the field of battle, nobly fighting for the cause of freedom, will be accepted by brave and patriotic Southern soldiers."[3]

Bragg tried to reduce the number of horses in the army to lessen the demand for forage and worried about the fact that only 44 percent of the aggregate force in the Army of Tennessee was listed as "effective." In other words, more than half of the men officially assigned to his army were not with it and able to do service. "This is frightful," Bragg told Davis. Desertion accounted for a part of this problem, and Bragg continued to react harshly any time the word was mentioned. "The deserters are an incumbrance to me and must be shot or they run off again," he told Joseph E. Johnston.[4]

Yet the general had room in his mind for social activities as well. "On Gen Bragg's invitation 14 ladies will be here tomorrow," Brent noted on November 21. Perhaps he invited the women of the area to headquarters because he was isolated from friendly discourse and missed his wife's company. Elise continued to live comfortably at Warm Springs but kept in touch with her husband through the mail. Taylor Beatty agreed to accompany her brother, Towson Ellis, on a visit to Warm Springs in late October. "Mrs. Bragg off driving & did not get back till dark," he reported upon arrival. The baths were too tempting to be resisted with mineral water at a temperature of 90 degrees and "Old Col. Mustian" taking good care of Elise.[5]

Mrs. Bragg acted as if the Army of Tennessee was destined to remain on Missionary Ridge for the season. "I am waiting to hear *where* your winter quarters will be established," she asked Braxton on November 23. "I scarcely hope you will be chivalrous enough to let me visit you." Elise noted that George Washington's wife stayed with her husband at Valley Forge and that Buell's wife stayed at Nashville and Rosecrans's wife at Murfreesboro, Banks's and Butler's wives at New Orleans. "I dare say Mrs. Grant is at Chattanooga." Braxton sent her clippings from the newspapers, and a Mr. Fairchild of New Orleans who was staying at Warm Springs also collected news items concerning her husband for Elise. She was disturbed that a prominent paper like the *Richmond Enquirer* came out so bitterly with anti-Bragg articles.[6]

Elise could not have known that the battle for Chattanooga began the day she penned this letter. Indications of a coming Union offensive had been brewing for some time, and Bragg was aware of them. He judged that the rate of Sherman's march from Memphis had been slowed by at least a month due to resistance engineered by Stephen D. Lee in northern Mississippi and Alabama, "a time of great value to us" he told Johnston. But Bragg did not improve on that opportunity. Longstreet continued to be stymied at Knoxville with no clear option for a quick victory, and Bragg did nothing at Missionary Ridge except to wait. The truth was he had no plan for the coming battle except to act strictly on the defensive, counting on the imposing heights of Missionary Ridge and Lookout Mountain as his only advantage. Reinforcements were unavailable. Bragg told Armand Beauregard early in October that he had 55,000 men; Longstreet later took away 12,000 to Knoxville, and Bragg dispatched an additional 2,500 to aid him in late November. He could count on only 41,500 men to oppose Grant's 70,000 troops when the fight at Chattanooga started.[7]

When Sherman finally arrived, Grant began to move. The first effort concerned a knoll called Orchard Knob that lay between the opposing lines and was held by Confederate skirmishers. Elements of the Fourth Corps in Thomas's Army of the Cumberland moved out on November 23 and easily captured the feature. Grant used it as a command post, and the new position offered Thomas a better jumping off place from which to move against Missionary Ridge if it became necessary.[8]

The next day, November 24, Joseph Hooker attacked Lookout Mountain with three divisions to oppose only two brigades that Bragg could spare on this huge eminence. The Federals moved along the steep, rugged side of the mountain, sweeping its slope until meeting stiff resistance where the point lay closest to Chattanooga. Although the fighting continued all day in worsening weather with lowered clouds that hid much of the action from observers below, the Federals pushed the Confederates back and cleared the sides and summit by dusk. The "Battle above the Clouds" as the action became known eliminated the left flank of Bragg's tenuous line. All that was left to the Confederates was the imposing height of Missionary Ridge. Grant intended his most intense push to take it the next day.[9]

Discussion at Bragg's headquarters followed these moves by the enemy. Hardee thought the Confederates should abandon their forward position and retire to the south side of Chickamauga Creek where they would have more options in terms of position and movement. Despite the commanding height it occupied, the Army of Tennessee was in a real sense pinned to the top of Missionary Ridge with little opportunity to move about. The ridge crest was narrow and the sides steep, which made it difficult to adjust the line or retire in order. Outnumbered, the Army of Tennessee also was susceptible to flanking movements. Bragg seriously considered Hardee's suggestion but thought it was now too late to evacuate. Breckinridge, who commanded the other corps in Bragg's army, was drunk during the conference, but he wanted to stay and fight. Bragg agreed that staying and fighting was the best course of action.[10]

"Though greatly outnumbered," Bragg told Samuel Cooper, "such was the strength of our position that no doubt was entertained of our ability to hold it." Initially it seemed as if Bragg's confidence was well placed. Grant planned to hit both flanks of the Confederate line, but operations failed to achieve much good. Hooker was delayed in crossing Lookout Creek and did not strike the southern end of the Rebel position until very late in the day. Sherman, after crossing the Tennessee River and positioning his men the previous night, struck Cleburne's Division on the north end of the ridge and ran into a bloody roadblock. Piecemeal attacks failed to drive the Confederates away.[11]

Grant's offensive was stalled, and the general called on Thomas to ease pressure on Sherman by conducting a limited attack on the Confederate front. Even though holding Missionary Ridge for two months, Bragg had failed to adequately plan his defense of the place. The Confederates had parceled out their limited manpower in not one but three lines; on top, midway up the slope, and at the foot of the eminence. Moreover, they had only recently constructed fieldworks on the ridge. Many of those works were not even sited properly to take advantage of the irregularities of the summit. As commander, Bragg bears the ultimate responsibility for all these problems.[12]

When Thomas attacked late on the afternoon of November 25, his men easily drove the enemy from the base of Missionary Ridge but then exceeded their orders by climbing the slope in pursuit. It was the right thing to do, for the opportunity to win a decisive victory was within their grasp. Rebel troops farther up the slope could not fire for fear of hitting their own men. The Federals met resistance as they continued, and there was some heavy fighting on parts of the line. But elsewhere the Confederate position crumbled, opening up wide gaps that the Federals were able to exploit.[13]

Bragg watched with satisfaction as Bate's Brigade repelled the initial Union advance on one part of the line and then rode among the troops to congratulate them. But he was surprised to hear that the line broke to right and left. "Every effort which could be made by myself and staff and by many other mounted officers availed but little," he told Samuel Cooper. "A panic which I had never before witnessed seemed to have seized upon officers and men, and each seemed to be struggling for his personal safety, regardless of his duty or his character." Sam R. Watkins of the 1st Tennessee recalled Bragg's effort in his memoirs. The general "was cursing like a sailor," Watkins asserted. When Bragg called out to the men, "Here is your commander," the troops yelled back "here is your mule" in derision. "I felt sorry for General Bragg," Watkins continued. "The army was routed, and Bragg looked so scared. Poor fellow, he looked so hacked and whipped and mortified and chagrined at defeat." Some of Watkins's comrades continued to deride him by saying "Bully for Bragg, he's h—l on retreat."[14]

The Army of Tennessee fled the top of Missionary Ridge in something close to a panic. Among the few units that remained intact was Cleburne's Division, which covered Bragg's retreat. Cleburne sent staff member Irving Buck to consult with Bragg, and Buck found the general at Catoosa Station at 4 A.M. of November 26. Army headquarters temporarily occupied a "large freight room" at the station where only a single candle lighted up a part of the room. When Buck told George Brent of his mission, he heard Bragg's voice emerge from the darkness asking who had arrived. Brent told him. "Anyone at all acquainted with General Bragg will remember that he was far from emotional," Buck recalled years later, "and not at all 'gushing' in his nature, and the younger officers stood in considerable awe of him." But Buck's arrival brought the general forth. As he approached, Bragg surprised and embarrassed Buck by extending his hands and "grasping my right one in both of his . . . He exhibited more excitement than I supposed possible for him. He had evidently not rested during the night." The cause of Bragg's emotional greeting was fear for his army. "'Tell General Cleburne to hold his position at all hazards, and keep back the enemy, until the artillery and transportation of the army is secure, the salvation of which depends upon him.'"[15]

Cleburne fulfilled his mission. On November 27 he bluntly repulsed Hooker's pursuit at Ringgold, and Grant called off further effort, sending 30,000 men under Sherman to relieve Burnside at Knoxville. Longstreet tried to break through the Union defenses by attacking Fort Sanders on November 29 but was bloodily repulsed in the effort. As soon as Sherman came within striking distance, Longstreet broke off his semi-siege of the city and retired toward the northeast.[16]

All of Bragg's plans ended in disaster, his army far worse off than it had ever been before. Chattanooga was lost forever, and the victory at Chickamauga wasted. If Grant had continued his pursuit beyond Ringgold, Bragg was prepared to retire all the way to Resaca thirty-five miles south of Chattanooga and use the Oostanaula River as a defensive line. That course proved unnecessary.[17]

Bragg had to report on November 29 that the disaster to his army was immense. He needed time to restore the troops' morale and order. "I deem it due to the cause and to myself to ask for relief from command and an investigation into the causes of the defeat," he told Cooper. Bragg could not explain what happened. He had naively trusted the topography of Missionary Ridge, even though he had made no effort to improve it with proper earthworks or astute placement of his lines. Also, Bragg had always trusted the rank and file. He had never seen them run before, and it shocked him. "No satisfactory excuse can possibly be given for the shameful conduct of our troops on the left in allowing their line to be penetrated. The position was one which ought to have been held by a line of skirmishers against any assaulting column." Bragg suggested that watching Union movements on the open ground near Chattanooga had demoralized "weak-minded and untried soldiers" in his army. He was determined to find out which units broke first and then to mete out punishment accordingly.[18]

But Bragg discovered another problem that concerned his generals. "*Drunkenness most flagrant*, during the whole three days of our trials, compels a *change* in the commander of the second corps" he wrote of Breckinridge. "We *are lost* if this continues. To correct it produces results almost as bad—as every *act of mine* is attributed to a *personal motive*." Bragg reminded Davis of Cheatham's similar problem at Stones River. "I can bear to be sacrificed myself, but not to see my country and my friends ruined by the vices of a few profligate men who happen to have an undue popularity."[19]

But nothing was done about Breckinridge because Davis finally relieved Bragg. On November 30, the Confederate president approved Bragg's request to be replaced. The news produced as much depression as joy for the beleaguered general. On December 1, he sent David Urquhart to Richmond with "a plain, unvarnished report" of the battle at Chattanooga and told Davis in writing that he was ready for other duty after "some little rest." He referred to the "shameful discomfiture" of Missionary Ridge. "The disaster admits of no palliation, and is justly disparaging to me as a commander. I trust, however, you may find upon full investigation that the fault is not entirely mine." Bragg confessed that both he and the president had "erred in the conclusion for me to retain command here after the clamor raised against me."[20]

St. John R. Liddell had by now become entirely disgusted with Bragg. After Missionary Ridge he had enough of the general's "purposeless plans and objects." Liddell missed the battle of Chattanooga while on leave but returned soon after the disaster on Missionary Ridge. He found Bragg "so much depressed that I had not an unkind word at hand to reproach him for his unmitigated follies."[21]

But Bragg continued to confide now and then in Liddell. He told him the president had consented to relieve him and mused on the irony of it. "'Here now,' said he, 'is Cheatham, drinking in Dalton and going around shaking his head when speaking of me, saying, "I told you so." But what more could be expected of a man whose occupation in Nashville before the war was to keep a drinking saloon and a stallion? I am disgusted with politicians for generals and executive officers. I have no dependence upon them. I shall retire to private station, I feel deeply distressed for our poor failing cause.'"[22]

Bragg went further and told Liddell he respected his opinion above all other officers in the Army of Tennessee. Liddell was surprised to hear such a comment. It had seemed to him that Bragg showed no inclination to follow his advice in the past, and he said so to the general. "I don't follow any views but my own," Bragg told him. "There are more ways than the council to obtain the views and opinions of those whom I respect, though I may not see proper to be governed by them."[23]

Planning to give up his command by December 2, Bragg requested orders to go to LaGrange and be with Elise at Warm Springs. He also requested that David Urquhart remain on his personal staff. The family friend was "almost a necessity in enabling me to bring up my records."[24]

But Bragg put in one note of optimism before leaving the army. On December 2 he again admitted to Davis, "No one estimates the disaster more seriously than I do, and the whole responsibility and disgrace rest on my humble head. But we can redeem the past." He then called up Beauregard's plan to assemble spare troops from less threatened quarters, reinforce the army, and take the offensive into Tennessee and Kentucky. This was the plan Armand Beauregard had discussed with Bragg early in October, the kind of plan Bragg rejected when Longstreet and others proposed it after Chickamauga. But Bragg's rejection was based on the fact that no troops could reinforce the army and nothing was done to remedy its logistical problems. Bragg's current endorsement of the plan rested on adequate preparation over several months. He even urged Davis to take the field and lead the effort in person. "With our greatest and best leader at the head, yourself, if practicable, march the whole upon the enemy and crush him in his power and his glory. I believe it practicable, and trust that I may be allowed to participate in the struggle which may restore to us the character[,] the prestige, and the country we have just lost."[25]

In general orders, Bragg took his leave of the army on December 2. "The associations of more than two years, which bind together a commander and his trusted troops, cannot be severed without deep emotion. A common cause and dangers shared on the many hard-fought fields from Pensacola to Chickamauga have cemented bonds which time even can never impair." He thanked his staff and credited it to "a great degree" with "what little of success and fame we have achieved." Bragg encouraged the army to serve Hardee well as he temporarily commanded until Davis found a replacement. He offered everyone "the blessing and the prayers of a gratified friend."[26]

Davis never blamed Bragg for the defeat at Missionary Ridge as he tried to work out a replacement for him. Lee suggested Beauregard but the Southern president preferred Lee himself. When asked if he could go to Dalton where the Army of Tennessee had established winter quarters, Lee questioned the wisdom of the move. It would result in no good unless he officially took command of the Army of Tennessee. "I also fear that I would not receive cordial co-operation," Lee admitted. "I have not that confidence either in my strength or ability as would lead me of my own option to undertake the command in question." Lee had created a successful team in northern Virginia, knew the region and his opponents well, and was so alarmed at reports of dissent in the Army of Tennessee that the thought of changing commands was daunting.[27]

Davis finally dropped the idea of transferring Lee to the west and decided on Johnston. Bragg, meanwhile, left the Army of Tennessee on the night of December 2 and made his way to Elise at Warm Springs. Taylor Beatty met him at Atlanta on December 3 and traveled with him to Newnan. Soon after that the exhausted ex-commander of the Army of Tennessee reached Mustian's spa.[28]

While Bragg enjoyed a much-needed rest, civilians and military personnel of the Confederacy tried to make sense of the last three months of his tenure in command of the army. Chickamauga impressed everyone as a major victory, especially coming so soon after the disasters at Vicksburg and Gettysburg. But soon many observers began to worry that it might result in nothing. The "people are still in a state of anxious suspense," Josiah Gorgas wrote on September 26, "fearing that all this bloodshed may have been in vain, and that Tennessee may after all not be recovered." The opening of the Cracker Line convinced Gorgas that nothing would be accomplished.[29]

Catherine Ann Devereux Edmondston, always critical of Bragg, had doubts about Chickamauga from the start. Bragg announced a complete victory, but she remembered his first report of Stones River and was "afraid to rejoice." Edmondston became thoroughly disgusted with him by November. "'*A little more grape—Captain* Bragg.' How much harm has that reputed speech of old Taylor's (for both Bragg & himself deny that he made it) done us! It made Bragg's reputation, gave him a wife, and to the nation an incompetent general. How many lives hung on those idle words." Missionary Ridge was, in her view, "a heavy blow to us, one under which the Confederacy staggers to the centre. . . . This General, this Bragg, & Mr. Davis' pertinacity in keeping him in command in spite of his repeated failures try my humility sorely!"[30]

Kate Cumming, the army nurse who had sympathized with Bragg, overheard two men discuss him soon after Chickamauga. One of them was highly critical but the other sarcastically asked him why, "because he had garnered the most brilliant victory of the war, or because he had *dared* to arrest General Polk?" If the latter was the case, then the unidentified supporter saw it as praise for the general, "as it showed, no matter how high the offender, he would be brought to justice." But Cumming quickly lost her patience with Bragg as the confrontation at Chattanooga stretched out indefinitely. "He seems to make no use of his victories."[31]

Mary Chesnut, whose husband served on Davis's staff, never had a kind word for Bragg. "I think a general worthless whose subalterns quarrel with him," she commented. "Something wrong with the man. Good generals are adored by their soldiers." She spared no sarcasm when assessing Bragg's wait-and-see policy after Chickamauga. "There sits Bragg—a good dog howling on his hind legs before Chattanooga, . . . and some Yankee Holdfast grinning at him from his impregnable heights. Waste of time." When hearing that he had been relieved of command, Chesnut commented that Bragg "has a winning way of earning everybody's detestation. Heavens, how they hate him."[32]

Robert Garlick Hill Kean, who headed the Bureau of War in Richmond, also kept close watch on developments in the West. By late October, reports indicated worsening problems in the Army of Tennessee. He bemoaned "the same state of hopeless distrust and disorganization in that army stated by so many . . . foreboding nothing but evil from Bragg's command of it. Yet the President seems fatally bent on retaining him." This presidential resolve stubbornly ignored what War Department clerk John B. Jones called "the tremendous prejudice against [the general] in and out of the army." News of Missionary Ridge shocked Jones's young son, who had admired Bragg.

He absent-mindedly "poured water into his sister's plate, the pitcher being near" when the girl asked for rice at the dinner table.[33]

Bragg's adult supporters found themselves on the ropes after Missionary Ridge, unable to ground their faith in the general on anything substantial. As Louis Trezevant Wigfall, the senator from Texas, put it, "they have not much margin on which to go."[34]

Newspaper reporting was largely against Bragg by this stage of his career but the *Memphis Appeal* tried to take an even-handed approach to him. The editor blamed Davis more than Bragg for his predicament. If the Confederate president wished to retain him at the head of the army, then the people should rally to the cause and support Bragg. But it was obvious even to the editor that this was a nearly hopeless situation.[35]

The *Appeal* editor was delighted to print a piece by a Tennessee man supporting Bragg in November, before the battle at Chattanooga. This unidentified friend argued that the Army of Tennessee continued to support him. The *Appeal* was happy to know this and criticized other papers such as the *Atlanta Confederacy* for their vicious attacks. The editor admitted that, even though flawed, Bragg was a better commander than the available replacements. He argued the general "has abundantly shown that he is as able to attack with vigor as to fall back upon occasion."[36]

When the final indignity of Missionary Ridge was visited upon the nation, the *Memphis Appeal* backed away gracefully from Bragg. The editor concluded that he was the victim of bad luck. "We have failed under his direction in enterprizes where the public voice with singular unanimity pronounces that we ought to have succeeded."[37]

Henry Watterson, editor of the *Chattanooga Rebel*, hated Bragg with a passion. His most vicious attack came after the battle of Chickamauga, leading Bragg to ban the newspaper within army lines. Owner Franc M. Paul then replaced Watterson as editor in an effort to restore the paper's circulation. "Paul was afraid to make the fight" against Bragg, Watterson told his fiancée. "Next to my love for you, the stoutest passion of my soul, is an intense loathing for this infamous character."[38]

John H. Linebaugh, another newspaper enemy, wrote for the *Memphis Appeal* under the name Ashantee. Bragg arrested him in mid-September 1863 for publishing information about the army's movements. Braxton's brother John provided the general much inside information about this man. Linebaugh had been a college classmate of Leonidas Polk, and the corps commander knew him well. In fact, John had been married by Linebaugh because, like Polk, the future newspaper correspondent was a minister. He moved through minor positions in the leadership of the Episcopal Church until compelled to give up the ministry due to his profanity and habitual drunkenness. Linebaugh attached himself to Polk's headquarters for a time during the war.[39]

Linebaugh was sent to several towns in northwest Georgia under arrest until he was released on a writ of habeas corpus. When he protested to Bragg's headquarters, the provost marshal on his staff explained that everyone was too busy to realize the correspondent had existed in a sort of limbo for two weeks without charges being filed. In fact, Bragg had no real intention of pursuing Linebaugh in court; he just wanted to get the writer out of his hair. "It is a singular thing," wrote Linebaugh, "that while the Army of Tennessee is the only one of our armies beset with troubles and disputes between the chief and subordinates, it is the only one in which there is any trouble between the chief and correspondents."[40]

The reactions of Bragg's men to his demotion were mixed. "It was sad for me to part with Bragg," admitted division commander W. H. T. Walker. "His enemies did their work. I hope they are satisfied." C. Irvine Walker of the 10th South Carolina had always admired the general and continued to do so throughout the fall of 1863. "Bragg . . . knows what he is about," Walker wrote soon after Chickamauga, "and I am perfectly willing to trust him." He rejoiced that Davis sided with Bragg in the revolt of the generals but worried that newspaper "critics will soon begin to show their generalship and tell Genl. B. what he should not have done. However I don't suppose he will care much about it."[41]

The 4th Louisiana reached Dalton on November 26, too late to participate in the battle of Chattanooga, but Samuel Lambert remained a staunch supporter of Bragg. He refused to blame either Bragg or the rank and file for the disaster. Commissary officer Benedict Joseph Semmes and ordnance officer Robert Lewis Bliss thought Bragg acted "splendidly" in efforts to stem the rout at Missionary Ridge and asserted that most men retained confidence in his leadership. Another commissary officer named Frank G. Ruffin was impressed by Bragg's character when he read that the general accepted responsibility for the Chattanooga defeat, believing him "an honest man, a good man, and an able man."[42]

While many of Bragg's old soldiers retained a degree of faith in his leadership, the men of Longstreet's two divisions overwhelmingly disliked him. "This army has no confidence in Bragg," commented James Morris Bivings to his father, "and I think the sooner he has been removed the better it will be for the Army of the West.[43]

Some of the men in the Army of Tennessee completely lost faith in Bragg by this time, although it would be unwise to assume that most of them fell into this category. Brigade leader Arthur M. Manigault later admitted it was a mistake not to have taken the offensive after Chickamauga, but he knew there were powerful reasons for not doing so. "General Bragg was overconfident in the strength of his position," Manigault concluded, "and underrated the number of his adversaries, and their fighting abilities. He had not men enough to make himself secure, besides which he was completely outgeneraled by the Yankee commander."[44]

Philip Daingerfield Stephenson of the 13th Arkansas found Bragg's actions in the weeks before the battle at Chattanooga inexplicable. The general "seemed to lose his head." While trying to rally the men at Missionary Ridge, no one paid attention to him. "It was then that he was made to feel the full force of his unpopularity. He had always been disliked. Now he found himself also distrusted. Placed in a position where the utmost influence as a loved and trusted leader was needed in order to control his men, he was made to see that to them he was nothing, absolutely nothing."[45]

Outside the Army of Tennessee, Confederate soldiers could either be decidedly hard on Bragg or be understanding of the man's troubles. Robert Ransom Jr., who commanded troops cooperating with Longstreet in East Tennessee, was highly critical of Bragg's handling of the Chickamauga phase of the campaign. He believed Rosecrans outmaneuvered him, and then Bragg had "to get back by hard fighting what he lost by bad maneuvering." But Hugh S. Gookin, who only recently joined a Confederate artillery unit stationed in Virginia, believed Bragg's only real fault was that he was unlucky.[46]

Soldier attitude toward Bragg in the Army of Tennessee was mixed. William Preston Johnston visited the army at Dalton to gauge its condition and told Davis the "feeling towards Bragg I find is stronger than I supposed, and almost every officer and man I have spoken to hopes he will yet return." Taylor Beatty found the same thing. "Have conversed with a good many men about Genl. Bragg's removal & find that there is an almost universal feeling of regret." Of course, Beatty was a friend and former staff member of Bragg's and Johnston was Davis's aide. In contrast, brigade leader Lucius Polk (a nephew of Leonidas Polk) spread the word that the battle of Chattanooga was a "blessing to us—inasmuch as it got rid of Bragg," according to civilian Kenneth Rayner in North Carolina.[47]

But a good number of Bragg's men wrote letters of support after his resignation. Capt. J. H. Fraser of the 50th Alabama addressed Bragg as a son would have written to his father. "The longer we remain with you the more we love you, and the more confidence we have in your skill and ability as a military captain. . . . Your old Army was never dissatisfied with you and we love you to day better." Surgeon M. I. Holt of the 2nd Tennessee remembered Bragg's kindness to him and the sick under his care at Pensacola in the early part of the war. He hoped his letter would "alleviate the pain inflicted by an ungrateful world." When Bragg's farewell order was read to the 5th Tennessee, Edwin Hansford Rennolds Sr. was impressed. "I think for one we are losing as good an officer as we can ever get, but having lost the confidence of the army it is noble in him to retire and certainly best."[48]

Quartermaster Edward Norphlet Brown of the 45th Alabama admitted to being a longtime admirer of the general, and he was distressed to see him leave. "Whenever he failed to whip the enemy he never failed to bring off his army in safety. It is my deliberate judgement that Braxton Bragg is the *greatest General of this revolution*. General Lee could loose as many men by his invasion of Pennsylvania as Bragg had in Kentucky yet Lee is *the* man & Bragg is reviled. Lee could have two or three Brigades gobbled up on the Rappahanoc & it is all right & if Bragg does not take captive the whole Army of Rosecrans his removal is demanded."[49]

After announcing his resignation but before leaving the army, Bragg was serenaded by the band of the 4th Florida in Bate's Brigade. Bate, in fact, was a consistent supporter of Bragg, and the general was very touched by the gesture. The crowd called on him for a speech, and he struggled through his emotions to tell the assembled men how he felt at leaving them. "In a most feeling and touching manner he took a long and sad farewell," wrote a newspaper correspondent.[50]

Several other brigade and division commanders held Bragg in high esteem. Edward C. Walthall sincerely regretted his resignation and partially blamed himself for it because his division was unable to hold Lookout Mountain. Joseph Wheeler, who owed much of his rise to Bragg's support, always was faithful to his benefactor. He hoped Bragg could return to the army soon. Samuel H. Stout deeply admired Bragg for the general's devotion to the sick and wounded of his army and the support he offered to its medical staff. Stout also praised Bragg's "patriotic intentions."[51]

Bragg's staff members, those who remained at army headquarters while his personal staff accompanied him to Warm Springs, wrote to tell their former chief how much they missed him. Harvey Washington Walter referred to Bragg as "my old chieftain & beloved commander" and assured him most of the men wanted him to return to the army. Col. J. P. Jones, the army's assistant inspector general, was certain "the more efficient and honest of the officers of rank prefer you to any other leader that could be sent here and would hail your return." The men "who desired you to give up the Army here stand isolated and with blank faces ask themselves the question 'Well who can fill his place?'"[52]

Several old comrades who had served under Bragg at Pensacola retained faith in him. Philip D. Roddey wrote from Tuscumbia, Alabama, to console his former commander by assuring him that no one could have accomplished more with the Army of Tennessee. Roddey told Bragg that his men would welcome him as their new superior if that could be arranged. James Chalmers owed much to Bragg for the supportive way the general had handled his ill-advised attack on Munfordville during the Kentucky campaign. Now Chalmers assured him that "I have seen no man in this war who looked, talked & acted on all occasions so much like my beau ideal of a General, as yourself." Chalmers accepted the fact that Bragg had to resign from the Army of Tennessee due to circumstances, "but those who made the circumstances—the political & military intriguers—who sought by constant defamation to weaken your influence with the army & the people—will have much to answer for" it.[53]

It would be dangerous to take these letters of support too seriously. Actually many men in uniform had many varied opinions about the general. The interesting point is that Bragg's defamers expressed themselves very publicly, while his supporters quietly offered their opinions in private letters. Except for Davis's support, Bragg had to fight his battles largely alone.

The opinion of historians on this phase of Bragg's career varies as well. Stanley Horn predictably blamed Bragg for the failure to prevent the Cracker Line. "Bragg could be trusted to bungle," Horn unfairly concluded, as if Longstreet had nothing to do with that failure. Don Seitz, who normally avoided negative conclusions about the general, could not understand "the supiness that followed the success" of Chickamauga. Thomas Robson Hay slammed Bragg for not handling his army better at Chickamauga. He identified poor health, a weak staff, and the creaky nature of army administration as the chief causes of Bragg's failure to capitalize on that victory.[54]

Recent historians have treated Bragg with more understanding. Peter Cozzens and Steven Woodworth accept Bragg's argument that the army was incapable of a strategic offensive after Chickamauga. Both men and Samuel Martin are highly critical of Longstreet for the failure to prevent Grant from creating the Cracker Line.[55]

Concerning the revolt of the generals, Thomas Connelly places at least part of the blame on the dissidents within the Army of Tennessee but also notes that Bragg should have deferred sacking so many generals to another time. Samuel Martin has noted that only a minority of the army's commanders signed the October 11 petition. Woodworth has pointed out that the Confederate president was largely responsible for the revolt because he failed to discipline the dissidents much earlier. "Davis was in an impossible situation. He had allowed Polk and his band of malcontents to undermine Bragg so completely that to support Bragg properly would now require sacking half the officer corps of the Army of Tennessee. The alternative was undermining discipline by granting a victory to insubordination, removing Bragg, and replacing him with someone who would very likely be inferior." Insisting on keeping Bragg in place while not punishing the dissidents, Davis created an insurmountable difficulty for Bragg.[56]

While historians tend to criticize Bragg for fighting with his generals when he should have been taking care of strategy after Chickamauga the truth is he did not ignore the latter. Bragg worked on both fronts simultaneously. He remained open to the possibility of a strategic offensive to bypass Chattanooga for some time but was daunted by the severe problems of such a move. A follow-up to Chickamauga would be much easier if he could march through, and not around, Chattanooga. In the end he opted for the less risky course of action, waiting to see if Rosecrans would leave the city or could be pried out. By the time it became apparent neither result was likely, Bragg decided firmly against a march around the city. His slim chance of starving the enemy out of Chattanooga was wrecked when Longstreet failed to stop Grant from opening the Cracker Line.[57]

By early November, Bragg could see no viable alternative to staying on Missionary Ridge and Lookout Mountain. He convinced himself that the terrain would compensate for the disparity of numbers and allowed more than two divisions to try a barely feasible expedition to Knoxville. If he could not risk a major strategic offensive into Middle Tennessee, he could afford a smaller, limited offensive into East Tennessee. But even that effort failed when Longstreet became stuck in the trenches outside Knoxville. As Peter Cozzens has pointed out, the outcome at Chattanooga was not inevitable. If Bragg had a reserve, he might have repelled Thomas's attack up Missionary Ridge and saved his position at least temporarily.[58]

Samuel Martin believes Bragg "was stunned" at how swiftly Davis accepted his offer to resign. He thinks that explained the general's suggestion that Davis take charge of the army for a new offensive. In my view, Bragg was not stunned but relieved by the quick acceptance of the resignation. His suggestion to reinforce the army and appoint a new leader, even the president himself, was consistent with the plan proposed by Beauregard and brought to Bragg's attention by Armand two months before. Bragg was not interested in taking command of that effort; like William Preston Johnston, he thought the president would make a good field commander. Bragg had an opportunity to comment on this plan in March 1864, and he strongly supported it then as well.[59]

It may seem ironic that the offensive Bragg refused to undertake after Chickamauga should find favor with him six months later, but he had liked the idea even when Armand explained it to him in October. The plan was feasible only if the Army of Tennessee was in proper shape for it and effective generals led its major units. There was no opportunity for rejuvenating the army in late 1863, but it was possible early in the spring of 1864. Bragg readily admitted he was not the man for the job. After commanding the army for twenty months—from April 1862 until December 1863—he was eager for rest but still hoped to offer his services to the Confederacy.

Military Adviser to the
Confederate President

Bragg traveled to Warm Springs in early December 1863 with Towson Ellis, Elise's brother, and Thomas Butler, her cousin. Surgeon T. G. Richardson, Lieut. F. Parker, and Col. David Urquhart completed the entourage. The party was "completely out of the world" at Warm Springs as Thomas Butler told his aunt, and Bragg reveled in it. By Christmas the general's health improved a great deal. Elise also seemed to be in much better health after nearly a year of struggling with typhoid fever. Warm Springs was quiet that winter season with only a handful of refugee families from New Orleans on the premises. Bragg's manservant, a soldier named Swartout, took care of the entourage's horses.[1]

The "quiet and perfectly retired life" at Warm Springs rejuvenated Bragg's health and spirits. It was in effect his refugee home because Bivouac had been taken away, "even to the wardrobes of himself and wife," as he put it in the third person. "The Genl bears his misfortunes with great patience and does not seem to feel the loss of his own reputation," Thomas Butler told his aunt, "but his whole thoughts are occupied with the unhappy condition of our country."[2]

Bragg's thoughts also dwelled on the circumstances of his leaving the army. "Men who are so ambitious or so venal as to forget their country in such a struggle as this and turn their energies to malignant distractions or personal advancement are not to be managed by conciliation," Bragg told Marcus J. Wright, commander of the arsenal in Atlanta. "I fought against advice and with a halter around my neck" because Davis would not fire everyone who opposed him. "But General," Bragg told Wright, "this world is full of bad men, and we must not be surprised at these things. Let us only pity the miserable miscreants, and strive to save our country from them."[3]

By the end of December Bragg felt that his "health has greatly improved, and I am now ready for any duty they may assign me," but he had no inkling what Davis wanted him to do. The Confederate president was working on that question. Beauregard suggested Bragg take over his position as the defender of Charleston so he could replace Edmund Kirby Smith in the Trans-Mississippi, but Davis did not take up the idea.[4]

Bragg retained a strong feeling of gratitude toward Johnston for sustaining him after the battle of Stones River, and according to Josiah Gorgas he was willing to serve as chief of staff in the Army of Tennessee. On one level the idea made sense. Bragg's work ethic, self-discipline, and familiarity with the army would have been an asset, but Johnston did not want Bragg. He thought it would be harmful to restore him in any way to his old command.[5]

Bragg never learned of Johnston's views on this matter and continued to respect and admire him. When Johnston wrote a note consoling him for the loss of Chattanooga and the army command, Bragg responded warmly. "I shall follow you and your noble comrades with prayers as fervent and hopes as strong as when I shared the toils and honors of the field, and no one of you will rejoice more than myself at the success which I trust awaits you."[6]

Controversy dogged Johnston's Civil War career almost as intensely as Bragg's, and his relationship with the recently deposed head of the western army contributed to it. Louis T. Wigfall chided his military friend for his glowing evaluation of Bragg's conduct at Stones River. Those who wanted to replace Bragg were not convinced by this to change their minds, and Johnston's friends were disappointed. "The real harm done was the irritation of those who were real friends of yours & who hated Bragg or honestly distrusted him," Wigfall complained.[7]

As Bragg's health and emotional stability returned, he corresponded with supporters. Joseph Wheeler fed him reports on the army's activities. William Bate admitted that he "had indulged the hope" Bragg would return soon. Such letters could only have increased Bragg's view that most of the army liked him, but of course he could not return unless Davis and Johnston approved.[8]

Bragg kept in touch with potential patrons. In a letter to Senator Thomas Jenkins Semmes of Louisiana, he called himself "the best abused man in the country" and likened himself to George Washington, the Duke of Wellington, and even Christ as historical figures vilified by their contemporaries. He expected his report of Stones River to be published soon and sent Semmes a copy of John Forsyth's Memorandum of Facts concerning the Kentucky campaign. "Where-ever I can serve the cause, in mind or body . . . there put me, and I will labor to the utmost of my ability."[9]

Davis was Bragg's most important ally in Richmond, and the general made sure he knew his views. Writing on December 8, soon after his arrival at Warm Springs, Bragg told Davis that Cheatham and Breckinridge "take to the bottle at once, and drown their cares by becoming stupid and unfit for any duty." He also confided to Wright at Atlanta that he found it impossible to command an army "when its Senior Generals can with impunity remain drunk for five successive days, as did Cheatham & Breckinridge about the time of our retreat at Missionary Ridge." He thought men such as this "have not the character or moral courage to deserve success in such a cause" as Confederate independence.[10]

Bragg blamed division commander Carter L. Stevenson's "utter imbecility" for losing Lookout Mountain. John K. Jackson was "equally as unreliable" in Bragg's view. He admitted to Davis that Stevenson and Jackson were among his "strongest personal friends," yet he could not avoid judging their military abilities truthfully. In part Bragg was trying to shift the blame for the terrible defeat at Chattanooga onto other shoulders.[11]

While Breckinridge gave up his demand for a court of inquiry to investigate Bragg's claims against him regarding Stones River, Cheatham could not keep quiet. "As I find the warfare on me has not ceased by Cheatham," Bragg wrote to Marcus J. Wright in early February, 1864, "and he still harps on the injustice done his command at Murfreesboro by my report," he revealed to Wright the full story of Cheatham's letter warning Bragg that the army was incapable of fighting on January 3. Bragg wanted Wright to use this information in countering Cheatham's denunciations but not to allow it to be published. There is no indication, however, that Wright tried to help Bragg.[12]

But it is important to keep in mind that while dealing with people like Cheatham, Bragg also found comfort in letters that arrived at Warm Springs. Samuel H. Stout wrote glowingly and it touched Bragg's heart. "One of the most pleasant associations of my official life has been with you and your corps of able assistants," he told Stout. To receive his approbation "is no small return to one whose stern discharge of duty more often offended than propitiated."[13]

Bragg replied with surprising candor when Gideon J. Pillow expressed "generous and distinguished sentiments." "Our acquaintance commenced, general, not without prejudices in my mind adverse to you," Bragg admitted. "But no influence, no power, and no clamor can ever suppress the admiration with which I have witnessed the intense labor and patriotic zeal with which you have served, and successfully served, our cause since you joined me more than a year ago." Bragg held a negative opinion of Pillow because of the latter's escape from Fort Donelson just before its surrender. But Pillow's energy in running a conscript bureau Bragg created within his Department of Tennessee after Stones River brought in men and redeemed Pillow's worth. The stern general had the ability to change his mind about people.[14]

Davis allowed Bragg nearly two months of rest before he began to call on his services. "Come to Richmond, if your health permits," he telegraphed on January 27. "I wish to confer with you." Bragg had no idea what Davis wanted of him, but he apparently traveled to Richmond more than once over the next month.[15]

In the meanwhile startling news came from the Army of Tennessee, resting in winter quarters at Dalton, Georgia. Patrick Cleburne proposed the arming of Southern slaves as a way to compensate for the Northern policy of arming blacks to serve in the Union army. Staying temporarily with his brother John near Montgomery, Alabama, Bragg was shocked by the idea. "Great sensation is being produced in the country where I have recently been by the Emancipation project of Hardee, Cheatham, Cleburne & Co.," Bragg wrote. He not only opposed such a policy but quietly delighted in the fact that his enemies in the Army of Tennessee were behind the unpopular suggestion. "It will kill them," he gloated. "They are agitators and should be watched."[16]

As yet Davis had no concrete plan for Bragg other than to consult him on an ad hoc basis, but rumors concerning his future continued to circulate. A story made the rounds that he would be given command of the Trans-Mississippi Department. The rumors were so strong that the Federals heard them. Nathaniel P. Banks reported from New Orleans that Bragg had crossed the Mississippi River with staff early in January in order to act as assistant secretary of war in superintending the actions of Kirby Smith. Some Confederates in the Trans-Mississippi welcomed the idea. "I hear every where the cry for *discipline*," wrote Thomas C. Reynolds, the exiled Confederate governor of Missouri. The report that Bragg was on his way produced "general expressions of delight." Above all generals in the Confederacy, he had the strongest reputation for imposing strict discipline.[17]

The rumor reported by Banks also reflected some degree of reality, for Beauregard had suggested that Bragg take up an important position in the Confederate government. He proposed Bragg replace Samuel Cooper as adjutant general. Then "all would yet go right," Beauregard thought.[18]

Although Davis rejected Beauregard's idea, he developed a habit of consulting with Bragg throughout February 1864. It is difficult to piece together how often the two met, but Bragg certainly was in Richmond during the middle of the month. Both the Senate and House of Representatives voted to offer him a seat on the floor to observe their proceedings. Bragg also dined with Josiah Gorgas on February 16. The meetings with Davis led to a formal assignment for Bragg "at the seat of government, and, under the direction of the President." He was "charged with the conduct of military operations in the armies of the Confederacy," according to General Orders No. 23 issued on February 24. The wording of the order seemed to offer Bragg something more than intended. It sounded as if he was made general-in-chief of all Confederate armies but without the explicit title. In reality, it became clear that his position was better defined as the Confederate president's military adviser for he had little real power. Davis often played this game, placing generals in position of apparent authority and then hedging their responsibilities by retaining the right to approve or disapprove what they did even in small matters. The operative phrase in General Orders No. 23 was "under the direction of the President," and Bragg realized he had to walk a thin line in order to serve the man who was his chief supporter. Bragg may have been his own man before; from now on he was Davis's man.[19]

Public reaction to the appointment naturally assumed Bragg was general-in-chief. The news caused "quite a buzz" in Richmond and elicited comments about the irony it provoked. A general who had so badly handled the Chattanooga campaign saw himself elevated rather than demoted. "Bragg the incapable, the Unfortunate, is Commander in Chief!," wrote an astonished Catherine Ann Devereux Edmondston. "Unhappy man, unhappy in his birth, for he is, I believe the son of his parents who was born in jail where his Mother was imprisoned on a charge of murder & the murder, too, of a negro." Edmondston found some comfort in the assurance that Bragg would fail in his new job and thus "rue the blind unreasoning friendship with which Mr Davis regards him."[20]

Even among those Southerners who assumed Bragg was their president's military adviser, a role played by Robert E. Lee earlier in the war, many considered it a poor move. John B. Jones in Richmond was disturbed by the thought that Davis made the appointment as a way to triumph over his critics and those of Bragg alike. "The President is naturally a little oppugnant," Jones wrote.[21]

Public opinion mattered little to Bragg at this time. He was rested and eager to help Davis. The general threw himself into the job without questioning the somewhat vague parameters of his authority. He appointed Col. John B. Sale as his military secretary. For the rest of his life Bragg called Sale "the most valuable and reliable Staff officer I had." As a forty-four-year-old lawyer, Sale had become captain of Company K, 27th Mississippi, but the Kentucky campaign dealt hard with his health. Suffering from persistent diarrhea, he secured appointment as judge of the military court of Hardee's corps. Bragg described him as "A good lawyer of irreproachable character a Christian gentleman of scrupulous integrity." Sale proved his loyalty when lobbying the Senate for the congressional vote of thanks to his commander for the Stones River campaign.[22]

Bragg focused on improving the bureaucratic functioning of the Southern military system. "The duties were almost entirely ministerial," he soon after reported, "and required an amount of labor, investigation and pressing both thankless and appalling." The last word in this quote indicates that Bragg was not entirely comfortable with his new position and all it entailed, but he did his best without complaint. Duty drove him forward, and a strong commitment to Davis provided the rest of his motivation.[23]

A wide variety of issues came into Bragg's range. George W. Brent and T. G. Richardson filed a report on the hospitals in and around Richmond that treated captured Union soldiers. The general was shocked at the bad conditions evident in these hospitals. They "compromised us in the treatment of our prisoners," thought Bragg. The general had "the interests of the hospitals very much at heart," Richardson told Stout. When the general received "a most touching letter" from the wife of a surgeon serving with the Army of Tennessee requesting he be assigned to hospital work at Columbus, Georgia, Bragg was so moved he asked Richardson to use his name in effecting the transfer.[24]

On the larger issue of prisoners of war, Bragg felt reform was needed. A report indicated that Confederate authorities kept inadequate records, and Bragg sought means to improve them. He also complained that too many Confederates deliberately gave themselves up and wondered how the authorities could identify and stop them.[25]

On the issue of blacks captured in Federal uniforms on the battlefield, however, Bragg acted as Davis's instrument. A number of such prisoners were taken when Robert F. Hoke captured Plymouth, North Carolina, on April 20, 1864. Bragg relayed Davis's wish that Governor Zebulon Vance take charge of the Union black soldiers and return them to their owners if any residents of North Carolina claimed them. He was to send the names of any blacks who were owned by residents of other states to Davis so the president could arrange for their return. Davis further instructed Vance, through Bragg, to keep all of this quiet so as not to arouse trouble with the Federal government, clearly recognizing that his actions regarding black Union soldiers were controversial.[26]

Davis asked Bragg's view concerning coordination of the railroads. He doubted the companies could be coerced into cooperating with each other, even at the risk of entire government supervision of their operations. There were many such issues that he had no authority to act upon. Bragg told Davis he had no hope that volunteering could bring more men into gray uniforms; only a more vigorous enforcement of the conscription act could do so. When a government official suggested Davis encourage European immigrants in the Union army to desert, Bragg weighed in with opinions of his own. He urged the recruitment of writers and editors to use Southern newspapers for this purpose and suggested the government print documents in German and French that offered haven for immigrants who wanted to escape the Union draft.[27]

When efforts to create a more centrally controlled system of staff officers for Confederate generals came about, Bragg demonstrated that he also was capable of changing his mind on important issues. He had reacted negatively to this idea in the summer of 1863 while leading the Army of Tennessee, arguing that a commander in the field should be allowed the freedom to choose his own staff members. Beauregard and Johnston agreed with that view. But after becoming the president's military adviser, Bragg changed his mind. He now agreed with administration views that a national staff system was needed, citing nepotism, favoritism, and ineffectiveness as chief faults of the old system. "Staff officers should be selected on grounds of military education and experience," historian June Gow has written of Bragg's new opinion, "organized in a staff corps directed by the War Department, and by it assigned to duty with a particular field command." Congress passed the staff bill in April 1864, but Samuel Cooper was never able to get it fully off the ground.[28]

Gow sees Bragg's handling of his staff in the field as old-fashioned and highly personal. For her the key point was defining the roles of staff officers. A chief of staff needed to be entrusted with a function separate from that of an assistant adjutant general, the chief record keeper. To be effective a chief of staff had to be an assistant to the commander with authority to issue orders in his name while he also coordinated the activities of other staff members. Bragg tended to avoid appointing chiefs of staff and saw each member's role as interchangeable with another as needed. Only when

Mackall served as chief of staff and Walter as adjutant general in the summer of 1863 did Bragg practice what Gow defines as the most effective division of authority. Generally Bragg preferred, as Gow puts it, "to act as his own chief of staff." Ironically Bragg had served as Albert Sidney Johnston's chief of staff for a time before Shiloh, and with authority to issue orders in the commander's name if needed, but he did not feel comfortable with that arrangement after acceding to chief command.[29]

Bragg tended to hoard power. As Davis relied on him not only for advice but to do things he could not do himself, Bragg tried to enlarge his authority. "The President appears to be making very general use of the Commanding General," Robert Garlick Hill Kean noted in his diary. This meant that Bragg began to issue orders on matters concerning the War Department but without consulting James Seddon. It became apparent to many in the government that Seddon was now less important to Davis, and the secretary was unhappy about it.[30]

Perhaps part of the friction developing between Seddon and Bragg stemmed from the general's frustration that his reports of the Kentucky campaign and Chickamauga still had not been cleared for publication. As Bragg testily wrote Seddon in May 1864, "I have rested patiently under the criticism and assaults of parties misrepresenting the facts of these campaigns, knowing the truth, when revealed, would be my best vindication." He asked that they be sent to Congress or at least that Seddon explain to him why they were not being sent. The secretary of war had a clear explanation; Jefferson Davis felt it would be "inexpedient" to publish Bragg's report of the Kentucky campaign, and the Chickamauga report had not been copied in time for the last meeting of congress. It would be ready for the legislators at the next congressional session. Bragg was convinced the reports were not made public "for fear of their killing off too many of our great men."[31]

Bragg tended to be abrasive when dealing with Seddon and Congress alike. Robert Kean noted the general's attitude and felt it was a mistake to treat legislators with scarcely veiled contempt. "If he brings his former bitterness to wound what he calls 'politicians' here as he has done, he will be in no end of trouble."[32]

But in dealing with Robert E. Lee, Bragg showed respect and deference. He created a limited relationship with Lee, receiving only six dispatches from him during the first four months of 1864. In contrast, Lee wrote twenty-seven dispatches to Jefferson Davis during that time period. Bragg recommended the promotion of Lee's son, G. W. C. Lee, to major general and command of the Richmond defenses in March 1864. He also tried to accommodate any other request Lee made of him. "I shall be truly happy to hear from you, general," Bragg told him, "and to receive your valuable suggestions and advice, together with all information you may obtain." There was never any prospect of Bragg's relationship with Davis supplanting the relationship Lee enjoyed with the Confederate president.[33]

Bragg was incensed when a Federal cavalry raid toward Richmond put some papers in his hands that seemed to confirm the "fiendish and atrocious conduct of our enemies." The Federals primarily sought to release Yankee prisoners held in Richmond, but Col. Ulric Dahlgren was killed during a skirmish. Papers found on his body indicated to Confederate authorities a secondary mission, to assassinate Jefferson Davis and the Rebel cabinet. Citing the "extraordinary and diabolical character" of the mission, Bragg urged that captured Union troopers be executed and the papers published as a way to justify their death. On this issue Seddon fully agreed with the general, but such action was not taken. Whether there was truly any official sanction by Federal authorities to assassinate Davis remains shrouded in mystery.[34]

Strong opinions such as this impressed some observers in Richmond. "Bragg's quick decided spirit is I believe felt here," Josiah Gorgas concluded. "His presence I have no doubt does good." But Gorgas criticized him after a conversation in late April. "His views are so startling & decided that I am tempted to think him a *little cracked*." Bragg worried that railroads leading into Richmond would be cut and the city would run out of food when the spring campaign opened. He wanted to remove government works and employees from the city, an idea Gorgas thought verged on panic, but it was done to a large degree.[35]

While Bragg dealt with an array of new issues he also contended with old problems. James Longstreet court-martialed his division commander Lafayette McLaws for the bloody failure to take Fort Sanders during the Knoxville campaign. Bragg sympathized with McLaws and offered to help. "I can assure you the evidence in my possession is ample to convict [Longstreet] of disobedience of orders[,] neglect of duty, and want of cordial cooperation and support, which resulted in all the disasters after Chicamauga," he told McLaws in March. Bragg held an equally negative opinion of Buckner as "a most perfect Jesuit & totally unreliable," in McLaws's words.[36]

Bragg had no occasion to provide McLaws with evidence because the court mostly exonerated him, and Samuel Cooper invalidated the guilty verdict it handed down for one of the charges. Another problem from the past emerged once again when a writer for the *Richmond Enquirer*, who had read Bragg's report of Chickamauga, summarized its contents for the newspaper. Thomas C. Hindman became angry when he realized Bragg blamed him for the failure at McLemore's Cove. Hindman called the report "false and slanderous," and demanded Bragg publicly disavow his statements. Bragg, of course, refused to do so and never responded to Hindman's letter.[37]

But other men from the past cherished fond memories of Bragg. Bate continued to send chatty letters, and his men also subscribed to present a sword to Bragg with an inscription that referred to their "special admiration for his personal gallantry witnessed by them amid the misfortune of the battle of Missionary Ridge." Bate also encouraged an officer who had witnessed what took place at McLemore's Cove to put the circumstances down in writing for Bragg's benefit, although the officer's signature was cut out of the letter that Bragg filed in his papers.[38]

Bragg was in an ironic position; as the president's agent, he dealt with Joseph E. Johnston, who had previously gone beyond the call of duty to support Bragg in the days following Stones River. But Davis and Johnston had not been able to see eye to eye on many issues since 1861. Bragg was placed in the uncomfortable position of serving as an intermediary between the two men, his loyalty potentially split between them. In Bragg's one-dimensional way of thinking, however, his duty was to the Confederate president. He did not see the ambiguity in the situation. Bragg became Davis's man, and it did not matter whether the issue involved an enemy or a friend.

The issue between Davis and Johnston in early 1864 revolved around whether the Army of Tennessee should take the offensive before the Federals mounted their spring push into Georgia. Bragg agreed with Davis that such a move promised rich dividends. He also thought the Army of Tennessee was now strong enough to undertake it. "The enemy is not prepared for us," he told Johnston on March 7, "and if we can strike him a blow before he recovers success is almost certain. The plan which is proposed has long been my favorite, and I trust our efforts may give you the means to accomplish what I have ardently desired but never had the ability to undertake."[39]

The plan, as Bragg explained it on March 12, was for Longstreet to join Johnston and strike for Nashville. Bragg believed Johnston would have something like 75,000 men, the largest force the Army of Tennessee ever mustered. He thought it was essential to reclaim "the provision country of Tennessee and Kentucky," and hoped thousands of men in both states would join Confederate ranks.[40]

But Johnston opposed such a move and preferred to await the enemy at Dalton. "His advance, should we be ready for it, will be advantageous to us," Johnston told Bragg, "and if we beat him we follow." Longstreet, who continued to occupy parts of East Tennessee and keenly supported an offensive, talked Lee into helping him argue for one. The pair traveled to Richmond on March 14 to confer with Davis, Bragg, and Seddon for several hours. The discussion faltered when Lee pressed for Johnston's views, and Davis and Bragg had to admit that Johnston did not like the idea. With this, it became obvious that nothing could be done.[41]

The pro-Bragg element in the Army of Tennessee complained of Johnston's policy. George W. Brent admitted the army still suffered from transportation and supply problems, but those problems were less serious than they had been the previous October. W. H. T. Walker, who had always admired Bragg, wanted Brent to tell the Rebel president's new military adviser "*to go ahead*" with plans for a major offensive. "I think General, I can safely say that you possess the confidence & affection of the Army of Tennessee," Brent concluded.[42]

Members of the Bolling Hall family certainly would have supported Brent's assertion. Capt. James A. Hall of the 24th Alabama believed that most men in the army would welcome Bragg's return. Hall believed officers had a duty "to instill into the men confidence in him. It was not long before my company were all Bragg *men* and when he left us they considered it a dark hour for Braggs army. They loved and respected him while they feared him."[43]

One of the strongest assets Bragg possessed in the army at Dalton was John Bell Hood. He admired the young man ever since Hood appeared at the head of his division at Chickamauga and lost a leg early on September 20. Hood also possessed the confidence and admiration of Davis, making for a powerful combination in favor of his promotion to corps command when he recovered in March 1864. Hood immediately began to write confidentially to Bragg. He urged him to unleash Longstreet and push Johnston to support a grand offensive with his own force. Hood wrote similarly to Davis and Seddon. "To regain Tennessee would be of more value to us than a half dozen victories in Virginia," Hood assured Bragg.[44]

While Hood won Bragg's devotion, the public mostly reacted negatively to Bragg's tenure as military adviser to the Southern president. "It is the general belief that Bragg is a failure" as a field commander, Louis T. Wigfall concluded, and the public could not make itself believe he would make a better adviser. Bragg made himself visible in Richmond, attending church services with other high-ranking army officers, but it did little to soften public attitudes. When an article appeared in the *Richmond Enquirer* defending Bragg, it was followed by another that severely condemned his record in the West. As it became increasingly clear that Grant would direct Union operations against Lee in Virginia, many Southerners became worried. "Pray God that Bragg may have nothing to do with the campaign against [Grant]," Catherine Ann Devereux Edmondston lamented in her journal. "He has been beaten too often by him already."[45]

Davis's Troubleshooter

From February until April 1864, Bragg concerned himself with a variety of administrative issues relating to the Confederate war effort. His work sometimes resulted in improvement of various systems and at other times had little effect on them. But with the onset of major Union offensives in Virginia and Georgia during the first week of May, Bragg's attention was drawn to operations in the field. Davis began to use him as he had used other members of his staff, as his eyes and ears in the field. Bragg's experience as commander of the Army of Tennessee was a powerful reason for the Confederate president to take his advice seriously. As a result, Bragg played important roles in some phases of the campaign in both Virginia and Georgia.

It is possible Bragg sensed that his job would become more difficult, for he established regulations concerning office procedure early in May, bracing for a flood of visitors and paperwork. He established office hours from 8:30 in the morning until 4 P.M. and instructed his staff to allow visitors from 10 A.M. until noon, with aides screening their wants in the anteroom and sending them to appropriate departments. Bragg consulted visitors only if they were on important business that could not be handled by others. All department and bureau heads were to be shown into his office at any time. Bragg relied on John Sale to maintain records associated with his position while David Urquhart superintended the reception of visitors with the help of Towson Ellis and Thomas Butler. F. S. Parker and John Strange assisted where needed. Bragg also had a black servant to clean up the office suite and a white messenger. By early May, he regularly signed correspondence as emanating from Headquarters, Armies of the Confederate States.[1]

The first major trouble that Bragg dealt with concerned his old friend P. G. T. Beauregard, who had been placed in command of the Department of North Carolina and Southern Virginia in April. Upon assuming command at Weldon, Beauregard received a memorandum from Bragg explaining all the "points of interest and importance in the department" so the new commander could quickly become familiar with them.[2]

While Grant directed the operations of the Army of the Potomac against Lee in the Overland Campaign, driving southward toward Richmond from the Wilderness, the Federal Army of the James under Benjamin Butler operated from the coast toward the area between Richmond and Petersburg. Beauregard's meager manpower was the only thing preventing Butler from capturing either city. The Federals made a lodgment on the railroad linking the two places and paused. Beauregard concocted a complicated plan to deal with Butler that involved having Lee fall back some sixty miles to the Chickahominy River and then detaching 15,000 men to reinforce his small army. With this force Beauregard hoped to crush Butler. Then he could send reinforcements to Lee, and the combined force would defeat Grant.[3]

Beauregard proposed this scheme in a dispatch to Bragg on May 14, but Bragg was not impressed. Instead, he urged on Davis a plan for Beauregard to attack Butler immediately with whatever manpower he possessed. Davis followed Bragg's advice, and Beauregard's offensive on May 16 soundly defeated the enemy, which retired to the tip of Bermuda Hundred where the Confederates constructed field works to contain them. Three days later Bragg committed to paper the reasons for his advice to the Confederate president. It would take too long to implement Beauregard's plan, allowing Butler to consolidate his position south of Richmond. Lee's retreat would have exposed much territory to Union occupation and depressed civilian morale. Bragg predicted that both Petersburg and the Shenandoah Valley would have fallen into enemy hands. Bragg's intervention and advice saved the Confederacy these setbacks. Very few people realized that Bragg played a role in repelling the first Union offensive against the capital that year.[4]

Lee conducted a fighting retreat from the Wilderness toward Richmond, his army enduring the hammering Grant launched at Spotsylvania and Cold Harbor. At the latter place, only about ten miles from the capital, both armies rested a few days in field works stretching across the sandy landscape. Concurrent Union operations had by this time cleared the Shenandoah Valley of Confederate troops, and a small army under David Hunter threatened Lynchburg, Virginia. Bragg urged that something be done to drive the enemy from the valley and then invade Maryland to threaten Washington, D.C. He envisioned only a small force doing this, but when Lee read Bragg's proposal, he thought he might be able to spare an entire corps for the job. "If it is deemed prudent to hazard the defense of Richmond," Lee wrote, "I will do so." Davis approved, and Lee's Second Corps under Jubal Early set out toward the upper valley. Early easily defeated Hunter, saved Lynchburg, and then moved down the valley to implement the scheme Bragg had suggested, crossing the Potomac River and driving to the outskirts of Washington by July 11. Only the timely arrival of the Sixth Corps from the Army of the Potomac at Petersburg saved the Federal capital.[5]

For an officer who had burned out under the stress of commanding the Army of Tennessee, Bragg seemed to have been reinvigorated. He acted with energy to influence military operations at key events in Virginia. Bragg earned his pay as Davis's military adviser in these incidents although he received no credit from the press or public for his work.

But Bragg had far less success in dealing with the problems faced by the Army of Tennessee in the Atlanta campaign. Johnston conducted a defensive policy, fortifying one position after another, but only rarely attempted small-scale attacks on William T. Sherman's army group. The Federals outnumbered him nearly two to one, and he preferred to give up ground rather than risk a general engagement.[6]

Bragg tried to encourage Johnston to be more aggressive. "Every disposable man has now been sent, and from the high condition in which your army is reported, we confidently rely on a brilliant success." In Bragg's view, Lee was conducting the kind of defensive action needed. Lee punished the Federals at every opportunity without unduly risking his command, forcing the Federals to pay a heavy cost in blood for their movement south. By early June, Bragg told Davis that the "condition of affairs in Georgia is daily becoming more serious." He felt that Lee had reduced the Federal manpower advantage in Virginia so as to render Grant less dangerous than Sherman. It was up to Johnston to do more to reduce the Union advantage in Georgia.[7]

Johnston resisted calls for aggressive action. He told Bragg that he could not stop the Federals from flanking him out of one position after another. The Yankees also approached his fieldworks with fortifications of their own, making frontal attacks against them prohibitively costly. While losing 9,000 men from the first week of May until late June, Johnston was sure he had inflicted at least that many casualties on Sherman. He argued that the best strategy was to unleash Confederate cavalry on the Federals' long and vulnerable line of communications, a single-track railroad stretching from the front to Louisville, Kentucky, some 350 miles away.[8]

Joseph Wheeler also urged Bragg to authorize a large-scale cavalry strike against the Federal railroad and wanted to lead it himself. Wheeler was directly under Johnston's orders but the army commander refused to send him on this mission because he needed his mounted troops for close cooperation with the infantry. Johnston constantly urged that Nathan B. Forrest's command in Mississippi be used to hit the railroad in Tennessee, but Union expeditions out of Memphis kept Mississippi in such a turmoil that Forrest could not be spared.[9]

Bragg was not moved by Johnston's explanations for his defensive policy and agreed with Davis that Forrest and other Confederate troops in Mississippi needed to protect that state rather than move north into Tennessee. "No doubt he is outnumbered by the enemy, as we are everywhere," Bragg wrote in reference to Johnston, "but the disparity is much less than it has ever been between those two armies."[10]

The Southern president's adviser seems never to have taken the idea of raiding Sherman's railroad seriously, probably because he had little regard for the effectiveness of long-range mounted operations. John Hunt Morgan, one of the most famous of all Confederate cavalry raiders, proposed yet another ride in the summer of 1864, and Davis sent his dispatch to Bragg for comment. Bragg disparaged the prospects. "Should he ever return with his command it will as usual be disorganized and unfit for service until again armed, equipped, and disciplined." Bragg downplayed the results to be gained by small mounted raids against well protected Union railroads. They most often resulted in repairable damage, interrupting the flow of supplies by only a few days.[11]

In the middle of important business, Bragg also dealt with problems stemming from his command of the western army. Daniel H. Hill again asked Bragg to put in writing that his relief from corps command was based on "personal grounds" and not any dereliction of duty by Hill. The disgruntled general told Bragg he did not regret anything he did while with the Army of Tennessee and only sought "simple justice." Bragg wearily reminded Davis that Hill had been relieved for trying to remove his superior officer from command of the army, and "in a manner both unmilitary and unofficer-like." Bragg had no intention of writing a statement of the kind Hill demanded.[12]

With regard to Bragg's handling of his job during the stirring days of May and June, opinions were mixed in interesting ways. Generally, the public and many soldiers who had no direct contact with him were uneasy. "They think if anything should happen to Lee that Bragg would be assigned," as Robert Garlick Hill Kean put it, "which they regard with universal consent as the ruin of the army and the cause."[13]

But there continued to exist within the Army of Tennessee a strong pro-Bragg contingent. His supporters were encouraged when Alexander P. Stewart, a stalwart division commander in the army, was named to replace Polk after the bishop general was killed at Pine Mountain on June 14. Polk had brought his troops from the Department of Mississippi and East Louisiana to join Johnston soon after the start of the Atlanta campaign. The command was incorporated into the Army of Tennessee as a third corps after Stewart was appointed to the position. Such promotions inspired and satisfied Bragg's friends, "who are daily increasing in this army," as Wheeler put it. There was no similar cabal against Johnston as had existed against Bragg the previous year. Nurse Kate Cumming's brother, who served in an artillery unit of the Army of Tennessee, told her the men were certain that the ample flow of food and other supplies during the campaign was due to Bragg's attention to his old command.[14]

Ironically, the Confederate public remained ignorant of Bragg's role in the Bermuda Hundred campaign against Butler and the operations against Hunter in the Shenandoah Valley. Instead the civilian public was overwhelmingly critical of Bragg as the spring campaigns intensified. Senator James L. Orr of South Carolina argued that Bragg's position was unnecessary, and many people felt irritated that a bill was working its way through congress allowing him a higher salary than Lee's. "The country was outraged and disgusted when this utterly 'played out' officer was made commanding general," commented the editor of the *Richmond Whig*. Bragg should have refused the appointment but "he was anxious to oblige the friend who had made him a very great man and determined to keep him great."[15]

Bragg paid no attention to public opinion in those busy days of early summer. The Atlanta campaign continued to go poorly for the South, with Johnston falling back to the Chattahoochee River by early July. Davis and Bragg became alarmed because Sherman's army group still had not been dealt a serious blow to reduce its fighting capacity. Bragg decided to act. He asked Davis for permission to visit the Army of Tennessee. As he later put it in the third person, the motive was to "see Gen'l Johnston, to whom he had ever been most friendly, with a view, if possible of obviating his removal." Davis authorized the trip on July 9, urging Bragg to "confer with General

Johnston in relation to military affairs there" but return to Richmond as soon as possible. Ironically, Johnston retired across the Chattahoochee River on the evening of July 9 and took a position only a couple of miles north of Atlanta. The campaign had reached a watershed, and the sense of foreboding increased in Richmond.[16]

Bragg's arrival at army headquarters early on July 13 attracted much attention. Everyone wondered at the significance of the visit. William Whann Mackall was now serving as Johnston's chief of staff and noted that Bragg "seemed a little disposed to be civil to me, that was all; it looked a good deal as if he thought he was magnanimous." On the other hand, W. H. T. Walker, who thought Bragg was "looking better than when he left this Army," jumped to the conclusion he had come to replace Johnston.[17]

Bragg sent a telegram to Davis immediately upon his arrival. He reported the Army of Tennessee was "sadly depleted" and had 10,000 fewer effectives than Johnston indicated a month before. Reports claimed that the Federals had already secured several crossing points on the Chattahoochee River but had not yet moved south of the stream in force. "I find but little encouraging," he told the president of the Confederacy.[18]

Bragg, Johnston, and the corps commanders spent ten hours conferring on July 13. According to all accounts, Bragg played his cards close to his chest, never mentioning the possibility of Johnston's removal. In fact, according to Johnston, Bragg claimed "to have no official business, to have made a casual visit on his way" to points west of Atlanta. He further told Johnston he intended to see if any reinforcements could be found for him. Bragg apparently had decided to see if Johnston himself would discuss his plans and wanted to gauge the level of hope and enthusiasm the commander held about his prospects. In this Bragg was disappointed because Johnston did not offer any insights into his thinking or emotions. "I thought him satisfied with the state of things, but not so with that in Virginia," Johnston later admitted. Hardee was a bit miffed that, despite his long association with Bragg and the Army of Tennessee, the president's military adviser did not consult with him about the course of events.[19]

On July 14, Bragg again consulted with Johnston, but he also quietly visited Hood at the latter's headquarters and had an intense discussion of the situation. Hood wrote a letter to Bragg and gave it to him with the intention of sharing it with Davis. In the letter Hood criticized Johnston for failing to take advantage of chances to attack the enemy all the way from Dalton down to the Chattahoochee River, losing 20,000 men to no purpose. "I have, general, so often urged that we should force the enemy to give us battle as to almost be regarded reckless by the officers high in rank in this Army, since their views have been so directly opposite."[20]

Hood's letter was the climax of a history of backbiting the young general had conducted ever since he took over a corps in the Army of Tennessee. The letter also was an outright lie, as Hood biographer Richard McMurry has frankly pointed out. The truth was that Hood had derailed Johnston's plans to attack the enemy more than once. At Cassville, Johnston attempted a major assault on one column of Federal troops approaching his position on May 19 only to call it off when Hood raised an alarm about the sudden presence of Federal troops to his flank. Later that day, Hood and Polk insisted their defensive position on a high ridge was vulnerable to enemy enfilading fire, compelling Johnston to retreat once again. When Hood took the offensive at Kolb's Farm during the Kennesaw Mountain phase of the campaign on June 22, he did so without authority from Johnston. Worse still, Hood failed to scout the terrain, ascertain exactly what lay ahead, or send out skirmishers. He blindly threw two divisions of his corps at a strong position, lost 1,000 men, and gained nothing for it except to halt a careful Union advance toward Johnston's left flank. He could have achieved that goal by merely taking position and digging in with no loss at all. Hood had not served his commander well in the field and had written private letters to Richmond authorities denigrating Johnston's conduct of the campaign.[21]

Bragg advised Davis to wait until he could send a full report of the situation, and he penned that report on July 15. It was damning of Johnston's conduct of the campaign. "As far as I can learn we do not propose any offensive operations, but shall await the enemy's approach and be governed, as heretofore, by the development in our front." Johnston removed supplies and machinery from Atlanta, and his constant retreats exposed Alabama to Union cavalry raids. "Much disappointment and dissatisfaction prevails," Bragg continued, "but there is no open or imprudent expression." Bragg now thought the army had lost 20,000 men thus far under Johnston's tenure.[22]

Bragg had his own opinion about what should be done. "There is but one remedy—offensive action." He admitted that Sherman had the advantage of position, troop strength, and morale "but not to an extent to make me despair of success. We should drive the enemy from this side of the river, follow him down by an attack in flank, and force him to battle, at the same time throwing our cavalry on his communications." This plan was

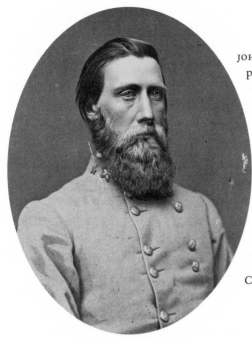

JOHN BELL HOOD. Bragg became a major patron of Hood's rise to prominence owing to his admiration of the young's man's qualities and his desperate search for new officers in the Army of Tennessee. He supported Hood's promotion to corps command and later aided in his elevation to lead the army in the middle of the Atlanta campaign. Bragg's evaluation of Hood was painfully flawed, and he helped to give the Confederacy an army leader whose failures doomed the Southern war effort. (Library of Congress, LC-DIG-cwpb-07468)

similar to what Bragg had done to Rosecrans at Stones River. He believed the rank and file "would hail with delight an order of battle." Although Bragg admitted that Johnston seemed "more inclined to fight" now than before, he offered Davis little hope that the current commander would take the offensive.[23]

Bragg did not recommend Johnston's removal, but he told Davis that if he had to be replaced, Hood was the best choice to head the Army of Tennessee. His opinion of Hood, "always high, has been raised by his conduct in this campaign," Bragg wrote. He obviously knew nothing of the details associated with Hood's deplorable role in the affair at Cassville or at Kolb's Farm. "Do not understand me as proposing him as a man of genius, or a great general, but as far better in the present emergency than any one we have available." The reason for such a high estimate was Hood's own shaping of his image. The young general "has been in favor of giving battle, and mentions to me numerous instances of opportunities lost." Hood assured Bragg that Polk agreed with him on that issue, while Hardee largely supported the constant fallbacks. A. P. Stewart also urged offensive action, according to Hood.[24]

Ironically, Bragg's thorough report reached Richmond too late to influence Davis; and yet the outcome was exactly what Bragg had suggested.

Bragg felt the report was too long and complicated to trust to telegraph wires, so he sent it to Richmond with Harvey Washington Walter. Before the report reached Davis, the Confederate president became alarmed by a small bit of news Bragg included in one of several short telegrams he sent on July 15. It related to an exaggerated report that the Federals were beginning to construct a line of earthworks from the Chattahoochee River toward the Georgia Railroad that linked Atlanta with Augusta to the east. For Davis, this was the last straw. He quickly sent a telegram to Johnston demanding to know his plans for dealing with the enemy "so specifically as will enable me to anticipate events." Johnston answered vaguely but honestly that he had no plan except to wait and see, "mainly to watch for an opportunity to fight to advantage." Davis decided therefore to act. Samuel Cooper sent a telegram relieving Johnston of his command on July 17 because "you have failed to arrest the advance of the enemy to the vicinity of Atlanta, . . . and express no confidence that you can defeat or repel him." Davis named Hood as Johnston's successor because of his opinion of Hood as an aggressive general, an opinion shaped by Hood himself in personal interactions with Davis and Bragg.[25]

When told of his new appointment Hood was stunned, indicating that he never really was angling for Johnston's position but had been playing a sophomoric game of backbiting tied up with his new-found personal friendships with powerful men in Richmond. He had played Polk's game thus far during the campaign and now found himself thrust into a position he did not want.[26]

Bragg remained unaware of the Southern president's decision to remove Johnston for several days. He visited the troops on July 15 and, according to Newton N. Davis of the 24th Alabama, was "greeted with loud & prolonged cheers. His old army are very much attached to him & many of them even now express a preference for him over any one else as a commander." With these cheers still ringing in his ears, Bragg left Atlanta on the night of July 15 and headed west, stopping at Montgomery to communicate with Edmund Kirby Smith in the Trans-Mississippi. "It was here that he heard with some surprise of the President's action in removing Gen'l Johnston," Bragg later wrote of himself, again in the third person. The surprise sprang not from the fact that Johnston was removed, for Bragg strongly tended to think that was a necessity, but that Davis did so without first consulting him. Very soon, Bragg received a visit from John Forsyth, friend and editor of the *Mobile Advertiser and Register.* H. D. Banks, a former staff member of Johnston's and current editor of the *Montgomery Mail*, and Leroy Pope Walker, former secretary of war and Confederate general, also visited Bragg in Montgomery. Banks and Walker especially were upset at Johnston's removal. Bragg tried to soothe them by explaining Davis's reasons for doing so and urging public opinion to support the Rebel president's decision.[27]

Bragg remained at Montgomery for several days to deal with a Union cavalry raid against the Montgomery and West Point Railroad led by Lovell H. Rousseau. The Federal horsemen, numbering 2,500 men, hit the line on July 17–18 and tore up thirty miles of track before riding toward Sherman's army group. As soon as that threat receded, Davis ordered Bragg on July 19 back to Atlanta for consultations with Hood, although Bragg did not receive the order immediately. He traveled to Columbus by July 22 and left the evening of the next day for Atlanta, arriving July 24. By that time Hood had done much, attacking George H. Thomas's Army of the Cumberland north of Atlanta in the battle of Peachtree Creek on July 20 and then flanking and nearly collapsing James B. McPherson's Army of the Tennessee east of Atlanta on July 22. The Confederates accomplished nothing more than to temporarily halt Sherman's moves around the city, which were designed to snip the rail lines feeding Hood's army. The Federals still managed to cut the Georgia Railroad east of Atlanta. Although McPherson was killed on July 22 and the Federals lost 5,600 men that day and on July 20, Hood suffered a combined loss of 6,900 troops in the two engagements.[28]

Bragg stretched the truth when he reported to Davis that the battle of July 22 was a "brilliant affair" which exerted "an admirable" effect on morale. He also misrepresented the details of the outcome. "I am happy to say our loss was small in comparison to the enemy's. He was badly defeated and completely failed in one of his bold flank movements, heretofore so successful." As a sponsor of Hood, Bragg felt the need to magnify his protégé's accomplishments. His second visit to Atlanta sparked interest even in the Union camp; Sherman knew of his arrival but of course had no clue as to the purpose of the visit.[29]

In fact, Bragg spent most of his time trying to support Hood concerning a myriad of problems the young commander had to deal with, and they largely resulted from the fallout concerning his appointment to head the Army of Tennessee. Bragg approved the transfer of Stephen D. Lee from his former command, the Department of Mississippi and East Louisiana, to take over Hood's Corps. Like Hood, Bragg saw Lee as a brilliant young general who had won a "very important victory" at Harrisburg, Mississippi, on July 14. That engagement, also known as the battle of Tupelo, actually resulted in the costly repulse of Lee's attack on Andrew Jackson Smith's Federal force, but Smith decided to retire after the battle for logistical reasons. The result was the turning back of yet another Union expedition designed to keep Lee and Forrest so busy they could not bother Sherman's rail line. When Lee arrived at Atlanta, Bragg assured John Sale that he was "most favorably received. Tone of army fine, and strength increasing daily."[30]

Hardee was a more difficult problem as far as Bragg was concerned. When Hood pointed out that Hardee was dissatisfied to serve under him (the two had never really got along), Bragg wanted to get Hardee out of the Army of Tennessee. Keenly remembering his own experience, Bragg assured Davis, "There does not exist that cordiality and mutual confidence and support necessary" among the high-ranking officers. He suggested bringing Richard Taylor in to replace Hardee. Bragg had always maintained a high opinion of Taylor even though the latter had yet to distinguish himself in largely administrative commands held in the Trans-Mississippi. But Bragg was certain that with Lee, Taylor, and Stewart to command the three corps under Hood, the Army of Tennessee "would be invincible." Davis did not take up Bragg's advice, preferring to console Hardee and encourage him to help Hood adjust to the demanding responsibilities of his new position.[31]

"General Hood has found much to do," Bragg told Davis on his second visit to Atlanta. In describing that work, Bragg also denigrated Johnston. "For want of administration the army was in sad condition" before Hood took command. There were too many staff officers in nearly all units and more wagons and mules had been allowed than were justified by regulations. Bragg tended to blame William Whann Mackall for this, also getting a shot at the chief of staff who had abandoned him just before the battle of Chattanooga. In the weeks following Hood's accession to command a number of changes took place, and Bragg approved them all. Hugh Mercer was deemed too old for his brigade command, so Bragg sent him home and brought Henry R. Jackson from Savannah to replace him. Thomas C. Hindman had not done well in division command during the campaign and left early in July, replaced with Bragg's hearty approval by James Patton Anderson. He had viewed Anderson as a stalwart in the Army of Tennessee ever since Stones River. When Mackall requested reassignment rather than serve under Hood, Bragg approved his request and the appointment of artillery chief Francis A. Shoup as the army's new chief of staff. "I trust my action in these cases has met your sanction," Bragg told Davis.[32]

The president of the Confederacy approved all of Bragg's work in this period and wanted him to do more. Davis wrote to Governor Thomas H. Watts of Alabama that his military adviser would brief him on the current situation in the wake of Rousseau's Raid. But Watts had a history of bad relations with Bragg. He had served under the general for five months, and the two had a falling out over some issue. Whatever caused the trouble, it is very evident that Watts had an absolutely poisonous attitude toward Bragg. "He has not one particle of *common sense* and he has less *heart* than any man I ever knew," the governor-elect wrote to Davis late in November, 1863. "He has less regard for law, and the proprieties of life than any general in the armies."[33]

With an attitude such as this, Watts was in no mood to meet Bragg. He wrote an icy letter to the general telling him "if I were to consult my private feelings alone, I should have no conference with you." But he respected Davis too much to ignore his wishes. Therefore, if Bragg could give him important facts he would "gladly receive them." Of course, Bragg felt the insult and decided not to meet him. Watts "never had the capacity to do good," Bragg thought, "and is now absorbed in striving to sustain his waning popularity by exemptions & appointments of State officers, that he is seriously injuring the cause." Instead of meeting Watts, Bragg went on to many other Southern cities in a roundabout return to Richmond.[34]

Bragg inadvertently made a bitter enemy of Joseph E. Johnston because of the way he handled the mid-July crisis facing the Army of Tennessee. Johnston was not surprised at Davis's firing him, for the two had a long history of misunderstanding and quarreling, but he had treated Bragg with consideration in early 1863. Bragg was not frank or honest with Johnston about the true reason for his visit to Atlanta. Even though he was surprised when he learned that Davis had relieved Johnston before he made a firm recommendation, it could not have been any surprise that Davis was inclined to do so. Moreover, Bragg also tipped the balance toward Hood as Johnston's replacement through his persistent praise of the young general and by secretly meeting with him while in Atlanta. Johnston felt betrayed by Bragg. "It is clear that his expedition had no other object than my removal," he told Dabney H. Maury. "A man of honor in his place would have communicated with me as well as with Hood on the subject."[35]

Even worse, Johnston heard reports about what Bragg told many people after leaving Atlanta. As soon as he learned of Davis's decision to drop Johnston, Bragg began to explain why this was done. In the process he criticized Johnston: at least those who heard him interpreted his explanation that way. In Johnston's view, Bragg spun the situation to favor the administration. He "exerted himself either falsely or unfairly to disparage me, exaggerating the losses of our Army without referring to what he had heard of those of the enemy, saying that I had disregarded the wishes & instructions of the administration that he had implored me to change my course. He did nothing of the sort." Johnston understood that on one level Bragg was merely supporting Davis "by way of reconciling people to the event" of his relief, but it stung and embittered him. He pointed out the irony associated with the situation. Bragg had lost Tennessee, suffered a humiliating defeat at Missionary Ridge, but soon after secured promotion to the "highest position in the Confederate armies." It was galling to be criticized by someone with a record such as Bragg's.[36]

While some members of the Army of Tennessee worried about Johnston's retreats, most of the troops loved him and were deeply upset by his removal. The army soldiered on under Hood, but for many of the men Bragg's role in their hero's removal was almost as galling as it was for Johnston. Douglas Cater of the 19th Louisiana remarked after the war that Bragg had worked his "magnetism" over Davis and "used his influence against our General Johnston, and recommended Hood." William Whann Mackall thought the influence worked the other way: Davis had "humbugged" Bragg and used him as a tool of his own designs. Andrew Jackson Neal of the Marion Light Artillery of Florida thought Bragg not only engineered the removal of Johnston but would do the same with Robert E. Lee for not damaging Grant even more. The image of Bragg assumed huge proportions. For good or ill, he was a more powerful, even malevolent figure in the minds of his former subordinates than ever before.[37]

Some of the men retained absolute faith in Bragg's judgment. C. Irvine Walker of the 10th South Carolina was one of those who feared Johnston's retreats would wreck the army. "I can't help thinking that Genl. Bragg would have conducted the campaign very differently and perhaps with other results," he mused.[38]

Walker may well have been right. Judging from Bragg's performance at Perryville, Stones River, and Chickamauga, where he ordered vigorous tactical offensives against the enemy, and given his views that Johnston ought to have been more aggressive from Dalton south, it is quite likely he would have conducted the Atlanta campaign with more spirit than Johnston. But the poisonous attitude many men still retained toward him would have wrecked Bragg's ability to lead the Army of Tennessee effectively after Missionary Ridge.

Bragg's role in the relief of Johnston has generated some controversy among historians. Thomas Robson Hay believes Bragg became a foe of Johnston in March 1864 when the latter resisted Davis and Bragg in their efforts to prod him into mounting an offensive before the Federals began their spring campaign. There is no evidence to support that view. Hay also argues that Hood was not a protégé of Bragg, but there is ample evidence to prove that Bragg was enamored of the young general and his assumed potential for greatness. Without a doubt, Bragg promoted Hood as the man of the hour and thereby played a large role in his ascension to command. Richard McMurry has wondered if Hood manipulated Bragg in order to remove Johnston, but there is no evidence for it. Bragg's long admiration for the young general, partly based on Hood's habit of writing confiding letters to him, was the reason that Bragg consulted with Hood after his conference with Johnston during the first Atlanta visit. There is ample evidence that Hood was genuinely surprised to be elevated to the army's command.[39]

Historians have noted the unsavory nature of Bragg's role in the removal of Johnston. It was "not at all creditable," according to Thomas Robson Hay. "To a certain extent he was under at least an ethical obligation to Johnston for the treatment he had received at Johnston's hands in the winter of 1862–1863." Hay correctly points out that Bragg should have fulfilled that obligation by being frank with Johnston about the mood in Richmond and the dangers of continuing to conduct his Fabian strategy against Sherman.[40]

In the wake of Johnston's removal, Bragg tried to persuade public opinion that the move was justified. In the process, he almost by necessity portrayed Johnston's tenure as commander of the Army of Tennessee as a failure. While this may seem callous considering Johnston's strong support of him in 1863, when faced with the choice, Bragg decided to support his boss in Richmond rather than his friend in Atlanta. However, he could have communicated with Johnston more honestly as Johnston himself pointed out. Bragg, however, saw nothing wrong in his own actions and praised them, in the third person again: "But in this, as in all other cases, he *never* hesitated as to his duty in supporting the government."[41]

15

Defeat

The last seven months of the war witnessed futile efforts by Bragg to stem the tide against almost inevitable defeat. As Federal strength remained relatively constant, Confederate strength and resources rapidly deteriorated with loss of territory and a dwindling manpower resource. The conflict became a race against time, numbers, and depressed morale as the Confederacy neared its ruin.

Following his extended journey west, Bragg returned to Richmond in late July and continued to offer advice on strategic problems. He resisted efforts by local commanders to have more troops shifted to their sectors and argued in favor of concentrating men to oppose only the main Union armies. He also pointed out that cavalry raids against Sherman's line of communications in Tennessee would not benefit the Rebel cause very much. "Raids are injurious to our troops and unprofitable in results," he told Davis. Bragg suggested enticing Union prisoners to enlist in the Confederate army, especially the foreign born who reportedly were disaffected. "It is possible we may obtain recruits who will at least do us no harm and may add to our strength," Bragg concluded.[1]

A problem associated with the past cropped up in September when Bragg's report of Chickamauga was printed. Looking over it, he was irritated that a mistake had been made in a crucial sentence. When judging Polk's explanations for the delay of his attack on September 20, Bragg had written "It is sufficient to say they are entirely unsatisfactory." The printed report, however, read "entirely satisfactory," completely reversing Bragg's meaning. He informed the clerk of the House of Representatives that he was sending his own clerk to correct this and other small mistakes in the printed version of the report.[2]

Public reaction to Bragg never softened during the summer months of 1864. It was a common saying among many that, in Mary Chesnut's words,

"Bragg is acting as lightning rod: drawing off some of the hatred of Jeff Davis to himself." Davis found himself the object of criticism when he publicly tried to defend Bragg. The Confederate president visited the Army of Tennessee after Hood lost Atlanta and authorized a strike northward to hit Sherman's railroad communications. While returning to Richmond, Davis gave many speeches and reportedly complained of "shafts of Malice" directed at himself and his military adviser. A few weeks later he denied saying such things and also denied praising Bragg's services to the nation.[3]

Inside the Confederate government, many bureaucrats were getting tired of Bragg. The Conscript Bureau and the Quartermaster's Department seemed to be riddled with problems. When Bragg complained of how the latter was run, Quartermaster Alexander R. Lawton responded angrily. Robert Garlick Hill Kean, head of the Bureau of War, lost his patience with the military adviser in October. "Bragg gets worse and worse, more and more mischievous. He resembles a chimpanzee as much in character as he does in appearance. He is engaged now in persecuting quartermasters who have clerks liable to military duty." Kean accused Bragg of quietly learning what new ideas Seddon was considering and then proposing them as his own to the Southern president. "Prying, indirection, vindictiveness, and insincerity are the repulsive traits which mark Bragg's character," Kean concluded.[4]

But historians have generally given Bragg high marks for his activity as Davis's military adviser. The array of issues and problems he tackled was staggering, and he steered a course that took little heed of people's criticism. Davis relied heavily on Bragg's advice, even though he did not act on everything recommended. Bragg's role in influencing field operations was decisive in three cases both East and West. As Thomas Connelly has put it, he exercised "a wide influence" in all manner of Confederate affairs both administrative and operational.[5]

Despite this heavy influence, Davis felt by mid-October that Bragg might be needed in the field. W. H. C. Whiting sent alarming reports that the Federals were preparing an expedition to capture Wilmington, North Carolina, closing the last major blockade-running port as well as one of the most important sources of supply for the Army of Northern Virginia. Davis wanted Bragg to take charge of affairs, leaving a staff officer to run his Richmond office. Bragg traveled south and assumed command of the defenses of Wilmington on October 22. After evaluating the situation, he concluded that Whiting's reports had been exaggerated, but the citizens in the area had lost all confidence in Whiting. Nevertheless, Bragg kept him as second in command to take advantage of his expertise. Bragg assured Davis and Lee that he could hold Wilmington.[6]

Public opinion continued to be negative regarding Bragg. When news of his transfer to North Carolina seeped in, observers assumed the pressure against him in Richmond was too much for Davis to bear. "Everybody fears that Wilmington will 'go up,'" thought Robert Garlick Hill Kean. But they were nevertheless delighted "that this element of discord, acrimony, and confusion is withdrawn from" Richmond. When Bragg's authority was extended so that he controlled all of North Carolina east of the Blue Ridge, War Department clerk John B. Jones saw it as a sign that the president of the Confederacy finally was giving up and cutting Bragg's ties to his former job in the nation's capital.[7]

Bragg assumed his enlarged command on November 17, but Davis quickly sent him on another assignment. Sherman had begun his March to the Sea from Atlanta two days before. Other than Joseph Wheeler's small cavalry division and some state militia, nothing stood in his way. The Rebel president sent Bragg to Augusta where he was to take charge of efforts to deal with Sherman. It was a nearly hopeless task, but Bragg left on the first train out of Wilmington. Taking a handful of troops with him, he telegraphed Mayor R. H. May of Augusta: "Exhort your people to be confident and resolute."[8]

Seddon wanted Bragg to take charge of all resources from Augusta to the coast, but the general was daunted by the assignment. He had no more than 6,000 men at his disposal (plus Wheeler's Division) and estimated Sherman had 30,000 troops. "I must candidly express my belief that no practicable combinations of my available men can avert disaster," he told Richmond on November 27. Ironically, Sherman possessed double the number of men Bragg estimated, making the prospects even gloomier. All Bragg could do was to repair the Georgia Railroad linking Augusta with Atlanta in order to reestablish Confederate control of the area Sherman was abandoning.[9]

The Federals bypassed Augusta and closed in on Savannah to open communications with the U.S. Navy by December 13. On that day, Davis advised Bragg to return to Wilmington. Bragg telegraphed Sale to have Elise join him there, for she had returned to Richmond when he left Wilmington.[10]

Bragg's futile trip to Augusta created more public criticism. John B. Jones was certain the general would "be crucified by the enemies of the President" for failing to stop Sherman even as Davis complained bitterly that prejudice against his military adviser hampered Bragg's ability to serve the nation. "I will say to you in confidence that since Bragg has gone I can get very little information of things about Richmond," Davis told Josiah Gorgas. "The murmurers & fault finders" refused to let Bragg alone. For their part, many Southern observers criticized their president for pushing forward Bragg while keeping Joseph E. Johnston on the shelf.[11]

There were some people in the Confederacy who still believed in Bragg. Many in the Trans-Mississippi continued to hope he would replace Edmund Kirby Smith in command of that region. Louisiana congressmen were heavily in favor of the idea, but the other congressmen from Arkansas, Texas, and Missouri seemed "violently opposed" to it. George W. Brent strongly urged that Bragg replace Kirby Smith in order to "organize and administer" the Trans-Mississippi.[12]

Some Confederates still hoped Bragg would return to the Army of Tennessee after Hood's disastrous invasion of that state. Robert C. Tyler, a former brigade commander in the army, believed the rank and file loved Johnston first and Bragg second. Tyler praised Bragg as a "gallant soldier, the Self Sacrificing Patriot [and] my beau ideal of a Soldier." He longed to serve under him again in the Army of Tennessee.[13]

When the Confederate congress created the position of general-in-chief and named Robert E. Lee to fill it, there was no hope that Bragg could continue to serve as Davis's military adviser. Sale had kept Bragg's Richmond office open until February, but now he needed to close it. Sale wanted his general to help him convince Davis that the staff should continue to serve him in the field, but Bragg could not leave Wilmington. He urged Sale to intercede with Davis on his behalf. Davis was willing to help, but he could allow Bragg to retain only three personal aides. The president of the Confederacy also asked Lee to allow Bragg a short visit to Richmond to wrap up the liquidation of his office and staff as military adviser.[14]

Bragg was once again in the center of important field operations. Grant ordered a major effort to reduce Fort Fisher, a massive earthen fort guarding the mouth of the Cape Fear River several miles downstream from Wilmington. The first Union offensive ended in abject failure. Commanded by Benjamin Butler, it involved an attempt to collapse the walls of Fort Fisher by exploding a powder boat in shallow waters near the work on December 24. That effort predictably failed, and Butler called off further action. The troops boarded their transports and returned to Virginia.[15]

Bragg had done comparatively little to win this victory. In a general order, he credited subordinates Whiting and William Lamb for the repulse of "one of the most formidable naval armaments of modern times." He further argued the repulse "proves that the superiority of land batteries over ships of war . . . has been re-established by the genius of the engineer; and the weaker party on the defensive may still defy the greater numbers and mechanized resources of an arrogant invader." Not only did Bragg persist in ad hoc comments on the morality of his enemy, but he proved to be mistaken about why Fort Fisher survived the attack. The Federals never landed a sufficient infantry force to attack the work.[16]

The second Union attempt to take Fort Fisher had an entirely different result. Butler was out, and Alfred H. Terry now commanded the army contingent cooperating with David D. Porter, who was in charge of the naval force. The second Fort Fisher expedition was pushed forward with consummate skill by both commanders. Davis encouraged Bragg, telegraphing, "We are trustfully looking to your operations," but there was little the general could do to stop the course of events. While Porter lay down a massive naval bombardment, Terry landed nearly 8,000 troops and attacked Fort Fisher on January 15. In fierce, often hand-to-hand fighting, the Federals drove the Rebel defenders out of the work and captured it within a few hours. Robert Hoke's Division had been shifted from Petersburg to Wilmington in the wake of the first Union expedition, but Bragg decided not to use it in an attempt to recapture the fort. "The enemy's enormous fleet alone would destroy us in such an attempt were we unopposed by the land force," he told Davis. Instead Bragg acted strictly on the defensive, holding lines to contain the Union landing within the vicinity of Fort Fisher.[17]

Not surprisingly, public opinion condemned Bragg for losing the fort. Whiting and Lamb, who were wounded and captured in the fight, also denounced Bragg for failing to help their beleaguered garrison. Bragg assumed responsibility for his actions. His judgment about holding Hoke's division to save Wilmington rather than to counterattack might well have been right, but it placed him in the position of a do-nothing general who sacrificed the garrison.[18]

Elise was with her husband at Wilmington during this time, but the couple found it difficult to live at this late stage of the war. In fact, Braxton asked his brother Thomas to send a barrel of flour. "Our only trouble is to get enough to eat, as we pay our board in kind. No one will take a boarder here or anywhere now for money," he told him. Braxton considered sending Elise to live with Thomas but worried that it would create alarm in

Wilmington when made public. She therefore remained with her husband, and it "has had a good effect on the weak and nervous," Bragg thought.[19]

Another Union offensive against Wilmington developed within a month after the fall of Fort Fisher. John M. Schofield transferred two divisions of the Twenty-third Corps from Tennessee to Annapolis, Maryland, where they boarded transports and headed for the mouth of the Cape Fear River. Joined by Terry's command, Schofield led 12,000 troops toward Wilmington, located twenty-three miles up from the river's mouth. Bragg had Hoke's 6,600 men and the garrison of Fort Anderson, part way upstream from the mouth and on the west side of the river. He positioned Hoke on the east side of the Cape Fear at Sugar Loaf and hoped to block the Federal advance. Schofield began his offensive by February 16, conducting careful moves to flank Fort Anderson and compel its evacuation without a battle, and continued doing the same against every Confederate position until Bragg ordered the evacuation of Wilmington on February 21. He sent Elise to Raleigh that evening as his men burned cotton and government supplies before leaving the city to his enemy.[20]

Bragg now recommended that all forces should concentrate with the intention of preventing a junction of Sherman and Schofield. "Divided we can do nothing," he concluded. Lee sanctioned the restoration of Joseph E. Johnston to command the Army of Tennessee, which now was hurrying to North Carolina. It was merely a remnant of the once mighty force that Bragg had led, but Lee authorized Johnston to take charge of any other Confederates he could find in the state. By March 5, Bragg's small command from Wilmington was merged into Johnston's force, and Bragg was not happy. He asked Davis to relieve him from this "embarrassing position" as he called it. "The circumstances constraining me to make this request are painful in the extreme, but I cannot blindly disregard them. You will find many abler servants to fill my place, but I feel the country has had none more seriously devoted." Bragg then for the first time signed a dispatch to the Southern president as "your friend and servant." Davis recommended that Bragg be sent to the Trans-Mississippi, but there was no opportunity for him to go.[21]

Before coming directly under Johnston's command, Bragg had the opportunity to fight one last battle on his own. Schofield sent two divisions under Jacob D. Cox to New Bern with orders to advance toward Kinston; the aim was to reach Goldsborough where Schofield hoped to contact Sherman. Bragg entrenched his men along Southwest Creek three miles east of Kinston. When Cox advanced to a place called Wise's Fork a short distance away, Bragg decided to strike. A small force under Daniel Harvey Hill had been added to Bragg's command, which now numbered 8,000 men. Bragg attacked Cox on March 8, drove the Federals a short distance, and captured 1,000 prisoners before the Federals stabilized their line. Receiving reinforcements, Cox skirmished with Bragg's men the next day, but the Confederates mounted another attack on March 10 only to be repulsed. Bragg retired over the course of the next few days, and Cox occupied Kinston on March 14.[22]

Bragg's initial report of the battle at Wise's Fork conveyed the good news that his attack had been successful up to a point. He also praised Hoke and Hill for "their usual zeal, energy, and gallantry in achieving this result." It was rather surprising, given his relations with Hill, that he should praise him, but perhaps Bragg saw his errant subordinate in a different light at Wise's Fork.[23]

Johnston gathered most of the Confederate troops in North Carolina for an attempt to stop Sherman near the small town of Bentonville. Bragg brought his men from the Department of North Carolina to join in the attempt. Included was Hoke's division of four brigades, plus a brigade of North Carolina Junior Reserves, and the 13th Battalion of North Carolina Light Artillery. For the planned attack on the van of Sherman's left wing, which had marched a little farther than supporting distance from the right wing, Johnston loaned Lafayette McLaws's Division to Bragg who positioned his command on Johnston's extreme left opposite the approach of William P. Carlin's division and James D. Morgan's division of the Fourteenth Corps.[24]

Bragg may have praised Hill for his performance at Wise's Fork, but Hill had not forgiven Bragg. Three days before the battle at Bentonville, Hill implored Johnston to assign him elsewhere. "He has made me a scape goat once & would do it again. I can't feel otherwise than unpleasantly situated." Johnston knew how Hill felt. He also had developed bitter feelings toward Bragg because of his relief from command of the Army of Tennessee. Johnston only reluctantly accepted Bragg as a subordinate. He loaned McLaws to Bragg after the latter pleaded with him for more strength to accomplish his part of the plan at Bentonville. Historian Mark L. Bradley has criticized Johnston for entrusting an important mission to Bragg and not supervising his actions.[25]

When the attack began on March 19, Bragg failed to move forward at the time stipulated by Johnston; his order to advance did not reach Hoke until an hour later. Bragg was to support the main advance by Hardee and Stewart to the right, but by waiting an hour he could offer comparatively little help. "Bragg . . . either misunderstood Johnston's order or he deliberately disobeyed it," concludes Bradley. Because Bragg never wrote a report of the battle, we do not know why he delayed the assault.[26]

Once started, Bragg's men achieved some level of success. Colquitt's Brigade, commanded by Charles T. Zachry, threw back Carlin's division. Hill blamed Bragg for pulling Zachry back in order to reposition Hoke's Division rather than following up the success. But Bradley does not agree. He notes that other Federal units stopped Zachry's advance before Bragg called the brigade back to reposition it for a second try.[27]

"Bragg's most serious blunder at Bentonville was in failing to utilize McLaws's Division while he had it," concludes Bradley. Attacking on time with both McLaws and Hoke in a coordinated fashion might have overwhelmed both Carlin and Morgan. Bentonville was the last battle of Bragg's career, and it ended in failure. But as Bradley points out, Johnston failed to compensate for Bragg's limitations. Johnston regretted it for many years. "It was a great weakness on my part, not to send him [away] on the 18th," he admitted six years later.[28]

Sherman brought up the right wing by March 20, and the two armies faced off behind extensive fieldworks. Johnston finally broke contact and retired on March 21, having accomplished little more than to delay Sherman a few days. In the aftermath of Bentonville, Bragg's star burned out. He was irritated that superiors sent orders directly to his subordinates rather than through his headquarters. Frustrated, Bragg told Hoke to take charge of the troops and then went to Raleigh. "I have nothing to do but mourn over the sad spectacle hourly presented of disorganization, demoralization, and destruction" he complained to Davis. "Officers seem paralyzed, men indifferent to everything but plunder, and the people, as they well may, appear disgusted and dismayed." Bragg could only observe events and move south "as necessity may require. My position is both mortifying and humiliating, but the example of your more trying one warns me to bear it with resignation."[29]

Several days later, the harried president of the Confederacy responded to Bragg's despair. On April 1, less than forty-eight hours before his own flight from Richmond, Davis unburdened himself in a long dispatch to his former military adviser. Grant had been positioned outside Petersburg since the previous June, trying to find a way to eject Lee's army from the earthworks protecting this railroad link thirty miles south of Richmond.

The battle of Five Forks on the evening of April 1 represented a turning point in that effort. Davis could not yet know this when he began his letter to Bragg, but he was keenly aware that if it was impossible to prevent a juncture of Sherman and Grant there was no hope of holding out in Virginia.[30]

Beyond the perilous situation, Davis commiserated with Bragg's agony over the failure of the cause. "I can readily understand your feelings," Davis told Bragg. "We both entered into this war at the beginning of it; we both staked everything on the issue, and have lost all which either public or private enemies could take away; we both bear the consciousness of faithful service, and, may I not add, the sting of feeling that capacity for the public good is diminished by the covert workings of malice and the constant iterations of falsehood. I have desired to see you employed in a position suited to your rank and equal to your ability. I do not desire to subject you to unfair opposition, when failure may be produced by it, and will not fail on the first fitting occasion to call for your aid in the perilous task which lies before us." Davis empathized with Bragg and felt a bond with him because of his own experience as a target of condemnation. For the first time the Southern president expressed himself to Bragg as "very truly, your friend."[31]

Two days after penning this letter, Davis, the Confederate government, and Lee's army evacuated Richmond and Petersburg. As the presidential party headed south, Lee retired westward while Grant mounted a vigorous pursuit of the Army of Northern Virginia. Sherman rested his men around Goldsborough in preparation for the last phase of his march to Petersburg, which now was unnecessary. Grant caught up with Lee and compelled his surrender at Appomattox Courthouse on April 9, but before the news spread Bragg decided to leave Raleigh and head south to join the refugee president of the Confederacy. Sale managed a party of men to accompany Bragg and Elise on the move from Raleigh to Charlotte. Communication was again opened with Davis, who authorized Bragg to move to Chester, South Carolina. "Present my best wishes to Mrs. Bragg and believe me to be as ever your friend," Davis concluded his note of April 20. Towson Ellis delivered the message to Bragg when the latter stopped at Monroe, North Carolina.[32]

Bragg moved on to Chester and waited for the presidential party to catch up. The two groups met near Cokesbury, South Carolina, on May 1 and traveled together for some distance south, accompanied by a sizable number of cavalry and loose men who had separated from their commands.

One of the latter, a soldier named Halcott Pride Jones who wanted to return to his home in Alabama, joined Bragg's group at Chester. He traveled with it into Georgia, crossing the Savannah River on May 3. The combined parties reached Washington, Georgia, on May 5 but then separated. "The President went one way some of his cabinet remained in town, others with Genl Bragg went home." For Halcott Jones it spelled the end of any hope; "our Govt went to pieces," he noted in his journal.[33]

The reason for this scattering was a report that Federal cavalry was closing in on Washington. James H. Wilson led a large force of Union mounted troops in a raid across Alabama and into western Georgia, defeating Forrest and smashing resources along the way. Wilson was well positioned to pursue the remnants of the Confederate government, and the best strategy for Davis and Bragg was to break into small groups. About 100 people accompanied Bragg and Elise on their journey toward Mobile. The group had three wagons with Hypolite Oladowski, former chief ordnance officer in the Army of Tennessee, in charge. Bragg and Elise traveled in an ambulance with Towson Ellis and a black servant to help them.[34]

The Federals obtained information about Bragg's movements. A Union soldier dressed in gray found Davis's party on the night of May 6 and rode with it before leaving early the next morning. He came across Bragg's party eight miles away near Salem, Georgia, and rode with it to Athens. As soon as the scout reported his findings, Col. William J. Palmer dispatched part of the 15th Pennsylvania Cavalry after Bragg while other troops sought Davis. Palmer and the regiment belonged not to Wilson's command but to units in George Stoneman's District of East Tennessee, whose forces were cooperating with Wilson. The Pennsylvania horsemen caught up with Bragg near Concord on the night of May 9.[35]

As the Federals approached, they saw Bragg on the porch of a cottage wearing a "discolored" gray uniform and trying to take off the buttons and insignia. Lieut. Samuel Phillips took Bragg a few yards away, and the two conversed for forty-five minutes while both sat on a fence rail. As a result, Phillips was convinced that Bragg and Elise meant to go to Mobile to live peacefully, and he decided to parole the general rather than take him into custody. The only condition of his parole was that Bragg should report to Wilson at Macon. Phillips's decision did not satisfy Palmer, who noted that the Bragg party had attempted to avoid detection. Palmer thought Bragg was trying to go to the Trans-Mississippi and continue resistance to the Federal government.[36]

Serg. Levi Sheffler and Corp. William Spang searched the party's wagons under the watchful eye of Bragg's black servant. They found field glasses, a sash, a number of woolen blankets and two U.S. uniforms. By this time Bragg returned to the wagons and asked to be allowed to keep the uniforms. They were gifts, he told the two Yankees, and he had never worn them. The pair also found a magnificent pair of spurs, "gold-mounted," and inscribed to Bragg "by the State of Georgia, for his gallantry at the battle of Missionary Ridge." Elise had occasion to lose her temper when the Federals brought out her trunk from the cottage. "She opened her batteries," recalled Spang, "by reminding us who we were, and said that she had never been so insulted in all her life as to have her effects searched by a set of Yankee hirelings." Elise tore a letter into small pieces as she let loose with her feelings. When the servant told either Bragg or Phillips that the two Federals had taken articles from the wagons, Phillips ordered them to return the spurs, sash, and field glasses.[37]

Phillips also assigned an escort of eight soldiers to accompany the Bragg party for a short distance south. Spang found Bragg to be "pleasant company, but reserved and very much of a gentleman." Having calmed down, Elise was now quiet too, and Spang thought "she was good looking, had black hair and eyes; in fact, a perfect type of a Southern brunette."[38]

Phillips had paroled Bragg in violation of standing orders, and Bragg never reported to Wilson as he promised. As late as May 24 Federal authorities considered arresting him, but Wilson gave up the idea. Fifty-four years later Wilson told Don Seitz that Bragg "never reached my headquarters. I sent word to him that he could go on home, provided he would remain thus on his parole of honor to abstain from all acts of hostility to the United States." That is exactly what Bragg intended to do when he and Elise reached Mobile where brothers Thomas and Dunbar were living.[39]

16

After the War

Bragg's troubled Civil War career led to a troubled postwar life. Finding it difficult to obtain satisfying employment, the ex-general went from one attempt at making a living to another. Throughout his waning years, Bragg fretted about history and his war record. He never wrote his memoirs but looked for someone to tell his story as he saw it. Bragg never found that someone.

Soon after reaching Mobile at war's end, Braxton and Elise moved to John Bragg's plantation near Lowndesboro about twenty-five miles southwest of Montgomery. Bragg bitterly complained of how Federal troops had treated John, "an aged and infirm citizen." According to Braxton, the Yankees roused him out of his home, burned the house and cursed him for having a "'d-d rebel brother, a general against us.'"[1]

Bragg and Elise settled into a difficult life near Lowndesboro managing what was left of John's estate. The couple lived in what Bragg called "our Negro cabin," but it really was the overseer's house. From there he oversaw the work of a dozen black laborers growing cotton along the Alabama River. Only a portion of the 3,000 acre plantation was under production. "We have plenty to eat," Bragg told Harvey Washington Walter, "and by moving about can find a dry spot when it rains. Our old Confederate clothing patched . . . still answers the necessities of life. Our great want, however, is food for the mind. To cultivated minds, a life without books, papers or society is next to purgatory."[2]

With time on his hands, Bragg thought of the terrible war he had survived. "We sowed & we have reaped," he told Walter. "We enjoyed four years of license, and are now paying for it." He blamed many Confederate leaders for assuming that victory was easy and especially pinpointed officials in the war department for impeding his efforts. "In trying to save them I lost myself, in saving themselves they lost me."[3]

John's plantation had few prospects, and Bragg felt too old and worn out from the war to invest the energy that had made Bivouac a success. He possessed no capital and no property of his own. The worst burden on his mind was Elise; she was used to luxurious living and now had to struggle for the bare necessities of life.[4]

Bragg did not have the money to attend a ceremony held near his birthplace in North Carolina to honor the daughter of Robert E. Lee. Anne Lee had died of typhoid at age twenty-three while staying at White Sulphur Springs, North Carolina, in October, 1862. She was buried in the family graveyard of William Duke Jones, owner of the springs and a cousin of Lee's wife. At some point late in the war, Bragg detailed an invalid Confederate soldier to construct a monument to Miss Lee, and Joseph Speed Jones organized an unveiling ceremony for the memorial in 1866. He invited Bragg to attend, but the general did not do so.[5]

Aching to put himself back on his feet financially, Bragg made efforts to retrieve something from the shattered remnants of Bivouac. Federal authorities had taken possession of the sugar plantation in October 1862 and later converted it into the Bragg Home Colony for Freedmen, operated by the Freedmen's Bureau right after the war. On January 3, 1866, government authorities released the property and sold it at an auction held in New Orleans. Sometime before moving from Mobile to Lowndesboro, Bragg had made his way to New Orleans by begging, as he put it, and tried to see if he could do something toward saving the place, but it was a futile trip.[6]

Members of the Moreau and Lorie families now owned Bivouac, but Bragg continued efforts to regain the land. He wrote to William T. Sherman asking his old friend's advice about the matter. Bragg assured Sherman he had a full accounting of all the property lost when the Federal army swept onto the place—300 hogsheads of sugar, 1,000 pounds of molasses, 8,000 bushels of corn, 50 beef cattle, 50 horses and mules, and much hay. As he had purchased Bivouac with Elise's money, Bragg argued the property was not subject to forfeiture due to his own actions in the war and that Elise could legally claim some compensation because she was not actively involved in the rebellion. Of course this was a hopeless line of argument, but Bragg worked hard to save the property he had not seen since December 1860. Late in his life Bragg still mourned the loss of Bivouac and the fate of his 125 slaves. In his perspective, they had been "happy and contented" before the war, but most of them were by 1875 dead "and the remainder in a State of Semi barbarism, half Starved and nearly naked," as he put it.[7]

Bragg devoted more than a year to making John's plantation work before he gave up the effort and found other employment. He and Elise

Jefferson Davis after the Civil War. The friendship between Bragg and the ex-president of the Confederacy blossomed by war's end and grew even stronger after the conflict. Bragg accepted a position selling life insurance, although the task did not suit his skills or inclinations, only because Davis was president of the company. In fact, Bragg's admiration for Davis in the postwar years amounted to hero worship. (Library of Congress, LC-DIG-ppmsca-23865)

moved to New Orleans in January 1867, where he worked for the New Orleans, Opelousos, and Great Western Railroad for eight months. He then became superintendent of the New Orleans waterworks in August but lost that job to a man appointed by the Republican city government.[8]

The next opportunity came from his former superior and late-war friend, Jefferson Davis, who now was president of the Carolina Life Insurance Company. Bragg accepted his offer to handle sales in the Louisiana district. Surgeon Samuel H. Stout correctly noted that such a job "did not suit his genius or taste," but Bragg could not refuse a request from Davis. "I accept the Agency you offer and can assure you the labor will be one of love," he told his new employer. "Having had no experience, you will have to indulge me, until the routine and details of duty can be mastered." Bragg told Davis how difficult it was to see him selling insurance instead of running an independent Southern nation. "Your life and services should properly belong to our people."[9]

Bragg entered his new duties with a determination to try his best. He marketed the Carolina Life Insurance Company as wholly Southern. "Chartered & located in the south, managed by southern men, supported by southern patronage, its assets all invested in the south." The company was headquartered at Memphis and employed a number of ex-Confederate officers. Bragg was offended when Northern insurance companies attacked the Carolina concern because Jefferson Davis was its president. He corresponded with other Southern-based insurance companies hoping to form a united front, "for defensive measures at least," and was eager to take the offensive in public relations against Northern critics of Davis. "We must know that our living is to come exclusively from the south," Bragg told the president of the Piedmont and Arlington Insurance Company, "and therefore no warfare with these fellows can hurt us." Bragg was ready to fight anyone who attacked "our old chief and martyr."[10]

But the going was rough. Bragg found by early 1870 that most people within his acquaintance had already purchased life insurance, and mostly from Northerners. "The use of Mr. Davis' name is to be our main strength, and reliance," he told the company secretary. Bragg proudly assured one of his early customers that after paying the first premium of $151.20, his $5,000 policy would be sent in the mail. "It is one of the first bearing the signature of Jeffn. Davis."[11]

Not long after starting the grinding business of selling insurance, Bragg considered moving to Egypt and offering his services to that nation's army. Several ex-Confederate officers were already doing so. He could not speak French, the common language of government and military service in Egypt, but Hypolite Oladowski did, and Bragg felt he could be persuaded to serve on his staff. The possibilities of growing sugar and cotton in Egypt also attracted Bragg, but in the end he did not make the move.[12]

Bragg sold insurance for nearly two years before giving up the job. He and Elise then moved to Mobile, where the ex-general superintended harbor and bay improvements beginning in August 1871. It suited his talents, but Federal government engineers changed the plans at the insistence of local contractors. Bragg could not approve the changes and resigned his position.[13]

The ever-pressing need for employment drove Bragg to contact ex-Confederates for their advice about opportunities. Writing to Daniel M. Frost in November 1873, he stated that civil engineering was his primary interest, in addition to administrative work in railroads or manufacturing. With the Panic of 1873 in full swing, business was slow in New Orleans, where he once again made his home. It was "impossible for one of my antecedents, who had his fortune stolen or confiscated, to make a decent and honorable support." Bragg had "only my head and my hands to rely on."[14]

By 1874, Bragg was bouncing from one position to another for various reasons. He supervised improvements at an inlet of the Gulf of Mexico near Pascagoula, Mississippi, before moving to Texas. Bragg served as chief engineer of the Gulf, Colorado, and Santa Fe Railroad until a dispute over his salary and accumulating arrears of pay compelled him to leave the company. For many months Bragg was unemployed, having failed to obtain the position of city surveyor for Galveston. According to Stephen D. Lee, "the old fellow looked mighty depressed." Edward O. C. Ord, a former Union general, thought Bragg would make an honest purchaser for the commissary department of the U.S. Army, but nothing came of it. From his home in Galveston Bragg speculated on finding a way to combat yellow fever, combining a business opportunity with a way to alleviate a dreaded fear among the residents of his adopted city. Contacting physician Joseph Jones at New Orleans, he wondered if wood impregnated with carbolic acid could be used effectively. Nothing came of the speculative venture, and as the months of idleness lengthened, Bragg became more despondent. "For nearly a year I have been simply burning the candle," he complained to a correspondent in March 1876.[15]

A few months later, he tried to secure appointment as inspector of railroads for the state of Texas. The prospects dimmed when Governor Richard Coke favored another candidate. Former Confederate general Samuel Bell Maxey, who had briefly led a brigade under Bragg, commiserated with his former commander. "Certainly if a man in the State is thoroughly qualified for the duties of Railway Inspector you are. I know your indomitable energy and feel sure this will be but a temporary inconvenience." Bragg finally received the appointment, but it would be the last job he held.[16]

Throughout the postwar period Bragg struggled not only to make a living but to come to grips with his Civil War career. It had disrupted some close friendships, forged new friendships, and created bitter feelings between himself and a host of other men. In some cases Bragg reconciled those bitter feelings, and in others the anger and hatred continued unabated. He also sought someone who could write the history of his campaigns in the way he thought it should be written, deciding not to author a memoir of his own. But his search for historical vindication failed.

Bragg considered William T. Sherman a close friend before the war, although Sherman did not fully reciprocate those feelings. But right after the war, Bragg saw Sherman only as a former enemy. In late 1865 he referred to the Union general as "the atrocious Sherman" because of his March to the Sea and through the Carolinas. It took the passage of a couple of years for Bragg to release that bitterness and feel comfortable resuming their correspondence, asking Sherman's advice about getting his plantation back. Sherman did nothing along that line, but Bragg no longer harbored resentment against him. When Sherman invited the Braggs to the wedding of

Braxton Bragg at Paint Rock. Located in Madison County, North Carolina, very near the Tennessee border, this popular tourist spot featured historic Native American trails through a deep gorge and exposed rock cliffs brightly colored by nature. Native American pictographs on the rock face have been dated to about 2500 B.C. Photographer Rufus Morgan exposed this previously unpublished view of Bragg and his party about 1872. (Photographic Collections, N-95-8-43, SANC)

his daughter in 1874, Bragg was touched "that we had not faded from your memory." He could not make the trip but signed his letter "In the kindly feeling of old." After conversing with the Northern general at a reunion held at West Point in the fall of 1876, Samuel Bell Maxey assured Bragg that Sherman retained fond memories of his prewar friendship.[17]

Ironically it was easier for Bragg to reconcile with his former war enemies than with his Confederate colleagues. While some Rebel officers retained their admiration for him into the postwar era, many others retained nothing but hatred. James Patton Anderson, for example, wrote glowingly to Bragg in 1867 that the Southern people were beginning to understand his accomplishments. He also praised Bragg's work ethic as a sure sign that he would succeed in any business venture. "I was always a great friend and admirer of Gen. Bragg," asserted James R. Chalmers after

Another View of Bragg at Paint Rock. Bragg was probably drawn to the area because of hot springs located near Paint Rock. Elise probably was with the party. This photograph depicting Bragg as a tourist, also the work of photographer Rufus Morgan, has never before been published. (Photographic Collections, N-95-8-44, SANC)

the war. Bragg could take a great deal of satisfaction from friends such as Anderson and Chalmers.[18]

But if he had occasion to discover what other men wrote and said about him, it would have chilled his heart. Randall L. Gibson remained one of the most vindictive enemies of Bragg. He never had a kind word to say about him since their relations soured while running contiguous sugar plantations in the late 1850s. After so many years of bitter acquaintance-ship, Gibson never understood why Bragg disliked him and tried to hinder his career. He bitterly complained throughout the war that being assigned to Bragg's command was a sentence of doom. Gibson's only clue was that, before the war, he had "somewhat" sided with the strongly pro-secession wing of the state Democratic Party while Bragg supported a more cautious approach to the national crisis. Bragg felt that anyone associated with the pro-secession wing "was more or less corrupt."[19]

Gibson spread wild stories about Bragg cowering behind trees at Shiloh and sending "orders without point, inapplicable, & incoherent." He told William Preston Johnston that Bragg was an "imbecile, coward, tyrant," and a "crazy man." If Albert Sidney Johnston had lived, "we should have had a Gentleman in command of that noble army," Gibson assured the slain general's son.[20]

Bragg never reconciled his feud with Gibson, but he tried to help John Bell Hood after the conflict. When Hood applied for a life insurance policy, Bragg endorsed it despite the former officer's infirmities. "His case is considered exceptional, and from my personal knowledge of his strong constitution, good health and excellent habits, . . . and his acceptance in several other companies, I do not hesitate to recommend him."[21]

John C. Breckinridge had bitterly resented Bragg's blaming him for much of the failure at Stones River and had demanded a court of inquiry. That court was never granted by the Richmond authorities, and Breckinridge went on to command a corps under Bragg at Chattanooga. Despite evidence that Breckinridge was intoxicated during the battle, Bragg did not press charges against him. Breckinridge went on to serve as the last Confederate secretary of war. Feelings mellowed between the two men. In 1869 Bragg wrote a short note to Breckinridge indicating the two held respectful feelings toward each other. Bragg noted that neither of them was willing "to take part in the affairs of our country," because of Reconstruction.[22]

Bragg and many other ex-Confederates disliked Longstreet after the war because the former Rebel general sided with the Republican Party during Reconstruction and wrote critically of Lee's performance at Gettysburg. Bragg thought Jubal Early's counterattacks against Longstreet "squelshes out the fellow, but he has neither sense nor sensibility to appreciate it." In a devastating letter to Andrew Kellar, editor of the *Memphis Avalanche*, Bragg characterized Longstreet as "well developed and full of animal or physical courage—but utterly destitute of moral or mental capacity courage or integrity." Fame in the war had "turned his head," and Bragg was not surprised that Longstreet allied with the Republican Party during the South's period of suffering and adjustment following Appomattox.[23]

In fact, Bragg detested Reconstruction and how it changed the South. He referred to the "Semi-Negro Semi-Military Legislature" of Louisiana and condemned the corruption of Grant's presidency, noting there would be clean government in Washington if "southern gentlemen" held the reins of power. Bragg mourned the loss of slavery. Ignoring the fact that it involved the oppression of other human beings, he thought it "the best and most humane" labor system ever known and did not know how Southern planters could replace it.[24]

The most absorbing issue on Bragg's mind, other than seeking meaningful employment, was the historical record of his career. As early as December 1865, while settling on John's plantation near Lowndesboro, Bragg expressed an interest in organizing his military papers. In fact, a New York publisher had already sent him a proposal to write his memoirs. "I prefer ... not being my own Historian," he told Peter Wellington Alexander, "knowing I could not be impartial." As he told Kellar in 1869, it had been "a rule with me since the war to keep out of all controversy and to confine myself to making a support for my family."[25]

Samuel H. Stout put it well when he wrote that Bragg had "an abiding faith in the impartial criticism of posterity." Bragg also was reluctant to initiate word wars with former enemies, although he indicated more than once that he was ready to respond if they initiated the conflict on their own. Henry D. Clayton, who commanded a brigade and division in the Army of Tennessee, was deeply disappointed that Joseph E. Johnson criticized Bragg in his memoirs for the latter's role in his removal. Clayton had read in a newspaper article that Bragg intended to respond, and he implored Bragg not to do so. "Like the great Lee, you and Mr Davis can afford to live and die in silence. Your good name & fame are fully established." Clayton thought that "our mutual sufferings & loss ought to close our mouth against any reproach, one of the other."[26]

To a degree, Bragg felt the same way but his concern for history led him to become active in memorializing the war. He helped to found the Southern Historical Society in New Orleans in 1869 and served as vice president and later president of the organization. Among other things, Bragg urged Stout to write a history of the medical services in the Army of Tennessee on the basis of Stout's huge collection of war papers.[27]

Bragg's potential as a historian was not lost on Jefferson Davis. As early as 1866 he identified him as the best man to write a history of the Army of Tennessee. When informed of this view by a third party, Bragg wrote to Mrs. Davis that he was open to the idea. "Such has been my fixed purpose though I have thought the results of my labors had best appear under some other name." Bragg tried to find someone who could write well and was willing to take his own line of interpretation. He thought he found such a man in William T. Walthall, who had served as major of the 12th Alabama and was employed by the Carolina Life Insurance Company. But Bragg's constant search for employment prevented the two from finding the time needed for collaboration.[28]

Walthall was intrigued by the prospects of working with Bragg to produce the general's memoirs, but he also was wary of him. While "greatly attached" to him personally, Walthall "was fully aware of his very positive, rugged, and somewhat angular character and disposition, of his strong prejudices and many antagonisms." The former major doubted if he could support Bragg as fully as the general wanted. After Bragg's death, Walthall continued to talk with Elise about the possibility of writing a biography of her husband. He would now have full control over the project, selecting which controversy to open for discussion, but in the end Walthall never moved forward with the work.[29]

But Bragg had several opportunities to influence postwar views of the conflict. When Beauregard began to claim credit for organizing the Army of the Mississippi and creating the plan used at the battle of Shiloh, Davis and Bragg were incensed. The ex-president of the Confederacy considered Bragg the most reliable source of information on the Shiloh campaign. "The time has arrived when you should spike the guns of this arrogant pretender," Bragg told Davis of Beauregard. He gave William Preston Johnston, who worked to keep the memory of his father alive, information about the campaign and, according to Davis, wrote "a monograph on the battle of Shiloh." While this paper seems to have been lost, Davis noted in his *Rise and Fall of the Confederate Government* that it frankly described Beauregard's advice to call off the attack before it even started. Bragg's connection with Beauregard had badly deteriorated. Beauregard's biographer believes the Creole general decided that Bragg had allied with Davis to become his enemy by the summer of 1864. He wrote sarcastically of Bragg in private letters for the rest of his life. Ironically, Bragg joined enemies and friends (Beauregard, Hood, Taylor and Longstreet) to serve as an honorary pallbearer when Johnston's remains were removed from New Orleans and reinterred at Austin, Texas, in January, 1867.[30]

Bragg was deeply concerned about Davis's welfare after the war. For a couple of years following his arrest, Federal authorities imprisoned Davis and considered trying him for treason. "We have been most anxious and distressed observers of the course of events since our separation from your martyr Husband," Bragg assured Varina Davis. Soon after his release, Davis and his wife visited Bragg in New Orleans. The general continued to sign his letters as "Your friend," and told Davis of his health problems—boils continued to plague him after the war. Bragg also tried to coax Davis to attend a convention of Mexican War Veterans of Texas at Austin during the spring of 1875.[31]

Bragg could not produce a major work of history on his own or through Walthall or through the aid of Jefferson Davis, but he had one more chance to work through a proxy. When Edward T. Sykes, a former captain in the 10th Mississippi and staff officer for Edward C. Walthall, was preparing to write a series of articles about Bragg's campaigns, the former general eagerly tried to help him. He offered his own papers, which he had "preserved from the general wreck." But Bragg made it clear that he did not want to write such a history. "It would do more harm than good, and I should again have to meet a howl of parasites." Bragg feared that many readers would assume the book was filled with "Braggs *prejudices*. I acknowledge myself prejudiced. I always was prejudiced against every species of dishonest knavery and treacherous selfishness." Every time he contemplated writing a book, Bragg came to the same conclusion. "*I dare not tell the* truth, and I dare not tell less."[32]

In his first letter to Sykes on February 8, 1873, Bragg felt he should have arrested Hill and Buckner for trying to unseat him as commander following Chickamauga. "Still, I am satisfied no good could have resulted. Our country was not prepared to sustain a military commander who acted on military principles, & no man could do his duty and sustain himself against the combined power of imbeciles, traitors, rogues and intriguing politicians." He continued to rail against the effort "to degrade & remove me for personal ends." In contrast to officers such as Hill and Hindman, Bragg praised Cleburne for his heroic stand at Ringgold to save the remnants of the army.[33]

Bragg also frankly discussed the problems associated with whiskey in the army. He related the story of Cheatham at Stones River and Breckinridge at Chattanooga. Having resolved his ill feelings toward the latter, Bragg now called him "as gallant and true a man as ever lived," but the truth had to be told. On the retreat from Missionary Ridge, Breckinridge staggered into Bragg's headquarters in the depot at Chickamauga Station and lay on the floor "*dead drunk*, and was so in the morning." Bragg told States Rights Gist to haul him away in a wagon if necessary to prevent him from being left behind. After the army retired to Dalton, Bragg relieved Breckinridge of his corps command. When the man sobered up, he acknowledged the justness of the action, but told Bragg that "it was the deepest mortification of his life."[34]

Ten days after his initial letter, Bragg sent a second message along with copies of several papers in his possession. He urged Sykes to consult John B. Sale for help and identified the *Southern Magazine* in Baltimore as a good home for his articles. "It is strongly southern and seems to be independent," Bragg thought. In the end, Sykes wrote a series of articles that were published in the *Southern Historical Society Papers*. They fell far short of what Bragg wanted and used only a small amount of the information he had fed Sykes. In fact, the articles are little more than brief resumes of the campaigns Bragg conducted. Sykes did argue that time would "give Bragg rank among the first Generals of the late war." But he refused to get involved in Bragg's controversies. The first article appealed to Kinloch Falconer, a longtime member of the Army of Tennessee staff. "The series will be of great value to those who followed the flag of Braxton Bragg," Falconer told Sykes.[35]

Battered by public criticism during the war, Bragg developed into a literary recluse. In an effort to avoid renewed controversy, he chose to remain silent on his war record. To a degree, he was right in thinking that the archives produced by the conflict would contain the material for future historians to write history that could vindicate his name, although the archival record also contains material used by historians to criticize him. As indicated by his association with Sykes, Bragg could not control what other people wrote, and that went for later historians as well. There is no substitute for a general's postwar view of his career; Bragg should have written his memoirs and braved whatever criticism came his way in the same fashion that he braved the storm of abuse directed at him during the war. We can piece together the general outline of what that memoir would have said, but it is not the same as having it from Bragg's own pen.

Bragg's story was not fully told when the former general died in Galveston on September 27, 1876. He met L. E. Trezevant, a veteran of the 26th Texas Cavalry who also lived in the city, and the two walked to the post office while chatting. At about 9 A.M., Bragg suddenly was seized and lost his balance, falling against Trezevant while the two crossed 20th Street. He fell without a word. Dr. J. F. Kerr happened to be near and came to his assistance. Helping hands carried him unconscious to the drugstore of Dr. J. G. Goadad on Post Office Street half a block away. Here, while lying on a sofa, Bragg died within ten minutes of his collapse. According to Trezevant, the general was in good spirits before the sudden blow to his heart. He was only fifty-nine years old.[36]

A grand jury concluded that Bragg died of heart failure, but a former subordinate of the general offered a different view. Stanford E. Chaillé of the Medical Department, University of Louisiana in New Orleans, had served as Bragg's Medical Director in 1862 and knew something of the general's health. He also relied on Professor Samuel Bemiss of the same university, who had examined Bragg's heart condition sometime after the conflict, to reach his conclusions. Chaillé believed Bragg died of degeneration of the cerebral blood vessels, a common form of death in those approaching old age. He also recalled treating Bragg about 1870 "for nervous disorder of left shoulder and arm." While this did not seem to have contributed to his death, Chaillé pointed out that Elise had mentioned her husband seemed afflicted by "symptoms of nerve lesion, such as impaired memory, head ache, tendency to sleep."[37]

Bragg's friends paid honor to "the dead hero" and supported Elise in her hour of grief. Bragg's remains lay in state at the armory of the Galveston Artillery on September 28. He was then transported to Mobile, where Elise wanted him to be buried. A funeral service took place at Christ Episcopal Church in Mobile followed by burial in Magnolia Cemetery on October 6. Col. T. K. Erwin of the 1st Alabama Militia assured Elise that many members of his regiment had served under Bragg during the war, and they wanted "to do all they can for their much loved Commander." He worked with Ann Toulmin Hunter, president of the Mobile Memorial Association, to select a plot that was "high & dry." A year after the burial, Elise contracted with a local marble firm to enclose her husband's grave in the section of Magnolia Cemetery called Soldier's Rest. Many years later, Elise described the plot where her husband lay as large with a grassy mound of earth. The marble company had erected "a stone balustrade" around the mound, and a stone block marked the entombment.[38]

Elise lived with her brother Towson Ellis in New Orleans "in strict retirement," as her friend Mrs. Ben Hardin Helm put it. She spent summers in the mountains of Virginia, but her life was so reclusive that editor Sumner A. Cunningham of the *Confederate Veteran* had no idea she existed until Mrs. Helm wrote him about her. When Cunningham met Mrs. Bragg, he urged her to visit Nashville, the hometown of the popular veterans' magazine. "I would gladly have accepted an invitation to the Chickamauga Park dedication," she told him. Cunningham then realized park organizers had been remiss in not inviting her or Mrs. Helm to the dedication in 1895, considering Elise's husband commanded the Confederate army there and Mrs. Helm's husband was killed in the battle. Elise had no finer admirer than Mrs. Helm. "Stately, dignified, a handsome woman," she described Bragg's wife, "remarkably courteous and elegant in her manner, a fine conversationalist, she interests herself in all the topics of the day."[39]

By the time of Bragg's death the Federal government instituted efforts to collect Confederate war records for publication. Many high-ranking Rebel officers loaned or donated their military papers to Washington, and Marcus J. Wright, a former brigade commander in Bragg's army, was hired as an agent in this effort. William Preston Johnston suggested to Elise that she sell her husband's papers rather than donate or loan them. She liked the idea as a way of raising capital to pay Walthall for writing a biography of the general. Walthall, however, thought the price discussed was too low. He advised her to retain ownership of the documents but let the government have certified copies of them. Elise could not understand this idea; according to Walthall, she thought the value lay in the content of the papers, not in the physical document itself, and disliked the idea of releasing the information without compensation. She lost faith in Walthall's advice and dropped the idea of encouraging him to write a biography.[40]

Relying on William Preston Johnston, Elise tried to interest the Federal government in her husband's archives. She sent some of them to Wright and hoped Congress would provide funds for the purchase of the entire collection. Wright was keenly interested, but Congress failed to pass the needed bill. Elise then hoped the legislators would provide funds for the publication of the papers, but that also failed. She retained the material for some time. Eventually, collector William P. Palmer bought the collection and donated it to the Western Reserve Historical Society in Cleveland, Ohio.[41]

Jefferson Davis survived Bragg by many years and continued to admire him. He praised the general in a speech at Mississippi City in July 1878 and continued to urge William Preston Johnston to seek information about Albert Sidney Johnston through Elise, who he thought was well posted in Bragg's knowledge of the famed general.[42]

John Bragg, Thomas's son and a telegrapher for his uncle during the Shiloh campaign, defended the general's memory. He praised an editorial by Samuel A' Court Ashe, Confederate veteran and postwar editor of the *Raleigh News and Observer*, for writing well of Bragg. John characterized his uncle as "the most roundly abused and terribly Columniated of all the Confederate Chief officers. All on account of being a strict disciplinarian. The 'pencil drivers' were ne'er his friends for he always drove them out of his army to preserve it from their espionage given to the yankees in their sheets."[43]

While John spoke up for his uncle, Bragg's manservant lived a quiet life in Columbia, Tennessee, until passing away in 1900. The local Confederate veterans' organization voted a resolution honoring him and provided the pallbearers at his funeral. The resolution called him "the faithful old negro man" but indicated he was popularly called Braxton Bragg rather than by his own name.[44]

Elise lived many years, passing away in New Orleans on September 25, 1908, at age eighty-three. The president of the United Daughters of the Confederacy called her "a woman of the sweetest and highest Southern type. Dignified in manner and speech, refined and cultured, patriotic and unselfish." The Braggs never had children so the direct line of the general vanished with her passing.[45]

Conclusion

Probably no other figure in the Confederate story was as controversial as Braxton Bragg. In an important way, this controversy has taken much of the humanity from his image. Far too often he becomes a stock figure exposed to ridicule instead of a man and a commander. Bragg was neither a hapless fool nor a brilliant general. He failed more often than succeeded in his Civil War career. He also was not the ogre who callously executed his own soldiers, nor was he friendless or cold toward his wife.

Public opinion in and out of the army shaped Bragg's image, making of him "the best-abused man in the world." Most editors and newspaper correspondents were far too ready to brand him as incompetent, tyrannical, or marked by a lack of good fortune. In turn, Bragg did not know how to deal with them except with contempt. He did have a friend in John Forsyth, but even Forsyth's own paper, the *Mobile Advertiser and Register*, often published negative stories about Bragg because one of the correspondents managed to slip his pieces past the editor. "Bragg scorned to use the press in his interest," Stout argued after the war, "hence the public discussion of his merits or demerits as a military man was almost wholly one sided." That is not entirely true; as seen in earlier chapters, Bragg made some effort after Stones River to influence newspaper reporting of his career but largely failed.[1]

Bragg did not know how to ingratiate himself with newspaper writers or with many other men. He did not have the political savvy to pull strings except to call on Davis to support him in controversies with his subordinates. That was a rather crude and heavy-handed way of dealing with recalcitrant officers, and he could not apply it to newspaper correspondents. One wonders why Bragg did not call on his family members for help in this way. Thomas Bragg was a well-placed member of Davis's cabinet early in the war and certainly made efforts to support his brother's career, even though Braxton never specifically asked him to do so. Thomas had developed a respectful relation with Jefferson Davis during their days in the U.S. Senate before the war and served him ably as attorney general from November 1861 until March 1862. Thomas had offered to resign if Davis felt the need to appoint someone who was politically connected to public elements that needed to be mollified. Davis took him up on that offer, appointing Thomas H. Watts in his place. Ironically, Watts was a fierce enemy of Braxton for personal reasons. He served as attorney general for a few months before winning election as governor of Alabama.[2]

The support that Thomas offered Braxton was quiet and largely ended after he left the Confederate cabinet. In many ways it was also unnecessary, for Davis firmly believed in Braxton and was his strongest supporter in the government. Other public men who supported Bragg did so quietly and in limited ways. Josiah Nott of Mobile privately believed in the general but never did anything to influence public opinion. John Forsyth wrote an effective defense of Bragg's Kentucky campaign and published it in his newspaper and in pamphlet form, but it made little headway against the surge of negative public opinion.[3]

Public opinion, indeed, was Bragg's biggest enemy. Formed mostly by men and women who knew the least about what he did and failed to do, unrestrained by balance or consideration for one working under tremendous stress and limited resources, civilians were free to say anything they wanted to say. Newspaper editors and writers in particular tended to use their positions to vent personal grievances against a man who readily made enemies. If a general won battles, he was a hero; if he lost, he was a fool or a traitor. On one level this is understandable. The Confederacy had only one chance to achieve independence, and racking up a string of half victories that resulted in no gain for Rebel armies was not the way to win it. Bragg had some newspaper friends and people who defended him by writing letters to the papers, but they became fewer and fewer as the war progressed. Overwhelmingly, Bragg lost the war with the Southern press and his reputation and effectiveness as a public figure was tremendously hurt in the process.

No strain in the public image hurt Bragg more than the idea that he was a man killer, too ready to shoot his own soldiers for minor infractions of discipline and often doing so without due process of military law. As explained in previous chapters, this idea sprang from three incidents. The first took place during the retreat from Corinth. Bragg initially wanted to shoot a soldier without due process for violating an order not to fire weapons during the retreat, but it is important to note that he was persuaded from doing so by the intercession of his staff. Despite the fact that the execution never took place, wild stories circulated so freely that the Confederate Senate came close to investigating Bragg's conduct.

The second incident concerned Corp. Asa Lewis of the 6th Kentucky who was executed even though he returned to the army on his own after dealing with family problems. While it is true that Lewis's death sentence was passed by a court-martial, Bragg could have disapproved it, as other officers strongly advised him to do. The third incident related to three men shot at Shelbyville. Despite many appeals for clemency, Bragg had the deserters executed to make an example of them.

Despite these three incidents, there is reason to believe that Bragg exercised restraint and sympathy concerning soldiers facing death sentences. It is important to note that army commanders did not sentence anyone to death; that was done by court-martial members who then submitted their findings and sentences to the army commander for approval. Recent examination of court-martial records by historians has revealed that Bragg was actually more lenient when it came to approving or disapproving death sentences as compared to other generals. From June 1862 until November 1863, Bragg reviewed at least forty-one death sentences for his soldiers and four for civilians. He remitted, commuted, or referred sentences to Davis for leniency in thirteen cases of the soldiers. In other words, Bragg approved the death sentence for twenty-eight soldiers while commanding the army. That amounted to one every twenty days of the time period under study. In contrast, Joseph E. Johnston approved one death sentence every seventeen days during the eight months he led the army.[4]

In fact, Thomas P. Lowry and Lewis Laska conclude that Bragg grew more lenient as time passed. They noticed "a trend away from death sentences" over the months that Bragg led the army. Many men charged with desertion failed to receive death sentences upon their conviction, and Bragg approved their more lenient sentences.[5]

Joseph E. Johnston was loved by his men, despite approving a higher percentage of executions than did Bragg, including what may have been the largest execution of Confederate soldiers on a single day during the entire war. Sixteen soldiers were scheduled to be shot on May 4, 1864; two received reprieves at the last minute, but fourteen were executed as planned. All of them had been convicted of desertion, and all of them belonged to North Carolina units in the Army of Tennessee. Thomas Owens asserted after the war that many men were so upset over this they came close to mounting a mutiny. "This punishment is about the only thing that detracted from the popularity of Gen. Joseph E. Johnston," he argued.[6]

Lowry and Laska also note that military justice was very harsh in Lee's Army of Northern Virginia. While they did not compare the rates of execution with those in the Army of Tennessee, Lee's army sentenced 12.4 percent of the men tried for desertion to death compared to only 4.8 percent in the Union army as a whole. The execution rate in the Army of Tennessee probably was much lower than in the Army of Northern Virginia.[7]

Yet Lee was enshrined as a Southern hero and Bragg blasted as a Southern despot. Texas senator Williamson S. Oldham expressed this theme well in his memoirs, referring to Bragg's "arbitrary and despotic military conduct, his absolute disregard of the constitution and laws of his country," as well as his "want of military capacity." Oldham argued after the war that the general was utterly unfit to lead an army "in the defence of the liberties of a free people."[8]

Interestingly, Bragg's men viewed him with a greater mix of hatred and respect than did civilian observers. After the war, Philip D. Stephenson considered him a failed general but admirably devoted to the cause. He was aware that Johnston executed more men than did Bragg, yet the troops loved Johnston. Sam Watkins was not a fan of Bragg but expressed in his own way fond memories of the general in his memoirs. "We had got sorter used to his ways," Watkins believed. "Bragg's troops would have loved him, if he had allowed them to do so, for many a word was spoken in his behalf, after he had been relieved of the command." Demonstrating his ambivalence, Watkins on another page of his memoirs declared that Bragg loved to break the spirit of his men by authorizing executions witnessed by thousands of them. "The more of a hang-dog look they had about them the better was General Bragg pleased. Not a single soldier in the whole army ever loved or respected him."[9]

Other men were not ambivalent about the man. "If Gen. Bragg ever did anything right," Douglas Cater of the 19th Louisiana put it after the war, "I never heard of it." The extreme view of Cater and the ambivalent view of Watkins were not the sum total of soldier commentary on Bragg after the war. Samuel Lambert of the 4th Louisiana thought he was "among the greatest Military leaders of the age."[10]

Bragg garnered more sympathy among some officers than among the rank and file, probably because they had more opportunities to see him work and knew more keenly than the enlisted men all the trials associated with high command. Cavalryman Basil Duke highly praised Bragg's ability to use the mounted arm in support of his infantry operations, especially at Stones River, ranking him as having no equal in employing cavalry in all ways during the conflict. Irving Buck, Cleburne's trusted staff officer, admired Bragg's ability to fight a battle even if he did not reap the full benefits of tactical success.[11]

Newcomers to the Army of Tennessee in the fall of 1863 often had a mixed perception of Bragg. Daniel H. Hill offered a surprisingly balanced view of him despite the bitterness engendered by his relief from corps command after Chickamauga. "I knew of the carping criticism of his subordinates and the cold looks of his soldiers, and knew that these were the natural results of reverses, whether the blame lay with the commander or otherwise." Hill understood that much of the negative soldier attitude toward Bragg was due to the lack of clear-cut victories and that Bragg's tendency to make scapegoats of his enemies tended to inhibit initiative among his subordinates. "Polk did not sustain Bragg & much of the paralysis upon the latter was due to his knowledge of the lack of confidence . . . between him & Polk & the lack of good feeling upon the part of the troops towards him. Bragg's was a sad case."[12]

Edward Porter Alexander also was struck by the fact that Bragg inspired nothing of the enthusiasm Lee called forth from his troops. He also thought Bragg had little in the way of intellect. According to Alexander, some men characterized him as "simply muddle headed & especially that he never could understand a map, & that it was a spectacle to see him wrestle with one, with one finger painfully holding down his own position."[13]

But Bragg received a fair evaluation from several old hands in the Army of Tennessee. Cavalry officer W. T. Martin knew that Hindman and Polk let Bragg down when the general was trying to take advantage of Rosecrans's approach to Chattanooga. Martin concluded that no other Rebel general was the target of so much misrepresentation "in regard to his acts and motives."[14]

Arthur M. Manigault had ample opportunity to observe Bragg from his position as a brigade commander and gave him high marks. No one exceeded Bragg as an administrator; he always fed his men well if that was at all possible, and the general handled the responsibilities of his position with energy and determination. Manigault admired Bragg's impartiality, meting out discipline to officers and enlisted men alike. "I think that the army under his command, all things considered, was in a higher state of efficiency whilst he ruled than ever before or after," Manigault concluded with justification. Personally, Manigault began by disliking Bragg but later changed his mind. "I learned to like him," he wrote after the war. Manigault also believed that most enlisted men felt the same way. They started by hating the general, and then "they found him out. . . . The rank and file of the army became much attached to him, and in spite of his misfortune parted with him with regret."[15]

It is possible Manigault's postwar comments are evidence that attitudes toward Bragg softened with time. But in order for such a transformation to happen, there must have been something to base it on, some degree of grudging respect and affection for Bragg among his men during the war that could germinate with the passage of time. There may have been some unstated comparison of Bragg with John Bell Hood's even worse tenure as head of the Army of Tennessee. Time and context tended to soften views of Bragg's career for some of his men.

The strongest and most persistent support for Bragg came from Louisiana soldiers and those who had served under him at Pensacola, but the general had friends in other units of the army as well. A significant group of generals, including Joseph Wheeler, James Patton Anderson, and William B. Bate, were devoted to Bragg through thick and thin, but they refused to speak out publicly for him. Bragg's enemies always were more vocal than his friends, supporting Mackall's and Liddell's contention that he did not know how to inspire his supporters to become open and avowed spokesmen for his cause.

Samuel H. Stout, however, strongly admired, supported, and loved Bragg from the stormy days of the war until he died in the early twentieth century. The basis of this feeling was Bragg's concern for the sick and wounded of his army. Stout recalled the anguish Bragg felt at leaving hundreds of his men at Murfreesboro, too badly wounded to be removed, when he fell back from Stones River. Stout also contended that Bragg anguished whenever duty compelled him to sign a death warrant for one of his men, but the general "took no pains to correct the impression his industrious enemies strove to make that he was unmerciful and tyrannical." Tennessee governor Isham G. Harris told Stout that he always was able to get Bragg to adopt a merciful course toward any soldier if the general was presented with an earnest appeal for clemency.[16]

From his position as head of Army of Tennessee hospitals, Stout observed Bragg's habits and personality. The general was a workhorse in his office, processing paperwork with a writing style that went to the heart of the issue. "General Bragg was industry personified," Stout wrote. Army headquarters staff members often worried that their commander did not eat enough, and they sent food to his office to remind him to take a break. "No one in his army was more temperate in eating and drinking than he," Stout recalled. "He was a pattern of sobriety and had not the slightest epicurean proclivity."[17]

An unidentified chaplain shared his impressions of Bragg with Stout, noting the general "never praises, never flatters, nor permits himself to be praised or flattered. Ah! If he only had a suavity of manner, commensurate with his self-denying patriotism and untiring industry[,] what a success he would be!" The chaplain often went to Bragg with a request and rarely was denied, but the general's manner was brief, to the point, and a bit gruff. He did not allow the supplicant time to offer thanks before dismissing him.[18]

Bragg was too single-minded, too focused on self-discipline, too little attuned to creating an impression with a variety of people for his own good. On the opposite side of the spectrum lay Joseph E. Johnston, a suave gentleman who could have taught lessons in civility. But Johnston lacked Bragg's hard-edged approach to duty. The lack of balance in a personality that saw life as duty and the cause as enlisting self-sacrifice turned many men's affections away from Bragg. Only those who saw through the outer crust and glimpsed the man inside that frowning face with the eyebrows uniting in a heavy tuft could understand and appreciate him.

St. John R. Liddell tried very hard to look into the inner man and often was frustrated at what he saw, although retaining a grudging admiration for Bragg. The two had been West Point cadets together, although Liddell never graduated from the academy. From the start of their Civil War association in July 1861, Liddell and Bragg disagreed on nearly everything. "I feared he was inclined to perverseness, which always will bias good judgment," Liddell thought. He often consulted Bragg during the time he led a brigade in the Army of Tennessee, and to a degree Bragg trusted and confided in him. But Liddell came to realize with some degree of truth that "Bragg did not know who to trust." The general rarely had an opportunity to select his subordinates and took whomever the circumstances of war brought his way. Liddell, however, doubted that Bragg even had the discernment to choose good subordinates. It appeared to him that favoritism rather than talent and performance were the basis for Bragg's preferment. "Bragg's manner made him malignant enemies and indifferent, callous friends," Liddell wrote in a devastating assessment of Bragg's prsonality.[19]

Richard Taylor knew Bragg from before the war and echoed many of these assessments. Taylor was impressed by Bragg's industry and patriotism but feared that generally poor health impeded the success of his efforts. Bragg was intolerant of anyone who did not match his vision of devotion to duty; he was good at discipline but exacted it so harshly as to make more enemies than friends. Winning clear-cut victories on the battlefield was the only way to overcome these deficiencies and gain the love of his army, but that rarely happened. Taylor marveled that the troops and subordinate officers followed Bragg as well as they did, given all these problems.[20]

Taylor was particularly disturbed by an incident that shed much light on Bragg's method of dealing with his subordinates. He visited army headquarters at Chattanooga just before the Kentucky campaign and dined with the general. When Taylor asked Bragg about a division commander who was an acquaintance, he was surprised at the response. "General ____ is an old woman, utterly worthless," Bragg crudely blurted. Taylor was shocked at such language in front of Bragg's staff. Later he privately asked him what he planned to do about it, and the general admitted he had no one better to replace the division leader. "I have but one or two fitted for high command, and have in vain asked the War Department for capable people." Taylor warned Bragg he could not expect cooperation from men he publicly abused, but the general refused to see the point. "I speak truth. The Government is to blame for putting such men in high position." Taylor thanked his stars that he was never assigned to duty under Bragg.[21]

The general's relations with his subordinates often were troubled, and much of it was due to his abrasive personality. But Bragg always felt differently toward the rank and file. There is every reason to believe that Bragg truly respected his men. "General, I have no children," he told Liddell the day before the battle of Stones River. "Hence, I look upon the soldiers of my army as my own—as *my* children." He wanted Liddell to tell his brigade what he had just said, "I am in earnest." Liddell wrote a circular to this effect, and his adjutant sent it around. Some of the men reacted with sarcasm. "He has a very large family," they said, "and sometimes causes his boys to be shot."[22]

Federal officers who knew Bragg before the war, or who heard stories of him dating from the Mexican conflict, offered conflicting visions of the Confederate general. Ulysses S. Grant had met Bragg in Mexico and always viewed him as honest and professional in his demeanor. "But he was possessed of an irascible temper, and was naturally disputatious." Grant correctly viewed Bragg as "always on the lookout to catch his commanding officer infringing his prerogatives" and "equally vigilant to detect the slightest neglect, even of the most trivial order." It was Grant who offered the world the entertaining story about Bragg arguing with himself when he served in two responsible positions at an army post, writing out one report and countering it with another. Grant thought it was "very characteristic of Bragg" to do something like this but admitted he could not verify its truthfulness.[23]

William T. Sherman knew Bragg more intimately than Grant and retained a quiet admiration for his good qualities. He also "had charity for his weaknesses," as Sherman put it in a postwar article. Sherman regretted that Bragg did not take the route of his colleague from Virginia, George H. Thomas, and opt for the Union cause. He "might have transmitted an honorable name to posterity."[24]

The premier publication by and for Southern veterans initially paid little attention to Bragg until editor Sumner A. Cunningham became aware of Elise. Cunningham published an article in the *Confederate Veteran* by Emilie Todd Helm about Elise and her husband. The article appeared in 1896, and Cunningham was taken with Elise and her situation as the widow of the most abused Southern general of the war. He admitted that he had been no fan of Bragg during the conflict but now praised him for his devotion to the cause. Emilie Helm, who was the half-sister of Abraham Lincoln's wife, characterized Bragg as reserved and dignified, his outer reticence hiding a kind heart. He sought no sympathy for the loss of his property or for the criticisms hurled his way during the war. When asked if he would write his memoirs, he refused and simply said, "Some day the truth will be known, and my acts will appear in a different light."[25]

The publication of Emilie Helm's article opened the *Veteran*'s pages to more discussion of Bragg. Cunningham had the year before printed a long article about Samuel Stout's *Reminiscences*, which reflected very positively on the general, but he made no editorial comment on Stout's views. After the publication of Helm's piece, Cunningham spoke out for Bragg. He printed M. R. Tunno's severe criticism of Bragg during the Shiloh campaign but inserted an editorial note that he doubted Tunno's assertion that "Gen. Bragg lost us that battle." Instead, Cunningham stressed the fact that Tunno admitted Bragg to be a true Southern patriot. That message was repeated in several articles by veterans. George B. Guild pointed out that Bragg directed the "most noted battles" fought by the Army of Tennessee. "Every soldier in his army knows that when Bragg made his arrangements to fight, somebody was sure to get hurt."[26]

Guild admitted that Bragg's inability to follow up his hard fighting and win important victories was problematic. John C. Stiles also asserted that "he was a famous scrapper with his subordinates." Some contemporaries noted Bragg's chronic health problems as explanations for his combative attitude toward officers. Richard Taylor thought the health angle explained much about Bragg. "He furnished a striking illustration of the necessity of a healthy body for a sound intellect. Many years of dyspepsia had made his temper sour and petulant." A weak constitution "unfitted him to sustain long-continued pressure of responsibility." Irving Buck believed Bragg's physical weakness prevented him from supervising operations during important battles.[27]

Judith Lee Hallock stressed Bragg's health as a key factor in understanding his Civil War career and wondered if he took opium for relief, even though she admitted that there is no evidence of it. Hallock also suggested that psychosomatic illness may have afflicted Bragg in times of great stress. Kenneth Noe emphasized the general's mood swings during the Kentucky campaign and placed greater stress on narcissistic personality disorder as an explanation for it than on self-prescribed medication. Although admitting it is impossible to prove it, Noe believed Bragg exhibited the symptoms of this disorder, which resulted from excessive parental expectations and an inability to meet them. In short, Bragg presented "a competent and idealized 'false self'" to the world, but quietly doubted his ability to fulfill that role. It led to dramatic mood swings and a tendency to find scapegoats when things went wrong.[28]

Hallock's and Noe's arguments are provocative but not provable, as both historians readily admit. In the end we have to take Bragg for what he was, even if we cannot thoroughly explain how he came to be. His contemporaries were scattered all across the spectrum when making sense of the general. Public opinion initially was split but began to sour when rumors of his willingness to execute soldiers for apparently trivial reasons spread. His supporters initially worked in public ways to help him, but even they became silent when Bragg made war on his chief subordinates after Stones River and Chickamauga.

When compared with the performance of other commanders of the main Rebel army in the West, Bragg's record shines more positively than negatively. Along with Beauregard, he was mostly responsible for organizing the Army of the Mississippi in March 1862. As its commander, Bragg took it on the first of only two strategic offensives the army ever conducted. He penetrated much farther into enemy territory, as Thomas Connelly has pointed out, than did Hood into Tennessee in 1864, and Bragg brought out the army in much better shape than did Hood.[29]

The Army of Tennessee won its most impressive tactical victories under Bragg. On October 8 at Perryville, December 31 at Stones River, and September 20 at Chickamauga, the Confederates achieved stunning successes even if they were not able to translate them into strategic victories. The only other tactical triumph the army achieved, on April 6 at Shiloh, was also in part contributed by Bragg.

In fact, if one tallied the results of the army's fighting in terms of days of success (for it won only one major battle in its history) versus days of failure, Bragg overwhelmingly comes out on top. The army achieved stunning tactical success on four days, and Bragg was responsible for three of them. It suffered tactical failure on fourteen days, and Bragg was responsible for four of them. In other words, he accounted for 75 percent of the Army of Tennessee's tactical success days but only 28.5 percent of its tactical failure days. None of the army's other commanders achieved a success rate remotely close to this. In contrast, John Bell Hood was responsible for 57.1 percent of the failure days.[30]

Bragg commanded the major western army for twenty months, from April 1862 until December 1863, much longer than any other man. Bragg took it to a higher standard of effectiveness than either Albert Sidney Johnston or P. G. T. Beauregard, each of whom held command for about a month. Under Joseph E. Johnston, who led it for eight months, the army worked efficiently, but its tactical prowess was dulled by continued retreats. Under John Bell Hood, who led it for five months, the command nearly fell apart. The army was at the peak of its effectiveness under Bragg. In short, the Army of Tennessee was Bragg's army.

Bragg was able to implant his own stamp on the Army of Tennessee only because Jefferson Davis believed in him and supported his tenure as commander through stormy times. The relationship between Bragg and Davis has often been misunderstood. Historians such as Thomas Robson Hay and Steven Woodworth have correctly pointed out that Bragg did not owe his position to his friendship with the Confederate president, for the two had never been friends either before or during that time period. While they knew each other since the Mexican War and shared a mutual respect, Bragg's attitude toward Davis soured when the latter, as secretary of war, tried to institute army reforms that seemed to destroy the efficiency of light artillery units. Bragg resigned rather than accept those changes. He continued to have a sour attitude toward Davis after the latter became president of the Confederacy, but Davis always retained his high opinion of Bragg and counted on him in the early months of the Civil War.[31]

Slowly it dawned on Bragg that he had a supporter in Richmond. That support was based not on Davis's friendship but on his appreciation for Bragg's administrative ability. It led to Bragg's elevation to command the chief Rebel army in the West. Just as importantly, Davis thought there was no one better suited for the job. These two factors were the foundation of Bragg's career. The general fully understood this and used the Southern president to strengthen his hand against dissident generals after Stones River and Chickamauga. Only after his elevation to serve as the president's military adviser did Bragg and Davis develop a personal friendship. The evidence of it appears only at the very end of the war, but that friendship lasted for the rest of their lives.

Davis had a strong tendency to stick with the generals he admired and shy away from those he did not. His continued support of Bragg added to the abuse he received from the public. Ironically, his support for Leonidas Polk, his true friend, greatly contributed to the army's troubles.

When Robert E. Lee gently offered to be replaced as head of the Army of Northern Virginia after Gettysburg, Davis refused to consider it. He did not take newspaper criticism of Lee seriously or think it reflected the mood of the soldiers. "There has been nothing which I have found to require a greater effort of patience than to bear the criticisms of the ignorant, who pronounce everything a failure which does not equal their expectations or desires," he assured Lee.[32]

The Confederate president also supported John C. Pemberton in the midst of public ridicule for the general's loss of Vicksburg. Davis expressed a thought that related not only to Pemberton's plight but to his own and Bragg's as well. "To some men it is given to be commended for what they are expected to do, and to be sheltered when they fail by a transfer of the blame which may attach; to others it is decreed that their success shall be denied or treated as a necessary result; and their failures imputed to incapacity or crime." For all three men, it seemed as if there was no possibility for public opinion to be fair or equitable.[33]

No general had the opportunity of winning the Confederate war singlehandedly. All labored under a matrix of problems compared to their opponents, starting with disparity of numbers, moving on to a miserable logistical system, a decrepit supply apparatus, waning morale, loss of territory, and severe problems of desertion. In every way, the Federals had many advantages, and as long as the Northern people's will to pursue the conflict to the bitter end remained strong, the South had decreasing chances of winning as the war continued.

This is why Bragg could win fights but not win campaigns—the Federals dominated the strategic context of military operations so thoroughly that victory on a large scale was nearly impossible to obtain. Confederate commanders in the west especially suffered in this regard because their opponents dominated the strategic context more thoroughly than in Virginia. Davis's government gave Lee nearly everything he wanted, amassing a larger proportion of Confederate strength to that small theater of operations than anywhere else in order to protect their national capital. Lee had the audacity to use that strength effectively and win many battles. In the process he created an aura of invincibility his western colleagues never attained. Despite all this, Lee could not win the war for Southern independence. The best he could do was stave off defeat for many months, giving Southerners what proved to be a vain hope of ultimate success until the Confederacy collapsed, first in the West and then in Virginia.

Edmund Ruffin perceptively noted this basic problem of the Confederate effort. "For it has been our remarkable misfortune throughout this war, that while we have defeated the enemy's forces in numerous great battles & have rarely been defeated in open field or pitched battle, all our victories have been barren of benefit or gain, except in obstructing & postponing the enemy's then aggressive movement[;] in no case have we been enabled . . . to roll back the wave of previous territorial conquest & occupancy permanently."[34]

Bragg was not alone in winning tactical success but giving up the field before the end of the battle. Beauregard did so at Shiloh, and Joseph E. Johnston did so at Bentonville. Lee racked up more tactical successes than any other Rebel general, but in the end he was unable to drain his enemy of willpower to continue fighting the larger war. Of all other Confederate generals, Bragg tried harder to achieve Lee's goal in the West than anyone else, especially in the era of Stones River. In part he could not achieve that goal because he had a more stubborn foe and less willing subordinates. Lee faced Hooker at Chancellorsville, while Bragg opposed Rosecrans at Stones River. Lee had Stonewall Jackson at Chancellorsville, while Bragg had Polk at Perryville, Stones River, and Chickamauga. Lee never had to deal with a situation where two of his division commanders wrote a note to him in the middle of a battle saying that virtually all units in his army were unreliable and could not fight any longer, a note endorsed by one of his two corps commanders. What would Lee have done in Bragg's situation at Stones River? Lee himself was afraid to go west and take command of the Army of Tennessee after Missionary Ridge, which must stand as the answer to the question.

It is probable that no army commander of either side in the Civil War had to deal with such insubordinate corps and division commanders as did Bragg. It is also true that no other army commander would have done what Bragg did in that situation; challenge them after Stones River and call in the president of the Confederacy to back him up. That was a mistake. However, Bragg did not create the bad blood within the Army of Tennessee; Polk did that, and he also corrupted Hardee into becoming a player of his corrosive game. But Bragg responded to the Polk challenge badly, and against the advice of his own staff, in sending the round-robin letter of January 11, 1863. That letter initiated a chain reaction that played itself out for the rest of his stormy tenure as commander. It made the situation far worse; in fact, the result was that Bragg's ability to command the army declined so rapidly that he endured one bitter disappointment after another. Polk destroyed his attempt to attack Rosecrans at Tullahoma; Hindman and Buckner unraveled his plan at McLemore's Cove; Hill and Polk derailed his effort to attack early on September 20. The next and worse round of warfare within the Army of Tennessee following Chickamauga took his ability to command to its nadir, and once again the Southern president was called in to restore a degree of order without harmony. The dismal lead-up to Chattanooga and the humiliation of Missionary Ridge were the legitimate fruits of Bragg's inability to give up a job that he had no hope of succeeding in, out of sheer stubbornness and a myopic desire to impose order and discipline on men he thought had forgotten everything about military subordination.

Bragg was ill-equipped to deal with the press; for that matter, many other public figures also had great difficulty dealing with it. Most Americans thought in simplistic, one-dimensional terms in the Civil War era, and their newspapers reflected that culture. Added to this was the partisan nature of journalism, with newspaper editors fighting vicious word battles against opponents of the political parties they supported. The result was a newspaper culture that too often saw generals merely as targets. Bragg's refusal to cozy up to correspondents doomed any chance he had to win support among the newspaper fraternity when simplistic, ill-informed, and often deliberately hostile writers took him on.

Public opinion was indeed Bragg's worst enemy; public opinion combined with a few high-ranking officers, who also made of him a convenient target and scapegoat for much that was wrong with the Confederacy. Given his prickly nature, Bragg bore his publicly assigned role as "the best-abused man" of the Confederacy with more resignation than one would expect. He trusted far too much in history and historians to tell his side of the story, failing to see it happen during his lifetime. He would have continued to be disappointed in the historical record for a long time after his death as well. Bragg was a fascinating mixture of good and bad qualities; his impact on Confederate history was enormous, and we are still grappling with it.

Notes

Abbreviations

ADAH	Alabama Department of Archives and History, Montgomery
ALPL	Abraham Lincoln Presidential Library, Springfield, Illinois
AM	Archives of Michigan, Lansing
AU	Auburn University, Special Collections and Archives, Auburn, Alabama
CHM	Chicago History Museum, Chicago, Illinois
CWM	College of William and Mary, Special Collections Research Center, Williamsburg, Virginia
CU	Columbia University, Rare Book and Manuscript Library, New York
DU	Duke University, Rubenstein Rare Book and Manuscript Library, Durham, North Carolina
EU	Emory University, Manuscript, Archives, Rare Book Library, Atlanta, Georgia
FHS	Filson Historical Society, Louisville, Kentucky
GLIAH	Gilder Lehrman Institute of American History, New York
HNOC	Historic New Orleans Collection, New Orleans, Louisiana
HSP	Historical Society of Pennsylvania, Philadelphia
HU	Harvard University, Houghton Library, Cambridge, Massachusetts
IHS	Indiana Historical Society, Indianapolis
IU	Indiana University, Lilly Library, Bloomington
LC	Library of Congress, Manuscript Division, Washington, D.C.
LSU	Louisiana State University, Louisiana and Lower Mississippi Valley Collections, Special Collections, Baton Rouge
MDAH	Mississippi Department of Archives and History, Jackson
MHM	Missouri History Museum, St. Louis
MHS	Massachusetts Historical Society, Boston
MOC	Museum of the Confederacy, Richmond, Virginia
MSU	Mississippi State University, Special Collections, Starkville
MU	Miami University, Walter Havighurst Special Collections, Oxford, Ohio
NARA	National Archives and Records Administration, Washington, D.C.
NC	Navarro College, Pearce Civil War Collection, Corsicana, Texas
OR	*War of the Rebellion: A Compilation of the Official Records of the Union and Confederate Armies*. 70 vols. in 128. Washington, D.C.: Government Printing Office, 1880–1901. Unless otherwise cited, all references are to series 1. *OR* citations take the following form: volume number (part number, where applicable):page number.
RBHPC	Rutherford B. Hayes Presidential Center, Fremont, Ohio

RL   Rosenberg Library, Galveston and Texas History Center, Galveston, Texas
SANC   State Archives of North Carolina, Raleigh
SRNB   Stones River National Battlefield, Murfreesboro, Tennessee
TSLA   Tennessee State Library and Archives, Nashville
TU   Tulane University, Special Collections, New Orleans, Louisiana
UA   University of Alabama, W. S. Hoole Special Collections Library, Tuscaloosa
UAF   University of Arkansas, Special Collections, Fayetteville
UF   University of Florida, Special and Area Studies Collections, Gainesville
UK   University of Kentucky, Special Collections, Lexington
UNC   University of North Carolina, Southern History Collection, Chapel Hill
US   University of the South, Department of Archives, Sewanee, Tennessee
USC   University of South Carolina, South Caroliniana Library, Columbia
USMA   United States Military Academy, Special Collections, West Point, New York
UTA   University of Texas, Dolph Briscoe Center for American History, Austin
UTC   University of Tennessee, Special Collections, Chattanooga
UTK   University of Tennessee, Special Collections, Knoxville
UVA   University of Virginia, Special Collections, Charlottesville
VHS   Virginia Historical Society, Richmond
WRHS   Western Reserve Historical Society, Cleveland, Ohio

Preface

1. Kirby Smith to wife, July 28, 1862, Edmund Kirby Smith Papers, UNC; Walter Bullock to mother, February 18, 1864, Bullock Family Papers, DU; Malone, *Memoir*, 122–24; Stephenson, "Missionary Ridge," 19.

2. Noe, *Perryville*, 15; McWhiney, *Braxton Bragg*, vii.

3. Seitz, *Braxton Bragg*, foreword; Hay, "Braxton Bragg," 267, 314–16.

4. Seitz, *Braxton Bragg*, foreword.

5. Horn, *Army of Tennessee*.

6. Ibid., 114.

7. Connelly, *Army of the Heartland*, 206.

8. Ibid.

9. Connelly, *Autumn of Glory*, 70.

10. McWhiney, *Braxton Bragg*, x–xi.

11. Ibid., 89.

12. Hallock, *Braxton Bragg*, 269.

13. Woodworth, *Jefferson Davis*, 92; Woodworth, "Braxton Bragg and the Tullahoma Campaign," 157–82; Woodworth, "'In Their Dreams,'" 50–67; Mendoza, "Censure of D. H. Hill," 68–83; Cozzens, *This Terrible Sound*, 5. Hay, "Braxton Bragg," 313, also points out that Davis and Bragg were not friends even though Connelly, *Army of the Heartland*, 182, continues to assert that they were and that this relationship explains Davis's support of Bragg.

14. Woodworth, *Jefferson Davis*, 94.

15. Woodworth, "Braxton Bragg and the Tullahoma Campaign," 176–78.

16. S. J. Martin, *General Braxton Bragg*, 1–2, 184, 473, 475.

17. Ibid., 2.

18. Grant, *Memoirs*, 449–50.

19. McWhiney, *Braxton Bragg*, 33–34. See also Gallagher, *Fighting for the Confederacy*, 591, n12.

20. William Dudley Gale to William M. Polk, March 28, 1882, Leonidas Polk Papers, US, also cited in Parks, *General Leonidas Polk*, 341.

21. Spence, *A Diary*, 66.

Chapter One

1. McWhiney, *Braxton Bragg*, 2, 4, 142.

2. S. J. Martin, *General Braxton Bragg*, 5; McWhiney, *Braxton Bragg*, 3.

3. McWhiney, *Braxton Bragg*, 25–27; S. J. Martin, *General Braxton Bragg*, 333; cards, Braxton Bragg Service Record, M331, NARA.

4. Cards, Braxton Bragg Service Record, M331, NARA; Bragg to George W. Cullum, September 1, 1859, Braxton Bragg Papers, USMA.

5. McWhiney, *Braxton Bragg*, 28–34; Keyes, *Fifty Years'*, 178.

6. Keyes, *Fifty Years'*, 178; Sherman, "Old Shady," 361–68.

7. McWhiney, *Braxton Bragg*, 35–38, 42; "Charges against 1st Lieut. B. Bragg 3rd Artillery," Braxton Bragg Papers, USMA.

8. McWhiney, *Braxton Bragg*, 51.

9. Bragg to George W. Cullum, September 1, 1858, Braxton Bragg Papers, USMA; McWhiney, *Braxton Bragg*, 54, 60, 64–71, 88, 90, 92; S. J. Martin, *General Braxton Bragg*, 57. See also Samuel G. French to Capers, July 2, 1901, Ellison Capers Papers, DU.

10. Davis to William W. S. Bliss, March 2, 1847, Crist, *Papers of Jefferson Davis*, 3:143.

11. Braxton Bragg to Sherman, March 4, 1848, William T. Sherman Papers, LC; Braxton Bragg to John, March 25, 1852, John Bragg Papers, UNC.

12. Bragg to Dear Friend, October 13, 1847, Braxton Bragg Papers, USMA; S. J. Martin, *General Braxton Bragg*, 59–60.

13. Helm, "Gen. and Mrs. Braxton Bragg," 102; McWhiney, *Braxton Bragg*, 108–9, 111, 118.

14. Elise Bragg quoted in McWhiney, *Braxton Bragg*, 119; Braxton Bragg quoted in Seitz, *Braxton Bragg*, 11–13.

15. Bragg to Dear General, March 8, 1854, and Bragg to George W. Cullum, September 1, 1859, Braxton Bragg Papers, USMA; Braxton Bragg to John, February 10, March 25, June 28, 1852, John Bragg Papers, UNC; Bragg to William Gates, November 22, 1847; Bragg to Trustees of University of Mississippi, June 26, 1848; and Bragg to J. Y. Mason, November 17, 1848, Braxton Bragg Papers, DU; McWhiney, *Braxton Bragg*, 130; Bridges, *Lee's Maverick General*, 19.

16. Bragg to wife, June 9, [1853], Braxton Bragg Papers, DU; Braxton Bragg to John, March 25, 1852, John Bragg Papers, UNC; Braxton Bragg to Sherman, June 3, 1855, William T. Sherman Papers, LC; "Prescription for Chronic Chill & fever," no date but in Braxton Bragg's handwriting, Confederate Military Leaders Collection, MOC.

17. McWhiney, *Braxton Bragg*, 139; S. J. Martin, *General Braxton Bragg*, 78, 80; Seitz, *Braxton Bragg*, 17–18; cards, Braxton Bragg Service Record, M331, NARA; Braxton Bragg to Stuart, May 31, 1856, George Hay Stuart Papers, LC.

18. McWhiney, *Braxton Bragg*, 139, 141, 143–44; Braxton Bragg to Sherman, June 3, 1855, William T. Sherman Papers, LC; affidavit by Braxton Bragg and Allan C. Story, January, no date, 1870, Braxton Bragg Papers, MHM; Braxton Bragg to Stuart, May 31, 1856, George Hay Stuart Papers, LC.

19. Affidavit by Braxton Bragg and Allan C. Story, January, no date, 1870, Braxton Bragg Papers, MHM; Bragg to wife, February 10, 1856, Braxton Bragg Letters, LSU.

20. Braxton Bragg to Sherman, May 23, 1856, December 16, 1859, June 14, 1860, William T.

Sherman Papers, LC; "My will & testament," June 25, 1858, Eliza Brooks Bragg Papers, CHM.

21. McWhiney, *Braxton Bragg*, 144; Bragg to George W. Cullum, September 1, 1859, Braxton Bragg Papers, USMA; Braxton Bragg to Sherman, December 16, 1859, June 14, 1860, William T. Sherman Papers, LC.

22. McWhiney, *Braxton Bragg*, 147; Braxton Bragg to Sherman, June 14, 1860, William T. Sherman Papers, LC; Sherman, *Memoirs*, 1:146.

23. Sherman, *Memoirs*, 1:143; Braxton Bragg to William T. Sherman, November 13, 1859, Fleming, *Sherman as College President*, 52.

24. Sherman, *Memoirs*, 1:146; Braxton Bragg to Sherman, December 16, 1859, February 13, 1860, William T. Sherman Papers, LC.

25. Braxton Bragg to G. Mason Graham, June 27, 1860, Fleming, *Sherman as College President*, 236–37; Braxton Bragg to Sherman, June 14, 1860, William T. Sherman Papers, LC.

26. Braxton Bragg to G. Mason Graham, June 27, 1860, July 6, 1860, Fleming, *Sherman as College President*, 237, 239; A. K. Craig to Braxton Bragg, June 29, 1860, William T. Sherman Papers, LC.

27. Braxton Bragg to Sherman, December 16, 1859, William T. Sherman Papers, LC.

28. Ibid.

29. Roland, *Louisiana Sugar Plantations*, 3–4, 16–18; Follett, *Sugar Masters*, 30–38.

30. Follett, *Sugar Masters*, 4–5, 8; Roland, *Louisiana Sugar Plantations*, 21.

31. Braxton Bragg to Stuart, May 31, 1856, George Hay Stuart Papers, LC; Helm, "Gen. and Mrs. Braxton Bragg," 103.

32. Bragg to Dear Sir, December 7, 1860, Braxton Bragg Letters, LSU.

33. Braxton Bragg to Sherman, December 26, 1860, William T. Sherman Papers, LC.

34. McWhiney, *Braxton Bragg*, 150–53; Bragg to wife, [January] 11, [1861], January 13, 1862, Braxton Bragg Papers, MHM; diary, January 14, 1861, Thomas Bragg Papers, UNC; Braxton Bragg to William T. Sherman, January 27, 1861, Fleming, *Sherman as College President*, 351.

35. Sherman to Thomas Ewing, January 8, 1861, and Sherman to Charles Anders, [ca. August 1863], Simpson and Berlin, *Sherman's Civil War*, 32–33, 510; Sherman, *Memoirs*, 1:161–62.

36. Sherman, *Memoirs*, 2:381–82.

37. Diary, February 18, 1861, Thomas Bragg Papers, UNC; Sherman to George Mason Graham, January 16, 1861, and Sherman to Boyd, February 23, 1861, Simpson and Berlin, *Sherman's Civil War*, 37, 57; Bragg to wife, February 8, 1860, Braxton Bragg Papers, RL; Walker to Bragg, February 25, 1861, *OR*, 1:608.

38. *Journal of the Congress*, 1:114; Howell Cobb to wife, February 20, 1861, Phillips, *Correspondence*, 544; Walker to Bragg, March 7, 1861, *OR*, 52(2):24.

Chapter Two

1. Walker to Bragg, March 7, 1861, *OR*, 52(2):24; Special Orders No. 1, Adjutant General's Office, March 7, 1861, and Orders No. 1, March 11, 1861, *OR*, 1:448, 449; Braxton Bragg to wife, March 7, [1861], Confederate Military Leaders Collection, MOC.

2. Braxton Bragg to wife, March 7, [1861], Confederate Military Leaders Collection, MOC.

3. Bearss, "Civil War Operations," 125, 129, 139, 141.

4. Ibid., 144, 146; McWhiney, *Braxton Bragg*, 157.

5. Davis to Bragg, April 3, 1861, and Bragg to Davis, April 7, 1861, Crist, *Papers of Jefferson Davis*, 7:86, 94–96; Bragg to Walker, April 6, May 6, 1861, and Walker to Bragg, April 30, 1861, *OR*, 1:457, 465; Bragg to wife, April 11 [1861], Braxton Bragg Papers, MHM.

6. Adams to Brown, May 13, 1861, and Bragg to Adams, May 14, 1861, *OR*, 1:413; W. Smith to Bragg, May 23, 1861; F.G.S. to Bragg, May 8, 1861; "A Southern Woman" to Bragg, April 24, 1861; and Bragg to Jefferson Davis, June 1, 1861, Braxton Bragg Papers, DU; Bragg to Davis, May 28, 1861, *OR*, 1:468; Jefferson Davis to Joseph E. Davis, June 18, 1861, Crist, *Papers of Jefferson Davis*, 7:204.

7. Bragg to wife, May 25, [1861], July 4, [1861], July 7, [1861], Braxton Bragg Papers, LC; McWhiney, *Braxton Bragg*, 182; Bragg to Benjamin, September 25, 1861, October 30, 1861, *OR*, 6:744, 759.

8. Bragg to Davis, July 9, 1861, Crist, *Papers of Jefferson Davis*, 7:230; July 23, 1861, Taylor Beatty Diary, UNC.

9. *Journal of the Congress*, 1:473; card, Braxton Bragg Service Record, M331, NARA; Bragg to Adjutant General, Confederate States Army, September 16, October 10, 1861; Bragg to Cooper, October 9, 29, 1861; and General Orders No. 108, Headquarters, Troops near Pensacola, October 10, 1861, *OR*, 6:438, 458–60; Bearss, "Civil War Operations," 145–47, 149, 153–54; Sykes, "A Cursory Sketch," pt. 1, 305–6; Thomas Butler to aunt, October 12, 1861, Butler Family Papers, LSU; Bragg to Davis, October 13, 1861, Crist., *Papers of Jefferson Davis*, 7:357.

10. Special Orders No. 173, Adjutant and Inspector General's Officer, October 7, 1861; General Orders No. 1, Headquarters, Department of Alabama and Western Florida, October 14, 1861; and Bragg to Adjutant General, Confederate Army, October 25, 28, 1861, *OR*, 6:751–52, 755–57; Bearss, "Civil War Operations," 156, 158.

11. Jackson to Davis, November 5, 1861, *OR*, 53:755; Benjamin to Bragg, December 27, 1861, *OR*, 6:788–89.

12. Benjamin to Bragg, December 27, 1861, *OR*, 6:788–89.

13. Bragg to Benjamin, January 6, 1862, *OR*, 6:797–98.

14. Beauregard to Johnston, December 9, 1861, *OR*, 5:990.

15. Bragg to Adjutant General, Confederate Army, November 25, 1861, *OR*, 6:488–89; Bearss, "Civil War Operations," 158–65; Thomas Butler to father, November 26, 1862, Butler Family Papers, LSU.

16. Elise to husband, [November] 28, 1861, Braxton Bragg Papers, UTA.

17. General Orders No. 130, Headquarters, Army of Pensacola, November 25, 1861, *OR*, 6:494; Bragg to wife, March 11, 1861, Braxton Bragg Papers, MHM; Lockett, "The Contrasts of War: Being Pen and Ink Pictures from the Life of a Soldier," 12, folder 48, Samuel Henry Lockett Papers, UNC.

18. Lockett, "The Contrasts of War: Being Pen and Ink Pictures from the Life of a Soldier," 13, folder 48, Samuel Henry Lockett Papers, UNC; Bragg to Adjutant General, Confederate Army, November 28, 1861, and Bragg to Benjamin, December 10, 1861, *OR*, 6:771, 777; Bragg to wife, September 1, 1861, Braxton Bragg Papers, MHM; Ada to editor, November 3, 1862, *Chattanooga Daily Rebel*, November 5, 1862.

19. Thomas Butler to sister, September 23, 1861, Butler Family Papers, LSU.

20. Bragg to Adjutant General, Confederate Army, January 3, 1862, *OR*, 6:497–98; Thomas Butler to father, January 3, 1862, Butler Family Papers, LSU.

21. Bragg to Adjutant General, Confederate Army, January 3, 1862, *OR*, 6:497–98; Braxton Bragg to Walter, January 7, 1862, Harvey Washington Walter Papers, UNC.

22. Bragg to Adjutant General, Confederate Army, January 4, February 1, 1862, *OR*, 6:793, 820.

23. Bragg to wife, March 11, 1861, Braxton Bragg Papers, MHM; editorial comment, Crist, *Papers of Jefferson Davis*, 7:170n; Bragg to wife, May 25 [1861], Braxton Bragg Papers, LC.

24. Bragg to wife, April 24, 1861, Braxton Bragg Papers, LC; Bragg to Henry J. Hunt,

April 21, 1861, Braxton Bragg Letters, GLIAH; Hunt to Braxton Bragg, April 23, 1861, Henry J. Hunt Letter, GLIAH.

25. Russell, *My Diary*, 149–50.

26. Bragg to wife, March 11, 1861, Braxton Bragg Papers, MHM; Thomas Butler to Father, June 22, 1861; Thomas Butler to aunt, December 16, 1861; and Thomas Butler to sister, February 2, 1862, Butler Family Papers, LSU.

27. Bragg to wife, March 11, 14, 1861, Braxton Bragg Papers, MHM. Bragg's photograph was taken at Theodore Lilienthal's Photographic Gallery and Studio on Poydras Street in New Orleans in early March 1861. The German-born photographer was just beginning to take advantage of a thriving market for photographic portraits of soldiers in the Civil War. See Van Zante, "Theodore Lilienthal," www.knowla.org/entry/806/.

28. Bragg to wife, April 19, May 28, [1861], Braxton Bragg Papers, LC; McWhiney, *Braxton Bragg*, 187; Elise to husband, August, no date, [1861]; and Elise to husband, no date [fall 1861], Braxton Bragg Papers, UTA; Chalmers to Bragg, January 3, 1861 [1862], James R. Chalmers Letter, LSU.

29. Elise to husband, October 18, 1861, Braxton Bragg Papers, UTA; McWhiney, *Braxton Bragg*, 179; diary, November 26, December 19, 1861, and January 20, 1862, Thomas Bragg Papers, UNC.

30. Diary, November 30, December 3, 1861, and January 8, February 25, 1862, Thomas Bragg Papers, UNC; General Orders No. 3, Adjutant and Inspector General's Office, January 9, 1862, *OR*, ser. 4, 1:834–35. With the state of Alabama, the important port city of Mobile, and thousands of untried soldiers under his command, Bragg's sense of self did not swell into unmanageable proportions. "My own ego will never be my guide in a crisis like [that facing my] beloved country," he wrote to a friend. That was true even after a music publisher in New Orleans issued sheet music for "Genl. Bragg Grand March" late in 1861. Draft of Bragg to My Dear Doctor, [November 11, 1861], Braxton Bragg Papers, WRHS; *Genl Bragg Grand March*, LSU.

31. Davis signed at least one letter to Bragg as "very truly, your friend," but not before the end of the war. See Davis to Bragg, April 1, 1865, *OR*, 47(3):740.

32. Chalmers to Davis, December 27, 1886, Rowland, *Jefferson Davis*, 9:515–16.

33. Diary, January 6, April 30, 1862, Thomas Bragg Papers, UNC; Woodworth, *Jefferson Davis*, 93.

Chapter Three

1. Bragg to Benjamin, February 15, 1862, *OR*, 6:826.

2. Benjamin to Bragg, February 18, 1862; Bragg to Beauregard, February 27, 1862; and Bragg to Jones, [March 1?, 1862], *OR*, 6:827, 836–37; Shorter to Bragg, February 26, 1862, *OR*, 7:914; Woodworth, *Jefferson Davis*, 94; McWhiney, *Braxton Bragg*, 204; Roman, *Military Operations*, 1:250.

3. Davis to Johnston, March 12, 1862, and Bradford to Davis, March 23, 1862, Crist, *Papers of Jefferson Davis*, 8:93, 113. Bradford had served with Bragg at Pensacola and told Davis a story about the massive bombardment of November 1861. When "a shell burst within a few paces of him . . . and as the sulphur gained our nostrils, he turned round to us and with a smile said 'Young gentlemen you smell your powder.'"

4. Sherman, *Memoirs*, 1:162; Daniel, *Shiloh*, 40–48.

5. David Urquhart to Thomas Jordan, August 25, 1880, David Urquhart Letter and Book, UNC; Bragg to Dear Sir, March 14, 1872, Braxton Bragg Papers, WRHS; McWhiney, *Braxton Bragg*, 204; Roman, *Military Operations*, 1:268–69.

6. Bragg to wife, March 25, 1862, Braxton Bragg Papers, MHM; John Walker to wife, March 8, 1862, Rice Family Papers, MSU; Bragg to Jordan, March 18, 1862, *OR*, 10(2):340.

7. Bragg to wife, March 20, [1862], Braxton Bragg Papers, DU; diary, March 14, 1862, Thomas Bragg Papers, UNC; Bragg to wife, March 25, 1862, Braxton Bragg Papers, MHM.

8. General Orders No. 1, March 4, 1862, *OR*, 7:920–21; General Orders, Headquarters of the Forces, March 29, 1862, *OR*, 10(2):370–71.

9. Bragg to Jordan, March 18, 1862, *OR*, 10(2):340; Bragg to wife, March 25, 1862, Braxton Bragg Papers, MHM; J. Davis, *Rise and Fall*, 2:54–55.

10. Elise to husband, February 16, 1862, Braxton Bragg Papers, UTA.

11. Elise to husband, February 21, March 7, 1862, Braxton Bragg Papers, WRHS; Elise to husband, March 3, 1861 [1862], Braxton Bragg Papers, UTA.

12. Elise to husband, February 21, March 7, 1862, Braxton Bragg Papers, WRHS; Elise to husband, March 12, 1862, Braxton Bragg Papers, UTA.

13. Bragg to wife, March 25, 1862, Braxton Bragg Papers, MHM; diary, March 10–11, 24, 1862, Thomas Bragg Papers, UNC.

14. Daniel, *Shiloh*, 118–23.

15. Bragg to wife, April 3, [1862], Braxton Bragg Letters, GLIAH.

16. Daniel, *Shiloh*, 119–20, 143–65.

17. Cooke to Kate Wilson, May 17, 1862, transcribed into Giles Buckner Cooke Diary, VHS; "For my mother," Giles Buckner Cooke Papers, VHS.

18. "For my mother," Giles Buckner Cooke Papers, VHS.

19. Ibid.

20. Bragg to wife, April 8, [1862], Braxton Bragg Papers, MHM; Webster, "Another Chapter on the Mystery," 341; diary, April 28, 1862, Thomas Bragg Papers, UNC.

21. Robertson to mother, April 9, 1862, Thomas Chinn Robertson Papers, NC; Cooper to Farley, April 22, 1862, James Cooper Papers, NC; undated fragment of letter, Given Campbell Papers, UNC.

22. McBride and McLaurin, *Randall Lee Gibson*, 56–60.

23. Randall L. Gibson to My Dear Doctor, September 7, 1874, Leonidas Polk Papers, UNC.

24. Bragg to Jordan, April 30, 1862, and Gibson to not stated, April 12, 1862, *OR*, 10(1):466, 480–81.

25. Gibson to Cooper, August 1, 1863, with endorsements by Cooper and Campbell; Allen to Gibson, June 17, 1863; and Dubroca to Gibson, August 3, 1863, *OR*, 10(1):482–84, 486–87.

26. Bragg to wife, April 8, [1862], Braxton Bragg Papers, MHM.

27. McBride and McLaurin, *Randall Lee Gibson*, 80–81.

28. Purvis, *Gallant Gladden*, 23, 44–51; Bragg to Mary Jane Minge, May 31, 1862, quoted in ibid., 133.

29. Daniel, *Shiloh*, 250–51.

30. J. C. Nott to Beauregard, November 6, 1869, Roman, *Military Operations*, 1:535.

31. Lockett, "Surprise and Withdrawal," 605; N. C. Hughes, *Liddell's Record*, 67.

32. T. H. Williams, *P. G. T. Beauregard*, 142; Le Baron to Davis, May 16, 1887, Rowland, *Jefferson Davis*, 9:560–61.

33. Daniel, *Shiloh*, 253–56.

34. Bragg to wife, April 8, [1862], Braxton Bragg Papers, MHM; Bragg to [Beauregard], April 8, 1862, 7:30 A.M. and 2 P.M., *OR*, 10(2):2, 398–99.

35. Bragg to wife, April 8, [1862], Braxton Bragg Papers, MHM; Bragg to Jordan, April 30, 1862, *OR*, 10(1):464, 469.

36. Elise to husband, April 16, 1862, Braxton Bragg Papers, UTA.

37. Ibid.

38. Elise to husband, April 20, 1862, Braxton Bragg Papers, UTA.

39. Elise to husband, May 9, 1862, Braxton Bragg Papers, UTA.

40. Seitz, *Braxton Bragg*, 106–22; McWhiney, *Braxton Bragg*, 240.

41. McDonough, *Shiloh*, 149; Sword, *Shiloh*, 251; Daniel, *Shiloh*, 213–14.

42. McWhiney and Jamieson, *Attack and Die*, 143–69; McDonough, *Shiloh*, 138.

43. Hess, *Rifle Musket*, 92–93, 107–15, 198–203.

44. Castel, "Mars and the Reverend Longstreet," 107–14.

45. S. J. Martin, *General Braxton Bragg*, 134–36, 147.

46. Sears, *Gates of Richmond*, 335.

Chapter Four

1. Hess, *Banners to the Breeze*, 1–2.

2. Braxton Bragg to Genl, no date, received at Headquarters morning of April 30, 1862, Braxton Bragg Service Record, M331, NARA.

3. "Soldiers," Headquarters, Second Corps, Army of the Mississippi, May 3, 1862, *OR*, 10(2):484.

4. General Orders No. 37, Headquarters of the Forces, May 6, 1862, *OR*, 10(2):500–501.

5. Diary, May 30, 1862, Thomas Bragg Papers, UNC; General Orders No. 4, Headquarters, Army of the Mississippi, May 12, 1862, *OR*, 52(2):314; card, Braxton Bragg Service Record, M331, NARA; *Journal of the Congress*, 2:158.

6. Bragg to [Beauregard], May 29, 1862, 11:30 A.M., and May 31, 1862, *OR*, 10(2):557, 570; Giles Buckner Cooke Diary, May 29, 1862, VHS.

7. Stout, *Reminiscences*, 13; Urquhart, "Bragg's Advance," 609; McMurry, *An Uncompromising Secessionist*, 79.

8. Giles Buckner Cooke Diary, May 30, 1862, VHS; Little and Maxwell, *Lumsden's Battery*, 8.

9. Giles Buckner Cooke Diary, May 30, 1862, VHS.

10. "Some of the Experiences of Giles B. Cooke during the war between the States 1861–1865," Giles Buckner Cooke Papers, VHS.

11. Moore to Davis, May 8, 1862, *OR*, 53:806; Davis to Pickens, June 12, 1862, *OR*, 14:560–61; Pickens to Davis, June 12, 1862, Crist, *Papers of Jefferson Davis*, 8:239.

12. J. Davis, *Rise and Fall*, 2:74–75; John Walker to wife, June 16, 1862, Rice Family Papers, MSU; T. H. Williams, *P. G. T. Beauregard*, 158–59.

13. J. Davis, *Rise and Fall*, 2:75; Bragg to Davis, June 19, 1862, *OR*, 52(2):815; Davis to Bragg, June 20, 1862, *OR*, 17(2):614; Bragg to William M. Browne, February 19, 1872, Braxton Bragg Papers, WRHS.

14. Bragg to Beauregard, July 22, 1862, *OR*, 52(2):331; Beauregard to editors of *Mobile Evening News*, July 16, 1862, Roman, *Military Operations*, 1:592.

15. Bragg to Beauregard, July 22, 1862, *OR*, 52(2):330–31.

16. Beauregard to Henry, August 18, 1863, *OR*, 28(2):291; Bragg memorandum, undated, Crist, *Papers of Jefferson Davis*, 8:274.

17. Beauregard to Mrs. O. W. LeVert, November 30, 1863, and Beauregard to William Preston Johnston, March 9, 1877, Beauregard Papers, MOC.

18. Curry to Davis, June 20, 1862, and Davis to Varina, June 25, 1862, Crist, *Papers of Jefferson Davis*, 8:256–57, 269; Davis to Bragg, July 26, 1862, *OR*, 17(2):658.

19. Bragg to Cooper, June 22, 1862, and Randolph to Bragg, June 23, 1862, *OR*, 16(2):701–2; Vaught to Mary, July 4, 1862, William C. D. Vaught Letters, HNOC; John Buie to J. C. Buie, September 30, November 14, 1862, John Buie Papers, DU.

20. General Orders No. 100, Headquarters, Department No 2, July 17, 1862, *OR*, 17(2):648; General Orders No. 93, headquarters, Department No. 2, July 5, 1862, *OR*, 17(1):12; [Bragg] endorsement on Adams to Jordan, July 1, 1862, dated July 2, 1862, *OR*, ser. 2, 2:1557.

21. Moore, *Conscription and Conflict*, 13–14.

22. McMurry, *An Uncompromising Secessionist*, 78–79.

23. Curry to Davis, June 20, 1862, Crist, *Papers of Jefferson Davis*, 8:257, 259n–260n.

24. Horn, *Army of Tennessee*, 157–58.

25. Cutrer and Parrish, *Brothers in Gray*, 104, 107–8; Tower, *A Carolinian Goes to War*, 20; McMurry, *An Uncompromising Secessionist*, 79; Bliss to mother, September 6, 1862, Robert Lewis Bliss Papers, ADAH.

26. White and Runion, *Great Things*, 5, 11; Spence, "Services in the Confederacy," 500.

27. Lowe, *Texas Cavalry Officer's Civil War*, 144; William Preston to William Preston Johnston, June 14, 1862, folder 20, box 10, Albert Sidney and William Preston Johnston Papers, TU.

28. Woodward, *Mary Chesnut's Civil War*, 413; Harwell, *Kate*, 47–48.

29. Clift, *Private War of Lizzie Hardin*, 202–3.

30. "Justice" to editor, *Mobile Advertiser and Register*, August 30, 1862, in *Chattanooga Daily Rebel*, September 13, 1862; diary, July 4, 1862, Thomas Bragg Papers, UNC.

31. Braxton Bragg to John Forsyth, July 17, 1862, box 1, folder 67, Samuel Richey Collection of the Southern Confederacy, MU.

32. *Journal of the Congress*, 2:264, 277, 279–80; diary, September 12, 1862, Thomas Bragg Papers, UNC.

33. McGrath to My Dear Judge, September 22, 1862, A. G. McGrath Letter, SANC.

34. Bragg to wife, July 22, 1862, Braxton Bragg Papers, MHM.

35. Bragg to Beauregard, June 12, 1862, and Bragg to Soldiers, June 27, 1862, *OR*, 17(2):594, 626.

36. Hess, *Civil War in the West*, 52–53; Hess, *Banners to the Breeze*, 3–6; Bragg to Beauregard, June 12, 1862, *OR*, 17(2):594.

37. Hess, *Civil War in the West*, 94–96; Hess, *Banners to the Breeze*, 22–24.

38. Bragg to Kirby Smith, July 20, 1862, *OR*, 17(2)651; Bragg to Davis, July 22, 1862, *OR*, 52(2):330–31.

39. Bragg to Cooper, July 23, 1862, *OR*, 17(2):655–56.

40. Connelly, *Army of the Heartland*, 200–201; Bragg to Johnston, September 21, 1861, *OR*, 4:419–20; Bragg to wife, September 27, 1861, Braxton Bragg Letters, UK; Hess, *Civil War in the West*, 94–96; Hess, *Banners to the Breeze*, 56–63.

41. Bragg to Cooper, July 23, 1862, *OR*, 17(2):655–56; Bragg to Cooper, August 1, 1862, *OR*, 16(2):741; Bragg to Davis, July 31, 1862, Crist, *Papers of Jefferson Davis*, 8:312, 313n; diary, July 18, 1862, Thomas Bragg Papers, UNC.

42. Editorial comment, Crist, *Papers of Jefferson Davis*, 8:313n–314n; cards, Thomas H. Watts Service Record, 17th Alabama, M311, NARA.

43. Bragg to Davis, July 31, 1862, and Davis to John Bragg, September 1, 1862, Crist, *Papers of Jefferson Davis*, 8:312, 313n, 370n–371n; diary, July 18, 1862, Thomas Bragg Papers, UNC.

44. Bragg to Davis, July 31, 1862, Crist, *Papers of Jefferson Davis*, 8:312–13.

45. Davis to Bragg, August 5, 1862, Crist, *Papers of Jefferson Davis*, 8:321–22; diary, August 8, 1862, Thomas Bragg Papers, UNC.

46. Bragg to Cooper, August 1, 1862, *OR*, 16(2):741; Kirby Smith, "Kentucky Campaign 1862," 4, folder 66, Edmund Kirby Smith Papers, UNC; diary, August 7–8, September 1, 1862, J. Stoddard Johnston Papers, FHS; Parks, *General Edmund Kirby Smith*, 201.

47. Clift, *Private War of Lizzie Hardin*, 202–3.

48. Diary, August 12, 14, 1862, Thomas Bragg Papers, UNC.

Chapter Five

1. Bragg to Cooper, May 20, 1863, *OR*, 16(1):1089.

2. Bragg to wife, September 2, 1862, Braxton Bragg Letters, Frederick M. Dearborn Collection, HU; Scarborough, *Diary of Edmund Ruffin*, 2:429. "Bragg is in command in the South west & censured for inactivity," wrote Catherine Ann Devereux Edmondston, in Crabtree and Patton, *"Journal of a Secesh Lady,"* 257. See also Miers, *Rebel War Clerk's Diary*, 89.

3. General Orders No. 128, Headquarters, Department No. 2, September 5, 1862, *OR*, 16(1):936–37; Kirby Smith, "Kentucky Campaign 1862," 5, folder 66, Edmund Kirby Smith Papers, UNC; Parks, *General Edmund Kirby Smith*, 202, 205–6, 211, 223.

4. General Orders No. 128, Headquarters, Department No. 2, September 5, 1862, *OR*, 16(1):936–37; Bragg note on back of General Orders No. 128, Headquarters, Department No. 2, September 5, 1862, Butler Family Papers, LSU.

5. Bragg to Cooper, September 12, 1862, *OR*, 16(2):815.

6. Bragg to Cooper, May 20, 1863, *OR*, 16(1):1090; Proclamation, Headquarters, Department No. 2, September 14, 1862, and Bragg to Cooper, September 12, 1862, *OR*, 16(2):815, 822.

7. Sears, "Fire on the Mountain," 4–63.

8. Hess, *Banners to the Breeze*, 64–66.

9. Bragg to Adjutant General, Confederate States Army, September 17, 1862; Bragg endorsement on Chalmers to Huger, September 19, 1862; and Bragg to Cooper, May 20, 1863, *OR*, 16(1):968, 980, 1090.

10. Bragg to Adjutant General, Confederate States Army, September 17, 1862, *OR*, 16(1):968; Hess, *Banners to the Breeze*, 67–68.

11. Bragg to Adjutant General, Confederate States Army, September 17, 1862, *OR*, 16(1):968; General Orders No. 6 and 7, Headquarters, Army of the Mississippi, September 17, 18, 1862, *OR*, 16(2):841–43.

12. Hess, *Banners to the Breeze*, 69–70.

13. Bragg to Adjutant General, Confederate States Army, September 17, 1862, *OR*, 16(1):968; Urquhart, "Bragg's Advance," 600–601.

14. Urquhart, "Bragg's Advance," 601; Bragg to Cooper, May 20, 1863, *OR*, 16(1):1090.

15. Bragg to Adjutant General, Confederate States Army, September 25, 1862, *OR*, 16(2):876.

16. Bragg to Adjutant General, Confederate States Army, September 25, 1862, *OR*, 16(2):876; Bragg to Cooper, May 20, 1863, *OR*, 16(1):1091.

17. Davis to Bragg, September 19, 1862, *OR*, 17(2):707; Hess, *Banners to the Breeze*, 75–76.

18. Horn, *Army of Tennessee*, 169, 171–72; Connelly, *Army of the Heartland*, 233–34; McWhiney, *Braxton Bragg*, 288–92; Woodworth, *Jefferson Davis*, 146.

19. Bragg to wife, September 18, 1862, Braxton Bragg Papers, MHM.

20. Burnett, *Pen Makes a Good Sword*, 135–36.

21. To the People of the Northwest, September 26, 1862, *OR*, 52(2):363–64.

22. To the People of Kentucky, September 29, 1862, *OR*, 52(2):367.

23. Diary, September 22, 1862, Thomas Bragg Papers, UNC; Bragg to Adjutant General, Confederate States Army, September 25, 1862, *OR*, 16(2):876.

24. Bragg to Adjutant General, Confederate States Army, September 25, 1862, *OR*, 16(2):876.

25. Hess, *Banners to the Breeze*, 25–26, 81.

26. Bragg to Cooper, May 20, 1863, *OR*, 16(1):1091.

27. Ibid.

28. Bragg to Davis, October 2, 1862, Crist, *Papers of Jefferson Davis*, 8:417.

29. Polk to Bragg, October 2, 1862, 10 A.M., and Polk to Bragg, October 3, *OR*, 16(2):898, 901.

30. Polk to Bragg, October 2, 1862, 1 P.M., *OR*, 16(2):897; Bragg to Cooper, May 20, 1863, *OR*, 16(1):1091.

31. Bragg to Cooper, May 20, 1863; Polk to Bragg, October 3, 1862, 3 P.M.; and Polk to Hardee, April 17, 1863, *OR*, 16(1):1091, 1095, 1101; Polk to Bragg, October 3, 1862, *OR*, 16(2):901; Robins, *Bishop of the Old South*, 178.

32. Bragg to Polk, October 3, 1862, 7 A.M. and 8. P.M., and Bragg to Polk, October 4, 1862, *OR*, 16(2):903–5. A manuscript copy of this dispatch is in Braxton Bragg Papers, USMA.

33. Bragg to Polk, October 4, 1862, *OR*, Vol. 16(2):905; Hess, *Banners to the Breeze*, 82–83.

34. Bragg to Adjutant General, Confederate States Army, October 12, 1862, *OR*, 16(1):1087; Hess, *Banners to the Breeze*, 83.

35. Bragg to Cooper, May 20, 1863, *OR*, 16(1):1092; Hess, *Banners to the Breeze*, 84.

36. Bragg to Adjutant General, Confederate States Army, October 12, 1862, and Bragg to Cooper, May 20, 1863, *OR*, 16(1):1087, 1092.

37. Bragg to Cooper, May 20, 1863; Bragg to Polk, October 7, 1862, 5:40 P.M.; Polk to Hardee, April 17, 1863; and Polk to Brent, November, no date, 1862, *OR*, 16(1):1092, 1096, 1102–3, 1110.

38. Bragg to Adjutant General, Confederate States Army, October 12, 1862; Bragg to Cooper, May 20, 1863; and Polk to Brent, November, no date, 1862, *OR*, 16(1):1087, 1092, 1110; George W. Brent Journal, October 8, 1862, Braxton Bragg Papers, WRHS; Parks, *General Leonidas Polk*, 269. For a postwar account of Bragg's arrival at Perryville by one of Simon Buckner's staff officers, see Claiborne, "Battle of Perryville," 225.

39. Noe, *Perryville*, 181–305.

40. Ibid., 369, 373; Bragg to Adjutant General, Confederate States Army, October 12, 1862, *OR*, 16(1):1087.

41. Claiborne, "Battle of Perryville," 226; George W. Brent Journal, October 8, 1862, Braxton Bragg Papers, WRHS; Bragg to Adjutant General, Confederate States Army, October 12, 1862, *OR*, 16(1):1088.

42. Bragg to Adjutant General, Confederate States Army, October 12, 1862, *OR*, 16(1):1088.

43. Hess, *Banners to the Breeze*, 82–85.

44. Bragg to Cooper, May 20, 1863, *OR*, 16(1):1093; Connelly, *Army of the Heartland*, 210, 219, 222, 234, 236, 246, 248, 269; Parks, *General Leonidas Polk*, 265–68; Robins, *Bishop of the Old South*, 167–68.

45. Connelly, *Army of the Heartland*, 208, 241; McWhiney, *Braxton Bragg*, 297–98; Woodworth, *Jefferson Davis*, 156–57.

46. Noe, *Perryville*, 369, 373; Bragg to Cooper, May 20, 1863, *OR*, 16(1):1093; Hess, *Banners to the Breeze*, 110–11.

47. George W. Brent Journal, October 12, 1862, Braxton Bragg Papers, WRHS; Bragg to Adjutant General, Confederate States Army, October 12, 1862, *OR*, 16(1):1088.

48. M. B. Morton, "Historic Conference between President Davis, General Bragg and

His Corps Commanders," *Nashville Banner*, December 4, 1909; Kirby Smith, "Kentucky Campaign 1862," 14–15, folder 66, Edmund Kirby Smith Papers, UNC.

49. M. B. Morton, "Historic Conference between President Davis, General Bragg and His Corps Commanders," *Nashville Banner*, December 4, 1909; Kirby Smith, "Kentucky Campaign 1862," 15–16, folder 66, Edmund Kirby Smith Papers, UNC; Claiborne, "The Campaign of 1862 into Kentucky of Gen'l Braxton Bragg," 19, folder 24, Thomas Claiborne Papers, UNC.

50. Bragg to Cooper, May 20, 1863, *OR*, 16(1):1093; George W. Brent Journal, October 18, 1862, Braxton Bragg Papers, WRHS; Hess, *Banners to the Breeze*, 111–13.

Chapter Six

1. Cooper to Bragg, October 20, 1862, and Bragg to Cooper, October 22, 1862, *OR*, 16(2):970, 974; Bragg to Davis, October 23, 1862, *OR*, 52(2):382.

2. Cooper to Bragg, October 23, 1862, *OR*, 16(2):976; diary, October 30, 1862, Thomas Bragg Papers, UNC; George W. Brent Journal, October 24, 1862, Braxton Bragg Papers, WRHS; Crist, *Papers of Jefferson Davis*, 8:470n–471n.

3. Randolph to Holmes, October 20, 27, 1862, *OR*, 13:890, 906; Randolph to Lee, October 25, 1862, *OR*, 19(2):682; McMurry, *An Uncompromising Secessionist*, 92; Hess, *Banners to the Breeze*, 112–14.

4. Davis to Bragg, October 17, 1862, Crist, *Papers of Jefferson Davis*, 8:448.

5. Davis to Kirby Smith, October 29, 1862, Crist, *Papers of Jefferson Davis*, 8:469; Cooper to Bragg, November 1, 1862, *OR*, 20(2):384–85; George W. Brent Journal, October 28, 1862, Braxton Bragg Papers, WRHS.

6. Diary, October 30, 1862, Thomas Bragg Papers, UNC.

7. Diary, October 31, 1862, Thomas Bragg Papers, UNC; Crist, *Papers of Jefferson Davis*, 8:470n–471n.

8. George W. Brent Journal, November 2, 1862, Braxton Bragg Papers, WRHS; Bragg to Cooper, November 3, 1862, *OR*, 20(2):386.

9. Weitzel to Strong, October 26, 29, 1862, *OR*, 15:166–69.

10. Deposition of Alvin N. Gardner, no date, Braxton Bragg Papers, MHM.

11. Helm, "Gen. and Mrs. Braxton Bragg," 102–3.

12. Bragg to wife, November 9, 1862, Braxton Bragg Letters, UK.

13. Ibid.

14. Strong to Weitzel, November 6, 1862, and Weitzel to Strong, November 5, 1862, *OR*, 15:164–66, 171–12.

15. Strong to Weitzel, November 6, 1862, *OR*, 15:166.

16. Bragg to Davis, November 24, 1862, *OR*, 20(2):423.

17. George W. Brent Journal, November 10, 13–14, 16, 1862, Braxton Bragg Papers, WRHS; Urquhart, "Bragg's Advance," 603.

18. Hess, *Banners to the Breeze*, 115–20.

19. Bragg to Cooper, November 22, 1862, and Bragg to Davis, November 24, 1862, *OR*, 20(2):416–17, 421–22; Isham G. Harris to Wright, November 23, 1862, Marcus Joseph Wright Papers, UNC.

20. Reid diary, October 21, 1862, Samuel Chester Reid Family Papers, LC; Vaught to sister, letter fragment, folder 18, William C. D. Vaught Letters, HNOC; William Preston to William Preston Johnston, November 22, 1862, box 10, folder 34, Albert Sidney and William Preston Johnston Papers, TU; Buie to J. C. Buie, November 14, 1862, John Buie Papers, DU;

Bliss to mother, October 24, 1862, Robert Lewis Bliss Papers, ADAH; Gustavus A. Henry to Wigfall, October 25, 1862, Louis Trezevant Wigfall Family Papers, LC.

21. Randall L. Gibson to My Dear Doctor, September 7, 1875, Leonidas Polk Papers, UNC; John Walker to wife, November 23, 1862, Rice Family Papers, MSU.

22. Buck, *Cleburne and His Command*, 117.

23. Editorial, *Richmond Examiner*, reprinted in *Memphis Daily Appeal*, October 30, 1862; "Gen. Bragg's Kentucky Campaign," *Mobile Tribune*, reprinted in *Chattanooga Daily Rebel*, November 2, 1862.

24. Pickens to Beauregard, November 5, 1862, *OR*, 14:667.

25. Taylor, *Destruction and Reconstruction*, 127.

26. Barton to William, October 27, 1862, Seth Barton Papers, NC.

27. Crabtree and Patton, *"Journal of a Secesh Lady,"* 280, 283, 286, 299, 301, 308–9; Robins, *Bishop of the Old South*, 190; Scarborough, *Diary of Edmund Ruffin*, 2:469–70, 478.

28. Davis to Kirby Smith, October 29, 1862, Crist, *Papers of Jefferson Davis*, 8:468–69.

29. Captain in the Army to editor, *Savannah News*, reprinted in *Memphis Daily Appeal*, November 12, 1862.

30. Ada to editor, *Chattanooga Daily Rebel*, November 5, 1862; Harwell, *Kate*, 73–74, 78, 140.

31. N. C. Hughes, *Liddell's Record*, 83–84, 98.

32. White and Runion, *Great Things*, 25–26, 35, 39, 49.

33. John K. Jackson to Frank, November 7, 1862, Charles Colcock Jones Papers, DU.

34. Kirby Smith to wife, October 20, November 8, 1862, folder 33, Edmund Kirby Smith Papers, UNC; Parks, *General Edmund Kirby Smith*, 245.

35. W. C. Davis, *Breckinridge*, 315, 325–27, 331–33.

36. Ibid., 328; Robert, "At Murfreesboro," 632.

37. John Forsyth remarks in *Atlanta Confederacy*, October 24, 1862, reprinted in *Memphis Daily Appeal*, October 28, 1862.

38. John Forsyth to Bragg, November 3, 1862, Braxton Bragg Papers, WRHS; Burnett, *Pen Makes a Good Sword*, 138.

39. John Forsyth, "Gen. Bragg's Kentucky Campaign," *Mobile Advertiser and Register*, November 11, 16, 1862.

40. [Forsyth], *Memoranda of Facts*, not paginated.

41. Ibid.

42. Burnett, *Pen Makes a Good Sword*, 139.

43. "Gov. Hawes' Letter," *Richmond Enquirer*, reprinted in *Mobile Advertiser and Register*, December 5, 1862.

44. John Forsyth, "The Kentucky Campaign," *Mobile Advertiser and Register*, December 5, 1862.

45. Diary, October 14–15, 19, 1862, Thomas Bragg Papers, UNC.

46. Diary, October 23, 1862, Thomas Bragg Papers, UNC.

47. Sears, *Landscape Turned Red*, 296; Noe, *Perryville*, 369.

48. Granger testimony, February 19, 1863, *OR*, 16(1):451–52.

49. Halleck endorsement on conclusion of Buell Commission, *OR*, 16(1):16.

50. Sherman to Ellen, August 20, 1862, and Sherman to Guthrie, August 14, 1864, Simpson and Berlin, *Sherman's Civil War*, 282, 694.

51. Taylor Beatty Diary, May 3, 1862, UNC; Bragg to Cooper, May 20, 1863, *OR*, 16(1):1094.

52. Urquhart, "Bragg's Advance," 600.

53. Ibid., 602–3.

54. Ibid., 600, 604.

55. Dyer, *"Fightin' Joe,"* 24–25, 39–40, 90; Wheeler, "Bragg's Invasion of Kentucky," 19–20, 25.

56. Polk, *Leonidas Polk*, 2:158–59.

57. J. Davis, *Rise and Fall*, 2:383–84.

58. Hay, "Braxton Bragg," 290–91; Horn, *Army of Tennessee*, 169, 171–72, 178; Wooster, "Confederate Success," 319–20, 323; McWhiney, *Braxton Bragg*, 301, 303, 305–6, 310, 319–20, 330.

59. McWhiney, *Braxton Bragg*, 333–34.

60. Noe, *Perryville*, 22, 102.

61. Ibid., 68, 102, 127–28. Samuel Martin writes supportively of Bragg in regard to the Kentucky campaign but offers no real analysis of his actions. Martin, *General Braxton Bragg*, 178, 183–84.

62. McWhiney, *Braxton Bragg*, 332–33.

Chapter Seven

1. Bragg to Beauregard, November 12, 1862, *OR*, 20(2):400.

2. Davis to Varina Howell Davis, December 15, 1862, Crist, *Papers of Jefferson Davis*, 8:548; Joseph E. Johnston to Louis T. Wigfall, December 15, 1862, Louis Trezevant Wigfall Family Papers, LC.

3. N. C. Hughes, *Liddell's Record*, 102; Bragg to Cooper, January 8, 1863, *OR*, 17(1):591–92.

4. Helm, "Gen. and Mrs. Braxton Bragg," 103.

5. Bragg to Wright, December 1, 1862, *OR*, ser. 2, 5:2–3.

6. Bragg to Rosecrans, December 3, 8, 1863, *OR*, ser. 2, 5:11, 13, 44.

7. Bragg to Rosecrans, December 11, 20, 1862, *OR*, ser. 2, 5:70, 102.

8. General Orders No. 12, 13, Headquarters, Army of Tennessee, December 12–13, 1862, Letters Sent, Chief of Engineers, Western Department, 1861–1862, and General Orders and Letters, Headquarters, Army of Tennessee, 1862–1864, chap. 3, vol. 8, RG109, NARA.

9. General Orders No. 15, 19, Headquarters, Army of Tennessee, December 13, 19, 1862, Letters Sent, Chief of Engineers, Western Department, 1861–1862, and General Orders and Letters, Headquarters, Army of Tennessee, 1862–1864, ch. 3, vol. 8, RG109, NARA.

10. General Orders No. 13, 14, 18, Headquarters, Army of Tennessee, December 13, 18, 1862, Letters Sent, Chief of Engineers, Western Department, 1861–1862, and General Orders and Letters, Headquarters, Army of Tennessee, 1862–1864, ch. 3, vol. 8, RG109, NARA.

11. General Orders No. 149, Headquarters, Department No. 2, November 17, 1862, *OR*, 20(2):407.

12. Bragg to Cooper, February 23, 1863, *OR*, 20(1):663; Cozzens, *No Better Place to Die*, 59–61.

13. Bragg to Cooper, February 23, 1863, *OR*, 20(1):663–64.

14. Cozzens, *No Better Place to Die*, 104–6, 171–72; Daniel, *Stones River*, 69–71, 96–103.

15. Bragg to Cooper, February 23, 1863, *OR*, 20(1):664.

16. Ibid.; Cozzens, *No Better Place to Die*, 76–77; Daniel, *Stones River*, 66–67, 72–95.

17. Cozzens, *No Better Place to Die*, 82–90, 104–8.

18. Bragg to Cooper, February 23, 1863, *OR*, 20(1):664.

19. Ibid., 665–66; Kniffin, "Battle of Stone's River," 626.

20. Bragg to Cooper, February 23, 1863, *OR*, 20(1):666; Cozzens, *No Better Place to Die*, 159–64; Daniel, *Stones River*, 160–68.

21. Rosecrans to Thomas, February 12, 1863, *OR*, 20(1):196.

22. Urquhart, "Bragg's Advance," 609.

23. Bragg to Cooper, February 23, 1863, *OR*, 20(1):667; Urquhart, "Bragg's Advance," 609.

24. Bragg to Cooper, February 23, 1863, *OR*, 20(1):667; Urquhart, "Bragg's Advance," 609.

25. Cozzens, *No Better to Die*, 159–66; Daniel, *Stones River*, 178–97.

26. Sykes, "Cursory Sketch," pt. 2, 473.

27. Diary, January 3, 1863, J. Stoddard Johnston Papers, FHS; Bragg to Cooper, February 23, 1863, *OR*, 20(1):669.

28. Cheatham and Withers to Bragg, January 3, March 21, 1863, and Polk endorsement on Cheatham and Withers to Bragg, January 3, 1863, *OR*, 20(1):700, 702.

29. W. B. Richmond endorsement on Cheatham and Withers to Bragg, January 3, 1863, and Polk to Hardee, January 3, 1863, *OR*, 20(1):700.

30. N. C. Hughes, *Liddell's Record*, 114–16; Bragg to Cooper, February 23, 1863, *OR*, 20(1):669.

31. Bragg to Cooper, February 23, 1863, *OR*, 20(1):669.

32. Ibid.

33. Diary, January 4–5, 1863, J. Stoddard Johnston Papers, FHS.

34. Bragg to Cooper, February 23, 1863, *OR*, 20(1):669.

35. Bragg to Ewell, January 8, 1863, *OR*, 52(2):404; Bragg to Adjutant General, January 17, 1863, *OR*, 20(1):983.

36. Bragg to Cooper, December 31, 1862, *OR*, 20(1):662.

37. Seddon to Lee, January 2, 1863; Beauregard to Smith, January 2, 1863; and Lee to Seddon, January 5, 1863, *OR*, 18:812–13, 820; Johnston to Bragg, January 2, 1863, *OR*, 20(2):476; Beauregard to Miles, January 5, 1863, *OR*, 53:270; Lowe, *Texas Cavalry Officer's Civil War*, 223.

38. Edward G. Butler to mother, January 6, 1863, Butler Family Papers, LSU.

39. Miers, *Rebel War Clerk's Diary*, 144–45; Crabtree and Patton, *"Journal of a Secesh Lady,"* 332, 335; Scarborough, *Diary of Edmund Ruffin*, 2:527, 530–31.

40. Crabtree and Patton, *"Journal of a Secesh Lady,"* 332, 338.

41. McWhiney, *Braxton Bragg*, 347–48.

42. Ibid., 352, 359–60, 363.

43. Ibid., 363–65, 367, 369–70.

44. Connelly, *Autumn of Glory*, 14–15, 23–24, 47, 49, 52–58, 61–64, 66–67, 71; Horn, *Army of Tennessee*, 205–6.

45. McDonough, *Stones River*, 73, 146, 148–51, 221–23; W. C. Davis, *Breckinridge*, 351; Symonds, *Joseph E. Johnston*, 195.

46. Cozzens, *No Better Place to Die*, 30, 60, 150; S. J. Martin, *General Braxton Bragg*, 220–43; Daniel, *Stones River*, 46–49, 162. While Joseph Wheeler's earlier biographer gave Bragg no credit for his use of cavalry in the Stones River campaign, his latest biographer corrects that by praising Bragg for the manner in which he employed his mounted arm. Dyer, *"Fightin' Joe,"* 72–73, 80–85, 173; Longacre, *Soldier to the Last*, 80.

47. Woodworth, *Jefferson Davis*, 169, 187, 189, 191–92, 194.

48. O'Reilly, *Fredericksburg Campaign*, 11, 33–35; Sears, *Chancellorsville*, 110–14; Rhea, *Battle of the Wilderness*, 8–10.

49. General Orders No. 151, Headquarters, Department No. 2, November 20, 1862, and Bragg to Cooper, November 22, 1862, *OR*, 20(2):411–12, 416; George W. Brent Journal, December 21, 1862, Braxton Bragg Papers, WRHS.

50. George W. Brent Journal, November 28 and December 2, 1862, Braxton Bragg Papers, WRHS.

51. Blegen, *Civil War Letters*, 158–59, 180; Kirk to wife, December 8, 1862, Edward Needles Kirk Correspondence, HSP.

52. [Garesche], *Biography of Lieut. Col. Julius P. Garesche*, 415, 425, 428, 430. Interestingly, none of the previous historians who have written about Stones River mention this sense of overwhelming confidence at Rosecrans's headquarters. See McDonough, *Stones River*, 64–79; Cozzens, *No Better Place to Die*, 44–47; and Daniel, *Stones River*, 28–32, for examples.

53. [Garesche], *Biography of Lieut. Col. Julius P. Garesche*, 38–39, 348, 363, 394.

54. Connelly, *Autumn of Glory*, 47, 49; McDonough, *Stones River*, 75; Bragg to not stated, January 1, 1863, *OR*, 52(2):402; Johnston to Bragg, January 1, 2, 1863, and Seddon to Kirby Smith, January 4, 1863, *OR*, 20(2):475, 476, 484; Street to Ninnie, January 3, 1863, John Kennedy Street Papers, UNC; Henry Watson to father and mother, January 22, 1863, 10th Texas Cavalry Regimental File, SRNB; White and Runion, *Great Things Are Expected of Us*, 45.

55. Post, *Soldier's Letters*, 181–82; Scribner, *How Soldiers Were Made*, 85; Guthrie to aunt, January 10, [1863], John Brandon Guthrie Papers, DU; Fisher to mother, January 7, 1863, Horace Newton Fisher Papers, MHS; Jones to wife and children, January 5, 1863, Willis Jones Papers, NC; George H. Berry to wife, January 12, 1863, 89th Illinois Regimental File, SRNB; William Roberts Stuckey to wife, January 20, 1863, 42nd Indiana Regimental File, SRNB; Bartholomew to Frank, January 5, 1863, Arza Bartholomew Letters, George G. Christman Collection, AM.

56. R. W. Williams and Wooster, "With Terry's Texas Rangers," 313; Heard, *Terry Ranger Writes Home*, page numbers not given, but letter to father and mother dated January 16, 1863, www.terrytexasrangers.org, accessed February 23, 2009; Goldman, "Letters from Three Members of Terry's Texas Rangers," page numbers not given, but Robert Edward Hill to sister, January 12, 1863, www.terrytexasrangers.org, accessed February 23, 2009; McDonall diary, January 4, 1863, Augustus O. McDonall Papers, UF; Charles George to Mary, January 24, 1864, George Family Papers, AU; Hafendorfer, *Civil War Journal*, 97; Buck, *Cleburne and His Command*, 84; Ingham, "Captain Valentine Merriwether M'Gehee," 144.

57. Clay, "'On the Right at Murfreesboro,'" 589; G. E. Goudelock to wife, January 7, 1863, 2nd Arkansas Regimental File, SRNB; John Euclid Magee Diary, January 5, 1863, *Supplement to the Official Records*, pt. 1, 3:645.

58. Anderson to Et, January 8, 1862 [1863], James Patton Anderson Papers, UF; Cutrer, *Our Trust Is in the God of Battles*, 115; Trimmier to wife, January 12, 1863, Theodore Gillard Trimmier Papers, TSLA; McMurry, *An Uncompromising Secessionist*, 120; Brown to Fannie, January 7, 11, 1863, Edward Norphlet Brown Letters, ADAH. For a reaction by a Confederate soldier in the Army of Northern Virginia to Bragg's handling of the Stones River battle, see Evans, *16th Mississippi*, 137–38.

59. Street to Ninnie, January 3, 1863, and January, no date, 1863, John Kennedy Street Papers, UNC; Bell to wife, January 11, 1862 [1863], Alfred W. Bell Papers, DU; Ambrose Doss to wife, January 8, 1863, 19th Alabama Regimental File, SRNB; D. H. Rogers to H. M. Lea, January 20, 1863, Lea Family Civil War Letters, MDAH; L. W. Hunter to sister, January 24, 1863, Horn Collection, MSU; W. L. Gammage to John H. Bonner, June, no date, 1863, Civil War Miscellany, UTA; "C" to editors, January 20, 1863, *Memphis Daily Appeal*, January 29, 1863; Leigh to editors, January 12, 1863, *Memphis Daily Appeal*, January 22, 1863; Rugely, *Batchelor-Turner Letters*, no page numbers given, but B. F. Batchelor to father, January 25, 1863, www.terrytexasrangers.org, accessed February 26, 2009; White and Runion, *Great Things*, 40, 47.

60. Bragg to Davis, January 17, 1863, and Harris to Davis, January 17, 1863, Crist, *Papers of Jefferson Davis*, 9:30, 33; William A. Brown memoirs, 86, Stanford's Mississippi Battery Regimental File, SRNB; McWhiney, *Braxton Bragg*, 374; Bragg to Ewell, January 8, 1863, *OR*, 52(2):404; Street to Ninnie, January, no date, 1863, John Kennedy Street Papers, UNC.

61. Dabney H. Maury to Samuel Cooper, January 14, 1863, Confederate Military Leaders Collection, MOC.

62. Beatty, *Memoirs of a Volunteer*, 156; Fred Knefler to Wallace, March 28, 1863, Lew Wallace Papers, IHS; Blegen, *Civil War Letters*, 171; Hascall, "Personal Recollections," 149, 151–54; John McAuley Palmer to Trumbull, January 11, 1863, Lyman Trumbull Collection, ALPL; Palmer to wife, January 21, 1863, John McAuley Palmer Collection, ALPL; Sheridan, *Personal Memoirs*, 1:244; Crittenden, "Union Left at Stone's River," 634. The origin of the phrase that cleverly expressed the difference between Bragg and Rosecrans at Stones River dates back to Samuel Johnson, who, in an issue of the *Rambler* (1750–52), wrote: "When I envied the finery of my neighbours, [my mother] told me that 'Brag was a good dog, but Holdfast was a better.'" See Woodward, *Mary Chesnut's Civil War*, 469n.

63. Crittenden, "Union Left at Stone's River," 633–34.

64. Bragg to "Soldiers of the Army of Tennessee," January 8, 1863, *OR*, 20(1):675. Joseph E. Johnston also issued congratulatory orders proclaiming Stones River "an exploit unparalleled in modern battles." General Orders No. 4, Headquarters, Johnston's Command, January 28, 1863, *OR*, 20(1):675.

65. "G" to editor, January 12, 1863, *Memphis Daily Appeal*, January 30, 1863; A. B. Flint to John Clark, February 24, 1863, Herbert Earle Buchanan Family Papers, UAF; M.H.S. to editor, January 13, 1863, *Selma Morning Reporter*, January 27, 1863; Anderson to Et, January 8, 11, 1862 [1863], James Patton Anderson Papers, UF; A. T. Gay to father, March 14, 1863, 31st Tennessee Regimental File, SRNB; Hannibal Paine to sister, January 10, 1863, Colville and Paine Family Letters, UTC; W. L. Gammage to John H. Bonner, June, no date, 1863, Civil War Miscellany, UTA; Crittenden to Bettie, January 20, 1863, John Crittenden Collection, AU.

66. Franklin, *Civil War Diaries*, 98–99; White and Runion, *Great Things*, 47; Rugely, *Batchelor-Turner Letters*, no pages given, www.terrystexasrangers.org, accessed February 26, 2009; R. W. Williams and Wooster, "With Terry's Texas Rangers," 314.

67. Rosecrans to Wright, January 6, 1863, and Rosecrans to Stanton, January 11, 1863, *OR*, 20(2):303, 317; Peterson to folks, January 10, 1863, Elisha A. Peterson Papers, DU; Culbertson to wife, January 7, 1863, William Culbertson Papers, DU; Fisher to John Ward, January 10, 1863, Horace Newton Fisher Papers, MHS; Jacques Martin to mother and brother, January 9 and 11, 1863, 6th Ohio Regimental File, SRNB; Samuel A. McClelland to cousin, January 25, 1863, 78th Pennsylvania Regimental File, SRNB; Hurd to brother, February 10, 1863, Benjamin Hurd Letters, UA; Robert Mitchell to Munn, February 22, 1863, Briggs-Mitchell Family Papers, CHM; Amos E. Wood to Robert, February 18, 1863, Robert H. Caldwell Papers, RBHPC; McGregor to Wiley, February 9, 1863, William McGregor Papers, NC; John E. Lane to Ellen Crist, February 9, 1863, Crist Manuscripts, IU; Tower, *A Carolinian Goes to War*, 58; Walter Gibson Peter to sister, May 12, 1863, Peter Family Papers, UVA.

68. Wood to Garfield, April 6, 1863, *OR*, 23(3):213.

69. Sears, *Chancellorsville*, 272–300.

70. Castel, *Decision in the West*, 191–95, 208, 258–60, 283–85, 333–34, 337–38, 363–65.

Chapter Eight

1. Connelly, *Autumn of Glory*, 73; Bragg to Clay, January 10, 1863, Clement Claiborne Clay Papers, DU.

2. Bragg to Ewell, January 7, 1863, *OR*, 2(2):488; Symonds, *Joseph E. Johnston*, 183–84, 188, 191.

3. Bragg to Johnston, January 11, 1863, *OR*, 20(2):492–93.

4. Ibid., and Johnston to Ewell, January 11, 1863, *OR*, 29(2):493.

5. Connelly, *Autumn of Glory*, 73–74.

6. Bragg to Polk, Hardee, Cleburne, Cheatham, and Breckinridge, January 11, 1863, *OR*, 20(1):699.

7. Ibid.; George W. Brent Journal, January 11–12, 1863, Braxton Bragg Papers, WRHS.

8. Breckinridge to Bragg, January 12, 1863; Hardee to Bragg, January 12, 1863; and Cleburne to Bragg, January 13, 1863, *OR*, 20(1):682–84.

9. Bragg to Benjamin S. Ewell, January 14, 1863, Confederate Military Leaders Collection, MOC.

10. Ibid.

11. Dent to wife, January 25, 27, 1863, Stouten Hubert Dent Papers, ADAH.

12. William Preston to Will, January 26, 1863, box 11, folder 4, Albert Sidney and William Preston Johnston Papers, TU.

13. Ibid.

14. Ibid.

15. Ibid.

16. Bragg to Davis, January 17, 1863, Crist, *Papers of Jefferson Davis*, 9:28.

17. Ibid.

18. Ibid., 28–29.

19. Bragg to John K. Jackson, January 24, 1863, Jackson and McKinne Family Papers, UNC.

20. Polk to Bragg, January 30, 31, 1863, and Bragg to Polk, January 30, 1863, *OR*, 20(1):701.

21. Polk to Davis, February 4, 1863, *OR*, 20(1):698.

22. Davis to Joseph E. Johnston, January 22, 1863, Rowland, *Jefferson Davis*, 5:420–21; William Preston to Will, January 26, 1863, box 11, folder 4, Albert Sidney and William Preston Johnston Papers, TU.

23. Copy of General Orders No., Headquarters, Chattanooga, January 28, 1863, Thomas Jenkins Semmes Papers, DU; Johnston to Davis, February 3, 1863, Crist, *Papers of Jefferson Davis*, 9:48–49. The original of Johnston's dispatch to Davis is in Joseph E. Johnston Papers, DU.

24. Johnston to Davis, February 3, 1863, Crist, *Papers of Jefferson Davis*, 9:49. There is an extract of Johnston's February 3 letter to Davis, written in Johnston's hand, filed in the Braxton Bragg Papers, WRHS. Apparently Bragg asked Johnston for it before the general left Tullahoma.

25. Johnston to Davis, February 12, 1863, Crist, *Papers of Jefferson Davis*, 9:59–60.

26. Johnston to Wigfall, February 14, 1863, Louis Trezevant Wigfall Family Papers, LC.

27. Davis to Johnston, February 19, 1863, Crist, *Papers of Jefferson Davis*, 9:66–67. After the war, Davis placed no blame on Bragg for the retreat from Murfreesboro, arguing that Rosecrans's numerical superiority caused it. He emphasized the damage inflicted on the Federals during the battle. See J. Davis, *Rise and Fall*, 2:385.

28. William Preston Johnston to William Preston, April 21, 1863, box 11, folder 14, and William Preston Johnston to Rosa, January 28, 1863, box 11, folder 5, Albert Sidney and William Preston Johnston Papers, TU.

29. Wigfall to Johnston, February 28, 1863, Louis Trezevant Wigfall Papers, UTA.

30. Bragg to Mackall, February 14, 1863, William Whann Mackall Papers, UNC.

31. Sears, *Gates of Richmond*, 67–145; Symonds, *Joseph E. Johnston*, 197.

32. John K. Jackson to Bragg, January 17, 1863, and Preston Smith to Bragg, January 13, 1863, Braxton Bragg Papers, WRHS. The assertion of Johnston's biographer that Davis and

Johnston were the only people in the Confederacy who believed Bragg was a good general is patently untrue. Symonds, *Joseph E. Johnston*, 198.

33. Bragg to Mackall, February 14, 1863, William Whann Mackall Papers, UNC.

34. Bragg to Davis, February 23, 1863, *OR*, 52(2):426.

35. Bragg to Cooper, February 23, 1863, *OR*, 20(1):664–66, 668, 670.

36. Ibid., 665, 670–71.

37. Ibid., 665.

38. Reid diary, August 22, 25, 30–31, September 5, 1862, Samuel Chester Reid Family Papers, LC.

39. Reid diary, January 18, 21, 1863, Samuel Chester Reid Family Papers, LC.

40. Johnston, "Theodore O'Hara," 67–70; Prichard, "Theodore O'Hara," 666–67; Connelly, *Autumn of Glory*, 73–74; Bragg to Mackall, February 14, 1863, William Whann Mackall Papers, UNC; Josiah C. Nott to Bragg, March 1, 1863, Braxton Bragg Papers, WRHS.

41. Bragg to Mackall, February 14, 1863, William Whann Mackall Papers, UNC. It is possible that Ora was a man named Shorter. See Bolling Hall Jr. to father, July 18, 1863, Bolling Hall Family Papers, ADAH.

42. Bragg to Mackall, February 14, 1863, William Whann Mackall Papers, UNC.

43. Josiah C. Nott to Bragg, March 1, 1863, Braxton Bragg Papers, WRHS.

44. Bragg to Mackall, February 14, 1863, William Whann Mackall Papers, UNC; Josiah C. Nott to Bragg, March 1, 1863, Braxton Bragg Papers, WRHS.

45. Johnston to Davis, March 2, 1863, *OR*, 52(2):816; Johnston to Wigfall, March 4, December 27, 1863, Louis Trezevant Wigfall Family Papers, LC.

46. Seddon to Bragg, March 16, 1863, *OR*, 23(2):698; George W. Brent Journal, March 18–19, 1863, Braxton Bragg Papers, WRHS; Johnston to Wigfall, December 3, 1863, Louis Trezevant Wigfall Family Papers, LC.

47. George W. Brent Journal, March 16, 25, April 1–2, 7, 1863, Braxton Bragg Papers, WRHS; Helm, "Gen. and Mrs. Braxton Bragg," 103; Johnston to Seddon, March 19, 1863, and Johnston to Davis, April 10, 1863, *OR*, 23(2):708, 745; Johnston to Wigfall, December 3, 1863, Louis Trezevant Wigfall Family Papers, LC. C. William Fackler of the 4th Alabama Cavalry told his sister of a rumor that Elise had passed away. "I assure you, had it of been him instead of her, there would have been rejoicing in the Southern Army as far as the privates are concerned. No one man, that ever lived, I don't believe ever had as much hatred expressed against him, as Bragg." Fackler to sister, March 26, [1863], C. William Fackler Papers, DU.

48. Varina Howell Davis to Jefferson Davis, [April 5, 1863], Crist, *Papers of Jefferson Davis*, 9:128.

49. Elliott, *Doctor Quintard*, 63.

50. George W. Brent Journal, March 25, 1863, and Milton Brown to Bragg, March 3, 1863, Braxton Bragg Papers, WRHS.

51. Connelly, *Autumn of Glory*, 88; Polk to Brent, November, no date, 1862, and Hardee to Williamson, December 1, 1862, *OR*, 16(1):1109–12, 1119–22.

52. Bragg to Hardee, April 13, 1863, and Hardee endorsement to Polk on Bragg to Hardee, April 13, 16, 1863, *OR*, 16(1):1098; George W. Brent Journal, April 14, 1863, Braxton Bragg Papers, WRHS. Connelly, *Autumn of Glory*, 88, claims that the circular letter was sent to fourteen men, but the *OR* citation above indicates only six.

53. Buckner to Bragg, April 26, 1863, *OR*, 16(1):1106–7.

54. Connelly, *Autumn of Glory*, 89; Woodworth, *Jefferson Davis*, 222.

55. Bragg to Cooper, February 23, 1863, *OR*, 20(1):668; Connelly, *Autumn of Glory*, 82;

W. C. Davis, *Breckinridge*, 353, 358. James Patton Anderson quietly admitted that Bragg gave him and his brigade too much credit for saving the Confederate line after Breckinridge's repulse on January 2. He thought "some partial friends of mine" fed Bragg exaggerated reports that led the army leader to this conclusion. But Anderson also was irritated that Breckinridge gave him no credit at all for his support at that critical moment. "Sketch of General Anderson's Life written by himself," James Patton Anderson Papers, UF.

56. Urquhart, "Bragg's Advance," 609n; Connelly, *Autumn of Glory*, 82–83; W. C. Davis, *Breckinridge*, 351–52.

57. George W. Brent Journal, April 2, 1863, Braxton Bragg Papers, WRHS; John C. Breckinridge to William Preston Johnston, May 6, 1863, Johnston Family Papers, FHS; Bragg to Walter, June 2, 1863, Harvey Washington Walter Papers, UNC; W. C. Davis, *Breckinridge*, 359–61; Johnson to Breckinridge, March 19, 1863, Jillson P. Johnson Service Record, M331, NARA.

58. *Chattanooga Daily Rebel*, May 13, 1863; William Preston to Will, January 26, 1863, box 11, folder 4, Albert Sidney and William Preston Johnston Papers, TU; Trabue to O'Hara, January 13, 1863, *OR*, 20(1):825–29.

59. Johnston to Breckinridge, May 18, 1863, William Preston Johnston Service Record, M331, NARA; Connelly, *Autumn of Glory*, 83–84.

60. Connelly, *Autumn of Glory*, 84–85.

61. Johnston to Davis, February 3, 1863, Crist, *Papers of Jefferson Davis*, 9:49.

62. Ibid.; N. C. Hughes, *Liddell's Record*, 119.

63. Bragg to wife, March 25, 1862, Braxton Bragg Papers, MHM; Bragg to Cooper, February 23, 1863; Hardee to Brent, February 28, 1863; and Ector to McCown, May 9, 1863, *OR*, 20(1):664, 774, 923; Connelly, *Autumn of Glory*, 81.

64. Bragg to Ewell, February 27, 1863; Special Orders No. 52, Headquarters, Army of Tennessee, February 27, 1863; Foote and Henry to Davis, March 8, 1863; Henry and Haynes to Seddon, March 16, 1863; and Special Orders No. 46, Headquarters, March 22, 1863, *OR*, 23(2):653–54, 673, 698, 722; Connelly, *Autumn of Glory*, 81.

65. Bragg to Davis, March 5, 1863, Crist, *Papers of Jefferson Davis*, 9:90.

66. Sale to Bragg, March 5, 1863, quoted in Seitz, *Braxton Bragg*, 284.

67. Ibid., 285–86.

68. Ibid.

69. James L. Pugh to Bragg, March 5, 1863, Braxton Bragg Papers, WRHS; *Journal of the Congress*, 3:112, and 6:139, 142, 149.

70. Johnson to Breckinridge, March 2, 4, 19, 1863, Jillson P. Johnson Service Record, M331, NARA.

71. Wigfall to Johnston, June 8, 1863, March 17, 1864, Louis Trezevant Wigfall Family Papers, LC.

72. Urquhart, "Bragg's Advance," 608; Isaac Alexander letter quoted in Haughton, *Training, Tactics and Leadership*, 113; N. C. Hughes, *Liddell's Record*, 107, 115–16; Tower, *A Carolinian Goes to War*, 58.

73. Josiah C. Nott to Bragg, March 1, 1863, Braxton Bragg Papers, WRHS.

74. Frank Campbell to Bragg, March 1, 1863, Braxton Bragg Papers, WRHS.

75. Richmond correspondence of the *Knoxville Register*, April 23, 1863, printed in *Memphis Daily Appeal*, May 6, 1863; Wiggins, *Journals of Josiah Gorgas*, 55; A. S. Lyon to Bragg, January 12, 1863, Braxton Bragg Papers, WRHS.

76. J. Q. Anderson, *Brokenburn*, 178–79; Trimble, "Behind the Lines in Middle Tennessee," 53–54.

77. Younger, *Inside the Confederate Government*, 42; sister to [James Fulker Kent], Janu-

ary 18, 1863, Kent-Amacker Family Papers, LSU; Kenneth Rayner to Ruffin, March 8, 1863, and David L. Swain to Ruffin, April 15, 1863, Hamilton, *Papers of Thomas Ruffin*, 3:304, 312.

78. N. C. Hughes, *General William J. Hardee*, 149.

79. J. M. Forsyth to Bragg, June 15, 1863, Braxton Bragg Papers, WRHS; Urquhart, "Bragg's Advance," 608–9.

80. Urquhart, "Bragg's Advance," 608–9; Buck, *Cleburne and His Command*, 124.

81. Woodworth, *Jefferson Davis*, 195, 197–99; Horn, *Army of Tennessee*, 226–27.

Chapter Nine

1. Marshall to wife, April 17, 1863, John H. Marshall Civil War Letters, MSU; Special Orders No. 103, Headquarters, Army of Tennessee, May 13, 1863, *OR*, 23(2):834–35.

2. Reid diary, June 8–9, 14, 1863, Samuel Chester Reid Family Papers, LC.

3. Bragg to wife, June 20, 1863, Braxton Bragg Papers, MHM.

4. Fremantle, *Three Months*, 145, 151–52.

5. "Three Deserters Shot at Shelbyville," 128.

6. Requisition for Forage for Public Horses, Mules, and Oxen, January 20–29, 1863, Braxton Bragg Service Record, M331, NARA; Bragg to Walter, June 2, 1863, Harvey Washington Walter Papers, UNC.

7. George W. Brent Journal, October 2, 1862, Braxton Bragg Papers, WRHS; Bragg to Cooper, May 8, 1863, George William Brent Service Record, M331, NARA; Boom, "'We Sowed & We Have Reaped,'" 75; Bragg to Mrs. Walter, May 7, 1863, Harvey Washington Walter Papers, UNC; Bragg to John Walker, May 18, 1863, Rice Family Papers, MSU; General Orders No. 17, Headquarters, Department No. 2, June 2, 1863, John J. Walker Service Record, M331, NARA; John M. Wampler to Bragg, July 30, 1863, Braxton Bragg Papers, USMA; Urquhart, "Bragg's Advance," 604n–605n; diary, June 1, 3, 1863, J. Stoddard Johnston Papers, FHS; Kinloch Falconer to E. T. Sykes, February 7, 1873, Confederate Military Leaders Collection, MOC.

8. Cards and Ellis to Adjutant General, Confederate States Army, March 30, 1861, Towson Ellis Service Record, M331, NARA.

9. Crabtree and Patton, *"Journal of a Secesh Lady,"* 410; Harwell, *Kate*, 103, 111, 139; Woodward, *Mary Chesnut's Civil War*, 495; C. J. Pope to Bragg, March 30, 1864, Braxton Bragg Papers, WRHS.

10. Thomas Butler to aunt, February 25, 1863, Butler Family Papers, LSU; George W. Brent Journal, April 13, 17, 1863, Braxton Bragg Papers, WRHS; Taylor Beatty Diary, January 11, March 3, 1863, UNC; Stickles, *Simon Bolivar Buckner*, 211.

11. Bragg to Mrs. J. J. Walker, [March, 1863], Braxton Bragg Papers, WRHS.

12. Urquhart, "Bragg's Advance," 609.

13. Elliott, *Doctor Quintard*, 69–70.

14. Ibid.

15. D. Coleman Diary, May 31, 1863, UNC; Elliott, *Doctor Quintard*, 69–70.

16. Woodworth, *While God Is Marching On*, 214; Rable, *God's Almost Chosen Peoples*, 3, 206–7, 303, 311.

17. Bragg to wife, June 20, 1863, Braxton Bragg Papers, MHM; Officers' Pay Account, July 1–31, 1863, Braxton Bragg Service Record, M331, NARA.

18. Taylor Beatty Diary, May 23, 1863, UNC; "Conundrum," February, 1863, Braxton Bragg Papers, RL.

19. Bragg to Davis, May 23, 1863, and Davis to Bragg, May 23, June 13, 1863, *OR*, 24(1):192, 196–97; Davis to Lee, May 26, 1863, Crist, *Papers of Jefferson Davis*, 9:192.

20. Bragg to [Johnston], June 22, 1863, *OR*, 52(2):500.

21. Ibid., 499.

22. Hallock, *Civil War Letters*, 83; Fremantle, *Three Months*, 145.

23. Connelly, *Autumn of Glory*, 115–16.

24. Woodworth, "Braxton Bragg and the Tullahoma Campaign," 160–62.

25. Ibid., 163–67, 169.

26. Notes of Lt. W. B. Richmond, *OR*, 23(1):621–23; Woodworth, "Braxton Bragg and the Tullahoma Campaign," 172–174; Parks, *General Leonidas Polk*, 313–14.

27. Woodworth, "Braxton Bragg and the Tullahoma Campaign," 172–74.

28. Hardee to Polk, July 1, 1863, 8:30 P.M., *OR*, 23(1):623–24.

29. Woodworth, "Braxton Bragg and the Tullahoma Campaign," 174–75.

30. Bragg to Johnston, July 3, 1863, *OR*, 23(1):584.

31. Elliott, *Doctor Quintard*, 76.

32. Bragg to [Johnston], July 22, 1863, *OR*, 23(2):925.

33. Woodworth, "Braxton Bragg and the Tullahoma Campaign," 175.

34. Bragg to Johnston, July 17, August 5, 1863, *OR*, 52(2):508, 514.

35. Bragg to Cooper, August 2, 5, 1863, *OR*, 23(2):948, 952–53.

36. Bragg to Davis, August 7, 1863, Crist, *Papers of Jefferson Davis*, 9:322; Elliott, *Isham G. Harris*, 1–59.

37. Draft of general orders, Headquarters, Army of Tennessee, August 7, [1863], Harvey Washington Walter Papers, UNC.

38. Polk to Davis, August 9, 1863, Crist, *Papers of Jefferson Davis*, 9:335n; Stickles, *Simon Bolivar Buckner*, 213.

39. Hill to Jack, no date, *OR*, 30(2):136; Hill, "Chickamauga," 638–39; Bridges, *Lee's Maverick General*, 195; Sketch of Daniel Harvey Hill, 13, box 3, folder 16, Archer Anderson Collection, MOC.

40. Hill, "Chickamauga," 641n.

41. Ibid., 640, 644–46.

42. Bolling Hall Jr. to father, July 18, 1863; Thomas B. Hall to father, August 31, 1863; Crenshaw Hall to father, July 10, 1863, and John E. Hall to father, September 30, 1863, Bolling Hall Family Papers, ADAH. When Bolling Hall Jr. died in 1866, Bragg wrote a touching condolence letter to his father. See Bragg to Bolling Hall Sr., February 12, 1866, Bolling Hall Family Papers, ADAH.

43. Taylor Beatty Diary, August 15, 1863, UNC; Hallock, *Braxton Bragg*, 34; Harwell, *Kate*, 129.

44. Harwell, *Kate*, 129–30.

45. Ibid., 130.

46. Eliza to husband, [August] 28, 1863, Braxton Bragg Papers, UTA.

47. Mackall to Hill, August 22, 1863, and Hill to Bragg, September 3, 1863, *OR*, 30(4):531, 588.

48. Bragg to Cooper, September 4, 11, December 28, 1863, *OR*, 30(2):21–22, 26–27; Cozzens, *This Terrible Sound*, 55, 70.

49. Bragg to Cooper, September 4, 1863, *OR*, 30(2):21.

Chapter Ten

1. Cozzens, *This Terrible Sound*, 31–33.

2. Ibid., 33, 42; Powell, *Failure in the Saddle*, 33–51, 231–32.

3. Cozzens, *This Terrible Sound*, 58.

4. George W. Brent Journal, September 8, 1863, Braxton Bragg Papers, WRHS; Woodworth, "'In Their Dreams,'" 52–54.

5. Woodworth, "'In Their Dreams,'" 55.

6. Ibid., 55, 59–60.

7. Hindman to Brent, October 25, 1863, *OR*, 30(2):294; Woodworth, "'In Their Dreams,'" 60.

8. Urquhart to not stated, November 21, 1863, *OR*, 30(2):311; copy of Bragg to E. T. Sykes, February 8, 1873, folder 18, J. F. H. Claiborne Papers, UNC; W. T. Martin, "Defence of General Bragg's Conduct," 204.

9. Woodworth, "'In Their Dreams,'" 60, 62, 66.

10. W. T. Martin, "Defence of General Bragg's Conduct," 204.

11. Hindman to Brent, October 25, 1863, *OR*, 30(2):295–96; Woodworth, "'In Their Dreams,'" 63–64.

12. Taylor Beatty Diary, September 11, 1862, UNC; Hindman to Brent, October 25, 1863, *OR*, 30(2):297; Woodworth, "'In Their Dreams,'" 65–66.

13. W. T. Martin, "Defence of General Bragg's Conduct," 205; Bragg to Cooper, December 28, 1863, *OR*, 30(2):27–31.

14. Connelly, *Autumn of Glory*, 186–87; Polk to Fannie, September 10, 1863, Leonidas Polk Papers, US; Polk, "General Bragg and the Chickamauga Campaign," 380–86.

15. Horn, *Army of Tennessee*, 249–50, 254; Woodworth, *Jefferson Davis*, 233; Cozzens, *This Terrible Sound*, 71–75, 81–85; Connelly, *Autumn of Glory*, 184; Hay, "Campaign and Battle of Chickamauga," 222–23; Symonds, *Stonewall of the West*, 142–43. Not surprisingly, Polk's early biographer completely exonerates his subject for the failure to attack Crittenden. Parks, *General Leonidas Polk*, 330.

16. George W. Brent Journal, September 15, 1863, Braxton Bragg Papers, WRHS; Connelly, *Autumn of Glory*, 189–90; Cozzens, *This Terrible Sound*, 87, 89; undated letter from Walker to wife, ca. August–September, 1863, W. H. T. Walker Papers, DU.

17. Rosecrans to [Adjutant General, U.S. Army], [October, no date, 1863], *OR*, 30(1):54–55; Cozzens, *This Terrible Sound*, 87.

18. Cozzens, *This Terrible Sound*, 86–87.

19. George W. Brent Journal, September 15–17, 1863, Braxton Bragg Papers, WRHS; Hill, "Chickamauga," 647; Cozzens, *This Terrible Sound*, 89.

20. Special Orders No. 245, Headquarters, Army of Tennessee, September 16, 1863; Falconer to [Polk], September 17, 1863, 3 A.M.; Falconer to Wheeler, September 17, 1863, 3 A.M.; and Brent to Wheeler, September 17, 1863, *OR*, 30(4):657, 660, 662; Cozzens, *This Terrible Sound*, 89–90, 92, 102.

21. Bragg to Cooper, September 24, 1863, *OR*, 30(2):23; Mackall to Minie, September 29, 1863, William Whann Mackall Papers, UNC.

22. Circular, Headquarters, Army of Tennessee, September 18, 1863, *OR*, 30(4):663; Bragg to Cooper, September 24, December 28, 1863, *OR*, 30(2):24, 31; Cozzens, *This Terrible Sound*, 92, 97.

23. Rosecrans to [Adjutant General, U.S. Army], [October, no date, 1863], *OR*, 30(1):55; Cozzens, *This Terrible Sound*, 113, 115, 119.

24. George W. Brent Journal, September 17–18, 1863, Braxton Bragg Papers, WRHS; Hay, "Campaign and Battle of Chickamauga," 250.

25. Foote to editor, *Richmond Whig*, August 26, 1863, and Williams to Davis, September 2, 1863, Crist, *Papers of Jefferson Davis*, 9:356, 365–66; Miers, *Rebel War Clerk's Diary*, 278, 281.

26. Thomas Butler to aunt, December 25, 1863, Butler Family Papers, LSU; Eliza to husband, September 8, 1863, Braxton Bragg Papers, UTA; John L. Mustian obituary, *Montgomery Advertiser*, May 26, 1881.

27. Eliza to husband, September 8, 17, 1863, Braxton Bragg Papers, UTA.

28. Ibid.

29. Cozzens, *This Terrible Sound*, 130–279.

30. Connelly, *Autumn of Glory*, 207–10; Hay, "Campaign and Battle of Chickamauga," 226–27; Mendoza, "Censure of D. H. Hill," 80.

31. Bragg to Cooper, December 28, 1863, *OR*, 30(2):33.

32. Polk, *Leonidas Polk*, 2:253–58; Polk to Brent, September 28, 1863, *OR*, 30(2):47; Parks, *General Leonidas Polk*, 336–37; Robertson, "A Tale of Two Orders," 134.

33. Polk, *Leonidas Polk*, 2:259; Hill to Jack, no date, *OR*, 30(2):140.

34. Polk, *Leonidas Polk*, 2:259–60, 264; Jack to Cleburne and Breckinridge, September 20, 1863, 5:30 A.M.; Hill to [Polk], September 20, 1863; Polk to Mackall, September 20, 1863, 7 A.M.; and Hill to Jack, no date, *OR*, 30(2):52–53, 141; Robertson, "A Tale of Two Orders," 133, 139.

35. Bragg to Cooper, December 28, 1863, *OR*, 30(2):33; Bragg to wife, September 22, 27, 1863, Braxton Bragg Papers, MHM.

36. Hay, "Campaign and Battle of Chickamauga," 228; D. H. Hill to Anderson, August 11, 1884, box 2, folder 8, and Sketch of Daniel Harvey Hill, 13, box 3, folder 16, Archer Anderson Collection, MOC; Bridges, *Lee's Maverick General*, 207–17.

37. Cozzens, *This Terrible Sound*, 300, 309–10; Connelly, *Autumn of Glory*, 220.

38. Hay, "Campaign and Battle of Chickamauga," 227n.

39. Hill, "Chickamauga," 653; copy of Bragg to E. T. Sykes, February 8, 1873, folder 18, J. F. H. Claiborne Papers, UNC; LeMonnier, "Gen. Leonidas Polk at Chickamauga," 17; Connelly, *Autumn of Glory*, 214–15, 217; Woodworth, *Jefferson Davis*, 235; Cozzens, *This Terrible Sound*, 306–7, 589n.

40. Cozzens, *This Terrible Sound*, 300–301.

41. Ibid.

42. Ibid., 357–509.

43. Longstreet, *From Manassas to Appomattox*, 451–52, 472; Longstreet to Hill, July, 1884, quoted in Hill, "Chickamauga," 659n; Cozzens, *This Terrible Sound*, 456.

44. Cozzens, *This Terrible Sound*, 488.

45. Longstreet to Hill, July, 1884, quoted in Hill, "Chickamauga," 659n; Connelly, *Autumn of Glory*, 228–29. See Robertson, "Bull of the Woods?," 132, 134–35, for a highly critical interpretation of Longstreet's performance at Chickamauga.

Chapter Eleven

1. Cozzens, *This Terrible Sound*, 512–13, 517; Hay, "Campaign and Battle of Chickamauga," 234.

2. Longstreet, *From Manassas to Appomattox*, 461; Sorrel, *Recollections*, 196; Reid diary, October 2, 1863, Samuel Chester Reid Family Papers, LC.

3. Longstreet, *From Manassas to Appomattox*, 462; Sorrel, *Recollections*, 197; Goggin, "Chickamauga," 222.

4. George W. Brent Journal, September 21, 1863, Braxton Bragg Papers, WRHS; Bragg to [Cooper], September 21, 1863, *OR*, 30(2):22. Bragg tended to place the number of troops engaged at Chickamauga as very low, 40,000 in fact. It is not easy to understand that unre-

alistically low figure. A. P. Stewart to Quintard, October 18, 1895, Charles Todd Quintard Papers, DU.

5. Bragg to wife, September 22, 1863, Braxton Bragg Papers, MHM.

6. Ibid.; George W. Brent Journal, September 22, 23, 1863, Braxton Bragg Papers, WRHS; Bragg to Cooper, September 23, 1863, OR, 30(2):23.

7. Longstreet, *From Manassas to Appomattox*, 462.

8. Bragg to Davis, September 25, 1863, Crist, *Papers of Jefferson Davis*, 9:405.

9. Ibid.

10. George W. Brent Journal, September 25, 1863, Braxton Bragg Papers, WRHS; Longstreet, *From Manassas to Appomattox*, 464; Thomas W. Patton to mother, September 28, 1863, James W. Patton Papers, UNC.

11. Longstreet to Seddon, September 26, 1863, OR, 30(4):705–6.

12. George W. Brent Journal, September 26, 1863, Braxton Bragg Papers, WRHS.

13. Bragg to wife, September 27, 1863, Braxton Bragg Papers, MHM; George W. Brent Journal, September 27, 28, 1863, Braxton Bragg Papers, WRHS.

14. Johnston to Bragg, September 23, 1863, OR, 30(4):696; Lee to Davis, September 23, 1863, OR, 29(2):742.

15. Oeffinger, *Soldier's General*, 203–4.

16. Bragg to Davis, September 25, 1863, Crist, *Papers of Jefferson Davis*, 9:405; Bragg to wife, September 27, 1863, Braxton Bragg Papers, MHM.

17. Brent to Polk, September 22, 25, 1863, and Polk to Brent, September 28, 1863, OR, 30(2):47, 54; George W. Brent Journal, September 25, 1863, Braxton Bragg Papers, WRHS; Polk to Davis, [September 27], 1863, Crist, *Papers of Jefferson Davis*, 9:410; Polk to Davis, October 6, 1863, Crist, *Papers of Jefferson Davis*, 10:11.

18. George W. Brent Journal, September 28–29, 1863, Braxton Bragg Papers, WRHS; Urquhart, "Bragg's Advance," 608n.

19. Bragg to Cooper, September 29, 1863; Cooper to Bragg, October 1, 1863; and Special Orders No. 249, Headquarters, Army of Tennessee, September 29, 1863, OR, 30(2):55–56; Davis to Bragg, September 30, 1863, and Bragg to Davis, October 1, 1863, OR, 52(2):533–34; George W. Brent Journal, October 1, 1863, Braxton Bragg Papers, WRHS.

20. Davis to Bragg, October 3, 1863, Crist, *Papers of Jefferson Davis*, 10:6.

21. Bragg to Cooper, October 6, 1863, OR, 30(4):731; Charges preferred against Lieut. Gen. L. Polk, OR, 30(2):55–56.

22. Polk to wife, October 3, 1863, quoted in Polk, *Leonidas Polk*, 2:298; Polk to Davis, October 6, 1863, Crist, *Papers of Jefferson Davis*, 10:12–13; Kenneth Rayner to Ruffin, November 26, 1863, Hamilton, *Papers of Thomas Ruffin*, 3:346.

23. Lee to Polk, October 26, 1863, OR, 30(2):69.

24. Hindman to Cooper, October 2, 1863; Davis to Seddon, November 20, 1863; and Charges and Specifications against Maj. Gen. T. C. Hindman, OR, 30(2):309–10.

25. Hindman to Cooper, April 27, 1864, and H. L. Clay endorsement, June 20, 1864, OR, 30(2):312–13; copy of Bragg memo, 1872, on back of copy of Charges and Specifications against Maj. Gen. T. C. Hindman, folder 18, J. F. H. Claiborne Papers, UNC.

26. Mackall letters, October 1, 3, 1863, quoted in Mackall, *Son's Recollections*, 180–81; George W. Brent Journal, October 1, 1863, Braxton Bragg Papers, WRHS; Bragg to Davis, September 29, 1863, Crist, *Papers of Jefferson Davis*, 9:414.

27. Bragg to Cooper, October 3, 1863, OR, 30(4):726.

28. Bragg to Cooper, December 28, 1863, OR, 30(2):37. Even as late as April 1864, the Army of Tennessee possessed too few wagons to make feasible an offensive across the

mountains into Middle Tennessee in the opinion of A. H. Cole, the chief of field transportation in the Confederate army. See Cole to Gibbon, April 11, 1864, *OR*, 32(3):772.

29. Bragg to Cooper, December 28, 1863, *OR*, 30(2):37.

30. William Preston to William Preston Johnston, October 3, 1863, box 11, folder 35, Albert Sidney and William Preston Johnston Papers, TU.

31. Otey, "Story of Our Great War," 343; Hill, "Chickamauga," 662.

32. Connelly, *Autumn of Glory*, 230–31, 233–34.

33. Hill, Brown, Preston, et. al. to Davis, October 4, 1863, *OR*, 30(2):65–66; Bridges, *Lee's Maverick General*, 235.

34. George W. Brent Journal, October 4, 1863, Braxton Bragg Papers, WRHS; Hill, Brown, Preston, et. al. to Davis, October 4, 1863, *OR*, 30(2):66; Horn, *Army of Tennessee*, 286–87; Longstreet, *From Manassas to Appomattox*, 465; D. H. Hill to Longstreet, February 11, 1888, and John C. Brown to Longstreet, April 14, 1888, James Longstreet Papers, DU; Avery, "Memorial Address," 144; D. H. Hill to Davis, October 30, 1886, Rowland, *Jefferson Davis*, 9:498; Elliott, *Soldier of Tennessee*, 77, 84–85, 140–42.

35. Polk to daughter, October 10, 1863, quoted in Polk, *Leonidas Polk*, 2:299.

36. William Preston Johnston to wife, October 18, 1863, Johnston Family Papers, FHS; Mackall to Minie, October 10, 1863, William Whann Mackall Papers, UNC; George W. Brent Journal, October 9, 1863, Braxton Bragg Papers, WRHS.

37. Cooper to Bragg, October 4, 1863, *OR*, 30(4):727.

38. Bragg memo, June 16, 1864, attached to copy of Hill to Bragg, June 11, 1864, Braxton Bragg Papers, WRHS; Davis to Bragg, June 29, 1872, Rowland, *Jefferson Davis*, 7:321.

39. Longstreet, *From Manassas to Appomattox*, 466–67.

40. Davis endorsement, November 28, 1863, on Ewing to Davis, November 22, 1863, Crist, *Papers of Jefferson Davis*, 10:530; Longstreet, *From Manassas to Appomattox*, 465; Buck, *Cleburne and His Command*, 159; M. B. Morton, "Historic Conference between President Davis, General Bragg and His Corps Commanders," *Nashville Banner*, December 4, 1909.

41. Longstreet, *From Manassas to Appomattox*, 468–69.

42. Mackall to Minie, October 12, 1863, William Whann Mackall Papers, UNC; diary, October 13, 1863, Edwin Hansford Rennolds Sr. Papers, UT.

43. Davis speech at Missionary Ridge, *Memphis Daily Appeal*, October 14, 1863, Crist, *Papers of Jefferson Davis*, 10:24; George W. Brent Journal, October 11, 1863, Braxton Bragg Papers, WRHS.

44. Armand to [G. T. Beauregard], October 10, 1863, *OR*, 30(4):735.

45. Armand to [G. T. Beauregard], October 10, 14, 1863, *OR*, 30(4):735, 746.

46. Armand to [G. T. Beauregard], October 14, 1863, *OR*, 30(4):746.

47. Ibid., 745–46.

48. Bragg to wife, September 22, 1863, Braxton Bragg Papers, MHM.

49. Eliza to husband, September 28, 1863, Braxton Bragg Papers, UTA.

50. Ibid.

51. George W. Brent Journal, October 14, 1863, Braxton Bragg Papers, WRHS; Davis speech at Selma, *Memphis Daily Appeal*, October 19, 1863, Crist *Papers of Jefferson Davis*, 10:29; Davis to Hardee, October 30, 1863, *OR*, 31(3):609; N. C. Hughes, *Liddell's Record*, 152–53.

52. Davis endorsement, November 28, 1863, on Ewing to Davis, November 22, 1863, Crist, *Papers of Jefferson Davis*, 10:530; Davis to Hill, December 4, 1867, ibid., 12:262; Davis to Bragg, June 29, 1872, ibid., 13:91; J. Davis, *Rise and Fall*, 2:434.

53. Bragg to Davis, September 25, 1863, Crist, *Papers of Jefferson Davis*, 9:405; Bragg memo, June 16, 1864, attached to copy of Hill to Bragg, June 11, 1864, Braxton Bragg Papers, WRHS.

54. Connelly, *Autumn of Glory*, 249; Sieburg, *Memoirs of a Confederate Staff Officer*, 45.

55. Mendoza, "Censure of D. H. Hill," 68, 76, 80; D. Coleman Diary, October 18, 1863, UNC.

56. Connelly, *Autumn of Glory*, 252; Stickles, *Simon Bolivar Buckner*, 223.

57. George W. Brent Journal, October 22, 24, November 1, 9, 1863, Braxton Bragg Papers, WRHS; Davis to Bragg, October 29, 1863, and Bragg to Davis, October 31, 1863, OR, 52(2):553–54, 557; Bragg to Cooper, November 8, 1863, OR, 31(3):650–51; Stickles, *Simon Bolivar Buckner*, 232, 237–42; Bragg to Wright, December 29, 1863, Marcus Joseph Wright Papers, UNC.

58. Forrest to Cooper, August 9, 1863; Bragg endorsement, August 14, 1863; Davis endorsement, no date; Forrest to Davis, August 19, 1863; and Davis endorsement, no date, OR, 30(4):507–10.

59. George W. Brent Journal, September 25, 1863, Braxton Bragg Papers, WRHS.

60. George W. Brent Journal, September 26, 29, 1863, Braxton Bragg Papers, WRHS; Brent to Forrest, September 28, 1863, and Forrest to [Wheeler], September 28, 1863, OR, 30(4):710–11; J. W. Morton, *Artillery*, 129–30.

61. N. C. Hughes, *Liddell's Record*, 150. A modern historian of Civil War cavalry agrees with Bragg's assessment of Forrest as a commander of mounted troops. See Eric Wittenberg's comments at http://civilwarcavalry.com/?p=21, accessed December 7, 2013.

62. J. W. Morton, *Artillery*, 130.

63. Ibid., 130–31.

64. Ibid., 131–33; Powell, *Failure in the Saddle*, 320; Wyeth, *That Devil Forrest*, 242–44; Mathes, *General Forrest*, 156; Lytle, *Bedford Forrest*, 237–39; Wills, *Battle from the Start*, 142–47; Ashdown and Caudill, *Myth of Nathan Bedford Forrest*, 24–26; S. J. Martin, *General Braxton Bragg*, 331–32.

65. Hallock, *Braxton Bragg*, 100–102; Powell, *Failure in the Saddle*, 321, 326.

66. J. W. Morton, *Artillery*, 129–32; George W. Brent Journal, October 20, 22, 24, 1863, Braxton Bragg Papers, WRHS.

67. J. W. Morton, *Artillery*, 131.

68. Davis to Forrest, October 29, 1863, and Bragg to Lee, October 13, 1863, OR, 31(3):604; J. W. Morton, *Artillery*, 131–32.

69. George W. Brent Journal, October 30, 1863, Braxton Bragg Papers, WRHS; Bragg to Davis, October 30, 1863, OR, 52(2):557.

70. Hood, *Advance and Retreat*, 62–63.

71. Bragg to Cooper, September 24, December 28, 1863, OR, 30(2):23, 35; Bragg to Davis, October 23, 1863, Crist, *Papers of Jefferson Davis*, 10:32; Davis to Bragg, October 29, 1863, OR, 52(2):555.

72. Mackall to Minie, September 29, October 5, 1863, William Whann Mackall Papers, UNC; Mackall letter, October 9, 1863, quoted in Mackall, *Son's Recollections*, 183.

73. Mackall to Minie, September 29, October 10, 1863, William Whann Mackall Papers, UNC; General Orders No. 2, Headquarters, Department of Tennessee, October 16, 1863, OR, 30(4):756–67.

74. Connelly, *Autumn of Glory*, 250–51; Woodworth, *Jefferson Davis*, 247.

75. Woodworth, *Jefferson Davis*, 247.

76. George W. Brent Journal, October 28, 1863, Braxton Bragg Papers, WRHS; Longstreet, *From Manassas to Appomattox*, 474–77; Woodworth, *Jefferson Davis*, 247–48.

77. George W. Brent Journal, October 28, 30, 1863, Braxton Bragg Papers, WRHS; N. C. Hughes, *Liddell's Record*, 156–57; Bragg to Davis, October 30, 1863, and Davis to Bragg, November 1, 1863, OR, 52(2):556, 558; Bragg to Cooper, December 28, 1863, OR, 30(2):36–37; Connelly, *Autumn of Glory*, 256–61.

78. George W. Brent Journal, October 29, 1863, Braxton Bragg Papers, WRHS; Davis to Bragg, October 29, 1863, *OR*, 52(2):555.

79. George W. Brent Journal, October 30, 1863, Braxton Bragg Papers, WRHS.

80. Bragg to Davis, October 31, 1863, *OR*, 52(2):557; Hess, *Knoxville Campaign*, 23–35; Connelly, *Autumn of Glory*, 262–67.

81. Longstreet, *From Manassas to Appomattox*, 481–83, 488.

82. N. C. Hughes, *Liddell's Record*, 157; Hess, *Knoxville Campaign*, 56–76, 95–123.

83. George W. Brent Journal, November 15, 1863, Braxton Bragg Papers, WRHS; Bragg to Davis, November 15, 1863, and Davis endorsement, no date, *OR*, 30(2):311.

84. Hill to Cooper, November 13, 1863; and Cooper to Hill, November 20, 1863, *OR*, 30(2):150–; Davis to Hill, December 24, 1886, Jefferson Davis Letter, GLIAH; Sketch of Daniel Harvey Hill, 15–16, box 3, folder 16, Archer Anderson Collection, MOC.

85. Ewing to Davis, November 22, 1863, Crist, *Papers of Jefferson Davis*, 12:529–30; George W. Brent Journal, November 1, 1863, Braxton Bragg Papers, WRHS; Losson, "Mutual Antagonists," 228-229.

86. Cobb to Davis, November 6, 1863, Crist, *Papers of Jefferson Davis*, 10:54–55.

87. Copies of T. G. Richardson to Stout, October 22, November 6, 1863, Samuel Hollingsworth Stout Papers, UNC.

88. N. C. Hughes, *Liddell's Record*, 148, 152.

89. Ibid., 150.

90. Mackall to Minie, September 29, October 5, 1863, William Whann Mackall Papers, UNC.

91. M. B. Morton, "Last Surviving Lieutenant General," 83.

92. Bragg to wife, September 22, 1863, Braxton Bragg Papers, MHM; Eliza to husband, September 28, 1863, Braxton Bragg Papers, UTA; John Bragg to sisters, October 12, 1863, Braxton Bragg Papers, USMA.

93. John Bragg to sisters, October 12, 1863, Braxton Bragg Papers, USMA.

94. Bragg to wife, November 14, [1863], Braxton Bragg Papers, LC.

95. When a Virginia lady wrote to ask him for a lock of his hair, Bragg did not know what to do. He had been keeping his hair so short lately that he used only a pocket comb to care for it. Bragg to wife, November 14, [1863], Braxton Bragg Papers, LC; Bragg to Walter, October 9, 1863, Harvey Washington Walter Papers, UNC.

Chapter Twelve

1. Copy of T. G. Richardson to Stout, November 6, 1863, Samuel Hollingsworth Stout Papers, UNC; George W. Brent Journal, November 8, 11–12, 1863, Braxton Bragg Papers, WRHS.

2. George W. Brent Journal, November 11, 1863, Braxton Bragg Papers, WRHS.

3. General Orders No. 205, 207, 208, Headquarters, Army of Tennessee, November 14–16, 1863, *OR*, 31(3):694–95, 700–701.

4. Bragg to Cooper, November 15, 1863, and Bragg to Davis, November 19, 1863, *OR*, 31(3):698, 716; Bragg to Davis, November 16, 1863, Crist, *Papers of Jefferson Davis*, 10:71–72.

5. George W. Brent Journal, November 21, 1863, Braxton Bragg Papers, WRHS; Taylor Beatty Diary, October 23–27, 1863, UNC.

6. Eliza to husband, November 23, 1863, Braxton Bragg Papers, UTA.

7. Johnston to Bragg, November 5, 1863, and Bragg to Johnston, November 15, 1863, *OR*, 31(3):639, 700; Armand to [G. T. Beauregard], October 10, 1863, *OR*, 30(4):735.

8. Cozzens, *Shipwreck of Their Hopes*, 126–35.

9. Ibid., 159–98.

10. George W. Brent Journal, November 24, 1863, Braxton Bragg Papers, WRHS; Cozzens, *Shipwreck of Their Hopes*, 196.

11. Bragg to Cooper, November 30, 1863, *OR*, 31(2):664–65; Cozzens, *Shipwreck of Their Hopes*, 199–243.

12. Cozzens, *Shipwreck of Their Hopes*, 257–81.

13. Ibid., 282–342.

14. Bragg to Cooper, November 30, 1863, *OR*, 31(2):665; Watkins, *Co. Aytch*, 117–18.

15. Buck, *Cleburne and His Command*, 177.

16. Cozzens, *Shipwreck of Their Hopes*, 369–84; Hess, *Knoxville Campaign*, 152–206.

17. Bragg to Cooper, November 29, 1863, *OR*, 31(2):682.

18. Bragg to Cooper, November 29, 30, 1863, and Bragg to Johnston, November 27, 1863, *OR*, 31(2):666, 681–82.

19. Bragg to Davis, November 30, 1863, Crist, *Papers of Jefferson Davis*, 10:92; Bragg to Davis, December 1, 1863, *OR*, 52(2):745.

20. Bragg to Davis, December 1, 1863, *OR*, 52(2):745–46; George W. Brent Journal, December 1, 1863, Braxton Bragg Papers, WRHS.

21. N. C. Hughes, *Liddell's Record*, 160.

22. Ibid., 164.

23. Ibid., 165.

24. Bragg to Cooper, December 1, 2, 1863, *OR*, 31(3):771–74; Bragg to Davis, December 1, 1863, *OR*, 52(2):745–46.

25. Bragg to Davis, December 2, 1863, *OR*, 52(2):568.

26. General Orders No. 214, Headquarters, Army of Tennessee, December 2, 1863, *OR*, 31(3):775–76.

27. J. Davis, *Rise and Fall*, 2:436; Lee to Davis, December 3, 1863; Davis to Lee, December 5, 1863; and Lee to Davis, December 7, 1863, *OR*, 31(3):779, 785, 792.

28. Walker to Mary, December 3, 1863, W. H. T. Walker Papers, DU; Taylor Beatty Diary, December 2–3, 1863, UNC.

29. Wiggins, *Journals of Josiah Gorgas*, 81, 86.

30. Crabtree and Patton, "*Journal of a Secesh Lady*," 469–70, 481, 495, 502, 506, 508.

31. Claiborne to wife, November 19, 1863, Thomas Claiborne Papers, UNC; Younger, *Inside the Confederate Government*, 105, 122; Harwell, *Kate*, 159–60, 171, 182.

32. Woodward, *Mary Chesnut's Civil War*, 469, 482, 496.

33. Younger, *Inside the Confederate Government*, 115; Miers, *Rebel War Clerk's Diary*, 301, 312.

34. Wigfall to Joseph E. Johnston, December 18, 1863, Louis Trezevant Wigfall Papers, UTA.

35. *Memphis Daily Appeal*, November 7, 1863.

36. Article by citizen of Tennessee in *Winchester Bulletin*, reprinted in *Richmond Sentinel*, and reprinted in *Memphis Daily Appeal*, November 13, 1863.

37. *Chattanooga Daily Rebel* quoted in *Memphis Daily Appeal*, December 4, 1863.

38. Hallock, *Braxton Bragg*, 162; Morris, "Chattanooga Daily Rebel," 16, 18, 20–24; Watterson to Rebecca Ewing, November 3, 1863, Henry Watterson Papers, FHS.

39. John H. Linebaugh letter, November 4, 1863, *Memphis Daily Appeal*, November 5, 1863; Braxton Bragg to Wright, March 6, 1864, (includes John Bragg to Braxton Bragg, February 6, 1864), Marcus Joseph Wright Papers, UNC.

40. John H. Linebaugh letter, November 4, 1863, *Memphis Daily Appeal*, November 5, 1863.

41. Walker to Mary, December 3, 1863, W. H. T. Walker Papers, DU; White and Runion, *Great Things*, 69, 72, 76.

42. Carleton, "A Record of the Late Fourth Louisiana," 258–60; Semmes to wife, December 3, 1863, Benedict Joseph Semmes Papers, UNC; Bliss to father and mother, December 5, 1863, Robert Lewis Bliss Papers, ADAH; Frank G. Ruffin to Thomas Ruffin, December 2, 1863, Hamilton, *Papers of Thomas Ruffin*, 3:348–49.

43. Edwin Kerrison to sister, October 8, 1863, Kerrison Family Papers, USC; Bivings to father, October 2, 1863, James Morris Bivings Papers, USC.

44. Tower, *A Carolinian Goes to War*, 101, 142, 158.

45. N. C. Hughes, *Civil War Memoir*, 137–39, 142, 148; Stephenson, "Missionary Ridge," 14.

46. Robert Ransom Jr. to Gordon, September 22, 1863, James B. Gordon Papers, SANC; Hugh S. Gookin to friend, December 3, 1863, Washington Artillery Letter, HNOC.

47. [Johnston] to Davis, December 26, 1863, Crist, *Papers of Jefferson Davis*, 10:136; Taylor Beatty Diary, December 1, 1863, UNC; Kenneth Rayner to Ruffin, December 31, 1863, Hamilton, *Papers of Thomas Ruffin*, 3:359–60.

48. Hallock, *Braxton Bragg*, 153–54; J. H. Fraser to Bragg, December 2, 1863, and M. I. Holt to Bragg, December 4, 1863, Braxton Bragg Papers, WRHS; diary, December 5, 1863, Edwin Hansford Rennolds Sr. Papers, UTK.

49. Brown to Fannie, December 2, 5, 1863, Edward Norphlet Brown Letters, ADAH.

50. *Memphis Daily Appeal*, December 3, 1863.

51. E. C. Walthall to Bragg, December 9, 1863; Joseph Wheeler to Bragg, December 15, 1863; and S. H. Stout to Bragg, December 5, 1863, Braxton Bragg Papers, WRHS.

52. H. W. Walter to Bragg, December 10, 1863, and J. P. Jones to Bragg, December 10, 1863, Braxton Bragg Papers, WRHS.

53. P. D. Roddey to Bragg, December 13, 20, 1863, and James Chalmers to Bragg, December 19, 1863, Braxton Bragg Papers, WRHS.

54. Horn, *Army of Tennessee*, 293; Seitz, *Braxton Bragg*, 406; Hay, "Campaign and Battle of Chickamauga," 236, 238, 246, 248–49.

55. Cozzens, *This Terrible Sound*, 518; Woodworth, *Jefferson Davis*, 237, 246–47; Cozzens, *Shipwreck of Their Hopes*, 35–36, 57–59, 67–71, 78–91; S. J. Martin, *General Braxton Bragg*, 345–47.

56. Connelly, *Autumn of Glory*, 235, 238; S. J. Martin, *General Braxton Bragg*, 334; Woodworth, *Jefferson Davis*, 242.

57. Cozzens, *Shipwreck of Their Hopes*, 31.

58. Ibid., 390.

59. S. J. Martin, *General Braxton Bragg*, 379.

Chapter Thirteen

1. Hallock, *Braxton Bragg*, 155; Bragg to Cooper, January 3, 1864, *OR*, 30(2):26; Thomas Butler to aunt, December 25, 1863, Butler Family Papers, LSU.

2. "Notes of Gen'l Bragg's services in the cause of the Confederacy after leaving the Army of Tennessee in Dec. 1863," Braxton Bragg Papers, WRHS.

3. Bragg to Wright, December 14, 29, 1863, March 6, 1864, Marcus Joseph Wright Papers, UNC.

4. Bragg to Wright, December 29, 1863, Marcus Joseph Wright Papers, UNC; Thomas Butler to aunt, December 25, 1863, Butler Family Papers, LSU; T. G. Richardson to Stout, December 21, 1863, Samuel Hollingsworth Stout Papers, UNC; Beauregard to Soulé, December 11, 1863, *OR*, 53:919–20.

5. Wiggins, *Journals of Josiah Gorgas*, 88; Joseph E. Johnston to Wigfall, December 27, 1863, Louis Trezevant Wigfall Family Papers, LC.

6. Bragg to Johnston, January 10, 1864, *OR*, 32(2):543; Bragg to Joseph E. Johnston, January 10, 1863 [1864], Braxton Bragg Papers, WRHS.

7. Wigfall to Joseph E. Johnston, December 18, 1863, Louis Trezevant Wigfall Papers, UTA.

8. Joseph Wheeler to Bragg, December 20, 1863, and William B. Bate to Bragg, January 25, 1864, Braxton Bragg Papers, DU.

9. Braxton Bragg to Semmes, December 31, 1863, Thomas Jenkins Semmes Papers, DU.

10. Bragg to Wright, December 14, 29, 1863, Marcus Joseph Wright Papers, UNC.

11. Bragg to Davis, December 8, 1863, Crist, *Papers of Jefferson Davis*, 10:104–5.

12. Braxton Bragg to Wright, February 5, 1864, folder 8, Marcus Joseph Wright Papers, UNC.

13. Braxton Bragg to Samuel H. Stout, January 2, 1864, quoted in Stout, "An Address," 441.

14. Bragg to Pillow, January 10, 1864, *OR*, 32(2):543.

15. Davis to Bragg, January 27, 1864, *OR*, 52(2):607; Bragg to Davis, January 28, 1864, Crist, *Papers of Jefferson Davis*, 10:210; Bragg to Wright, February 5, 1864, folder 8, Marcus Joseph Wright Papers, UNC.

16. Bragg to Wright, February 5, March 6, 1864, folder 8, Marcus Joseph Wright Papers, UNC.

17. Cooke to Stone, January 23, 1864, and Banks to Halleck, February 2, 1864, *OR*, 34(2):135, 216; Reynolds to Davis, February 20, 1864, Crist, *Papers of Jefferson Davis*, 10:249.

18. Beauregard to Miles, February 7, 1864, *OR*, 53:307.

19. *Journal of the Congress*, 3:755, and 6:825; Wiggins, *Journals of Josiah Gorgas*, 93; General Orders No. 23, Adjutant and Inspector General's Office, February 24, 1864, *OR*, 32(2):799.

20. Younger, *Inside the Confederate Government*, 138; Butler to Stanton, February 29, 1864, *OR*, 33:618; Crabtree and Patton, *"Journal of a Secesh Lady,"* 531–32.

21. Scarborough, *Diary of Edmund Ruffin*, 3:351; Miers, *Rebel War Clerk's Diary*, 341.

22. Taylor Beatty Diary, March 4, 1864, UNC; Bragg to Baker, December 30, 1864, *OR*, 44:1005; copy of Bragg to E. T. Sykes, February 8, 1873, folder 18, J. F. H. Claiborne Papers, UNC; Sale to George W. Randolph, November 10, 1862; Bragg to Davis, April 24, 1863, and copy of extract of Special Orders No. 33, Headquarters, Department of Tennessee, March 3, 1864, John B. Sale Service Record, M331, NARA.

23. "Notes of Gen'l Bragg's services in the cause of the Confederacy after leaving the Army of Tennessee in Dec. 1863," Braxton Bragg Papers, WRHS; Hallock, *Braxton Bragg*, 218.

24. Brent and Richardson to Bragg, March 14, 1864, and Bragg endorsement, March 18, 1864, *OR*, ser. 2, 6:1048–50; T. G. Richardson to Stout, March 10, 26, 29, 1864, Samuel Hollingsworth Stout Papers, UNC.

25. Bragg endorsement, May 29, 1864, on Chilton to Cooper, May 26, 1864, *OR*, ser. 2, 7:173–74.

26. Bragg to Vance, April 21, 1864, *OR*, ser. 2, 7:78.

27. Bragg endorsement, April 20, 1864, on Northrop to Cooper, April 7, 1864, *OR*, 51(2):851–52; Bragg endorsement, May 18, 1864, on Polk to Davis, May 5, 1864, *OR*, 39(2):580; Bragg to Johnston, April 14, 1864, *OR*, 52(2):659; Bragg endorsement, August 22, 1864, on Hayes to Davis, January 6, 1864, *OR*, ser. 4, 3:4–6.

28. Gow, "Theory and Practice," 121–22; Bragg to William Preston Johnston, April 22, 1864, *OR*, ser. 4, 3:316.

29. Gow, "Chiefs of Staff," 343–45, 359–60.

30. Younger, *Inside the Confederate Government*, 142; Miers, *Rebel War Clerk's Diary*, 358.

31. Bragg to Seddon, May 20, 1864, and Seddon endorsement, May 20, 1864, *OR*, 30(2):39;

Seddon to Bragg, May 23, 1864, vol. 3, no. 101, 92–93, Samuel Richey Collection of the Southern Confederacy, MU; Bragg to Wright, March 6, 1864, Marcus Joseph Wright Papers, UNC.

32. Younger, *Inside the Confederate Government*, 142.

33. See Lee to Davis and Lee to Bragg, various dates, *OR*, vol. 33, 1061–1331; Bragg to Davis, March 21, 1864, Crist, *Papers of Jefferson Davis*, 10:284; Bragg to Lee, April 8, 1864, *OR*, 51(2):1077.

34. Bragg to Seddon, March 4, 1864, and Seddon to Lee, March 5, 1864, *OR*, 33:217–19; Hallock, *Braxton Bragg*, 170.

35. Wiggins, *Journals of Josiah Gorgas*, 97, 101; Hallock, *Braxton Bragg*, 174; Goff, *Confederate Supply*, 201–2.

36. Copy of Bragg to Lafayette McLaws, March 4, 1864, Braxton Bragg Papers, WRHS; Bragg to McLaws, March 4, 1864, *OR*, 52(2):634; Oeffinger, *Soldier's General*, 219, 227–28.

37. Thomas C. Hindman to Bragg, March 21, 1864, Braxton Bragg Papers, WRHS.

38. William B. Bate to Bragg, March 17, 1864; J. J. Finley and Joseph C. Smith to Bragg, March 15, 1864; and unidentified correspondent to Bragg, March 19, 1864, Braxton Bragg Papers, WRHS.

39. Bragg to Johnston, March 4, 7, 1864, *OR*, 32(3):584, 592.

40. Bragg to Johnston, March 12, 1864, *OR*, 32(3):614–15.

41. Longstreet to Johnston, March 16, 1864, and Johnston to Bragg, March 18, 1864, *OR*, 32(3):637, 649; Bragg to Lee, April 8, 1864, *OR*, 51(2):1076–77; Longstreet, *From Manassas to Appomattox*, 544–46; Hess, *Knoxville Campaign*, 232–37.

42. George William Brent to Bragg, April 16, 1864, Braxton Bragg Papers, WRHS.

43. James B. Hall to father, January 31, 1864, Bolling Hall Family Papers, ADAH.

44. Hood to Bragg, March 10, April 13, 1864, *OR*, 32(3):607–8, 781; Hood to Bragg, April 3, 13, 1864, Braxton Bragg Papers, WRHS.

45. Wigfall to Johnston, March 17, 1864, Louis Trezevant Wigfall Papers, UTA; Woodward, *Mary Chesnut's Civil War*, 585–86; Younger, *Inside the Confederate Government*, 142–43; Crabtree and Patton, *"Journal of a Secesh Lady,"* 545.

Chapter Fourteen

1. "Regulations for the Office of Gen. Bragg: Richmond May 1864," Braxton Bragg Papers, WRHS; Bragg to Cooper, May 7, 1864, *OR*, 35(2):476.

2. Bragg endorsement May 9, 1864, on Beauregard to Cooper, April 27, 1864, *OR*, 33:1317.

3. Beauregard to Bragg, May 14, 1864, and Bragg endorsement, May 19, 1864, *OR*, 36(2):1024–25.

4. Bragg endorsement, May 19, 1864, on Beauregard to Bragg, May 14, 1864, *OR*, 36(2):1024–25; Miers, *Rebel War Clerk's Diary*, 386–87; T. H. Williams, *P. G. T. Beauregard*, 214–16.

5. Bragg endorsement, no date, and Lee endorsement, June 11, 1864, on Breckinridge to Bragg, June 10, 1864, *OR*, 51(2):1003.

6. Wright to Bragg, May 23, 1864, *OR*, 52(2):672.

7. Bragg to Johnston, May 23, 1864, *OR*, 52(2):671–72; Bragg to Johnston, June 2, 7, 1864, and Bragg to Davis, June 4, 1864, *OR*, 38(4):755, 762.

8. Johnston to Bragg, 13, June 27, 1864, *OR*, 38(4):772, 795–96.

9. Joseph Wheeler to Bragg, July, no date, 1864, Braxton Bragg Papers, DU.

10. Bragg to Davis, June 29, 1864, *OR*, 38(4):805.

11. Bragg endorsement, July 2, 1864, on Morgan to Marshall, May 29, 1864, *OR*, 39(1):76.

12. Hill to Bragg, June 11, 1864, and Bragg endorsement, June 16, 1864, *OR*, 52(2):677.

13. Miers, *Rebel War Clerk's Diary*, 375; Younger, *Inside the Confederate Government*, 155.

14. Joseph Wheeler to Bragg, July, no date, 1864, Braxton Bragg Papers, DU; Harwell, *Kate*, 207.

15. *Richmond Enquirer*, as reported in *Richmond Whig* and in *Memphis Daily Appeal*, June 2, 1864; Wiggins, *Journals of Josiah Gorgas*, 112.

16. "Notes of Gen'l Bragg's services in the cause of the Confederacy after leaving the Army of Tennessee in Dec. 1863," Braxton Bragg Papers, WRHS; Davis to Bragg, July 9, 1864, *OR*, 39(2):695–96; Wright to Bragg, July 10, 1864, *OR*, 52(2):691.

17. Taylor Beatty Diary, July 13, 1864, UNC; Mackall letter, July, 1864, quoted in Mackall, *Son's Recollections*, 217; Walker to daughter, July 15, 1864, and Walker to Mary, July 18, 1864, W. H. T. Walker Papers, DU.

18. Bragg to Davis, July 13, 1864, *OR*, 38(5):878.

19. Bragg to Davis, July 15, 1864, *OR*, 39(2):712; Joseph E. Johnston to Dabney Herndon Maury, September 1, 1864, in Maury, *Recollections*, 147–48; Joseph E. Johnston to Dear General, August 27, 1864, Louis Trezevant Wigfall Family Papers, LC; Johnston to Cooper, October 20, 1864, *OR*, 38(3):620–21; Hardee to wife, September 27, 1864, Crist, *Papers of Jefferson Davis*, 11:67.

20. Hood to Bragg, July 14, 1864, *OR*, 38(5):879–80.

21. Castel, *Decision in the West*, 198–206, 242–43; Hess, *Kennesaw Mountain*, 28–46.

22. "Notes of Gen'l Bragg's services in the cause of the Confederacy after leaving the Army of Tennessee in Dec. 1863," Braxton Bragg Papers, WRHS; Bragg to Davis, July 15, 1864, *OR*, 39(2):713.

23. Bragg to Davis, July 15, 1864, *OR*, 39(2):713–14; Bragg to Davis, July 15, 1864, *OR*, 38(5):881.

24. Bragg to Davis, July 15, 1864, *OR*, 39(2):713–14.

25. Bragg to Sale, July 15, 1864, *OR*, 52(2):707; Davis to Johnston, July 16, 1864; Johnston to Davis, July 16, 1864; and Cooper to Johnston, July 17, 1864, *OR*, 38(5):882–83, 885.

26. Hood, *Advance and Retreat*, 126.

27. Davis to Bettie, July 16, 1864, Newton N. Davis Papers, ADAH; Walker to Mary, July 16, 1864, W. H. T. Walker Papers, DU; Bragg to Davis, July 15, 1864, *OR*, 39(2):713; "Notes of Gen'l Bragg's services in the cause of the Confederacy after leaving the Army of Tennessee in Dec. 1863," Braxton Bragg Papers, WRHS; editorial comment, Crist, *Papers of Jefferson Davis*, 10:543n.

28. Bragg to Sale, July 17, 23, 24, 1864, *OR*, 38(5):887, 904, 907; Davis to Bragg, July 19, 1864, *OR*, 52(2):709; Bragg to Sale, July 22, 1864, *OR*, 39(2):721; Castel, *Decision in the West*, 348, 381, 411–12, 417.

29. Sherman to Halleck, July 28, 1864, and Bragg to Davis, July 25, 1864, *OR*, 38(5):279, 908.

30. Bragg to Lee, July 17, 1864, folder 3, Stephen D. Lee Papers, UNC; Bragg to Sale, July 26, 1864, *OR*, 38(5):911.

31. Bragg to Davis, July 27, 1864, Braxton Bragg Papers, DU.

32. Ibid.; Bragg to Davis, July 27, 1864, *OR*, 52(2):713.

33. Watts to Davis, November 27, 1863, Crist, *Papers of Jefferson Davis*, 10:90–91; T. H. Watts to Bragg, July 22, 1864, Braxton Bragg Papers, DU.

34. T. H. Watts to Bragg, July 22, 1864, and Bragg to Davis, August 16, 1864, Braxton Bragg Papers, DU; Bragg memorandum, August 16, 1864, Crist, *Papers of Jefferson Davis*, 10:613; Bragg to Sale, August 3, 1864, *OR*, 39(2):751.

35. Johnston to Maury, September 1, 1864, Maury, *Recollections of a Virginian*, 148; Joseph E. Johnston to Wigfall, August 27, 1864, Louis Trezevant Wigfall Family Papers, LC.

36. Joseph E. Johnston to Wigfall, August 27, 1864, Louis Trezevant Wigfall Family

Papers, LC; Joseph E. Johnston to Beverly Johnston, August 28, 1864, R. M. Hughes, "Some War Letters," 321; Johnston to Cooper, October 20, 1864, *OR*, 38(3):620; Johnston to Maury, September 1, 1864, Maury, *Recollections of a Virginian*, 147.

37. Cater, *As It Was*, 168, 184, 186; Mackall to Minie, July 15, [1864], William Whann Mackall Papers, UNC; Neal to Pa, July 20, 1864, Andrew Jackson Neal Papers, EU.

38. White and Runion, *Great Things*, 128; Dent to wife, September 10, 1864, Stouten Hubert Dent Papers, ADAH.

39. Hay, "Davis, Bragg, and Johnston," 39–41; McMurry, *John Bell Hood*, 118.

40. Hay, "Davis-Hood-Johnston Controversy," 65n, 82; Symonds, *Joseph E. Johnston*, 325.

41. "Notes of Gen'l Bragg's services in the cause of the Confederacy after leaving the Army of Tennessee in Dec. 1863," Braxton Bragg Papers, WRHS.

Chapter Fifteen

1. Bragg endorsement, September 3, 1864, on Jones to Cooper, August 22, 1864, *OR*, 35(1):127–28; Bragg to Davis, September 29, 1864, *OR*, 52(2):748; Bragg to Lee, September 27, 1864, *OR*, 42(2):1296.

2. Bragg to Lamar, September 22, 1864, *OR*, 30(2):40.

3. Woodward, *Mary Chesnut's Civil War*, 643; *Telegraph* (Macon)— October 20, 1864, Crist, *Papers of Jefferson Davis*, 10:53n–54n.

4. Bragg to Davis, September 7, October 13, 1864, *OR*, ser. 4, 3:624–25, 724; Younger, *Inside the Confederate Government*, 175.

5. Woodworth, *Jefferson Davis*, 156; editorial comment, Crist, *Papers of Jefferson Davis*, 10:252; Connelly, *Autumn of Glory*, 411, 415, 438–39; Hallock, *Braxton Bragg*, 181, 186, 189.

6. Davis to Bragg, October 15, 1864; General Orders No. 1, Defenses of Wilmington, October 22, 1864; Bragg to Davis and copy to Lee, October 22, 1864; Bragg to Davis, October 25, 1864; and Bragg to Lee, October 25, 1864, *OR*, 42(3):1149, 1160, 1171–72.

7. Miers, *Rebel War Clerk's Diary*, 436, 447; Younger, *Inside the Confederate Government*, 177; Special Orders No. 269, Adjutant and Inspector General's Office, November 11, 1864, *OR*, 42(3):1209.

8. Sale memorandum, November 15, 1864; General Orders No. 1, November 17, 1864; Davis to Bragg, November 22, 1864; and Bragg to Davis, November 22, 1864, *OR*, 42(3):1217–18, 1225; Bragg to May, November 22, 1864, and Bragg to Sale, November 25, 1864, *OR*, 44:881, 895.

9. Seddon to Bragg, November 27, 1864, and Bragg to Sale, November 27, 30, 1864, *OR*, 44:901.

10. Davis to Bragg, December 13, 1864, and Bragg to Davis, December 17, 1864, *OR*, 42(3):1271, 1278; Bragg to Sale, December 13, 15, 1864, *OR*, 44:954, 958.

11. Miers, *Rebel War Clerk's Diary*, 461; Wiggins, *Journals of Josiah Gorgas*, 146; Crabtree and Patton, *"Journal of a Secesh Lady,"* 646.

12. Snead to [Price], January 10, 1865, *OR*, 48(1):1321; Brent to Beauregard, December 8, 1864, *OR*, 45(2):665.

13. Robert E. Tyler to Bragg, January 22, 1865, Braxton Bragg Papers, WRHS.

14. Sale to Bragg, January 26, 27, 1865, and Bragg to Sale, January 27, 1865, *OR*, 46(2):1142, 1153; Bragg to Davis, February 15, 1864 [1865], Towson Ellis Service Record, M331, NARA; Sale to Bragg, February 2, 8, 1865; Bragg to Davis, February 3, 1865; Bragg to Sale, February 3, 1865; and Bragg to Lee, February 9, 1865, *OR*, 47(2):1083, 1088, 1129, 1138.

15. Fonvielle, *Wilmington Campaign*, 93–172.

16. General Orders No. 17, Headquarters, Department of North Carolina, December 29, 1864, *OR*, 42(1):999.

17. Davis to Bragg, January 15, 1865; Davis to Bragg, January 16, 1865; and Bragg to Davis, January 16, 1865, *OR*, 46(2):1061, 1078; Bragg to Thomas Bragg, January 20, 1865, "Defence and Fall of Fort Fisher," 346–49; Fonvielle, *Wilmington Campaign*, 249–309.

18. Crabtree and Patton, *"Journal of a Secesh Lady,"* 663; Hallock, *Braxton Bragg*, 237, 240; Bragg to Davis, February 1, 1865, Crist, *Papers of Jefferson Davis*, 11:369.

19. Bragg to Thomas Bragg, January 20, 1865, "Defence and Fall of Fort Fisher," 349.

20. Fonvielle, *Wilmington Campaign*, 331–460; Bragg to Baker, February 21, 1865, *OR*, 47(2):1244.

21. Bragg to Beauregard, February 25, 1865, and Bragg to Davis, March 5, 1865, *OR*, 47(2):1279, 1328; Hallock, *Braxton Bragg*, 249–50. As late as April 7, Varina urged her husband not to send Bragg to the Trans-Mississippi. "I am satisfied that the country will be ruined by its intestine feuds if you do so," she wrote. Varina Davis to Jefferson Davis, April 7, 1865, Rowland, *Jefferson Davis*, 6:539.

22. Hallock, *Braxton Bragg*, 251–152; Bradley, *Last Stand*, 75.

23. Bragg to Johnston, March 8, 1865, *OR*, 47(1):1078.

24. Bradley, *Last Stand*, 442–44.

25. D. H. Hill to Johnston, March 16, 1865, Joseph E. Johnston Papers, CWM; Bradley, *Last Stand*, 301.

26. Bradley, *Last Stand*, 204–5, 222–23.

27. Ibid., 301–2.

28. Ibid., 232, 302, 412; S. J. Martin, *General Braxton Bragg*, 460–61; Johnston to Hoke, January 27, September 27, 1871, Robert F. Hoke Papers, SANC. McLaws did not indicate that he thought Bragg handled his troops badly at Bentonville. See Oeffinger, *Soldier's General*, 268–70.

29. Bragg to Davis, March 26, 1865, *OR*, 53:415–16.

30. Davis to Bragg, April 1, 1865, *OR*, 47(3):740.

31. Ibid.

32. Sale to Gordon, April 10, 1865, *OR*, 47(3):785; Davis to Bragg, April 20, 1865, Crist, *Papers of Jefferson Davis*, 11:551.

33. Davis to Bragg, April 24, 1865, *OR*, 47(3):836; Halcott Pride Jones Journal, March 24, April 27–May 5, 1865, SANC.

34. Wilson to Sherman, May 8, 1865, *OR*, 49(2):663; S. J. Martin, *General Braxton Bragg*, 462–65; Hallock, *Braxton Bragg*, 258.

35. Palmer to Bascom, May 12, 1865, *OR*, 49(1):550; S. J. Martin, *General Braxton Bragg*, 465.

36. Palmer to Bascom, May 12, 1865, *OR*, 49(1):550–51; Colton and Smith, *Column South*, 308–9.

37. Colton and Smith, *Column South*, 309–10.

38. Ibid., 310.

39. Smith to Wilson, May 19, 1865; Wilson to Smith, May 19, 1865; and Hough to Moore, May 24, 1865, *OR*, 49(2):840; Wilson to Seitz, December 14, 1919, Seitz, *Braxton Bragg*, 542.

Chapter Sixteen

1. S. J. Martin, *General Braxton Bragg*, 466; Hallock, *Braxton Bragg*, 260; Bragg to Alexander, December 10, 1865, Peter Wellington Alexander Papers, CU. John Bragg was more than the brother of a Confederate general. As an Alabama legislator, he was involved in

the state's transition from the Union as evidenced by information in John Bragg to McRae, January 21, 1861, Colin J. McRae Papers, ADAH.

2. Bragg to Alexander, December 10, 1865, Peter Wellington Alexander Papers, CU; Bragg to Walter, April 8, 1866, Harvey Washington Walter Papers, UNC; tax document, 1866, folder 17, John Bragg Papers, UNC.

3. Bragg to Walter, April 8, 1866, Harvey Washington Walter Papers, UNC. This letter has been published in Boom, "'We Sowed & We Have Reaped,'" 74–79.

4. Bragg to Walter, April 8, 1866, Harvey Washington Walter Papers, UNC.

5. Copy of unsigned letter to Bragg [July 17, 1866], and copy of Mrs. Joseph S. Jones et al. letter to Robert E. Lee, [July 17, 1866], Howard Jones Papers, SANC.

6. Hallock, *Braxton Bragg*, 260; Bragg to Walter, April 8, 1866, Harvey Washington Walter Papers, UNC; Bragg to Alexander, December 10, 1865, Peter Wellington Alexander Papers, CU.

7. Bragg to Sherman, January 25, 1867, William T. Sherman Papers, LC; Helm, "Gen. and Mrs. Braxton Bragg," 102–3; Allan C. Story to Bragg, May 13, 1870, March 8, 1872, Braxton Bragg Papers, MHM; Bragg to J. A. Furling, February 12, 1875, Braxton Bragg Letters, LSU; Hallock, *Braxton Bragg*, 261.

8. Bragg to M. G. Ludlow, April 15, 1869, Braxton Bragg Papers, DU; Stout, *Reminiscences of General Braxton Bragg*, 19.

9. Copy of Bragg to Jefferson Davis, December 1, 1869, Braxton Bragg Papers, RL; Hallock, *Braxton Bragg*, 261; Stout, *Reminiscences of General Braxton Bragg*, 19.

10. Copy of Bragg to Jefferson Davis, December 1, 1869; Bragg to Kenneth Baillio, June 6, 1870; and Bragg to W. C. Carrington, January 29, 1870, Braxton Bragg Papers, RL.

11. Bragg to W. S. Boyle, January 21, 1870, and Bragg to Will Bainbridge, January 27, 1870, Braxton Bragg Papers, RL.

12. Bragg to D. W. Adams, April 12, 1870, Confederate Personnel, Louisiana Research Collection, TU; W. W. Appleton to Sherman, December 10, 1875, William T. Sherman Papers, LC; Hallock, *Braxton Bragg*, 261.

13. Hallock, *Braxton Bragg*, 262; Stout, *Reminiscences of General Braxton Bragg*, 19.

14. Bragg to Daniel M. Frost, November 12, 1873, Graham-Frost Family Papers, MHM.

15. Bragg to Jones, February 24, 1875, Joseph Jones Papers, TU; Bragg to Chilton, March 30, 1876, Robert H. Chilton Collection, MOC; E. O. C. Ord to Sherman, June 2, 1876, William T. Sherman Papers, LC; Davis to Varina Howell Davis, March 31, 1876, Crist, *Papers of Jefferson Davis*, 13:362; Hallock, *Braxton Bragg*, 262; Stout, *Reminiscences of General Braxton Bragg*, 19.

16. Samuel B. Maxey to Bragg, September 16, 1876, Braxton Bragg Papers, MHM; Helm, "Gen. and Mrs. Braxton Bragg," 102; Hallock, *Braxton Bragg*, 263.

17. Bragg to Alexander, December 10, 1865, Peter Wellington Alexander Papers, CU; Bragg to Sherman, October 1, 1874, William T. Sherman Papers, LC; Samuel B. Maxey to Bragg, September 16, 1876, Braxton Bragg Papers, MHM.

18. Harwell, *Kate*, 139; James Patton Anderson to Bragg, April 16, 1867, Braxton Bragg Papers, MHM; James R. Chalmers to Davis, December 27, 1886, Rowland, *Jefferson Davis*, 9:516.

19. Randall L. Gibson to William Preston Johnston, March 1, 9, September 3, 1863, folder 9–10, 32, box 11, Albert Sidney and William Preston Johnston Papers, TU.

20. Randall L. Gibson to William Preston Johnston, November 26, 1872, folder 28, box 15; Gibson to Johnston, April 2, 1886, folder 7, box 25; and Gibson to friend, February 1, 1876, folder 17, box 3, Albert Sidney and William Preston Johnston Papers, TU.

21. Bragg to W. S. Boyle, August 3, 1870, Braxton Bragg Papers, RL.

22. Bragg to John C. Breckinridge, June 22, 1869, item 18575, container 269, Breckinridge Family Papers, LC.

23. Bragg to Chilton, March 30, 1876, Robert H. Chilton Collection, MOC; Bragg to Andrew G. Kellar, April 15, 1869, Braxton Bragg Letter, HNOC.

24. Bragg to D. W. Adams, April 12, 1870, Confederate Personnel, Louisiana Research Collection, TU; Bragg to Chilton, March 30, 1876, Robert H. Chilton Collection, MOC.

25. Bragg to Alexander, December 10, 1865, Peter Wellington Alexander Papers, CU; Bragg to Andrew G. Kellar, April 15, 1869, Braxton Bragg Letter, HNOC.

26. Stout, *Reminiscences*, 21; Henry D. Clayton to Bragg, May 11, 1874, Braxton Bragg Papers, MHM.

27. Hallock, *Braxton Bragg*, 264; Coulter, "What the South Has Done," 19–20; Bragg to Stout, June 20, 1870, Stout, "An Address concerning the History of the Medical Service," 442.

28. Davis to wife, January 24, 1866, Crist, *Papers of Jefferson Davis*, 12:101; Walthall to Davis, November 26, 1874, March 20, 1875, Crist, *Papers of Jefferson Davis*, 13:252, 268; Bragg to Varina Davis, September 11, 1866, Davis Family Collection, MOC; Helm, "Gen. and Mrs. Braxton Bragg," 104.

29. W. T. Walthall to Wright, October 1, 1880, Marcus Joseph Wright Papers, UNC.

30. Davis to Bragg, March 4, 1872; Bragg to Davis, March 14, 1872; Davis to William Preston Johnston, November 27, 1874; and Johnston to Davis, December 8, 1874, Crist, *Papers of Jefferson Davis*, 13:76–77, 252, 255; P. G. T. Beauregard to William Preston Johnston, March 9, 1877, Beauregard Papers, MOC; Bragg to William Preston Johnston, December 16, 1874, January 7, 1875, folder 27–28, box 16, Albert Sidney and William Preston Johnston Papers, TU; J. Davis, *Rise and Fall*, 2:59–60; C. L. Le Baron to Davis, May 16, 1887, Rowland *Jefferson Davis*, 9:561; T. H. Williams, *P. G. T. Beauregard*, 238; Beauregard to Roman, May 21, 1887, Alfred Roman Papers, LC; Roland, *Albert Sidney Johnston*, 353.

31. Bragg to Varina Davis, September 11, 1866, and Bragg to Davis, March 9, 1870, December 21, 1871, February 16, 1875, Davis Family Collection, MOC; editorial comment, Crist, *Papers of Jefferson Davis*, 12:278n.

32. Bragg to E. T. Sykes, February 8, 18, 1873, Confederate Military Leaders–Western Theater Collection, MOC. Reliable copies of both letters are in folder 18, J. F. H. Claiborne Papers, UNC.

33. Bragg to E. T. Sykes, February 8, 1873, Confederate Military Leaders–Western Theater Collection, MOC.

34. Bragg to E. T. Sykes, February 8, 18, 1873, Confederate Military Leaders–Western Theater Collection, MOC. Breckinridge's biographer does not accept the charge that the general was drunk during the Chattanooga campaign. He points out that Bragg provided the only concrete evidence for it and concludes that "while it cannot positively be denied that Breckinridge was drunk during those four days, Bragg's charge is hardly sufficient to warrant the assumption that the Kentuckian was under such influence." W. C. Davis, *Breckinridge*, 394–96.

35. Bragg to E. T. Sykes, February 18, 1873, Confederate Military Leaders–Western Theater Collection, MOC; Sykes, "The Army at Dalton," 4–5; Kinloch Falconer to E. T. Sykes, February 7, 1873, Confederate Military Leaders–Western Theater Collection, MOC.

36. Seitz, *Braxton Bragg*, 543; Hallock, *Braxton Bragg*, 265.

37. Helm, "Gen. and Mrs. Braxton Bragg," 102; Stanford E. Chaillé to Mrs. Bragg, November 22, 1876, Braxton Bragg Papers, WRHS.

38. Felix H. Robertson to John Fee, September 27, 1876, Braxton Bragg Papers, RL; Seitz, *Braxton Bragg*, 543–44; T. K. Erwin to Mrs. Bragg, October 9, 1876, and Ann Toul-

min Hunter to T. K. Erwin, October 9, 1876, Braxton Bragg Papers, USMA; bill from Mr. McDonald, marble dealer, September 21, 1877, Eliza Brooks Bragg Papers, CHM; Elise Bragg letter quoted in *Confederate Veteran*, 7:296.

39. Helm, "Gen. and Mrs. Braxton Bragg," 102–3.

40. William Preston Johnston to Wright, October 26, 1878, and W. T. Walthall to Wright, October 1, 1880, Marcus Joseph Wright Papers, UNC.

41. W. T. Walthall to Wright, July 30, 1878; William Preston Johnston to Wright, October 30, 1880, and March 3, 1881; and Elise Bragg to Wright, March 12, July 5, 1881, Marcus Joseph Wright Papers, UNC.

42. Davis to William Preston Johnston, August 25, 1877, and Davis speech, July 10, 1878, Crist, *Papers of Jefferson Davis*, 13:430, 494.

43. John Bragg to Samuel A' Court Ashe, July 30, 1881, J. Bragg Letter, SANC.

44. "Gen. Braxton Bragg's Old Servant," 233.

45. Seitz, *Braxton Bragg*, 544; "Mrs. Braxton Bragg," 586.

Conclusion

1. Harwell, *Kate*, 103, 111; Stout, *Reminiscences*, 16.

2. Editorial comment, Crist, *Papers of Jefferson Davis*, 8:63n; diary, March 17, 1862, Thomas Bragg Papers, UNC; Davis to Braxton Bragg, February 19, 1872, Crist, *Papers of Jefferson Davis*, 13:74.

3. Horsman, *Josiah Nott*, 1–2, 266–67, 273, 281–82, 335; John Forsyth, "Gen. Bragg's Kentucky Campaign," *Mobile Advertiser and Register*, November 11, 16, 1862; [Forsyth], *Memoranda of Facts*, not paginated.

4. Lowry and Laska, *Confederate Death Sentences*, 49–53.

5. Ibid., 53.

6. Ridley, "Camp Scenes around Dalton," 66–67; Erwin to mother, May 5, 1864, George Phifer Erwin Papers, UNC; Owens, "Penalties for Desertion," 235.

7. Lowry and Laska, *Confederate Death Sentences*, 3–4.

8. Jewett, *Rise and Fall of the Confederacy*, 177.

9. Stephenson, "Missionary Ridge," 17, 20–21; N. C. Hughes, *Civil War Memoir*, 152; Watkins, *Co. Aytch*, 48–49, 118, 125, 129.

10. Cater, *As It Was*, 136, 165; Carleton, "Record," 259.

11. Duke, *History of Morgan's Cavalry*, 343; Buck, *Cleburne and His Command*, 186.

12. Hill, "Chickamauga," 639, 640n, 646; A. Anderson, "Campaign and Battle of Chickamauga," 397; D. H. Hill to Anderson, August 11, 1884, box 2, folder 8, Archer Anderson Collection, MOC.

13. Gallagher, *Fighting for the Confederacy*, 307.

14. W. T. Martin, "Defence of General Bragg's Conduct," 201–2.

15. Tower, *A Carolinian Goes to War*, 158.

16. Stout, *Reminiscences*, 21–22.

17. Ibid., 7.

18. Ibid., 8.

19. N. C. Hughes, *Liddell's Record*, 13, 29–31, 113–14, 116–17.

20. Taylor, *Destruction and Reconstruction*, 125, 126, 128.

21. Ibid., 124–26.

22. N. C. Hughes, *Liddell's Record*, 106.

23. Grant, *Memoirs*, 449–50.

24. Sherman, "Old Shady," 365.

25. Helm, "Gen. and Mrs. Braxton Bragg," 103–4; Tunno, "Criticism of Gen Bragg at Shiloh," 116.

26. "Tributes to Gen. Braxton Bragg," 132–33; Tunno, "Criticism of Gen Bragg at Shiloh," 116; Helm, "Gen. and Mrs. Braxton Bragg," 104.

27. Helm, "Gen. and Mrs. Braxton Bragg," 104; Stiles, "Missionary Ridge," 14; Taylor, *Destruction and Reconstruction*, 125–126; Buck, *Cleburne and His Command*, 186.

28. Hallock, *Braxton Bragg*, 4–5, 25, 33, 270–72; Noe, *Perryville*, 18, 104–6, 124–25.

29. Connelly, *Autumn of Glory*, 278; Hallock, *Braxton Bragg*, 268; Stout, *Reminiscences*, 23.

30. Tactical success days were counted as April 6, 1862, October 8, 1862, December 31, 1862, and September 20, 1863. Tactical failure days were counted as April 7, 1862, January 2, 1863, November 23, 24, 25, 1863, July 20, 22, 28, 1864, August 31, 1864, September 1, 1864, November 30, 1864, December 15, 16, 1864, and March 19, 1864. This was guided by a desire to choose engagements that came close to being general battles rather than small fights involving only part of the Army of the Mississippi/Army of Tennessee. Army commanders had more opportunity to influence the outcome of a general battle than that of a local, impromptu battle of the kind that often happened during the Atlanta campaign, such as New Hope Church or Pickett's Mill.

31. Connelly, *Army of the Heartland*, 182; Hay, "Braxton Bragg," 313; Woodworth, *Jefferson Davis*, 92.

32. Cooper, *Jefferson Davis*, 52–53; Lee to Davis, August 8, 1863, and Davis to Lee, August 11, 1863, Rowland, *Jefferson Davis*, 5:585–86, 589.

33. Davis to Pemberton, August 9, 1863, Rowland, *Jefferson Davis*, 5:588.

34. Scarborough, *Diary of Edmund Ruffin*, 2:676–77.

Bibliography

Archives

Abraham Lincoln Presidential Library, Springfield, Illinois
    John McAuley Palmer Collection
    Lyman Trumbull Collection
Alabama Department of Archives and History, Montgomery
    Robert Lewis Bliss Papers
    Edward Norphlet Brown Letters
    Newton N. Davis Papers
    Stouten Hubert Dent Papers
    Bolling Hall Family Papers
    Colin J. McRae Papers
Archives of Michigan, Lansing
    Arza Bartholomew Letters, George G. Christman Collection
Auburn University, Special Collections and Archives, Auburn, Alabama
    John Crittenden Collection
    George Family Papers
    Chicago History Museum, Chicago
    Eliza Brooks Bragg Papers
    Briggs-Mitchell Family Papers
College of William and Mary, Special Collections Research Center,
      Williamsburg, Virginia
    Joseph E. Johnston Papers
Columbia University, Rare Book and Manuscript Library, New York
    Peter Wellington Alexander Papers
Duke University, Rubenstein Rare Book and Manuscript Library, Durham,
      North Carolina
    Alfred W. Bell Papers
    Braxton Bragg Papers
    John Buie Papers
    Bullock Family Papers
    Ellison Capers Papers
    Clement Claiborne Clay Papers
    William Culbertson Papers
    C. William Fackler Papers
    John Brandon Guthrie Papers
    Joseph E. Johnston Papers

Charles Colcock Jones Papers
James Longstreet Papers
Elisha A. Peterson Papers
Charles Todd Quintard Papers
Thomas Jenkins Semmes Papers
W. H. T. Walker Papers
Emory University, Manuscript, Archives, Rare Book Library, Atlanta, Georgia
Andrew Jackson Neal Papers
Filson Historical Society, Louisville, Kentucky
J. Stoddard Johnston Papers
Johnston Family Papers
Henry Watterson Papers
Gilder Lehrman Institute of American History, New York
Braxton Bragg Letters
Jefferson Davis Letter
Henry J. Hunt Letter
Harvard University, Houghton Library, Cambridge, Massachusetts
Frederick M. Dearborn Collection
Historic New Orleans Collection, New Orleans, Louisiana
Braxton Bragg Letter
Hugh S. Gookin Letter (Washington Artillery Letter)
William C. D. Vaught Letters
Historical Society of Pennsylvania, Philadelphia
Edward Needles Kirk Correspondence
Indiana Historical Society, Indianapolis
Lew Wallace Papers
Indiana University, Lilly Library, Bloomington
Crist Manuscripts
Library of Congress, Manuscript Division, Washington, D.C.
Braxton Bragg Papers
Breckinridge Family Papers
Samuel Chester Reid Family Papers
Alfred Roman Papers
William T. Sherman Papers
George Hay Stuart Papers
Louis Trezevant Wigfall Family Papers
Louisiana State University, Louisiana and Lower Mississippi Valley Collections,
    Special Collections, Baton Rouge
Braxton Bragg Letters
Butler Family Papers
James R. Chalmers Letter
Genl Bragg Grand March. P. Rivinac. New Orleans: A. E. Blackmar and Brother, 1861
Kent-Amacker Family Papers
Massachusetts Historical Society, Boston
Horace Newton Fisher Papers
Miami University, Walter Havighurst Special Collections, Oxford, Ohio
Samuel Richey Collection of the Southern Confederacy
Mississippi Department of Archives and History, Jackson
Lea Family Civil War Letters

Mississippi State University, Special Collections, Starkville
    Horn Collection
    John H. Marshall Civil War Letters
    Rice Family Papers
Missouri History Museum, St. Louis
    Braxton Bragg Papers
    Graham-Frost Family Papers
Museum of the Confederacy, Richmond, Virginia
    Archer Anderson Collection
    Beauregard Papers
    Robert H. Chilton Collection
    Confederate Military Leaders Collection
    Confederate Military Leaders–Western Theater Collection
    Davis Family Collection
National Archives and Records Administration, Washington, D.C.
    Compiled Service Records of Confederate General and Staff Officers,
        and Non-Regimental Enlisted Men, M331, RG109
        Braxton Bragg Service Record
        George William Brent Service Record
        Towson Ellis Service Record
        Jillson P. Johnson Service Record
        William Preston Johnston Service Record
        John B. Sale Service Record
        John J. Walker Service Record
    Compiled Service Records of Confederate Soldiers Who Served in Organizations
        from the State of Alabama, M311, RG109
        Thomas H. Watts Service Record, 17th Alabama
    Letters Sent, Chief of Engineers, Western Department, 1861–1862, and General
        Orders and Letters, Headquarters, Army of Tennessee, 1862–1864, Chapter 3,
        Volume 8, RG109
Navarro College, Pearce Civil War Collection, Corsicana, Texas
    Seth Barton Papers
    James Cooper Papers
    Willis Jones Papers
    William McGregor Papers
    Thomas Chinn Robertson Papers
Rosenberg Library, Galveston and Texas History Center, Galveston, Texas
    Braxton Bragg Papers
Rutherford B. Hayes Presidential Center, Fremont, Ohio
    Robert H. Caldwell Papers
State Archives of North Carolina, Raleigh
    J. Bragg Letter
    James B. Gordon Papers
    Robert F. Hoke Papers
    Halcott Pride Jones Journal
    Howard Jones Papers
    A. G. McGrath Letter
Stones River National Battlefield, Murfreesboro, Tennessee
    George H. Berry Letter, 89th Illinois Regimental File

William A. Brown Memoirs, Stanford's Mississippi Battery Regimental File
Ambrose Doss Letter, 19th Alabama Regimental File
A. T. Gay Letter, 31st Tennessee Regimental File
G. E. Goudelock Letter, 2nd Arkansas Regimental File
Jacques Martin Letters, 6th Ohio Regimental File
Samuel A. McClelland Letter, 78th Pennsylvania Regimental File
William Roberts Stuckey Letter, 42nd Indiana Regimental File
Henry Watson Letter, 10th Texas Cavalry Regimental File
Tennessee State Library and Archives, Nashville
    Theodore Gillard Trimmier Papers
Tulane University, Special Collections, New Orleans, Louisiana
    Confederate Personnel, Louisiana Research Collection
    Albert Sidney and William Preston Johnston Papers, Louisiana Research
        Collection
    Joseph Jones Papers, Louisiana Research Collection
United States Military Academy, Special Collections, West Point, New York
    Braxton Bragg Papers
University of Alabama, W. S. Hoole Special Collections Library, Tuscaloosa
    Benjamin Hurd Letters
University of Arkansas, Special Collections, Fayetteville
    Herbert Earle Buchanan Family Papers
University of Florida, Special and Area Studies Collections, Gainesville
    James Patton Anderson Papers
    Augustus O. McDonall Papers
University of Kentucky, Special Collections, Lexington
    Braxton Bragg Letters
University of North Carolina, Southern History Collection, Chapel Hill
    Taylor Beatty Diary
    John Bragg Papers
    Thomas Bragg Papers
    Given Campbell Papers
    J. F. H. Claiborne Papers
    Thomas Claiborne Papers
    D. Coleman Diary
    George Phifer Erwin Papers
    Jackson and McKinne Family Papers
    Stephen D. Lee Papers
    Samuel Henry Lockett Papers
    William Whann Mackall Papers
    James W. Patton Papers
    Leonidas Polk Papers
    Benedict Joseph Semmes Papers
    Edmund Kirby Smith Papers
    Samuel Hollingsworth Stout Papers
    John Kennedy Street Papers
    David Urquhart Letter and Book
    Harvey Washington Walter Papers
    Marcus Joseph Wright Papers

University of South Carolina, South Caroliniana Library, Columbia
    James Morris Bivings Papers
    Kerrison Family Papers
University of the South, Department of Archives, Sewanee, Tennessee
    Leonidas Polk Papers
University of Tennessee, Special Collections, Chattanooga
    Colville and Paine Family Letters
University of Tennessee, Special Collections, Knoxville
    Edwin Hansford Rennolds Sr. Papers
University of Texas, Dolph Briscoe Center for American History, Austin
    Braxton Bragg Papers
    W. L. Gammage Letter, Civil War Miscellany
    Louis Trezevant Wigfall Papers
University of Virginia, Special Collections, Charlottesville
    Peter Family Papers
Virginia Historical Society, Richmond
    Giles Buckner Cooke Diary and Papers
Western Reserve Historical Society, Cleveland, Ohio
    Braxton Bragg Papers

Newspapers

Atlanta Confederacy	*Mobile Tribune*	*Richmond Whig*
Chattanooga Daily Rebel	*Montgomery Advertiser*	*Savannah News*
Knoxville Register	*Nashville Banner*	*Selma Morning Reporter*
Memphis Daily Appeal	*Richmond Enquirer*	*Telegraph (Macon)*
Mobile Advertiser and	*Richmond Examiner*	*Winchester Bulletin*
Register	*Richmond Sentinel*	

Websites

Van Zante, Gary. "Theodore Lilienthal." In *KnowLa Encyclopedia of Louisiana*, edited by David Johnson. December 14, 2010. http://www.knowla.org/entry/806/. Accessed June 17, 2015.

Eric Wittenberg Comments on Nathan Bedford Forrest. http://civilwarcavalry.com/?p=21. Accessed December 7, 2013.

Books and Articles

Anderson, Archer. "Campaign and Battle of Chickamauga." *Southern Historical Society Papers* 9 (1881): 385–418.

Anderson, John Q., ed. *Brokenburn: The Journal of Kate Stone, 1861–1868*. Baton Rouge: Louisiana State University Press, 1955.

Ashdown, Paul, and Edward Caudill. *The Myth of Nathan Bedford Forrest*. Lanham, Md.: Rowman and Littlefield, 2005.

Avery, H. C. "Memorial Address on the Life and Character of Lieut. General D. H. Hill." *Southern Historical Society Papers* 21 (1893): 133–50.

Bearss, Edwin C. "Civil War Operations in and around Pensacola." *Florida Historical Quarterly* 36, no. 4 (October 1957): 125–65.

Beatty, John. *Memoirs of a Volunteer, 1861–1863*. New York: W. W. Norton, 1946.

Blegen, Theodore G., ed. *The Civil War Letters of Colonel Hans Christian Heg*. Northfield, MN: Norwegian-American Historical Association, 1936.

Boom, Aaron M., ed. "'We Sowed & We Have Reaped': A Postwar Letter from Braxton Bragg." *Journal of Southern History* 31, no. 1 (February 1965): 74–79.

Bradley, Mark L. *Last Stand in the Carolinas: The Battle of Bentonville*. Campbell, Calif.: Savas Woodbury, 1996.

Bridges, Hal. *Lee's Maverick General: Daniel Harvey Hill*. New York: McGraw-Hill, 1961.

Buck, Irving A. *Cleburne and His Command*. Jackson, Tenn.: McCowat-Mercer Press, 1959.

Burnett, Lonnie A. *The Pen Makes a Good Sword: John Forsyth of the Mobile Register*. Tuscaloosa: University of Alabama Press, 2006.

Carleton, Mark T., ed. "A Record of the Late Fourth Louisiana Reg't, C.S.A. It's Service, ETC." *Louisiana History* 10, no. 3 (Summer 1969): 255–60.

Castel, Albert. *Decision in the West: The Atlanta Campaign of 1864*. Lawrence: University Press of Kansas, 1992.

———. "Mars and the Reverend Longstreet; or, Attacking and Dying in the Civil War." *Civil War History* 33, no. 2 (June 1987): 103–14.

Cater, Douglas. *As It Was: Reminiscences of a Soldier of the Third Texas Cavalry and the Nineteenth Louisiana Infantry*. Abilene, Tex.: State House Press, 2007.

Claiborne, Thomas. "Battle of Perryville, KY." *Confederate Veteran* 16 (1908): 225–27.

Clay, H. B. "'On the Right at Murfreesboro.'" *Confederate Veteran* 21 (1913): 588–89.

Clift, G. Glenn, ed. *The Private War of Lizzie Hardin: A Kentucky Confederate Girl's Diary of the Civil War in Kentucky, Virginia, Tennessee, Alabama, and Georgia*. Frankfort: Kentucky Historical Society, 1963.

Colton, J. Ferrell, and Antoinette G. Smith, eds. *Column South: With the Fifteenth Pennsylvania Cavalry from Antietam to the Capture of Jefferson Davis*. Flagstaff, Ariz.: Northland Press, 1960.

Connelly, Thomas Lawrence. *Army of the Heartland: The Army of Tennessee, 1861–1862*. Baton Rouge: Louisiana State University Press, 1967.

———. *Autumn of Glory: The Army of Tennessee, 1862–1865*. Baton Rouge: Louisiana State University Press, 1971.

Cooper, William J., Jr. *Jefferson Davis and the Civil War Era*. Baton Rouge: Louisiana State University Press, 2008.

Coulter, E. Merton. "What the South Has Done about Its History." *Journal of Southern History* 2, no. 1 (February 1936): 3–28.

Cozzens, Peter. *No Better Place to Die: The Battle of Stones River*. Urbana: University of Illinois Press, 1990.

———. *The Shipwreck of Their Hopes: The Battles for Chattanooga*. Urbana: University of Illinois Press, 1994.

———. *This Terrible Sound: The Battle of Chickamauga*. Urbana: University of Illinois Press, 1992.

Crabtree, Beth G., and James W. Patton, eds. *"Journal of a Secesh Lady": The Diary of Catherine Ann Devereux Edmondston, 1860–1866*. Raleigh: Division of Archives and History, 1979.

Crist, Lynda Lasswell, ed. *The Papers of Jefferson Davis*. 17 vols. Baton Rouge: Louisiana State University Press, 1971–2008.

Crittenden, Thomas L. "The Union Left at Stone's River." In *Battles and Leaders of the Civil War*, vol. 3, edited by Robert Underwood Johnson and Clarence Clough Buel, 632–34. New York: Thomas Yoseloff, 1956.

Cutrer, Thomas W., ed. *Our Trust Is in the God of Battles: The Civil War Letters of Robert Franklin Bunting, Chaplain, Terry's Texas Rangers, C.S.A.* Knoxville: University of Tennessee Press, 2006.

Cutrer, Thomas W., and T. Michael Parrish, eds. *Brothers in Gray: The Civil War Letters of the Pierson Family.* Baton Rouge: Louisiana State University Press, 1997.

Daniel, Larry J. *Battle of Stones River: The Forgotten Conflict between the Confederate Army of Tennessee and the Union Army of the Cumberland.* Baton Rouge: Louisiana State University Press, 2012.

———. *Shiloh: The Battle that Changed the Civil War.* New York: Simon and Schuster, 1997.

Davis, Jefferson. *The Rise and Fall of the Confederate Government.* 2 vols. New York: Thomas Yoseloff, 1958.

Davis, William C. *Breckinridge: Statesman, Soldier, Symbol.* Baton Rouge: Louisiana State University Press, 1974.

"Defence and Fall of Fort Fisher." *Southern Historical Society Papers* 10 (1882): 346–49.

Duke, Basil W. *History of Morgan's Cavalry.* Cincinnati: Miami Printing, 1867.

Dyer, John P. *"Fightin' Joe" Wheeler.* Baton Rouge: Louisiana State University Press, 1941.

Elliott, Sam Davis, ed. *Doctor Quintard, Chaplain C.S.A. and Second Bishop of Tennessee: The Memoir and Civil War Diary of Charles Todd Quintard.* Baton Rouge: Louisiana State University Press, 2003.

———. *Isham G. Harris of Tennessee: Confederate Governor and United States Senator.* Baton Rouge: Louisiana State University Press, 2010.

———. *Soldier of Tennessee: General Alexander P. Stewart and the Civil War in the West.* Baton Rouge: Louisiana State University Press, 1999.

Evans, Robert G., ed. *The 16th Mississippi Infantry: Civil War Letters and Reminiscences.* Jackson: University Press of Mississippi, 2002.

Fleming, Walter L., ed. *General W. T. Sherman as College President.* Cleveland, Ohio: Arthur H. Clark, 1912.

Follett, Richard. *The Sugar Masters: Planters and Slaves in Louisiana's Cane World, 1820–1860.* Baton Rouge: Louisiana State University Press, 2005.

Fonvielle, Chris E., Jr. *The Wilmington Campaign: Last Rays of Departing Hope.* Mechanicsburg, Pa.: Stackpole Books, 1997.

Forsyth, John. "Gen. Bragg's Kentucky Campaign." *Mobile Advertiser and Register,* November 11, 16, 1862.

[———]. *Memoranda of Facts Bearing on the Kentucky Campaign.*

Franklin, Ann York. Compiler. *The Civil War Diaries of Capt. Alfred Tyler Fielder, 12th Tennessee Regiment Infantry, Company B, 1861–65.* Louisville, Ky.: Ann York Franklin, 1996.

Fremantle, Arthur James Lyon. *Three Months in the Southern States: April–June, 1863.* Lincoln: University of Nebraska Press, 1991.

Gallagher, Gary W., ed. *Fighting for the Confederacy: The Personal Recollections of General Edward Porter Alexander.* Chapel Hill: University of North Carolina Press, 1989.

[Garesche, Louis]. *Biography of Lieut. Col. Julius P. Garesche, Assistant Adjutant-General, U.S. Army.* Philadelphia: J. B. Lippincott, 1887.

"Gen. Braxton Bragg's Old Servant." *Confederate Veteran* 8 (1900): 233.

Goff, Richard D. *Confederate Supply.* Durham, N.C.: Duke University Press, 1969.

Goggin, James N. "Chickamauga—A Reply to Major Sykes." *Southern Historical Society Papers* 12 (1884): 219–24.

Goldman, Pauline S., ed. "Letters from Three Members of Terry's Texas Rangers, 1861–1865." M.A. thesis, University of Texas, 1930. www.terrystexasrangers.org, Accessed February 23, 2009.

Gow, June I. "Chiefs of Staff in the Army of Tennessee under Braxton Bragg." *Tennessee Historical Quarterly* 27, no. 4 (Winter 1968): 341–60.

———. "Theory and Practice in Confederate Military Administration." *Military Affairs* 39, no. 3 (October 1975): 119–23.

Grant, Ulysses S. *Memoirs and Selected Letters.* 2 vols. in 1. New York: Viking, 1990.

Hafendorfer, Kenneth A., ed. *Civil War Journal of William L. Trask: Confederate Sailor and Soldier.* Louisville, Ky.: KH Press, 2003.

Hallock, Judith Lee. *Braxton Bragg and Confederate Defeat.* Vol. 2. Tuscaloosa: University of Alabama Press, 1991.

———, ed. *The Civil War Letters of Joshua K. Callaway.* Athens: University of Georgia Press, 1997.

Hamilton, J. G. DeRoulhac, ed. *The Papers of Thomas Ruffin.* 4 vols. Raleigh: Edwards and Broughton, 1920.

Harwell, Richard Barksdale, ed. *Kate: The Journal of a Confederate Nurse.* Baton Rouge: Louisiana State University Press, 1959.

Hascall, Milo S. "Personal Recollections and Experiences Concerning the Battle of Stone River." In *Military Essays and Recollections: Papers Read before the Commandery of the State of Illinois, Military Order of the Loyal Legion of the United States*, 4:148–70. Chicago: Cozzens and Beaton, 1907.

Haughton, Andrew. *Training, Tactics and Leadership in the Confederate Army of Tennessee: Seeds of Failure.* Portland, Ore.: Frank Cass, 2000.

Hay, Thomas Robson. "Braxton Bragg and the Southern Confederacy." *Georgia Historical Quarterly* 9, no. 4 (December 1925): 267–316.

———. "The Campaign and Battle of Chickamauga." *Georgia Historical Quarterly* 7, no. 3 (September 1923): 213–50.

———. "Davis, Bragg, and Johnston in the Atlanta Campaign." *Georgia Historical Quarterly* 8, no. 1 (March 1924): 38–48.

———. "The Davis-Hood-Johnston Controversy." *Mississippi Valley Historical Review* 11, no. 1 (June 1924): 54–84.

Heard, Jesse Burke, ed. *Terry Ranger Writes Home: Letters of Pvt. Benjamin F. Burke Written While in Terry's Texas Rangers, 1861–1864.* N.p.: n.p., 1965. www.terrystexasrangers.org. Accessed February 23, 2009.

Helm, Mrs. Ben Hardin. "Gen. and Mrs. Braxton Bragg." *Confederate Veteran* 4 (1896): 102–4.

Hess, Earl J. *Banners to the Breeze: The Kentucky Campaign, Corinth, and Stones River.* Lincoln: University of Nebraska Press, 2000.

———. *The Civil War in the West: Victory and Defeat from the Appalachians to the Mississippi.* Chapel Hill: University of North Carolina Press, 2012.

———. *Kennesaw Mountain: Sherman, Johnston, and the Atlanta Campaign.* Chapel Hill: University of North Carolina Press, 2013.

———. *The Knoxville Campaign: Burnside and Longstreet in East Tennessee.* Knoxville: University of Tennessee Press, 2012.

———. *The Rifle Musket in Civil War Combat: Reality and Myth.* Lawrence: University Press of Kansas, 2008.

Hill, Daniel H. "Chickamauga—The Great Battle of the West." In *Battles and Leaders of the Civil War*, vol. 3, edited by Robert Underwood Johnson and Clarence Clough Buel, 638–62. New York: Thomas Yoseloff, 1956.

Hood, J. B. *Advance and Retreat: Personal Experiences in the United States and Confederate States Armies.* Philadelphia: Burk and M'Fetridge, 1880.

Horn, Stanley F. *The Army of Tennessee: A Military History*. Indianapolis: Bobbs-Merrill, 1941.

Horsman, Reginald. *Josiah Nott of Mobile: Southerner, Physician, and Racial Theorist*. Baton Rouge: Louisiana State University Press, 1987.

Hughes, Nathaniel Cheairs, Jr., ed. *The Civil War Memoir of Philip Daingerfield Stephenson, D.C.* Conway: University of Central Arkansas Press, 1995.

———. *General William J. Hardee: Old Reliable*. Baton Rouge: Louisiana State University Press, 1965.

———, ed. *Liddell's Record: St. John Richardson Liddell, Brigadier General, CSA, Staff Officer and Brigade Commander, Army of Tennessee*. Dayton, Ohio: Morningside, 1985.

Hughes, Robert M. "Some War Letters of General Joseph E. Johnston." *Journal of the Military Service Institution of the United States* 50, no. 175 (January–February 1912): 318–28.

Ingham, Howard M. "Captain Valentine Merriwether M'Gehee." *Publications of the Arkansas Historical Association* 4 (1917): 140–51.

Jewett, Clayton E., ed. *Rise and Fall of the Confederacy: The Memoirs of Senator Williamson S. Oldham, CSA*. Columbia: University of Missouri Press, 2006.

Johnston, J. Stoddard. "Sketch of Theodore O'Hara." *Register of the Kentucky Historical Society* 11, no. 33 (September 1913): 67–72.

Journal of the Congress of the Confederate States of America. 7 vols. New York: Kraus Reprint, 1968.

Keyes, E. D. *Fifty Years' Observation of Men and Events, Civil and Military*. New York: Charles Scribner's Sons, 1884.

Kniffin, Gilbert C. "The Battle of Stone's River." In *Battles and Leaders of the Civil War*, vol. 3, edited by Robert Underwood Johnson and Clarence Clough Buel, 613–32. New York: Thomas Yoseloff, 1956.

LeMonnier, Y. R. "Gen. Leonidas Polk at Chickamauga." *Confederate Veteran* 24 (1916): 17–19.

Little, George, and James R. Maxwell. *A History of Lumsden's Battery, C.S.A.* Tuscaloosa, Alabama: R. E. Rhodes Chapter, United Daughters of the Confederacy, n.d.

Lockett, S. H. "Surprise and Withdrawal at Shiloh." In *Battles and Leaders of the Civil War*, vol. 1, edited by Robert Underwood Johnson and Clarence Clough Buel, 604–6. New York: Thomas Yoseloff, 1956.

Longacre, Edward G. *A Soldier to the Last: Maj. Gen. Joseph Wheeler in Blue and Gray*. Washington, D.C.: Potomac Books, 2007.

Longstreet, James. *From Manassas to Appomattox: Memoirs of the Civil War in America*. Bloomington: Indiana University Press, 1960.

Losson, Christopher. "Mutual Antagonists: Braxton Bragg, Frank Cheatham, and the Army of Tennessee." In *Border Wars: The Civil War in Tennessee and Kentucky*, edited by Kent T. Dollar, Larry H. Whiteaker, and W. Calvin Dickinson, 214–37. Kent, Ohio: Kent State University Press, 2015.

Lowe, Richard, ed. *A Texas Cavalry Officer's Civil War: The Diary and Letters of James C. Bates*. Baton Rouge: Louisiana State University Press, 1999.

Lowry, Thomas P., and Lewis Laska. *Confederate Death Sentences: A Reference Guide*. N.p.: Booksurge, 2008.

Lytle, Andrew. *Bedford Forrest and His Critter Company*. New York: McDowell, Obolensky, 1960.

Mackall, William W. *A Son's Recollections of His Father*. New York: E. P. Dutton, 1930.

Malone, Thomas H. *Memoir of Thomas H. Malone: An Autobiography Written for His Children*. Nashville: Baird-Ward, 1928.

Martin, Samuel J. *General Braxton Bragg, C.S.A.* Jefferson, N.C.: McFarland, 2011.

Martin, W. T. "A Defence of General Bragg's Conduct at Chickamauga." *Southern Historical Society Papers* 11 (1883): 201–6.

Mathes, J. Harvey. *General Forrest.* New York: Appleton, 1902.

Maury, Dabney Herndon. *Recollections of a Virginian in the Mexican, Indian, and Civil Wars.* New York: Charles Scribner's Sons, 1894.

McBride, Mary Gorton, and Ann Mathison McLaurin. *Randall Lee Gibson of Louisiana: Confederate General and New South Reformer.* Baton Rouge: Louisiana State University Press, 2007.

McDonough, James Lee. *Shiloh—In Hell before Night.* Knoxville: University of Tennessee Press, 1977.

———. *Stones River—Bloody Winter in Tennessee.* Knoxville: University of Tennessee Press, 1980.

McMurry, Richard M. *John Bell Hood and the War for Southern Independence.* Lexington: University Press of Kentucky, 1982.

———, ed. *An Uncompromising Secessionist: The Civil War of George Knox Miller, Eighth (Wade's) Confederate Cavalry.* Tuscaloosa: University of Alabama Press, 2007.

McWhiney, Grady. *Braxton Bragg and Confederate Defeat.* Vol. 1, *Field Command.* New York: Columbia University Press, 1969.

McWhiney, Grady, and Perry D. Jamieson. *Attack and Die: Civil War Military Tactics and the Southern Heritage.* Tuscaloosa: University of Alabama Press, 1982.

Mendoza, Alexander. "The Censure of D. H. Hill: Daniel Harvey Hill and the Chickamauga Campaign." In *The Chickamauga Campaign,* edited by Steven E. Woodworth, 68–83. Carbondale: Southern Illinois University Press, 2010.

Miers, Earl Schenck, ed. *A Rebel War Clerk's Diary.* New York: Sagamore Press, 1958.

Moore, Albert Burton. *Conscription and Conflict in the Confederacy.* New York: Macmillan, 1924.

Morris, Roy. "The Chattanooga Daily Rebel." *Civil War Times Illustrated* 23, no. 7 (November 1984): 16–18, 20–24.

Morton, John Watson. *The Artillery of Nathan Bedford Forrest's Cavalry.* Nashville: M. E. Church, 1909.

Morton, M. B. "Historic Conference between President Davis, General Bragg and His Corps Commanders." *Nashville Banner,* December 4, 1909.

———. "Last Surviving Lieutenant General." *Confederate Veteran* 17 (1909): 61–64, 83–85.

"Mrs. Braxton Bragg." *Confederate Veteran* 16 (1908): 586.

Noe, Kenneth W. *Perryville: This Grand Havoc of Battle.* Lexington: University Press of Kentucky, 2001.

Oeffinger, John C, ed. *A Soldier's General: The Civil War Letters of Major General Lafayette McLaws.* Chapel Hill: University of North Carolina Press, 2002.

O'Reilly, Francis Augustin. *The Fredericksburg Campaign: Winter War on the Rappahannock.* Baton Rouge: Louisiana State University Press, 2003.

Otey, Mercer. "Story of Our Great War." *Confederate Veteran* 8 (1900): 342–43.

Owens, Thomas. "Penalties for Desertion." *Confederate Veteran* 2 (1894): 235.

Parks, Joseph Howard. *General Edmund Kirby Smith, C.S.A.* Baton Rouge: Louisiana State University Press, 1954.

———. *General Leonidas Polk, C.S.A.: The Fighting Bishop.* Baton Rouge: Louisiana State University Press, 1962.

Phillips, Ulrich B., ed. *Correspondence of Robert Toombs, Alexander H. Stephens, and Howell Cobb: Annual Report of the American Historical Association for the Year 1911.* 2 vols. Washington, D.C.: Government Printing Office, 1913.

Polk, W. M. "General Bragg and the Chickamauga Campaign—A Reply to General Martin." *Southern Historical Society Papers* 12 (1884): 378–90.

———. *Leonidas Polk: Bishop and General.* 2 vols. London: Longmans, Green, 1915.

Post, Lydia Minturn, ed. *Soldier's Letters, from Camp, Battle-Field and Prison.* New York: Bunce and Huntington, 1865.

Powell, David A. *Failure in the Saddle: Nathan Bedford Forrest, Joseph Wheeler, and the Confederate Cavalry in the Chickamauga Campaign.* El Dorado Hills, Calif.: Savas Beatie, 2010.

Prichard, James M. "Theodore O'Hara." In *The Encyclopedia of Louisville*, edited by John E. Kleber, 666–67. Lexington: University Press of Kentucky, 2001.

Purvis, Edith Anthony. *The Gallant Gladden: The Life and Times of General A. H. Gladden, South Carolinian, 1810–1862.* Columbia, S.C.: Palmetto Bookworks, 1996.

Rable, George C. *God's Almost Chosen Peoples: A Religious History of the American Civil War.* Chapel Hill: University of North Carolina Press, 2010.

Rhea, Gordon C. *The Battle of the Wilderness, May 5–6, 1864.* Baton Rouge: Louisiana State University Press, 1994.

Ridley, B. L. "Camp Scenes around Dalton." *Confederate Veteran* 10 (1902): 66–68.

Robert, Charles E. "At Murfreesboro Just before the Battle." *Confederate Veteran* 16 (1908): 631–32.

Robertson, William G. "Bull of the Woods? James Longstreet at Chickamauga." In *The Chickamauga Campaign*, edited by Steven E. Woodworth, 116–39. Carbondale: Southern Illinois University Press, 2010.

———. "A Tale of Two Orders: Chickamauga, September 20, 1863." In *Gateway to the Confederacy: New Perspectives on the Chickamauga and Chattanooga Campaigns, 1862–1863*, edited by Evan C. Jones and Wiley Sword, 129–58. Baton Rouge: Louisiana State University Press, 2014.

Robins, Glenn. *The Bishop of the Old South: The Ministry and Civil War Legacy of Leonidas Polk.* Macon, Ga.: Mercer University Press, 2006.

Roland, Charles P. *Albert Sidney Johnston: Soldier of Three Republics.* Austin: University of Texas Press, 1964.

———. *Louisiana Sugar Plantations during the Civil War.* Baton Rouge: Louisiana State University Press, 1997.

Roman, Alfred. *The Military Operations of General Beauregard in the War between the States, 1861 to 1865.* 2 vols. New York: Harper and Brothers, 1884.

Rowland, Dunbar, ed. *Jefferson Davis, Constitutionalist: His Letters, Papers and Speeches.* 10 vols. New York: J. J. Little & Ives, 1923.

Rugely, H. J. H., ed. *Batchelor-Turner Letters, 1861–1864.* Austin, Tex.: Steck, 1961. www.terrystexasrangers.org. Accessed February 26, 2009.

Russell, William Howard. *My Diary North and South.* Philadelphia: Temple University Press, 1988.

Scarborough, William Kauffman, ed. *The Diary of Edmund Ruffin.* 3 vols. Baton Rouge: Louisiana State University Press, 1972–89.

Scribner, B. F. *How Soldiers Were Made; or, The War as I Saw It under Buell, Rosecrans, Thomas, Grant, and Sherman.* Chicago: Donohue and Henneberry, 1887.

Sears, Stephen W. *Chancellorsville.* Boston: Houghton Mifflin, 1996.

———. "Fire on the Mountain: The Battle of South Mountain, September 14, 1862."
  Blue & Gray 4 (1987): 4–63.

———. *Landscape Turned Red: The Battle of Antietam*. New Haven, Conn.: Ticknor &
  Fields, 1983.

———. *To the Gates of Richmond: The Peninsula Campaign*. New York: Ticknor & Fields,
  1992.

Seitz, Don D. *Braxton Bragg: General of the Confederacy*. Columbia, S.C.: State Company,
  1924.

Sheridan, P. H. *Personal Memoirs*. 2 vols. Wilmington, N.C.: Broadfoot, 1992.

Sherman, William T. *Memoirs*. 2 vols. New York: D. Appleton, 1875.

———. "Old Shady, with a Moral." *North American Review* 147 (October 1888): 361–68.

Sieburg, Evelyn Ratchford, ed. *Memoirs of a Confederate Staff Officer from Bethel to
  Bentonville*. Shippensburg, Pa.: White Mane Books, 1998.

Simpson, Brooks D., and Jean V. Berlin, eds. *Sherman's Civil War: Selected Correspondence of
  William T. Sherman, 1860–1865*. Chapel Hill: University of North Carolina Press, 1999.

Sorrel, G. Moxley. *Recollections of a Confederate Staff Officer*. New York: Neale, 1905.

Spence, John C. *A Diary of the Civil War*. Murfreesboro, Tenn.: Rutherford County
  Historical Society, 1993.

Spence, Philip B. "Services in the Confederacy." *Confederate Veteran* (1900): 500–501.

Stephenson, P. D. "Missionary Ridge." *Southern Historical Society Papers* 31 (1914): 8–22.

Stickles, Arndt M. *Simon Bolivar Buckner: Borderland Knight*. Chapel Hill: University of
  North Carolina Press, 1940.

Stiles, John C. "Missionary Ridge." *Confederate Veteran* 25 (1917): 14.

Stout, S. H. "An Address concerning the History of the Medical Service in the Field and
  Hospitals of the Army and Department of Tennessee." *Southern Practitioner* 24, no. 8
  (August 1902): 434–54.

———. *Reminiscences of General Braxton Bragg*. Hattiesburg, Miss.: Book Farm, 1942.

Supplement to the Official Records of the Union and Confederate Armies. 100 vols. Wilmington,
  N.C.: Broadfoot, 1995–99.

Sword, Wiley. *Shiloh: Bloody April*. Dayton, Ohio: Morningside Bookshop, 1983.

Sykes, E. T. "The Army at Dalton." *Southern Historical Society Papers* 12 (1884): 1–5.

———. "A Cursory Sketch of General Bragg's Campaigns." Pt. 1. *Southern Historical
  Society Papers* 11 (1883): 304–10.

———. "A Cursory Sketch of General Bragg's Campaigns." Pt. 2. *Southern Historical
  Society Papers* 11 (1883): 466–74.

Symonds, Craig L. *Joseph E. Johnston: A Civil War Biography*. New York: W. W. Norton,
  1992.

———. *Stonewall of the West: Patrick Cleburne and the Civil War*. Lawrence: University
  Press of Kansas, 1997.

Taylor, Richard. *Destruction and Reconstruction: Personal Experiences of the Late War in the
  United States*. Edinburgh: William Blackwood and Sons, 1879.

"Three Deserters Shot at Shelbyville." *Confederate Veteran* 16 (1908): 128.

Tower, R. Lockwood, ed. *A Carolinian Goes to War: The Civil War Narrative of Arthur
  Middleton Manigault, Brigadier General, C.S.A.* Columbia: University of South Carolina
  Press, 1983.

"Tributes to Gen. Braxton Bragg." *Confederate Veteran* 3 (1895): 132–33.

Trimble, Sarah Ridley, ed. "Behind the Lines in Middle Tennessee, 1863–1865." *Tennessee
  Historical Quarterly* 12, no. 1 (March 1953): 48–80.

Tunno, M. R. "Criticism of Gen. Bragg at Shiloh." *Confederate Veteran* 11 (1903): 116.

Urquhart, David. "Bragg's Advance and Retreat." In *Battles and Leaders of the Civil War*, vol. 3, edited by Robert Underwood Johnson and Clarence Clough Buel, 600–609. New York: Thomas Yoseloff, 1956.

The War of the Rebellion: A Compilation of the Official Records of the Union and Confederate Armies. 70 vols.in 128. Washington, D.C.: Government Printing Office, 1880–1901.

Watkins, Sam R. *Co. Aytch: A Side Show of the Big Show*. New York: Collier, 1962.

-Webster, J. T. "Another Chapter on the Mystery." *Confederate Veteran* 29 (1921): 341–42.

Wheeler, Joseph. "Bragg's Invasion of Kentucky." In *Battles and Leaders of the Civil War*, vol. 3, edited by Robert Underwood Johnson and Clarence Clough Buel, 1–25. New York: Thomas Yoseloff, 1956.

White, William Lee, and Charles Denny Runion, eds. *Great Things Are Expected of Us: The Letters of Colonel C. Irvine Walker, 10th South Carolina Infantry, C.S.A*. Knoxville: University of Tennessee Press, 2009.

Wiggins, Sarah Woolfolk, ed. *The Journals of Josiah Gorgas, 1857–1878*. Tuscaloosa: University of Alabama Press, 1995.

Williams, Robert W., Jr., and Ralph A. Wooster, eds. "With Terry's Texas Rangers: The Civil War Letters of Dunbar Affleck." *Civil War History* 9, no. 3 (September 1963): 299–319.

Williams, T. Harry. *P. G. T. Beauregard: Napoleon in Gray*. Baton Rouge: Louisiana State University Press, 1955.

Wills, Brian Steel. *A Battle from the Start: The Life of Nathan Bedford Forrest*. New York: Harper Collins, 1992.

Woodward, C. Vann, ed. *Mary Chesnut's Civil War*. New Haven: Yale University Press, 1981.

Woodworth, Steven E. "Braxton Bragg and the Tullahoma Campaign." In *The Art of Command in the Civil War*, edited by Steven E. Woodworth, 157–82. Lincoln: University of Nebraska Press, 1998.

———. "'In Their Dreams': Braxton Bragg, Thomas C. Hindman, and the Abortive Attack in McLemore's Cove." In *The Chickamauga Campaign*, edited by Steven E. Woodworth, 50–67. Carbondale: Southern Illinois University Press, 2010.

———. *Jefferson Davis and His Generals: The Failure of Confederate Command in the West*. Lawrence: University Press of Kansas, 1990.

———. *While God Is Marching On: The Religious World of Civil War Soldiers*. Lawrence: University Press of Kansas, 2001.

Wooster, Ralph A. "Confederate Success at Perryville." *Register of the Kentucky Historical Society* 59, no. 4 (October 1961): 318–23.

Wyeth, John A. *That Devil Forrest: Life of General Nathan Bedford Forrest*. Baton Rouge: Louisiana State University Press, 1989.

Younger, Edward, ed. *Inside the Confederate Government: The Diary of Robert Garlick Hill Kean*. New York: Oxford University Press, 1957.

Index

Robertson, Felix, 117, 129, 134
Robertson, Thomas Chinn, 35
Roddey, Philip D., 211
Rosecrans, William S., 79, 94, 96, 108–10, 139, 146, 159, 171, 190, 297 (n. 62)
Rousseau, Lovell H., 235–37
Ruffin, Edmund, 58, 278
Ruffin, Frank G., 208
Ruggles, Daniel, 16, 18
Russell, William Howard, 24

Sale, John B., 133, 134, 219, 226, 236, 243, 262
Schofield, John M., 245
Scribner, Benjamin, 107
Sears, Claudius W., 9
Seddon, James, 221–22, 224, 242
Seitz, Don C., xiii–xiv, 211, 250
Semmes, Benedict Joseph, 208
Semmes, Thomas Jenkins, 134, 215
Seven Pines, battle of, 123
Sheffler, Levi, 249–50
Shenandoah Valley campaign, 227–28, 230
Sherman, William T., 3, 9–10, 12–14, 88, 192, 200, 228, 235, 242, 252, 255–56, 274
Shiloh, battle of, 28, 32–42, 51, 187, 260, 274, 276, 278
Shorter, John Gill, 28
Shoup, Francis A., 236
Sims, William E., 134
Smith, Preston, 74, 123
Southern Historical Society, 259
Southern Historical Society Papers, 262
Southern Magazine, 262
Spang, William, 249–50
Spence, John C., xix
Spence, Philip B., 50–51
Starke, P. B., 176
Stephenson, Philip D., xiii, 209, 269
Stevenson, Carter L., 216
Stewart, Alexander P., 133, 230, 233, 236
Stiles, John C., 274
Stone, Kate, 136
Stoneman, George, 249
Stones River, battle of, xv, xvii, xix, 79, 96–138, 140, 148, 152, 206, 215–16, 233, 238, 266, 270–71, 276, 278, 296 (n. 52), 297 (n. 62), 297 (n. 64), 298 (n. 27), 300 (n. 55)

Stout, Samuel H., xv, 210, 216, 259, 266, 271–72, 274
Strange, John, 226
Street, John Kennedy, 107–9
Strong, George C., 78
Sword, Wiley, 40
Sykes, Edward T., xx, 100, 261–62

Taylor, Richard, 18, 81, 236, 260, 272–73, 275
Taylor, Zachary, 4, 206
Tennessee units
   1st, 180
   12th, 95
Terry, Alfred H., 244
Thomas, George H., 6, 190, 201, 274
Trabue, Robert P., 130–31
Trezevant, L. E., 262
Tullahoma campaign, xvii, xix, 145–49, 279
Tunno, M. R., 274
Tupelo, battle of, 235–36
Tyler, Robert C., 243

Urquhart, David, 29, 62, 88, 119, 129, 135, 138, 141–42, 155, 174, 203–4, 214, 226

Vance, Zebulon, 219–20
Van Dorn, Earl, 43, 46, 54, 63
Vaught, William C. D., 49, 80

Walker, C. Irvine, 50, 83, 109–10, 208, 238
Walker, John, 30, 80, 141–42
Walker, Leroy P., 13, 17, 23, 234–35
Walker, W. H. T., 155, 158, 208, 224, 231
Walter, Harvey W., 19, 39, 74, 140, 197, 210, 221, 234
Walthall, Edward C., 133, 137, 210, 261
Walthall, W. T., xx, 259–61, 264
Wampler, John M., 141
Warm Springs, Georgia, 161
Watkins, Sam R., 201–2, 269
Watterson, Henry, 207
Watts, Thomas H., 56, 237, 267
Wauhatchie, battle of, 191
Weitzel, Godfrey, 77–78
Western Reserve Historical Society, 264
Wheeler, Joseph, 90, 97, 100, 137, 146, 153, 176, 185
Whiting, W. H. C., 241–44